THE

# LYON IN MOURNING

OR A COLLECTION OF SPEECHES LETTERS JOURNALS ETC. RELATIVE TO THE AFFAIRS OF PRINCE CHARLES EDWARD STUART

BY THE REV. ROBERT FORBES, A.M.

BISHOP OF ROSS AND CAITHNESS

1746-1775

Edited from his Manuscript, with a Preface by

HENRY PATON, M.A.

IN THREE VOLUMES

I

# CONTENTS

# PREFACE

*The Lyon in Mourning* is a collection of Journals, Narratives, and Memoranda relating to the life of Prince Charles Edward Stuart at and subsequent to the Jacobite Rebellion of 1745. The formation of this collection was to a great extent the life-work of the Rev. Robert Forbes, M.A., Bishop of Ross and Caithness.

He was the son of Charles Forbes, a schoolmaster in the parish of Rayne, Aberdeenshire, and of Marjory Wright, and was born there in 1708, his baptism being recorded in the parochial register as having taken place on 4th May of that year. He must have been a studious youth, as he was sent to Marischal College, Aberdeen, in or about 1722, at the early age of fourteen, and graduated there as Master of Arts in 1726. He then proceeded to qualify himself for orders in the Scottish Episcopal Church, and coming to Edinburgh in June 1735, he was there ordained priest by Bishop Freebairn. In December of that year he became assistant to the Rev. William Law at Leith, and soon afterwards, at the request of the congregation, was appointed his colleague. At Leith, it may be said, he lived and laboured for the remainder of his life.

Like most of the Episcopalians of that day, he was an ardent Jacobite, indeed one of the most ardent, and but for a timely interposition of the 'hated Hanoverian' government would not improbably have shared the fate of some of his brethren whose end he chronicles. In that case there would have been no *Lyon in Mourning*, and it is but fair to say that (though

*The Lyon* can never be considered, and does not pretend to be, an impartial relation of the events with which it deals, our literature of the Rebellion of 1745 would have been greatly the poorer by its absence. Nay, it may even be said that, but for the continuous energy and single-eyed purpose of Bishop Forbes in this work, much of what is now known on this subject would never have come to light.

On hearing of the advent of Prince Charles Edward in the West Highlands, Mr. Forbes, with two Episcopalian clergymen and some other gentlemen, started off with the intention of sharing his fortunes, but all were arrested on suspicion at St. Ninians, near Stirling, and imprisoned. He notes the fact in the Baptismal Register of his congregation, as follows: 'A great interruption has happened by my misfortune of being taken prisoner at St. Ninian's, in company with the Rev. Messrs. Thomas Drummond and John Willox, Mr. Stewart Carmichael and Mr. Robert Clark, and James Mackay and James Carmichael, servants, upon Saturday, the seventh day of September 1745, and confined in Stirling Castle till February 4th, 1746, and in Edinburgh Castle till May 29th of said year. We were seven in number, taken upon the seventh day of the week, the seventh day of the month, and the seventh month of the year, reckoning from March.'[1] An incident of the roping of these prisoners at their removal from Stirling to Edinburgh is narrated by the author.[2]

After his release from imprisonment Mr. Forbes appears to have been invited to reside in the house of one of the most wealthy members of his congregation, Dame Magdalene Scott,

---

[1] *Journals, etc., of Bishop Forbes*, by the Rev. J. B. Craven, 1886, p. 12. This register is still extant, and one of its counterparts, the register of marriages performed by the Bishop, is printed in the *Scottish Antiquary*, vol. viii. pp. 125-129. See also p. 169. One of the baptisms was that of John Skinner, author of 'Tullochgorum,' who on 8th June 1740 went to Mr. Forbes in his room, and was re-baptized, declaring that 'he was not satisfied with the sprinkling of a laymaß, a Presbyterian teacher, he had received in his infancy.'

[2] See ff. 916, 987.

Lady Bruce of Kinross, the widow of Sir William Bruce of Kinross. She resided in the Citadel of Leith, and was a strong Jacobite; Mr. Forbes tells how her house was on more than one occasion the special object of the Government's concern, as the Prince himself was supposed to be concealed there.[1] For this lady Mr. Forbes cherished the highest esteem, speaking of her as 'the worthy person, the protection of whose roof I enjoy.'[2] She died in June 1752, aged 82; but before that event took place he had left her house, on the occasion of his marriage to his first wife, Agnes Gairey. This was in 1749,[3] and the lady died on 4th April of the following year.[4] He afterwards married, as his second wife, Rachel, second daughter of Ludovick Houston of Johnstone, in Renfrewshire, of whom he makes frequent mention in *The Lyon*. She was in fullest sympathy with her husband's Jacobite proclivities, and occasionally sent presents to the Prince abroad.

In 1762 Mr. Forbes was chosen and appointed Bishop of Ross and Caithness, and in 1767 he was elected Bishop of Aberdeen by a majority of the local clergy, but the College of Bishops disallowed the election in his case, and another was appointed. How keenly Mr. Forbes felt this action will be seen from his conversation and correspondence with Bishop Gordon of London. He twice visited his diocese in the north, and kept full journals of his progresses.[5] They are similar to a diary of his visit to Moffat, which is inserted in *The Lyon*,[6] and which was doubtless so inserted because of its concern with certain Jacobite matters; but it is also of interest on other accounts.

In later life, when, from having less to chronicle, he was not so taken up with this work, Bishop Forbes was an

---

[1] See ff. 940, *et seq.* [2] See f. 325. [3] See f. 1749.

[4] Craven's *Journals, etc.*, p. 11.

[5] These have been printed, along with a sketch of his life and a history of the Episcopal Church in Ross, in the work by the Rev. J. B. Craven, pp. 139-327.

[6] See ff. 1915, *et seq.*

occasional contributor to the *Edinburgh Magazine*, in which he published a number of topographical and antiquarian articles. Several of these, relating to Roslin Chapel, were collected and printed in 1774, under the *nom de plume* of *Philo-Roskelynsis*. He died at Leith on 18th November 1775 and was buried in the Maltman's Aisle in South Leith parish church. He does not appear to have had any children.

The origin of this collection, *The Lyon in Mourning*, probably dates from the author's imprisonment in Stirling Castle or Edinburgh Castle. In the latter place he was brought into contact with some of those who had taken an active share in the cause of Prince Charles, and it was, doubtless, while listening to their narratives that he was inspired with the idea of committing them to writing. Why he called his collection by the name it bears, he nowhere explains. It has been suggested that it was 'in allusion to the woe of Scotland for her exiled race of princes;' the Lyon being the heraldic representative of the nation. Bishop Forbes, in his own mind, no doubt, identified the Scottish nation with the comparatively few Jacobites within the country.

But whatever may be said about the title, the Bishop's purpose was, as he declared, to make up 'a Collection of Journals and other papers relative to the important and extraordinary occurrences of life that happened within a certain period of time,' and which, he adds, 'will serve to fix a distinguishing mark upon that period as a most memorable æra to all posterity. . . . I have,' he proceeds to say, 'a great anxiety to make the Collection as compleat and exact as possible for the instruction of future ages in a piece of history the most remarkable and interesting that ever happened in any age or country.' Nor was it only what particularly concerned that 'certain YOUNG GENTLEMAN' (as they were wont to style the Prince) that Bishop Forbes set himself to gather information, but also whatever could be gleaned about those who followed his fortunes. He was even desirous that every act of kindness performed by the victorious Hanoverians towards their vanquished enemies, should be cherished with the names of the doers, that they with the others 'may be carefully recorded and transmitted to posterity, according to truth and justice.'

And thus, though it be a purely Jacobite Collection, it is evident throughout that the author was most scrupulous with regard to the truth of the facts he relates. Hence, in seeking for narratives of the different episodes in the rebellion, his endeavour was to get them at first-hand from participators therein. 'I never chuse,' he says, 'to take matters of fact at second-hand if I can by any means have them from those who were immediately interested in them.'[1] Where this could not be obtained, he instructed his correspondents to 'have a particular attention to dates, and to names of persons and places;' for, he adds, 'I love a precise nicety in all narratives of facts, as indeed one cannot observe too much exactness in these things. . . . I love truth, let who will be either justified or condemned by it. . . . I would not wish to advance a falsehood upon any subject,' not even on Cumberland himself, for any consideration whatsoever.

His assiduity in the work is likewise noteworthy. Assuming that he began collecting in the end of 1746, by September 1747 he records that he has covered between twenty-four and thirty sheets, which by 19th April following had increased to about forty, by 4th July 1748, to sixty sheets, and by the following month about seventy, which he had bound up in several octavo volumes. These (from the point at which he mentions this[2]) would be at this time four in number, for by 'sheets,' Bishop Forbes means a sheet of paper which, when folded, yields sixteen pages, and the number of pages in these first four volumes amount in the aggregate to 868 pages. He was now well advanced with another, the fifth, which ends with page 1112. The sixth volume is also dated on its title-page '1748,' volume seventh, 1749, and volume eighth, 1750.

[1] f. 1231. [2] f. 1052, 1067.

This eighth volume, however, could only have been begun in that year, as there is reference in it, near the end, to an event which happened in 1761. But as the seven volumes contain 1598 pages, or, as the author would have put it, ninety sheets, we have a pretty fair estimate of his diligence in the collecting, sometimes drafting, and in all cases transcribing his materials. Naturally, as the main facts of the Rebellion receded from public view by the progress of time and other events, interest would abate, and materials fall off, and this is evident enough from the compilation of volume eighth taking ten or eleven years, while the previous seven were accomplished in three or four. Volume ninth, again, gave the collector employment for at least fourteen years, for though it is dated in 1761, it contains correspondence down to April 1775. This volume, while it yields a few papers respecting the Rebellion of 1745, is chiefly occupied with a correspondence maintained by Bishop Forbes with other Jacobites, in which a most lively interest is taken in the daily life and affairs of Prince Charles on the Continent of Europe, and schemes suggested and devised for the realisation, some time or other, of Jacobite hopes. This correspondence is continued in the tenth and last volume, which, however, is only partly filled up, the rest of the volume consisting of blank pages. It was commenced in 1775, and goes on to October of that year, the death of Bishop Forbes occurring in the following month. Here, however, there is no lack of interest in the persons to whom we are introduced as engaged in the Cause along with Bishop Forbes. They are almost all Episcopalians. Indeed, the members of the Scottish Episcopal body were practically identified with the Stuart Cause from the Revolution onwards, until in despair, they, by a formal declaration, professedly severed themselves from it in or about 1780. Bishop Forbes did not live to see this, but even some time before his death evil tidings had frequently arrived and given rise to sad forebodings of shattered hopes, and the wrecking of long-cherished expectations.

To publish his Collection, Bishop Forbes could never be induced. He rightly judged it imprudent to print what could only be construed as a censure of the Government of the day, and which, accordingly, was likely to draw resentment not only upon himself, but upon any of the surviving actors whose names it was his desire to immortalise in story. Urged to it by one of his correspondents (Dr. John Burton of York, who, being himself a sufferer on the Prince's account, published a pamphlet narrative of the Prince's adventures and escape, and also of his own sufferings), Bishop Forbes always replied that he 'waited a seasonable opportunity.' His mind, as to this, further appears from the way in which he expresses himself to a brother in office in reference to Dr. Burton's publication. It has made its appearance, he says, 'contrary to my earnest and repeated remonstrances. I have resisted many solicitations, and I am well aware that this is far from being a proper time for the publication of truths of so much delicacy and danger, and therefore, for my part, I am resolved to wait for a more seasonable opportunity;' and when that would occur he could not imagine. This was in 1749, and, as the result shows, the opportunity never came for him. He did print a short account of the Prince's adventures at a later date, copies of which he sent to the Prince and others abroad; but this was only a trifle in comparison with what he had collected.

Naturally, *The Lyon in Mourning* was one of his most valued possessions, and he guarded it with the most jealous care. Only on one occasion would he allow it out of his own hands. He would show his friends the external bulk of it, but they were not permitted to pry within. One young relative, who did not apparently stand very high in the author's favour, had the temerity to ask that the 'black-edged volumes' might be sent to him in London for completing a narrative which he and another were preparing for publication, and in reply got the rebuff, that there was much room for doubting his competency for the task he had undertaken, while as for the loan of the Manuscript, he had asked what the author would not have granted to his own father. However, Bishop Forbes judged it expedient to part with them for a time when his residence was threatened with a search. He had this to plead as an excuse to Dr. Burton, who begged the Bishop to furnish from his collection some materials to make his own proposed publication more perfect. 'I was obliged,' he replies, 'to secret my collection, having been threatened with a search for papers. I have therefore put my collection out of my own custody into the keeping of a friend, where I cannot have access to it without some difficulty, and I resolve to keep it so, that so I may defy the Devil and the Dutch.' Indeed, this was his usual way with it, for he writes to another, 'I keep my collection in a concealment always, so that I am not afraid of its being seized by enemies; and it is not every friend I allow to see only the bulk and outside of my favourite papers.'[1]

The volumes are bound in sombre black leather, and have their edges blackened, while around each title-page is a deep black border. Some relics, which are, or have been, attached to the volumes for preservation, call for some notice. They are most numerous on the insides of the boards of the third volume. First, there is a piece of the Prince's garters, which, says Bishop Forbes, 'were French, of blue velvet, covered upon one side with white silk, and fastened with buckles.'[2] Next there is a piece of the gown worn by the Prince as Betty Burke, which was sent to Bishop Forbes by Mrs. MacDonald of Kingsburgh. It was a print dress, and from this or other pieces sent the pattern was obtained, and a considerable quantity of print similar to it made by Mr. Stewart Carmichael, already mentioned. Dresses made from this print were largely worn by Jacobite ladies, both in Scotland and England, for a time. Thirdly, there is a piece of tape, once part of the string of the apron which the Prince wore as part of his female attire. Bishop Forbes secured this relic from the hands of Flora

---

[1] f. 1426. [2] f. 197.

MacDonald herself, who brought the veritable apron to Edinburgh, and gave the Bishop the pleasure of girding it on him. To keep company with these, another relic has been added to this board by the late Dr. Robert Chambers, and which, consequently, Bishop Forbes never saw. It is a piece of red velvet, which once formed part of the ornaments of the Prince's sword-hilt, and was obtained, as that gentleman narrates, in the following way. On his march to England, the Prince rested on a bank at Faladam, near Blackshiels, where the sisters of one of his adherents, Robert Anderson of Whitburgh, served him and his followers with refreshments. Before he departed, one of the young ladies begged the Prince to give them some keepsake, whereupon he took out his knife, and cut off a piece of velvet and buff leather from the hilt of his sword. Up till 1836 at least, this was preciously treasured at Whitburgh; and it was from Miss Anderson of Whitburgh, of a later generation of course, that Mr. Chambers at that time obtained the scrap which he placed with the Bishop's relics. On the inside of the back board of this volume are pieces of tartan, parts, respectively, of the cloth and lining of the waistcoat which the Prince received from MacDonald of Kingsburgh, when he relinquished his female garb. This he afterwards exchanged with Malcolm MacLeod for a coarser one, as it was too fine for the rôle of a servant, which he was then acting. Malcolm MacLeod hid the waistcoat in the cleft of a rock until the troubles should be over; but when he went to recover it, as it had lain there for a year, he found it all rotted, save a small piece, which, with two buttons, he forwarded to Bishop Forbes.

On the inside of the back board of the fourth volume the Bishop has had two small pieces of wood, one of which has now disappeared. The remaining piece is about one inch long, less than half an inch broad, and about one-eighth of an inch in thickness. These, says the author, are pieces of that identical eight-oared boat, on board of which Donald MacLeod, etc., set out with the Prince from Boradale, after the battle of Culloden, for Benbecula, in the Long Isle. The bits of wood were obtained and sent by MacDonald of Glenaladale. Then, finally, there are pieces of one of the lugs of the brogues or shoes which the Prince wore as Betty Burke, stuck on the inside of the back board of volume fifth. But the Bishop seems to have had the brogues themselves, and he and his Jacobite friends were wont to use them as drinking vessels on special occasions. This was reported to the Prince, who heartily enjoyed the idea, and remarked concerning Bishop Forbes, 'Oh, he is an honest man indeed, and I hope soon to give him proofs how much I love and esteem him.'

After the death of Bishop Forbes *The Lyon in Mourning* remained a possession treasured by his widow for fully thirty years, she alone knowing of what value it had been in the eyes of her husband. With advancing years, however, she fell into poverty, and was obliged in 1806 to part with the Collection, a suitable purchaser having been found in Sir Henry Steuart of Allanton, who had set himself the task of preparing 'An Historical Review of the different attempts made to restore the Stewart family to the throne from the Revolution in 1688 to the suppression of the Rebellion in 1745.' Ill-health frustrated his design, and *The Lyon in Mourning* lay past unknown and unheeded at Allanton until it was unearthed by Dr. Robert Chambers. He purchased it from Sir Henry Steuart, and in 1834 published a number of the papers and narratives contained in it in his work entitled *Jacobite Memoirs of the Rebellion of* 1745. On an average computation it may be said that Dr. Chambers printed about a third part of what is contained in *The Lyon*, sometimes weaving one narrative with another, in order to present in fuller form, so far as possible, the entire history of the Prince in his adventures. But what Dr. Chambers there gave in the personal narratives of the contributors to *The Lyon in Mourning*, and what he has written in his admirable popular *History of the Rebellion*, on information derived chiefly from the same source, have but increased the desire of the historical student to have before him the complete text of *The Lyon in Mourning* as it stands in the original manuscript. This desire the present publication will gratify. The Council of the Scottish History Society originally proposed merely to print what Dr. Chambers had left unprinted. But consideration of the fact just stated, and the undesirability of the reader being required to compare two works in order to ascertain the real contents of the *Lyon*, led to the resolution to print the full text of the Bishop's manuscript, especially also as the *Jacobite Memoirs* is now a somewhat scarce book.

Dr. Chambers bequeathed this Manuscript Collection of Bishop Forbes to the Faculty of Advocates, Edinburgh, in whose library it now remains. He had previously attached to the first volume the following writing, to declare the genuineness and history of the work :—

'EDINBURGH, *May* 5, 1847.

'I hereby certify that the accompanying manuscript, in ten volumes, entitled *The Lyon in Mourning*, was purchased by me in 1833 or 1834 from the late Sir Henry Steuart of Allanton, Baronet, by whom I was informed that he had bought it about thirty years before from the widow of Bishop Forbes of the Scottish Episcopal Church, the compiler, who had died in 1775.

'The volume contains, in a chronological progress, many documents and anecdotes respecting the civil war of 1745, and the individuals concerned in it. On this account I desired to possess it, as I designed to make use of its contents for the improvement of a history of the insurrection which I had written.

(Signed) 'ROBERT CHAMBERS.'

By a 'chronological progress' the reader is not to understand that the events of the Prince's life, or of the Rebellion, will be found related in order of time in the following pages. It can only mean that Bishop Forbes proceeded in a chronological progress from 1746 or 1747 till his death, in building up his Collection, telling us from time to time the dates of his receiving his information, which he enrols as he receives it, without any other regard to chronology than its coming to him. But to enable the reader to follow the chronological sequence of events, a brief chronological digest of the narratives contained in the Collection will be given as an Appendix in the third volume. In that volume also will be found an Index to the whole work. Into the plots and scheming prior to the actual outbreak of the insurrection, Bishop Forbes's materials do not lead us. It is, however, satisfactory to learn that the Scottish History Society has in hand the publication of the Journal of the Prince's Secretary, John Murray of Broughton, which promises to throw light upon much that was taking place anterior to the actual outbreak, as well as in other respects to supply the deficiencies of *The Lyon in Mourning*.

It only remains to acknowledge the kindness of the Faculty of Advocates in placing *The Lyon in Mourning* at the disposal of the Society for publication, and the uniform courtesy of Mr. Clark and his assistants in the Advocates' Library in facilitating the progress of this work. Our acknowledgments are also due to the indefatigable Secretary of the Society, Mr. T. G. Law, and to his ever-willing assistants in the Signet Library, for their ready furtherance in the labours of reference and research.

# The LYON in Mourning

or,

A Collection (as exactly made as the Iniquity of the Times would permit) of Speeches, Letters, Journals, &c. relative to the Affairs, but more particularly the Dangers & Distresses, of ..'

Vol: 1st.

Eheu! quanta tenent Scotos mala? quanta Doloris
Copia! qui Patriam luctus ubique premit?

1747.

FACSIMILE OF ORIGINAL TITLE-PAGE

# THE LYON IN MOURNING

OR

A COLLECTION (AS EXACTLY MADE AS THE INIQUITY OF THE TIMES WOULD PERMIT) OF SPEECHES, LETTERS, JOURNALS, ETC., RELATIVE TO THE AFFAIRS, BUT MORE PARTICULARLY THE DANGERS AND DISTRESSES OF

VOL. I

Eheu ! quanta tenent Scotos mala ! quanta doloris
Copia ! qui Patriam luctus ubique premit !

1747

# Copy of a Letter from the Rev. Mr. Robert Lyon[1] to his Mother and Sisters.

My dear mother and my loving sisters,—How ever great a shock to nature I presently feel in writing you upon this occasion, and the great trouble and affliction it must give you all in reading my last, yet I could not allow myself, having warning of my approaching fate, to leave this miserably wicked world, without bidding you farewel and offering you my advice. *fol.* 1. 1746 23 Oct.

It has pleased Almighty God in His unsearchable Providence for some time past to afflict me with grievous and sore troubles, everything that could be look'd on as comfortable in this world being denied me that was in the power of my enemies to grant or refuse. But blessed be my merciful God, they could not stop the inward consolations of God's Holy Spirit, which has hitherto supported me in health and vigour under all this miserable scene of calamities, for which I have the greatest reason, while I live, to bless and adore His glorious name. The miseries I have already undergone, and humanly speaking, am still to suffer, are undoubtedly inflicted upon me as a just reward and punishment for my manifold sins and iniquities, and I trust they have been dispensed as the chastisements of a *fol.* 2. merciful Father to a prodigal child in order to draw me to a nearer acquaintance with Himself, to wean my heart from all

[1] Mr. Lyon was incumbent of the Episcopal Church in Perth, being elected thereto as colleague to the Rev. Laurence Drummond (whom he mentions in this letter) in or about 1738. When Prince Charles and his army passed through Perth on his way south, Mr. Lyon joined himself to them, especially as the most influential part of his congregation had gathered to the Prince's standard. He was appointed chaplain of Lord Ogilvie's regiment. After his arrest he was imprisoned at Montrose, and thereafter at Carlisle, where he was tried, and sentenced to be executed. He accordingly suffered death at Penrith on 28th October 1746. For further particulars about Mr. Lyon the reader may consult the *Episcopal History of Perth*, by the Rev. George T. S. Farquhar, M.A., 1894, pp. 131-186.

13 Oct. inordinate affections to the follies and vanities of the world, to enlarge my heart with desires of being with Jesus, my Saviour, of the freedom from sin and of the fruition of my God to all eternity. This is the proper influence His afflicting hand should have had upon me. And, if my heart deceives me not, I have made it my endeavour, tho' with a great mixture of weakness during my long confinement, it should have its due effect.

Before this will reach you (my dear mother and sisters) the last fatal scene of my sufferings will be over and I set at liberty (even by my enemies themselves) from the heavy load of irons and chains I have so long drag'd. Lord, loose me from the burden of my sins! Assist me in my last and greatest trial! Receive my soul, and bring me into the way of eternal happiness and joy! Grieve not for me, my dearest friends, since I suffer in a righteous and honourable cause, but rather rejoice that God has assisted me by His grace, the most unworthy of
*fol.* 3. His servants, to act agreeably to my conscience and duty by bearing testimony to truth and righteousness, religion and loyalty in midst of a wicked and irreligious, perverse and rebellious generation. Let this consideration, the motives of Christianity, and the hopes and assurances which our holy religion so plentifully affords, allay in you all immoderate grief, and make you thoroughly resign'd to God's holy will in all His wise dispensations; which howsoever harsh at present they may appear to flesh and blood, yet they shall all be made to work together for good to them that love and fear Him, and put their trust in His mercy.

I am very sensible how much easier it is to give advice against affliction and trouble in the case of others than to take it in my own. It hath pleased God to exercise me of late with very sore trials, in which I do, I think, perfectly submit to His good pleasure, firmly believing that He does always that which is best. And yet tho' my reason was satisfied, my passion was not so soon appeas'd; for to do this is a work of some labour and time.

But since that God hath thought fit to warn me of my own mortality by giving me a summons to die a violent and barbarous death by the hand of man, I thank God for it; it hath occasion'd in me no very melancholy reflections. But this perhaps is more owing to my natural temper than wise considerations. But yet, methinks, both reason and religion do offer you, my dear mother and sisters, considerations of that solidity and strength, as may very well support you under all the afflictions of this present life. Pray then consider:— 23 Oct. fol. 4.

That God is perfect love and goodness; that we are not only His creatures, but His children, and as dear to Him as to ourselves; that He does not afflict willingly nor grieve the children of men, and that all evils of afflictions which befal us, are intended for the cure and prevention of greater evils, of sin and punishment. And therefore we ought not only to submit to them with patience as being deserved by us, but to receive them with thankfulness as being design'd by Him to do us that good and to bring us to that sense of Him and ourselves which perhaps nothing else would have done. That the sufferings of this present life are but short and light compar'd with those extreme and endless miseries which we have deserved, and with that exceeding weight of glory which we hope for in the other world, if we be careful to make the best preparations for death and eternity. Whatever hardships and afflictions we suffer for our attachment to truth and righteousness bring us nearer to our everlasting happiness, and how rugged soever the way may be, the comfort is that it leads to our Father's house where we shall want nothing that we can wish for. fol. 5.

But now you labour under affliction for the death and loss of your only son, and all of you of your dearest earthly friend. Consider then that, if you be good Christians, God who is your best friend, who is immortal and cannot die, will never leave you nor forsake you, but will provide both for your temporal and spiritual concerns beyond what you can either ask or think. But nature, you say, is fond of life. I acknowledge it. But then consider, to what purpose should we desire a long life? since with the usual burdens and infirmities and misfortunes that attend it, it is but the same thing over again or worse, so many more nights and days, summers and winters, with less pleasure and relish, every day a return of the same and greater pains and troubles, but perhaps with less strength and patience to bear them.

23 Oct. These, and the like considerations, have under my present calamities entertain'd me not only with contentment but comfort, tho' with great inequality of temper at several times, and with much mixture of human frailty, which will in some degree stick to us while we are in this world. However by this kind of thoughts afflictions and death itself will become more familiar to us, and keep us from starting at the one or repining
fol. 6. at the other.

I acknowledge I find in myself a great tenderness in parting with you, my dearest relations, which I must confess doth very sensibly touch me. But then I consider, and so, I hope, with all of you, that this separation will be but a very little while, and that tho' I shall leave you in a very wicked world, yet you are all under the care of a good God who can be more and better to you than I and all other relations whatever, and will certainly be so to all those that love Him and hope in His mercy.

It likewise gives me no small uneasiness that I should leave you in a worse way as to your worldly circumstances than I could have wished or once expected, having spent my own and made some encroachments upon poor Cicie's[1] stock. But then I must say in my own vindication, this was not by any luxury or riot, as you can bear me witness, but rather owing to a small yearly income, an expensive place for living, and being too liberally disposed upon certain occasions; but, above all, by my being engag'd in the late glorious cause of serving my King and country. You'll easily see it was no mercenary view, but purely obedience to conscience and duty that made me take
fol. 7. part in the fate of my royal prince and country when I tell you that I never received a farthing of his Royal Highness's money, nor was assisted in the least penny by any engaged in his service. So that this undertaking consum'd no small part of my private stock; and I hope you'll readily grant it could not have been better bestow'd, altho' all of you must feel the want of it. But God who has formerly done wonderful things for us all will, I trust, provide for you the necessaries of life.

And even poverty rightly weigh'd is not so very sad a condition. For what is it but the absence of a very few super-

[1] Mr. Lyon's favourite sister.

fluous things which please wanton fancy rather than answer need, without which nature is easily satisfied, and which, if we do not affect, we cannot want? What is it but to wear coarse cloaths, to feed on plain and simple fare, to work and take some pains, to sit or goe in a lower place, to have few friends and not one flatterer? And what great harm in this? If I had time to compare it with the many dangers and temptations to which wealth is expos'd,—pray consider that poverty is a state which many have born with great chearfulness. Many wise men have voluntarily embrac'd it. It is allotted by Divine wisdom to most men, and the very best of men do often endure it. God has declared an especial regard to that state of life. The mouth of truth hath proclaimed it happy. The Son of God dignified it by His own choice, and sanctified it by His partaking deeply thereof. And can such a condition be very disagreeable to any of you (who were never over-prosperous in the world)? Or can it reasonably displease you?

23 Oct.

*fol.* 8.

My dear mother and sisters, these considerations, I hope, thro' the Divine assistance, will be a mean to support you under your present and future afflictions, and preserve you from repining at my fate and your own loss.[1]

[Before I end this letter I must take this opportunity to acquaint you of one thing that none on earth knows but the person immediately concern'd. The matter is this. Had it pleased God that I should have surviv'd my dear mother, and been provided of any tolerable subsistence in this world, I design'd and propos'd to make Stewart Rose (whom I know to be a virtuous, wise, good, and religious young woman), partner of my life and fortune. I am too sensible of what she suffers on my account, and which would make her affliction sit the harder upon her, the natural modesty she is mistress of, would

[1] The paragraph following in brackets was at first omitted by Mr. Forbes, with this explanatory note inserted at the end of the letter. '*N.B.*—In the original of the above letter there was a paragraph about a very particular concern of Mr. Lyon's which I did not chuse to transcribe.' But he afterwards supplied it by writing it on the inside of the front board of the volume, with the following: '*N.B.*—Finding that Mr. Lyon's own relations and Mrs. Stewart Rose made no secret of the mutual affection that had been betwixt the young lady and her departed friend, I obtain'd a true copy of the paragraph and transcrib'd it as above.—ROBERT FORBES, A.M.'

Oct. never allow'd her to give vent to her grief, had not I mention'd it to you. I therefore recommend her to you, my dear mother, always to look upon her as your daughter, and to you, my dear sisters, to treat her always as your own sister, she being really so in my most serious intention and fix'd resolution. And I am persuaded there are none of you but will bear so far a regard to my memory as to value, esteem, and, as far as in your power, cherish and comfort the person on whom I had so deservedly settled my love and affection. I am sensible that all of you esteem'd her before on your acquaintance with her and her own proper merit, and am convinc'd that my discovering my mind thus far will more and more increase and not lessen your love and regard to her. May Almighty God support and comfort her and you all, and make you with humble submission resign'd to the Divine will.]

I must next acknowledge with all the tender-heartedness of a brother, the grievous troubles and afflictions both of body and mind my dear sister, Cicie, hath undergone, in order to be of use and comfort to me under my severe trials. Her firm love to me has made her follow my fate too far, and be a witness of more of my troubles than I could have wish'd. But whatever she has suffer'd on my account, which indeed cannot be express'd, she has been of unspeakable service to me. May Almighty God reward her, and whatever love all of you bore to her formerly I hope it will be enlarged to her on this very account.

*fol. 9.* I cannot conclude without offering my best wishes (as they have always had my prayers) to Mr. Drummond, my colleague, and every individual person a member of our congregation. May Almighty God bless all of them both in their temporal and spiritual concerns, and of His infinite goodness reward them for their love and kindness, their attachment and concern for me in the several difficulties I have undergone! May the same God in His due time afford them authoriz'd guides to perform Divine offices amongst them, to administer to them the means of grace and bread of life, that they may be no longer as sheep without a shepherd. Till which time may the Holy Spirit direct every one of them into the way of truth, and assist them earnestly to contend for the faith once delivered to the saints, in unity of spirit, in the bond of peace, and in righteousness of life. And finally, may the same merciful Lord save them and bless them, make them to the end of their lives stedfast in the faith, unblameable in holiness and zealous of good works. 23 Oct.

You 'll be pleased to offer my hearty and sincere good wishes to Balgowan[1] and all that worthy family. I gratefully acknowledge their remarkable and undeserved favours. May Almighty God return them sevenfold into their bosom! *fol.* 10.

I sincerely pray that Almighty God may reward the family of Moncrief, Mr. Smyth's, Mr. Stirling's, Dr. Carmichael's, Mr. Graeme's, ladies of Stormont, Lady Findal's, and all other my kind benefactors and well-wishers with you (who have so bountifully ministred to my necessities) with His eternal and everlasting good things.

As I expect and earnestly desire forgiveness from God of all my sins and transgressions, thro' the merits and mediation of my only Saviour and Redeemer Jesus Christ, so from the very bottom of my heart I forgive all my enemies, persecutors, and slanderers, and particularly Clerk Millar,[2] who, I have reason to believe, has prosecute me to death, and whom, to my knowledge, I never injured in thought, word, or deed. May God grant him repentance that he may obtain forgiveness at the hands of our heavenly Father. And with the same earnestness I desire all of you to forgive him, and tho' it should be in your power, never in the least degree to resent it against him or his.

And now, my dear mother and sisters, it is my dying exhortation to you, as well as to every particular person, who (by the providence of God) was committed to my spiritual care, stedfastly and constantly to continue in the faith and communion of our holy persecuted mother, the Church of Scotland, in which I have the honour to die a very unworthy priest, whatever temporal inconveniences and hardships you may wrestle with in so doing. Nothing must appear too hard which tends to the salvation of your souls; and the disciple is *fol.* 11.

[1] John Grahame of Balgowan.

[2] George Miller, town clerk of Perth, who seems to have taken an active part in the prosecution of his townsmen who engaged in the rebellion. See fol. 27.

Oct. not to expect better treatment than his Lord and Master. For as they persecuted Him, even so will they persecute you. Strenuously adhere then, in spite of all opposition, to those doctrines and principles, which thro' the grace of God and my own weak abilities, I endeavoured to teach publickly and inculcate upon you in my private conversation, I mean the doctrines of the Holy Scriptures, with their only genuine and authentick comment, the universal doctrines and practices of Christ's Church in her purest ages, even the three first centuries, before the manifold errors of Popery, on the one hand, or Presbyterian enthusiasm, on the other, prevail'd; both of which have been dangerous to the souls of many. Let no worldly consideration
f. 12. prevail with any of you to join with schismaticks of whatever kind; and more especially be not deceived by those who may come unto you in sheep's cloathing, having the appearance of sanctity and righteousness more than others, but in Divine offices offer up to God unlawful petitions and immoral prayers.

And, as you know, the man cannot be perfectly happy without the reunion of soul and body (in consequence of which principle it was my practice, in my family devotions to commemorate the souls of my deceas'd friends who died in the Lord), so I earnestly beg and intreat when you approach the throne of grace that you 'll pray for rest and peace, light and refreshment to my soul, that I may find mercy in the day of the Lord, and that I may be partaker of perfect consummation and bliss both in body and soul in God's eternal and everlasting glory. May our good and wise ecclesiastical governours, with the Divine assistance, contribute their endeavours to restore this and all other primitive and apostolic practices in due form to the publick offices of our Church, which would be a mean to administer comfort and great consolation to many a pious and devout soul. I cannot finish this subject
f. 13. without putting up my petitions in the same words of our holy mother, the Church, as she appoints the very day[1] on which it is determined I should suffer: 'O Almighty God, who hast built thy Church upon the foundation of the apostles and prophets, Jesus Christ himself being the head corner-stone,

[1] St. Simon and St. Jude's Day, F. [F. denotes that the notes are the author's].

grant us so to be joined together in unity of spirit by their doctrine that we may be made an holy temple, acceptable unto Thee through Jesus Christ, our Lord. Amen.' 23 Oct.

And now, my dear mother and sisters, I must conclude this my too long letter with my prayers for you. May our most gracious God pardon all your offences and correct whatever is amiss in any of you. May He preserve you all in health, peace, and safety, and, above all, in mutual love to one another. May He pour down upon you His spiritual blessings, and vouchsafe you also such a measure of temporal blessings as He sees most convenient for you. May He of His infinite mercy let you want nothing either for life or for godliness. I pray God to fit us all for that great change which we must once undergoe; and if we be but in any measure prepared, sooner or latter makes no great difference. I commend you all to the Father of Mercies and the God of all consolation and comfort, beseeching Him to increase your faith, patience, and resignation, and to stand by you in all your conflicts, difficulties, and troubles, that when ye walk thro' the valley of the shadow of death you may fear no evil, and when your heart fails you may find Him the strength of your heart and portion for ever. *fol.* 14.

Farewel, my dear mother! Farewel, my loving sisters! Farewel, every one of you for ever! And let us fervently pray for one another that we may have a joyful and happy meeting in another world, and there continue in holy fellowship and communion with our God and one another, partakers of everlasting bliss and glory to the endless ages of eternity.

The grace of our Lord Jesus Christ and the love of God and the communion of the Holy Ghost be with you all evermore, is the prayer and blessing of, my dear mother, your obedient and affectionate son, and my loving sisters, your affectionate and loving brother, while

Robert Lyon.

*Carlisle Castle, October 23d,* 1746.
*To my mother and sisters.*

## The Last and Dying Speech of Robert Lyon, A. M. Presbyter at Perth.[1]

fol. 15. 18 Oct. The death I am now to suffer by the hands of violence the partial and unthinking world will doubtless be ready to imagine a sign of guilt and a stain upon the character with which I am invested.

But would the hardships of a close confinement and the time permit me to explain and vindicate my principles, I am persuaded I could prove them just and my conduct guiltless in the things for which I am to die.

That I may not, however, leave a natural curiosity on such occasions quite ungratified I shall briefly run over the principal passages of my past life, and represent my genuine sentiments in some material points. Which I hope will have the greater weight and effiicacy upon you, my dear fellow-subjects and beloved countrymen, as I am just about to step into eternity where, at the greatest tribunal, on the last day I know I must be judged according to the works I have already done. And

fol. 16. First. It will be very proper to inform you that I have the honour to be more immediately descended from one of those Scottish clergymen,[2] who unhappily surviv'd our flourishing Church and prosperous nation at the late Revolution; by which means it was my lot, by the wise providence of God to be early train'd up in the school of adversity, inasmuch as he underwent the common fate of our other spiritual pastors and dear fathers in Christ who were by merely secular, and what is worse, unlawful force thrust away from their charges and depriv'd of that maintenance to which they had a general and divine right as well as a legal title by our Constitution. And this in many instances was executed with the utmost rigour and severity, attended with every wicked and aggravating circumstance. For how could it be otherwise when allowed to

[1] This speech was printed in *Blackwood's Magazine* for May 1819 (No. 26, vol. v. p. 164), and in *Stephen's Episcopal Magazine* for 1836, pp. 10, 111.

[2] Thought to be the Rev. James Lyon, a native of Forfarshire, who was ordained under the patronage of the Earl of Strathmore, and became incumbent at Kirkwall, whence he was ejected after the Revolution (*Episcopal History of Perth*, p. 135).

be done by an ungovern'd mob, distracted with enthusiasm and misguided zeal, but whose deed received its sanction by some subsequent pretended laws. 28 Oct.

Into this once glorious but now declining part of the Church Catholick I was thro' the care and piety of my loving parents enter'd by a holy baptism. For which inestimable benefit, as my judgment ripen'd and my reason improv'd I ever found *fol.* 17.
greater cause to bless the happy instruments, and to thank my God, as it clearly appeared upon impartial enquiry that this Church for purity of doctrine, orthodoxy in the faith, perfection of worship and her apostolical government, equals, if not excels, any other church on the earth. And therefore I persisted by Divine grace an unworthy member in her faithful communion till thro' various instances of the goodness and care of Heaven manifested in the wonderful support and preservation of our family, I received a pious and liberal education (tho' my father, wore out with sufferings, lived not to see it half compleated), and at length arrived at that age when by the canons of the Church I could be admitted into holy orders; which I received at a time no earthly motive could influence me, but a sincere intention to serve God and to my power to do good offices to men.

Both which I, tho' most unworthy of the sacred character, have ever honestly endeavour'd to the utmost of my weak ability, by enforcing and practising, as far as circumstances and my station in the Church would permit, that golden and glorious rule for the conduct of a Christian, and for every *fol.* 18.
church whereby to reform itself, and moreover which alone can unite the differing parts of Christendom, I mean the Holy Scriptures, with their only genuine and authentick comment, the universal doctrines and practices of Christ's Church in her first three centuries. Which that it may again universally obtain God Almighty grant for his sake who purchas'd the Church with the effusion of his blood.

In perfect consistency with this Catholick and noble rule I declare upon this aweful occasion, and on the word of a dying man, that I ever abhor'd and detested and *do* now *solemnly* disclaim the many errors and corruptions of the Church of Rome; as I do with equal zeal the distinguishing principles of

28 Oct. Presbyterians and other dissenting sectaries amongst us who are void of every support in our country but ignorance and usurping force, and whom I always considered as the shame and reproaeh of the happy Reformation, and both alike uncatholick and dangerous to the soul of a Christian.

I must further declare that by the same method I found out
*fol.* 19. the absurdities of these two differing parties, I was soon determin'd from rational and solid arguments to embrace the doctrines of passive obedience, the divine right of kings, and in particular the indefeasible and hereditary title of our own gracious sovereign, James the Eighth and Third, and of his royal heirs, whom God preserve and restore.

For these I am thoroughly convinc'd are doctrines founded upon the best maxims of civil government and on the Word of God; and besides the very essence of our own Constitution and municipal laws. And therefore I could never view that Convention which pretended to depose King James the Seventh, our King's royal father, and dispose of his crown; I could never, I say, view that unlawful and pack'd Assembly in any other light but as traitors to their country and rebels to their King.

And as our then injured King and his undoubted heirs have from time to time uninterruptedly claim'd their right and asserted their dominion, I am so far from thinking that the
*fol.* 20. royal misfortunes loose the subjects from their obedience, that I rather apprehend they loudly call for a steadier allegiance and more faithful duty.

In which sentiments I have been still more and more confirm'd by the lamentable consequences of the opposite opinion, and by that sad affliction and load of misery, which a long usurpation has brought upon my country and which it is needless for me here to insist upon, as our numerous grievances, too heavy to be born, have been strongly, but alas! in vain, represented and loudly proclaimed even in some late pretended parliaments.

But what more naturally falls to my share to consider, and what I fear has been still less regarded in the long persecuted state of my dear mother, the Church of Scotland, that Church of which it is my greatest honour to be a member and a priest, tho' very undeserving of either; a Church, national and independent of any other and of every power upon earth, happily govern'd by her own truly primitive bishops, as so many spiritual princes, presiding in their different districts, and in them, accountable to none but God for the administration of her discipline; a church, whose creeds demonstrate her soundness in the faith, and who is blest with a liturgy (I mean the Scots Liturgy,[1] compil'd by her own bishops) nigher to the primitive model than any other church this day can boast of (excepting, perhaps, a small but I believe a very pure church in England[2] who, I am told, has lately reformed herself in concert with the forementioned and infallible rule)—in one word a church very nearly resembling the purest ages, and who (after more than half a century groaning under persecutions and mourning in her own ashes, but all the while distinguishing herself no less by forbearance and charity to her bitterest enemies than by her steadiness to principle and Catholick unity) is now at last, alas! devoted, in the intention of her adversaries to utter destruction; which I fervently pray God to prevent.

28 Oct.

*fol.* 21.

Her oratories have been profan'd and burnt, her holy altars desecrated, her priests outragiously plundered and driven from their flocks, some of them imprison'd and treated with uncommon cruelty, her faithful members almost depriv'd of the ordinary means of their salvation, and this mostly done without so much as a form of law, by a hostile force specially appointed by him who calls himself the Duke of Cumberland, and who (God grant him a timely repentance and forgive him) has occasion'd the painful and untimely death of many innocent and inoffensive persons; and by wilful fire and sword, by every means of torment and distress—barbarity exceeding

*fol.* 22.

[1] A copy of part of this 'Liturgy' in print is inserted here in the manuscript. It is entitled 'The Communion Office for the use of the Church of Scotland, as far as concerneth the ministration of that Holy Sacrament. Authorised by King Charles I. Anno 1636, Edinburgh, printed by Mr. Thomas Ruddiman, MDCCXXIV.' The signature of 'Robert Lyon' is on the title-page, and the following note by Mr. Forbes on the back of the title-page, 'This is the identical copy which the Rev. Mr. Robert Lyon made use of in consecrating the Holy Eucharist in Carlisle Castle.' It consists of 24 pp. 12mo. The Liturgy referred to is better known as Laud's Liturgy, the enforcing of which gave rise to the Second Reformation in Scotland.

[2] This church, which he called 'The True British Catholic Church,' was founded by Dr. Deacon, concerning whom see footnotes at fols. 37 and 40.

28 Oct. Glencoe massacre itself—has brought a dreadful desolation upon my dear country.

All which evidently shews that there is nothing, however necessary and dear to mankind, however sacred and near allied to Heaven; that must not give way to their resentment and to the better establishing their ill-got power, and that no lasting security even to the present established Church of England can reasonably be expected from this ruinous and usurped government. And indeed the reigning impiety and that flood
*fol. 23.* of wickedness which the kindly influence and encouragement of a corrupted court has drawn upon us must speedily deface the very form of religion and give the finishing stroke to virtue, tho' no harsher methods were us'd by them.

But may the gracious hand of Heaven interpose and stop the wide destruction! May our Church once more resume her antient lustre, her priests be cloathed with righteousness and her saints yet sing with joyfulness! May her members yet be multiplied, blessed with peace and felicity in this world, and crown'd with immortality in that which is to come!

And now, my dear fellow-subjects, you cannot be at a loss to apprehend the reason of my appearance on this occasion, and of the death I am to suffer. For when our brave and natural-born Prince (a Prince endued with every virtue proper to grace a throne, and a stranger to every vice that high life is most subject to, in a word a Prince adorn'd with every quality that could attract the hearts of a wise people or make a nation
*fol. 24.* happy) generously hazarded his own valuable person to relieve us from slavery and to retrieve his father's crown; and every steady patriot who had courage to resolve to conquer or suffer in the way of duty, according to the will of God, join'd his royal standard; thither many, to whom I was attach'd by relation, friendship and several other ties, dutyfully resorted, and kindly invited and earnestly importun'd me to attend them as their priest, while they were laudably engaged in their king and country's cause; which agreeably to my now profess'd principles I readily consented to, as I plainly foresaw that I could not discharge my function with more safety in that congregation to which I have a spiritual and peculiar relation where part of the Prince's forces always lay, than in

going along with my worthy friends in their glorious expedition. 28 Oct.

And here I must declare that while I accompanied my brave countrymen in their noble enterprise I saw a decency and order maintain'd amongst them, equal if not superiour to any regular disciplin'd force. And if any hardship or severity was committed I am fully persuaded it was unknown to, and very cross to the inclination of their merciful and royal leader. *fol.* 25.

And in particular I do believe that the destruction of St. Ninian's[1] was merely by accident and without any order from his royal highness. And this is the more evident since the person who had the fatal occasion of it lost his own life in the conflagration. But it was maliciously represented and put in the worst light to vindicate the malicious procedure of the Usurper's forces; whose conduct let it be compar'd with that of our King's army and then you may form as ready and just a judgment of the true and pretended father of the country, as Solomon by a like experiment did of the true and pretended mother of the child.

And for my own particular, I do solemnly affirm that during this expedition I never bore arms, for this I thought inconsistent with my sacred character. I never prayed in express terms for any king (because for many years it has not been the practice of our Church, and to make such a change in her offices I thought incompetent for me without the appointment, or at least the permission of my superiours) and preach'd the plain truths of the Gospel without touching on political subjects. This confession, by surprize, and the advice of my council I was forced to make at the Bar, upon which my pretended judges declar'd, and the jury found me guilty of high treason and levying war, for my barely accompanying the royal army as before mentioned. And this their rigorous procedure they founded upon a pretended new Act of Parliament made since I was personally engaged in the royal cause, *fol.* 26.

[1] See fuller references to this incident of the war at f. 155. According, however, to detailed accounts from the other side, it was deliberately done, and caused the death of several of the poorer townspeople, who were allured into the church in the hope of getting stores the rebels could not carry away.—*Scots' Magazine*, 1746, p. 221.

28 Oct. and for what I know since I was a prisoner: which plainly
*fol. 27.* shews that whatever my private sentiments have been my life has been greedily sought and unjustly taken away, in as much as they pass'd their sentence without any other overt act of high treason (even in their own sense) being prov'd against me.

But in obedience to the precept, and after the divine example of my blessed Master, Jesus Christ, I heartily and cheerfully forgive them, as I do all my adversaries of whatever kind, particularly George Millar, Clerk of Perth, who, I have reason to believe, has prosecute me to death, and whom to my knowledge I never injur'd in thought, word, or deed. Lord, grant him repentance that he may find forgiveness of God.

And more especially I forgive the Elector of Hanover by virtue of whose unlawfull commission I am brought to this violent and publick death, and whom I consider as my greatest enemy, because he is the enemy of my holy mother, the Church, of my King and of my Country.

*fol. 28.* I do here acknowledge publickly with a strong and inward sense of guilt that thro' fear, human frailty, the persuasion of lawyers and the promise and assurance of life, I was prevail'd upon, contrary to the sentiments of my conscience and my openly profess'd principles, to address the Elector of Hanover for mercy and my life. Which address or petition or anything of that kind I have sign'd, derogatory to the royal cause, or our undoubted lawful sovereign's right and title, I hereby retract, and wish from the bottom of my heart I had never done any such thing; and with the sorrow and contrition of a dying penitent, most humbly beg forgiveness of my heavenly Father for this my great offence. God be merciful to me a sinner. I likewise beg forgiveness of all those good, religious and loyal persons to whom my inconsistent conduct in this particular has given just
*fol. 29.* occasion of scandal and offence. And I humbly confess the justice of God for bringing to nought the devices of men when aim'd at or sought after by undue means and unlawful methods. But hereby the unmerciful disposition of the Hanoverian family appears the more evident, and the injustice and cruelty of the Elector's Council at law in this, that they

indicted, arraign'd, tried and condemn'd a person[1] whom I had forc'd by a subpœna to attend my trial at Carlisle as an exculpatory evidence, notwithstanding he had long before delivered himself up in consequence of the pretended Duke of Cumberland's proclamation, had obtain'd a protection and got a pass. This the more deeply concerns me in case any of his friends should imagine I had any design against him by forcing him to run such a hazard. But I here call God to witness, I esteemed the man, and as I thought him perfectly safe, I had no other view in bringing him this length than to do myself justice. 28 Oct.

I farther acknowledge and humbly adore the justice of God's holy providence, the sovereign disposer of all things, in permitting the execution of the sentence of death against me, confiding that He of his mercy and goodness, through the blood and mediation of his dear and only Son, will accept of this my suffering in the cause of truth and righteousness, and reward it with the joys of his eternal kingdom. I heartily give thanks to Him for vouchsafing me the honour and felicity of dying for the sake of conscience, and of sealing with my blood those heavenly truths I have maintain'd, particularly that of loyalty to my king and prince. *fol.* 30.

And I do declare upon this aweful and solemn occasion I feel no sting of conscience for the part I have acted in our civil discords; and do sincerely profess before God and the whole world that had He of his infinite wisdom thought proper to prolong my life, I should have ever, by His all-powerful aid and grace, steadily persisted in the same faith and *fol.* 31. principles, in the hearty and zealous belief and open profession of which I now die, and with fervent charity to all men; imploring the pardon and forgiveness of all my sins thro' the merits and mediation of my crucified Saviour, our Lord Jesus Christ; earnestly exhorting you, my dearest fellow-subjects, and most beloved countrymen, speedily to repent and to turn to your duty in every point, and, in particular, to that fidelity and allegiance which you owe to your native and only rightful sovereign.

---

[1] William Baird in Perth. See f. 464 for the history of this case.

8 Oct. Consider, I beseech you, consider the evils already felt, the impending ruin of your country. Consider the crying injustice and indignity offered to the best of princes. Above all, consider the guilt and high demerit of violating God's laws and resisting His ordinance. And let these powerful and prevailing motives excite you quickly to amend your ways, to make a thorough change in your life and conversation, and to
fol. 32. continue for ever firm and unshaken in your duty and subjection to the power ordain'd of God, not only for wrath, but also for conscience sake. So shall ye arrest the vengeance and just wrath of Heaven which has gone out against us. Ye shall be the happy instruments yet to preserve your wishing country from entire destruction, and save your souls in the day of the Lord.

For which glorious and noble ends, Do Thou, O God Almighty! by Thy Holy Spirit, turn the hearts of the disobedient to the wisdom of the just, the hearts of parents to their children, of children to their parents, the hearts of priests and kings to their people, of people to their kings and priests, the hearts of all to one another and all together unto Thee, their God, thro' Jesus Christ!

I conclude in the words of our holy mother, the Church, as she piously appoints in the office for this day,[1] and in that of the protomartyr, St. Stephen :—

fol. 33. 'O Almighty God, who has built thy church upon the foundation of the apostles and prophets, Jesus Christ himself being the head corner stone, grant us so to be joined together in unity of spirit by their doctrine, that we may be made an holy temple acceptable unto Thee, through Jesus Christ our Lord, Amen.

'Grant, O Lord, that in all our sufferings here upon earth for the testimony of thy truth, we may stedfastly look up to Heaven, and by faith behold the glory that shall be revealed; and being fill'd with the Holy Ghost may learn to love and bless our persecutors by the example of the first martyr, St. Stephen, who prayed for his murderers, to Thee, O blessed Jesus, who standest at the right hand of God, to succour all

---

[1] St. Simon and St. Jude's Day.—F.

those that suffer for Thee, our only Mediator and Advocate, Amen.' 28 Oct.

Good Lord, lay not innocent blood to the charge of this people and nation.

Lord Jesus, receive my spirit! *fol.* 34.

Such are the genuine dying sentiments and fervent humble prayers of ROBERT LYON, A.M.,
*priest of the persecuted and afflicted Church of Scotland.*

*Penrith*, 28 *October* 1746.

On the 18th of October Mr. Francis Buchanan of Arnprior, after he was taken from prison return'd again and spoke to me the following words or to the same purpose:

As I have obtain'd a few minutes longer to stay here I desire to spend them with you in prayer and conversation. After prayers he proceeded and said: I am much oblig'd to Mr. Wilson[1] (one of the clergymen belonging to the Cathedral) for suggesting one thing which I forgot to speak of, being conscious of my own innocence. He says my being slander'd with the murder of Mr. Stewart of Glenbuckie[2] did me harm on my trial. Now I take this opportunity to declare publickly to you *fol.* 35.
and my fellow prisoners that Glenbuckie and I liv'd many years in close friendship together, and altho' he was found dead in my house, yet, upon the word of a dying man, I declare I myself had no hand in his death, nor do I know any other person that had. And I am persuaded I can likewise answer for every one of my servants, since all of them were acquainted with and had a particular love to that gentleman. So that I declare it to be my opinion that he was the occasion of his own death. ROBERT LYON.

*N.B.*—As Mr. Lyon frequently administred the holy Eucharist to his fellow-prisoners in Carlisle Castle, so particularly upon Wednesday, October 15th, he had the happiness to communicate above fifty of them, among

[1] Probably Mr. Thomas Wilson, then prebendary, afterwards dean in 1764.

[2] See a narrative of Mr. Buchanan's case at f. 100, and about the death of Mr. Stewart, f. 107.

28 Oct. which number were Mr. Thomas Coppoch, the English clergyman, and Arnprior, and upon the 26th of the
fol. 36. same month, being the 22nd Sunday after Trinity, he had above thirty communicants. He suffer'd at Penrith upon Tuesday, October 28th, the festival of St. Simon and St. Jude, 1746, and perform'd the whole devotions upon the scaffold, with the same calmness and composure of mind and the same decency of behaviour, as if he had been only a witness of the fatal scene. He delivered every word of his speech to the numerous crowd of spectators. Mr. Lyon never saw the speeches of Mr. Deacon and Mr. Syddal,[1] which some might imagine from their agreement in some points. He bore all his own charges in the expedition. The above *N.B.* was taken from the mouth of Mrs. Cecilia Lyon, who did not come from Carlisle till after her brother had suffered death. ROBERT FORBES, A.M.

fol. 37. The SPEECH of MR. THOMAS THEODORE DEACON.[2]

30 July 1746 MY DEAR FELLOW-COUNTRYMEN,—I am come here to pay the last debt to nature, and I think myself happy in having an opportunity of dying in so just and so glorious a cause. The deluded and infatuated vulgar will no doubt brand my death with all the infamy that ignorance and prejudice can suggest. But the thinking few who have not quite forsaken their duty to God and their king, will I am persuaded look upon it as being little inferiour to martyrdom itself, for I am just going to fall a sacrifice to the resentment and revenge of the Elector

[1] These follow on this and subsequent pages.

[2] See a letter to his father on the same occasion, f. 381 *infra*. According to Bishop Forbes, Mr. Deacon was the son of Dr. Thomas Deacon, who, he adds, (f. 40 *infra*), was a non-jurant bishop in Manchester. But another contemporary authority describes him as the son of an eminent and wealthy doctor of medicine in Manchester, and states that Thomas was educated at the university to qualify him for the same professions.—'History of the Rebellion,' extracted from the *Scots' Magazine*, 1755, pp. 294-301. The fact is that Dr. Deacon engaged in both professions. Three of his sons joined the Prince. Thomas was appointed a lieutenant in the Manchester Regiment, and so was his brother Robert, while Charles, the youngest, aged about seventeen, was made an ensign. All were taken at the surrender of Carlisle, and sent prisoners to London. Robert

of Hanover and all those unhappy miscreants who have openly espoused the cause of a foreign German usurper and withdrawn their allegiance from their only rightful, lawful and native sovereign, King James the 3d. It would be trifling here to expatiate on the loss of so many brave subjects' lives who have had the courage to appear in defence of their native King; the vast, the immense treasure squandered away in defence of the Usurper; the heavy load of taxes and debts under which the nation groans; the prevalence of bribery and corruption; the preference of strangers to natives, and innumerable other inconveniencies which must necessarily attend a foreigner's sitting on the throne of Great Britain, and which must be too obvious to every impartial, unprejudiced Englishman. 30 July *fol.* 38.

Moreover, I think it is very evident that the very mercy of the Usurper is no less than arbitrary power, and the freedom of Parliament, bribery, and corruption; from which unhappy circumstances nothing else can restore this nation and bring it to its former happiness and glory but inviting King James the 3d to take possession of his undoubted right.

I profess I die a member, not of the Church of Rome, nor yet that of England, but of a pure Episcopal Church which has reform'd all the errors, corruptions and defects that have been introduc'd into the modern Churches of Christendom—a church which is in perfect communion with the antient and universal Church of Christ, by adhering uniformly to antiquity, universality and consent, that glorious principle which if once strictly and impartially pursued would, and which alone can, remove all the distractions and unite all the divided branches of the Christian Church. This truly Catholick principle is *fol.* 39.

---

became so ill on the way that he was left at Kendal, and died there. Charles was reprieved, though he was taken to the place of execution under a military guard to see his brother and others suffer. The head of Thomas Deacon, with others, was sent to Manchester to be stuck up on the Exchange there. His father was the first to come and gaze upon it, and saluting it, thanked God that he had had a son who could die for his lawful prince. Dr. Deacon only survived his son about six years, and the inscription on his tombstone is worthy of note:—'Here lie interred the remains (which through mortality are at present corrupt, but which shall one day surely be raised again to immortality and put on incorruption) of Thomas Deacon, the greatest of sinners and most unworthy of primitive bishops, who died 16th February 1753, in the 56th year of his age.—Axon's *Annals of Manchester*, pp. 89-90.

July agreed to by all the Churches, Eastern and Western, Popish and Protestant, and yet is unhappily practised by none but the Church in whose holy communion I have the happiness to die. May God of his great mercy daily increase the members thereof. And if any would enquire into its primitive constitution, I refer them to our Common Prayer-Book, intitled 'A compleat Collection of Devotions, both publick and private,
ol. 40. taken from the Apostolick constitutions, antient Liturgies, and the Common Prayer-Book of the Church of England, printed at London. 1734.[1]

I sincerely declare I forgive all my enemies, who have raised on me any false or scandalous reports, the pretended Court by which I was tried, and all those who were witnesses against me, particularly the unfortunate, deluded Mr. Maddox,[2] who has added the sin of unparallel'd ingratitude to those of treachery to his fellow-subjects, perfidiousness to his lawful prince and perjury against his God, having sworn away the lives of those very persons who chiefly supported him while he attended on the Prince's army, and for a month after he was taken prisoner. And further, I affirm on the word of a dying man he perjured himself in the evidence he gave against me at my trial, as I verily believe he did in what he swore against
ol. 41. most if not all of the others.[3]

Lastly, I most freely forgive my two principal enemies, the Elector of Hanover and his son, who claims the pretended title of Duke of Cumberland, who are actually guilty of murder in putting me with many others to death, after the latter had granted a regular, formal capitulation in writing;

---

[1] This book was compiled by Mr. Deacon's father, a non-jurant bishop in Manchester.—F.

[2] Samuel Maddock or Maddox, an apothecary's apprentice in Manchester. He was appointed ensign in the Manchester Regiment, and after being taken prisoner became king's evidence. Some witnesses averred that Maddox held a bad character; that as apprentice he had wronged his master, and was not worthy of credence even upon his oath.—'History of the Rebellion,' extracted from the *Scots' Magazine*, 1755, pp. 279 *et seq*. See also ff. 91, 98 *infra*.

[3] Maddox deponed against Mr. Deacon, that he 'sat at the table at the Bull-head at Manchester, took down the names of such as enlisted in the Pretender's service, and received a shilling for each; and when he was writing he employed himself in making blue and white ribbons into favours, which he gave to the men who enlisted.'—'History of the Rebellion,' *ut supra*, p. 289.

which is directly contrary to the laws of God and nations, and 30 July
I hope will be a sufficient warning to all those who shall hereafter have spirit, honour and loyalty enough to take up arms in defence of their lawful sovereign, King James the 3d, or any of his successors against the Usurper and his descendants. I say, I hope it will be a sufficient warning for them never to surrender to Hanoverian mercy, but to die bravely with swords in their hands. Not but I submit with the utmost chearfulness and tranquility to this violent death, being thoroughly convinc'd that thereby I shall be of much more service to my *fol.* 42.
beloved country and fellow-subjects as well as my only lawful king, my dear, brave Prince of Wales and the Duke of York (whom God of his infinite mercy bless, preserve and restore!), than all I could do by fighting in the field or any other way.

I publickly profess that I heartily repent of all my sins, but am so far from reckoning the fact for which I am to die one of them that I think I shall thereby be an honour to my family, and if I had ten thousand lives would chearfully and willingly lay them down in the same cause. And here I solemnly affirm that malicious report to be false and groundless which has been spread (merely with design to involve my relations in inconveniencies), that I engaged in this affair thro' their persuasion, instigation and even compulsion. On the contrary, I was always determin'd to embrace the first opportunity of performing my duty to my Prince, which I did with- *fol.* 43.
out consulting or being advised to it by any friend on earth.

And now, my dear countrymen, I have nothing more to say than to advise you to return to your duty before it be too late and before the nation be entirely ruin'd. Compare the paternal and tender affection which your King has always shewn for this, his native country, with the rashness of the Usurper, and his great regard to his German dominions, the interest of which has been always preferr'd to that of England. Compare the extraordinary clemency and humanity of the ever glorious Prince Charles with the horrid barbarities and cruelties of the Elector's son which he perpetrated in Scotland. Remember what solemn promises have been given by both our King and Prince Charles to protect you in your laws, religion and liberties. Has not the Prince thrown himself into your

30 July arms? Has he not given sufficient proof of his abilities in the
*fol.* 44. Cabinet, as well as bravery in the field? In fine, he has done his part, and consequently the sin must lye at your door if you do not yours.

May God be pleased to bless this land and to open the eyes of the people that they may discern their duty and true interest, and assist in restoring their only natural King to his indisputable and just right! God bless and prosper him, and guide him in all his undertakings! So prayeth

THOMAS THEODORE DEACON.

Lord, have mercy upon me!
Christ, have mercy upon me!
Lord, have mercy upon me!
Lord Jesu, receive my soul!

*Wednesday, July 30th, 1746, upon Kennington Common.*

*fol.* 45.

## The SPEECH of MR. THOMAS SYDDAL.[1]

30 July 1746 FRIENDS, BRETHREN AND COUNTRYMEN,—Since I am brought here to be made a sacrifice for doing the duty of a Christian and an Englishman, it may be expected I should give some account of myself and the cause for which I suffer. This expectation I will gladly indulge. And I wish the whole kingdom might be inform'd of all that I now say at the hour of death when there is the least reason to doubt my sincerity.

I die a member, not of the Church of Rome, nor yet of that of England, but of a pure Episcopal Church, which hath reformed all the errors, corruptions and defects that have been introduced into the modern Churches of Christendom—a church which is in perfect communion with the ancient and universal Church of Christ by adhering uniformly to antiquity, universality and consent, that glorious principle which if once
*fol.* 46. strictly and impartially pursued would, and which alone can, remove all the distractions and unite all the divided branches

[1] Thomas Syddall was a barber in Manchester and acted as adjutant of the Manchester regiment. Some interesting particulars about him and his family will be found in *Manchester Collectanea*, vol. lxviii. of the Chetham Society, pp. 208-225, where this speech is also printed.

of Christendom. This truly Catholick principle is agreed to by all Churches, Eastern and Western, Popish and Protestant, and yet unhappily is practised by none but the Church in whose holy communion I have the happiness to die. May God in His great mercy daily increase the members thereof! And if any would enquire into its primitive constitution I refer them to our Common Prayer Book which is intitled 'A compleat Collection of Devotions, both publick and private, taken from the Apostolical Constitutions, the ancient Liturgies, and the Common Prayer Book of the Church of England, printed at London in the year 1734.' 30 July

I most humbly and heartily offer up my praises and thanksgiving to Almighty God that He hath been pleased of His great goodness to give me grace to follow the pious example of my father,[1] who enduring hardships, like a good soldier of *fol.* 47 Jesus Christ, was martyred under the government of the late Usurper in the year 1715, for his loyal zeal in the cause of his lawful King.

And I solemnly declare that no mean, wicked motives of revenging my father's death (as hath been uncharitably said) induced me to join in attempting a restoration of the royal family. I think I had no occasion to be displeased with his murderers, when I reflect (as I firmly believe) that instead of punishing they sent him to his everlasting rest sooner than he would have gone according to the course of nature. And so far from doing an injury to his family, they pointed him out by his sufferings an excellent example of Christian courage, and contributed by that means to the good of his innocent children.

Neither was I tempted to enter into the army commanded by the Prince of Wales by any ambitious or self-interested *fol.* 48. views. I was easy in my circumstances and wanted no addition of riches to increase my happiness. My desires were limited

[1] Thomas Syddall, a blacksmith, who on 10th June 1715, the anniversary of the birthday of the Old Pretender, headed a party of rioters in Manchester, and wrecked Cross Street Chapel. He was seized and sentenced to the pillory and imprisonment in Lancaster Castle. The Jacobite army, however, released him and some of his comrades, but he was retaken at Preston, and after trial at Liverpool was executed at Manchester on 11th February 1716.—Axon's *Annals of Manchester*, p. 76.

30 July within reasonable bounds, and what I thought I had occasion for (I bless God) I was able to procure. And to make my joy as full as in this world ought to be wish'd, I was blessed with an excellent, faithful, religious, loving wife, and five children, the tender objects of our care and affection. In this situation I was void of ambition and thankful to God for His gracious disposal of me.

My motive for serving in the Prince's army was the duty I owe to God, the King and the country, in endeavouring the restoration of King James the Third and the royal family; which I am persuaded is the only human means by which this nation can ever become great and happy. For altho' I have never had the honour of seeing his Majesty, yet I am well
*fol.* 49. assur'd by others of his excellent wisdom, justice and humanity and that he would think it his greatest glory to rule over a free and happy people without the least innovation of their religion or liberties.

For this we have not only the royal promise of the King himself (than which a reasonable people cannot desire a greater security) but we have also the word of a young Prince who is too great and good to stoop to a falsity or to impose upon any people—a Prince blessed with all the qualities which can adorn a throne, and who may challenge his keenest enemies to impute to him any vice which can blacken his character, whom to serve is a duty and a pleasure, and to die for an honour.

And here I cannot but take notice that if his Royal Highness had any of that cruelty in his temper which hath so abundantly displayed itself in his enemy, the pretended Duke of Cumber-
*fol.* 50. land, he would have shewn it upon Mr. John Weir,[1] when he had him in his power, and knew that he had been a spy upon the royal family abroad and upon the Prince at home, almost from the time of his first landing. But the brave unfortunate young heroe, with noble compassion, spared that life which hath since been employed in our destruction. If I might presume to say that the gallant good Prince hath any fault it would be that of an ill-timed humanity. For if he had

[1] Captain John Vere, or Weir, in service under the Duke of Newcastle. He had been taken prisoner by the rebels about the time they held Carlisle, and was employed by them in negotiating the terms of capitulation.

been so just to himself and the righteous cause wherein he was engag'd as to have made examples of some of those who betrayed him, in all human probability he had succeeded in his glorious undertaking and been reserved for a fate to which his unequall'd virtues justly entitle him. 30 July

There is one thing I am bound in justice to others to take notice of in respect to Mr. Samuel Maddox, who for prudential *fol.* 51. reasons was not produced upon my trial to imbrue his hands in my blood, as well as in that of my fellow-sufferers. Yet I solemnly declare in the presence of Heaven (where I hope shortly to be) that in the trial of Mr. Thomas Deacon and Mr. John Berwick,[1] I heard him perjure himself, as I verily believe he did in every trial upon which he was produced as an evidence. To this sin of perjury he hath also added the odious crime of ingratitude, for to my own knowledge he was under great obligations to the very people against whom he has falsly sworn, and was supported and kept from starving by them and me for a considerable while in prison when nobody else would assist him.

I heartily forgive all who had any hand in the scandalous surrender of Carlisle; for as it was the opinion of every one of the garrison who had been in foreign service that the place was *fol.* 52. tenable many days, and as the Elector's troops then lying before the town were in a bad condition, it is highly probable that a gallant defence (which I strenuously insisted upon) would have procured us such terms as to have prevented the fate to which we are now consign'd. I also forgive the pretended Duke of Cumberland for his dishonourable and unsoldierly proceeding in putting us to death in violation of the laws of nations after a written capitulation to the contrary, and after the garrison, upon the faith of that capitulation, had surrendred the place and faithfully performed all the conditions required of them.

I pray God to forgive and turn the hearts of the bishops and their clergy who, prostituting the duty of their holy profession, have departed from their function as messengers of peace, and

[1] Or Beswick. A Manchester linen-draper, aged about thirty-one years. He was known by the soubriquet of 'Duke' in the rebel army.—'History of the Rebellion' in *Scots' Magazine*, pp. 295-299.

10 July scandalously employed themselves in their pulpits to abuse the
fol. 53. best Prince engaged in the most righteous cause in the world, and against their own consciences and opinions, represented him and his army in a disadvantageous and false light, in order to get the mob on their side and spirit up an unthinking people to a blood-thiristy, cruel and unchristian disposition. I could heartily wish these men would prefer suffering to sinning, and consider how contrary it is to the character of a truly Christian pastor to receive instructions about what doctrine to preach from the baneful Court of an impious Usurper. The credulous, deluded mob, who have been thus set on by their teachers, I also pray God to forgive for the barbarous insults I received from them when in chains. Father, forgive them, for they know not what they do!

As I have before given thanks to Almighty God for the example of my honest father, so I beseech him that the same
fol. 54. Christian, suffering spirit may ever be in all my dear children; praying that they may have the grace to tread the same dangerous steps which have led me to this place, and may also have the courage and constancy to endure to the end and despise human power when it stands oppos'd to duty.

I pray God of his great mercy and goodness that he would be pleased to pour down the choicest of his blessings upon the sacred head of his Majesty, King James the Third, and his royal sons, the Prince of Wales, and the Duke of York; and (although England be not in a disposition to deserve so great a blessing, yet for the sake of justice and the love which Nature and duty prompt me to bear my native country) to restore them soon to their lawful, natural and undoubted rights, and in the meanwhile to inspire them with Christian patience and firmness of heart to bear their undeserved misfortunes.

It would be an unspeakable satisfaction to me if my manner
fol. 55. of dying, or anything I now say, would contribute to the removing those unhappy and unreasonable prejudices with which too many of my countrymen are mislead. Danger of Popery and fear of French power are the idle pretences that wicked and ill-designing men make use of to misguide and stir up the passions of unwary (though perhaps honest) people. But if Englishmen would seriously consider that those who

make the most noise about Popery are remarkably void of any religion at all, and dissolute in their morals; that Atheism, infidelity, profaneness and debauchery are openly avowed and practised even within the walls of that very Court whence they derive all their fancied religious and civil liberties. If they would reflect (when they talk of French influence) that they seek protection from a German Usurper, who is hourly aggrandizing himself and raising his foreign dominions upon the ruines of the deluded people of England. If they would reflect that I and my fellow-sufferers are now murdered in order to weaken the cause of loyal virtue, and to strike a terror into the minds of all such as have the honest inclination to do their King, their country and themselves justice. If they would reflect upon the calamities, the massacres, the desolation of Scotland, which presage the destruction of this already more than half-ruined country, surely they would find but little cause to be pleased with their situation—a situation so extremely distant from honour and happiness that it would be uncharitable and misbecoming a dying man to wish even his most inveterate enemies to continue in it, and which I therefore pray God, of his infinite mercy, to deliver all Englishmen from.

30 July

*fol.* 56.

If, my dear countrymen, you have any regard to your own happiness, which, in charity, I have endeavoured to point out in my dying moments, let me beseech you, in the name of God, to restore your liege sovereign, and with him the glorious advantages of an excellent constitution under a lawful government. This is every man's duty to aim at. And if your honest attempts should fail, remember it is a great blessing to die for the cause of virtue, and that an almighty power can and will reward such as suffer for righteousness sake.

*fol.* 57.

To that God, infinite in his goodness and eternal in his providence, I commend my soul, imploring his forgiveness of all my sins, and hoping for a speedy translation to eternal joy through the merits and sufferings of Jesus Christ.—Amen! Amen! Amen! THO. SYDDAL.

*Upon Kennington Common, Wednesday, July* 30, 1746.

fol. 58. ## THE SPEECH of the Right Honourable ARTHUR, LORD BALMERINO.[1]

18 Aug. 1746. I WAS bred in Anti-Revolution principles which I have ever persevered in, from a sincere persuasion that the restoration of the royal family and the good of my country are inseparable.

The action of my life which now stares me most in the face is my having accepted a company of foot from the late Princess Anne, who I know had no more right to the crown than her predecessor, the Prince of Orange, whom I ever consider'd as an usurper.

In the year 1715 as soon as the King landed in Scotland I thought it my indispensible duty to join his standard, tho' his affairs were then in a desperate condition.

I was in Switzerland in the year 1734, where I received a letter from my father, acquainting me of his having procured me a remission and desiring me to return home. Not thinking
fol. 59. myself at liberty to comply with my father's desire without the King's approbation, I wrote to Rome to know his Majesty's pleasure, and was directed by him to return home; and at the same time I received a letter of credit upon his banker at Paris, who furnished me with money to defray the expense of my journey and put me in proper repair.

I think myself bound upon this occasion to contradict a report which has been industriously spread and which I never heard of till I was a prisoner, 'That orders were given to the Prince's army to give no quarters at the battle of Culloden.'

---

[1] Arthur Elphinstone, sixth and last Lord Balmerino and fourth Lord Coupar, only succeeded his half-brother in these peerages on 5th January 1746. As he indicates in his speech, he forsook the service of King George the First in 1715, and joined the Earl of Mar, escaping abroad after the battle of Sheriffmuir. His father secured his pardon, and returning home he married Margaret, daughter of Captain John Chalmers (or Chambers) of Gogar, in Midlothian, but by her had no issue. An account of his trial and execution, with some notice of his life and family, and a portrait of him at the time of his death, was published in pamphlet form (12mo, pp. 50) at London in 1746. A fuller report of the above speech is given at f. 108, some panegyrical verses at ff. 112 and 403 *et seq.*; and a singular letter addressed to Lord Balmerino three days before his death with a later reference to Lady Balmerino in connection therewith at f. 561 *et seq.* Lady Balmerino died at Restalrig, near Edinburgh, on 24th August 1765.

With my eye upon the block (which will soon bring me before 18 Aug.
the highest of all tribunals) I do declare that it is without all manner of foundation; both because it is impossible it could have escap'd the knowledge of me, who was Captain of the Prince's Life-guards, or of Lord Kilmarnock, who was Colonel of his own regiment; but still much more so because it is entirely inconsistent with the mild and generous nature of that brave Prince, whose patience, fortitude, intrepidity and *fol.* 60.
humanity, I must declare upon this solemn occasion, are qualities in which he excells all men I ever knew, and which it ever was his greatest desire to employ for the relief and preservation of his father's subjects. I believe rather that this report was spread to palliate and excuse the murders they themselves committed in cold blood after the battle of Culloden.

I think it my duty to return my sincere acknowledgments to Major White and Mr. Fowler for their human and complaisant behaviour to me during my confinement. I wish I could pay the same compliment to Governor Williamson who used me with the greatest inhumanity and cruelty. But having taken the sacrament this day I forgive him as I do all my enemies.

die in the religion of the Church of England which I look upon as the same with the Episcopal Church of Scotland in *fol.* 61.
which I was brought up.

When he laid his head upon the block, he said: God reward my friends and forgive my enemies! Bless and restore the King, the Prince, and the Duke, and receive my soul. Amen!

*Upon Towerhill, Monday, August* 18*th*, 1746, *in the* 58*th year of his age.*

•

From the *Constitutional Journal*, September 27th, 1746.

Lord Balmerino taking leave of his fellow-sufferer, Lord 1746
Kilmarnock, generously said: He was sorry to have his com- 18 Aug.
pany in such an expedition, and that he wished he alone might pay the whole reckoning. He was himself asked by one of the spectators, Where Lord Balmerino was. To whom he answered,

27 Sept. 'I am here, Sir, at your service.' His manner of undressing occasion'd most to say of him with Shakespear—

> 'He was
> A bridegroom in his death, and run into 't
> As to a lover's bed.'

He gave something to one who had behaved well to him in his confinement, whom he singled out of the crowd. He laid himself on the wrong side of the block, but on information immediately rectified it without the smallest appearance of disorder or confusion.

## The Speech of Donald MacDonell of Tiendrish, of the Family of Keppoch.[1]

*fol.* 62. As I am now to suffer a publick, cruel, barbarous and (in
1746 the eyes of the world) an ignominious and shameful death, I
18 Oct. think myself obliged to acknowledge to the world that it was principle and a thorough conviction of its being my duty to God, my injured king and oppressed country, which engaged me to take up arms under the standard and magnanimous conduct of his royal highness, Charles, Prince of Wales, etc. It was always my strongest inclination as to worldly concerns to have our ancient and only rightful royal family restored, and even (if God would) to lose my life chearfully in promoting the same. I solemnly declare I had no by-views in drawing my sword in that just and honourable cause, but the restoration of my king and prince to the throne, the recovery of
*fol.* 63. our liberties to this unhappy island which has been so long loaded with usurpation, corruption, treachery and bribery; being sensible that nothing but the king's restoration could make our country flourish, all ranks and degrees of men happy,

---

[1] He was the son of Ronald Mor of Tir-na-dris, second son of Archibald MacDonald of Keppoch, and so nephew to the famous 'Coll of the Cows.'—*History of the MacDonalds*, p. 490. He suffered death at Carlisle. See f. 106. He is said to be the original of Sir Walter Scott's Fergus MacIvor in *Waverley*. His sword, a genuine *Andrew Ferrara*, afterwards came into the possession of the Howards of Corby Castle.

and free both Church and State from the many evil consequences of Revolution principles. 18 Oct.

I must here let the world know that the whole evidences, to the number of six or seven, brought against me at my trial by the Elector's council were perjured. What they aim'd to prove was only relative to the battle of Gladesmuir, and in this they swore the greatest untruths, and did not declare one word of truth. I earnestly pray for their repentance that God may forgive them, as I sincerely do, not only them but all other my enemies in general.

I own indeed I was engaged in said battle and saw a great slaughter on all hands where I was posted. But sure I am the *fol.* 64.
evidences that appeared against me did not see one step of my behaviour that day.

I thank God ever since I drew my sword in that just and honourable cause, I acted not only in obedience to the merciful commands of my glorious prince but in compliance with my own natural disposition, with charity and humanity to my enemies, the Elector's troops, when prisoners and in my power, without receding at the same time from that duty and faithfulness I owed to my prince and the common cause.

My being taken prisoner at the battle of Falkirk[1] was more owing to my own folly or rashness than the bravery or valour of the enemy, whom I saw before I was taken entirely routed and chased off from the field of battle. I fell into their hands *fol.* 65.
by supposing them at a distance, and in the twilight, to be Lord John Drummond's regiment and French picquets; but too late, to my sad experience, found out my fatal mistake. And here I refer to my enemies to declare my behaviour on that occasion.

Now though I am presently to die a cruel death, yet when I consider the justice of the cause for which I suffer, it puts a stop to every murmuring reflection; and I thank Almighty God I resign my life to Him, the giver, with chearfulness and submission to his Divine and all-wise providence.

I here declare I die an unworthy member of the Roman Catholick Church, in the communion of which I have lived,

---

[1] See ff. 979-982.

18 Oct. however much her tenets be spoken against and misrepresented fol. 66. by many; and in that I now expect salvation through the sufferings and merits and mediation of my only Lord and Saviour Jesus Christ. But I hereby declare upon the word of a dying man that it was with no view to establish or force that religion upon this nation that made me join my Prince's standard, but purely owing to that duty and allegiance which was due to our only rightful, lawful and natural sovereign, had even he or his family been heathen, Mahometan, or Quaker.

I am hopeful and am persuaded that my valorous prince, by the blessing of God, will at last be successful, and when in his power, will, under God, take care of my poor wife and family. And as I have no worldly fortune to leave my dear son, I recommend him to the blessing and protection of Almighty God, as the best legacy I can give him, and earnestly require his fol. 67. obedience to my last and dying command, which is to draw his sword in his King's, his Prince's and his country's service, as often as occasion offers and his lawful sovereign requires. As I have the honour to die a Major in our King's service, I am hopeful, if my dear child deserves it, he will succeed me at least in the same office, and serve his Prince with the same honour, integrity and faithfulness I have all along endeavoured, to which his royal highness is no stranger.

I conclude with my blessing to my dearest wife and all my relations and friends, and humbly beg of my God to restore the King, to grant success to the Prince's arms, to forgive my enemies and receive my soul. Come, Lord Jesus, come quickly! Into thy hands I resign my spirit!

Donald MacDonell.

fol. 68. *At Carlisle, upon Saturday, October* 18*th, the festival of St. Luke, the Evangelist,* 1746.

*N.B.*—Major MacDonell was the first that drew blood in the cause. He with only twelve or thirteen Highlanders under his command had the courage to attack two companies of soldiers (being eighty or ninety in number), whom he chas'd for seven or eight miles in Lochabar, and at last forced them to lay down their arms and surrender themselves prisoners of war; among whom were Captain John Scott, son of Scotstarvet; and Captain James Thomson, brother to Charlton. Captain Scott had a very pretty gelding which Major MacDonell made a present of to the prince. There was not the least mark of a wound upon the Major or any of his worthy few, tho' many firings had been exchanged in the chase and severals of the soldiers were wounded. 18 Oct. *fol.* 69.

I had a particular account of this gallant and surprizing action (oftener than once) from the Major's own mouth. He was a brave, undaunted, honest man, of a good countenance and of a strong, robust make. He was much given to the pious acts of devotion, and was remarkably a gentleman of excellent, good manners. That submission and chearfulness of temper with which he bore up under all his sufferings may easily be discovered from the following copies of letters which are faithfully transcrib'd from the Major's own hand-writ, with a return to one of them, transcrib'd from an holograph of the writer.[1]

Robert Forbes, A.M.

## Copy of a Letter to Mr. Robert Forbes at My Lady Bruce's[2] lodgings at Leith. *fol.* 70.

Dear Sir,—After making offer of my compliments to yourself and the Leith ladies, no doubt you have heard before now that our trials come on the ninth of September next; and may God stand with the righteous! The whole gentlemen who came from Scotland are all together in one floor with upwards of one hundred private men; so that we are much thronged. They have not all got irons as yet; but they have not forgot 1746 24 Aug.

[1] See further references to the Major, and his presenting the Prince with the first horse he rode in the war, the capture he had made in this first skirmish, ff. 357, 360, 641.

[2] Dame Magdalene Scott, widow of Sir William Bruce of Kinross, a noted Jacobite, in whose family Mr. Forbes lived until his marriage.

Aug. me, nor the rest of most distinction, but the whole will be soon provided. You'll make my compliments to Lady Bruce and Mr. Clerk's[1] family, but especially to Miss Mally Clerk,[2] and tell her that notwithstanding of my irons I could dance a
fol. 71. Highland reel with her. Mr. Patrick Murrey makes offer of his compliments to you, and I hope we'll meet soon. I am sincerely, my dear sir, your affectionate and most obliged servant, DONALD MACDONELL.

*Castle Carlisle, Aug. 24th,* 1746.

## COPY of a RETURN to the ABOVE.

1746 7 Aug. DEAR SIR,—Your kind letter of the 24th instant I gladly received, and it gives me no small pleasure to find you are in so much good health, amidst the many distressing circumstances of your present situation. The friends mentioned in your letter make a return of their compliments, and best wishes to you with as much affection and earnestness as friendship is capable of. In a word, that worthy person, my lady, gives you her blessing.

fol. 72. Some charitable and well-disposed persons in Edinburgh are employing their good offices in raising a contribution for what is needful amongst the poor prisoners with you; and I hope their laudable endeavours will meet with success. For certainly human nature in distress, be the case what it will, is always a just object of pity and compassion, except to those selfish and barbarous persons who are proof against all the tender feelings of sympathy.

Your friends in the Castle of Edinburgh are ever mindful of you. Kellie[3] is put into the room with your companions, and poor Kingsburgh[4] is close confin'd by himself in the

---

[1] Captain Hugh Clerk, in Leith. [2] His daughter, Mary.

[3] Alexander Erskine, fifth Earl of Kellie. He had taken part in the Rebellion, but surrendered to the Government, and after over three years' imprisonment in Edinburgh Castle, was released without being brought to trial.

Alexander MacDonald of Kingsburgh, in Skye, factor to Sir Alexander MacDonald. For concealing the Prince in his house he was arrested, carried to Fort Augustus, and sent by a party of Kingston's Horse to Edinburgh. He was committed prisoner to the Castle on 2nd August. See his own history in the sequel.

solitary room where Kellie formerly was, and is not allowed to step over the threshold of the door; a situation not at all agreeable to his taste, for he loves a social life. 27 Aug.

That honest soul,[1] Cowley, glad am I to hear of his welfare. Pray remember me in the kindest manner to him and all my acquaintances with you, particularly Mr. Robert Lyon, whose passing thro' Edinburgh I am heartily sorry I knew nothing about; for I should have used my utmost endeavours to have seen him. *fol.* 73.

Let me know the issue of your case whatever it be, for you may assure yourself of a place in the prayers and good offices of, dear sir, your friend and servant, ROBERT FORBES.

*August 27th*, 1746.

*P.S.*—The lady prisoners in the Castle are well. Adieu.

*N.B.*—When the Major was in the Castle of Edinburgh he happened to run scarce of monie, when I was so happy as to make out for him among my acquaintances upon July 20th and 21st, 1746, ten pounds sterling.

Upon the approach of winter, collected for MacGregor of Glengyle and some men with him, fifteen pounds sterling. To Mr. James Falconar, clergyman, fifty shillings sterling. To a brother of Kinloch Moidart, who had been bred a sailor, a guinea and a half. Isabel Shepherd's effects, given that way, eight pounds sterling. Total, 37. 1. 6. ROBERT FORBES, A.M.

## COPY of a LETTER to MR. JOHN MOIR, Merchant in Edinburgh, and Mr. ROBERT FORBES in Leith. *fol.* 74.

MY DEAR GENTLEMEN,—These are letting you know that I was yesterday on my trial, and after long and most eloquent pleadings, was brought in guilty. Really, there never came a more eloquent discourse out of men's mouth, and more to the purpose than what my good and worthy friend Mr. Lockheart[2] 1746 16 Sept.

[1] Patrick Murray, silversmith. [2] Lord Covinton.—F.

16 Sept. spoke, and he would tear them all to pieces if justice or law was regarded. I have wrote to my dear wife, but did not let her into the whole, and I have recommended to her in the strongest manner to goe forthwith home, and to manage her affairs at home in the best way possible. And I recommend to you both as ever you can oblige me (whose former favours I can never forget) that you back what I have wrote her, and that you pre-
fol. 75. vail with her to goe directly home. I never will forgive either of you if you do not manage this point. For tho' she would come here 'tis probable she would get no access. And even tho' she would get no access, our parting would be more shocking to me than death. My trust was still on the Almighty's providence, and as that is still the case with me, I hope for the best and prepare for the worst. In a word, I am afraid there are few here will escape being brought in guilty. Before this Court there were the most villainous proofs laid in against me by four of Colonel Leef's men and a dragoon, of facts that I never was guilty of, not the least circumstance of what they charged me with. But may God stand with the righteous, for I freely forgive them. You shall hear from me
fol. 76. as oft as I can. And for God's cause, see my wife fairly on her way home. You'll make my compliments to the worthy ladies of my acquaintance, and all other friends in general, and your selves both in particular, and I am, with the greatest sincerity and affection, Dear gentlemen, your most obliged humble servant, DONALD MACDONELL.

*Carlisle Castle, September 16th*, 1746.

*P.S.*—If you see it advisable that my wife, with some ladies of distinction, wait of General Husk—do in this as you see proper. I believe the half of our number will plead guilty. Pray give my service to Mrs. Jean Cameron, and excuse my not writing her.

fol. 77. ## COPY of a LETTER to MR. ROBERT FORBES at my LADY BRUCE's lodgings, Leith.

DEAR SIR,—Wishing from my whole heart that these may

find you and your Leith friends in good health, I have had a little bit fever some days past. But God be blessed I am now in good health, heart and spirits, and if it is my fate to goe to the scaffold, I dare say that I 'll goe to death as a Christian and a man of honour ought to do. But it is possible that a broken ill-us'd Major may be a Colonel before he dies. You 'll make my compliments to my Lady Bruce, Mr. Clerk's family, but Miss Mally in particular, and the rest of the honest folks in that city, and accept of the same from him who is with the greatest sincerity, affection, and esteem, my dear sir, your most affectionate and obedient servant, while 28 Sept.

DONALD MACDONELL.

*Carlisle Castle, September 28th,* 1746.

*P.S.*—I wrote you and Mr. Moir a joint letter about ten days agoe. *fol.* 78.

## COPY of a LETTER to MR. JOHN MOIR, Merchant in Edinburgh.

MY DEAR SIR,—I received yours yesterday of the 11th current, and as I am to die to-morrow this is my last Farewel to you. May God reward you for your services to me from time to time, and may God restore my dear Prince, and receive my soul at the hour of my death. You 'll manage what money Mr. Stewart is due me as you see proper, for my poor wife will want money much to pay her rents and other debts. I have given Mr. Wright fourteen pounds sterling and half a dozen shirts, in order to be sent my poor wife by Mr. Graham at Multrees of Hill. I have wrote just now to Mr. Graham, and sent letters inclosed to my poor wife and my brother. My dear Sir, manage Mr. Stewart's money as you best advise, and fail not to write to my wife of same. I conclude with my blessing to yourself and to all the honourable honest ladies of my acquaintance in Edinburgh, and to all other friends in general, and in particular those in the Castle. And I am, with 1746 17 Oct. *fol.* 79.

17 Oct. love and affection, My dear Sir, yours affectionately till death, and wishes we meet in Heaven. DONALD MACDONELL.

*Castle Carlisle, October 17th, 1746.*

*P.S.*—Remember me in particular to my dear Mr. Robert Forbes.

*N.B.*—Several persons, particularly the lawyers, agents and writers, insisted much with the Major that he should plead guilty, that being the only probable chance left him for saving his life. He resisted all their importunities without the least wavering. And when they press'd him very hard to comply with their advice he
*fol.* 80. boldly declar'd that he had far rather be taken out and hanged at the Bar, in the face of those judges before whom he was soon to be tried, than do any such thing as they desired. Upon which they gave over arguing with him upon the point, and promis'd to exert themselves to the utmost to save so valuable a life.

*N.B.*—The following narrative is so doubtful that it is not to be relied upon.[1]

Mr. Burnet of Monboddo, Advocate, talking to one of the judges at Carlisle, said that he thought the Government should treat these condemned men with humanity and in a different way from those who are really downright rebels; because, said he, they were influenced in the matter by a principle of conscience, being firmly persuaded in their minds that they were endeavouring to do right to one that was injur'd, and whom they look'd upon as their only lawful sovereign, having no ill design at all against the person, family or estate of King George, but wishing him to return to his own place; and therefore their rising in arms could not strictly be look'd upon as proceeding from a spirit of rebellion. The judge answered: 'Sir, If you design to plead the cause or to soften the case of your countrymen, you hit

[1] This narrative is accordingly scored through by Mr. Forbes.

upon the worst argument in the world, for the Government is positively determin'd by all means to extirpate these folks of principle.' This happen'd in a private conversation. 17 Oct.

ROBERT FORBES, A.M.

## The SPEECH of DAVID MORGAN,[1] Esquire. *fol.* 81.

IT having been always deem'd incumbent on every person in my situation to say something of himself and the cause he suffers for, I could not decline it, however disagreeable to my persecutors, when I once held it my duty. 1746 30 July.

The cause I embarked in was that of my liege sovereign, King James the Third, from an opinion I long since had of his just right; an opinion, founded on the constitution, and strongly recognised and established by an Act of Parliament, now in its full vigour, which neither the people collectively nor representatively have any power or authority to subvert or alter. [See the Statute of Charles 2d.] Nor can that law be repealed but by a free Parliament summoned to meet by a lawful king, not by a Convention commanded by a foreign prince and *fol.* 82. usurper, and intimidated and directed by him at the head of a foreign army.

To this Convention we owe the Revolution; to the Revolution we owe the accession of the family of Hanover; and to this accession all our present ills, and the melancholy and certain prospect of the entire subversion of all that is dear and valuable to Britons.

My opinion of the King's title to the imperial crown of these realms, thus uncontrovertible, received additional strength and

[1] David Morgan was a member of a good family in Monmouthshire, was about fifty years of age, and educated for the Bar. Not succeeding to his expectation in that profession he retired to his estate, and lived as a country gentleman until he joined the Prince's army at Preston. He was evidently consulted by the Prince and his officers as to their procedure, for he got the name of 'the Pretender's Councillor.' He accompanied the army to Derby. He was among the first lot of prisoners executed on Kennington Common, and there being no clergyman appointed to attend them on the scaffold, Mr. Morgan, 'with his spectacles on' for about half an hour, 'read prayers and other pious meditations to them out of a book of devotion.'—'History of the Rebellion,' *Scots' Magazine*, pp. 291, 295, 298, 300.

30 July satisfaction from his character and qualifications, confirmed to me by persons of the strictest honour and credit, and demonstrated to me, that his establishment on the throne of his ancestors would be an incident as productive of happiness to the subject as of justice to the sovereign; since his Majesty's confess'd superiour understanding is absolutely necessary to extricate our country out of that most desperate state she has
*fol.* 83. been declining to since the Revolution, and has precipitately fallen into since the accession.

On this declension and ruine of our country have the favourers and friends of both Revolution and accession built vast and despicable fortunes, which possibly they may entail (with the conditions of slavery annexed) on their betrayed and abandoned issue; it being much more clear that slavery will descend from generation to generation than such fortunes so acquired.

Have we not seen parliaments in a long succession raise supplies sufficient to surfeit avarice? Do we not see that avarice heaping up millions for the nurture and support of foreign dominions on the ruines of that country that grants them? Nor can this move the least compassion or even common regard
*fol.* 84. for her welfare and interest from that ungrateful avarice. British Councils since the Usurper's accession have had foreign interest their constant object, and the power and finances of the imperial crown of Great Britain have been betrayed, prostituted, and squandered for the convenience and support of the meanest Electorate in Germany; and the Elector's conduct has been more destructive and detrimental to our country than all the finesse, treachery and force that the French or any other adversary's council and power could have attempted or effected. Land armies only can sustain and cover dominions on the Continent. These are raised in the country protected, and maintained by the country protecting. Here Great Britain has all the burden and Hanover all the advantage: whereas navies are the British bulwarks, which have by the Elector been neglected, misapplied, or employed to her disadvantage, and can alone guard and protect her dominions and commerce.

*fol.* 85. If the present convention had any regard to self-preservation or that of their constituents they would this session have made new laws for the further security of privilege. The panick, diffused universally over the Electoral family, would have prepared an easy assent, to any law in the subject's favour. But even here these representatives omitted this second opportunity of securing and improving the happiness of their electors; and instead thereof have given additional power to the Usurper to suspend the bulwark of liberty, and invert the order and method of trials for treason—precedents they will have occasion one day to repent of, since they very probably may fall victims to them. 30 July

The false glosses and fears of Popery universally propagated have deluded unthinking, vulgar minds, and diverted all attention to reason; when it is clear to any just reflection that his Majesty can have no happiness but what results from his Britain, who he must know from melancholy experience will not be tempted to part with the doctrines and exercise of the religion established in her. His Majesty must know that a lawful king must adhere to the constitution in Church and State, and show a most inviolable attachment to those laws that were made for the security of both, whatever indulgences and concessions are made by conventions to an usurper for the breach of all. A lawful king is a nursing father who would protect us, and demand no more supplies than the immediate services required, and those from the riches of the country, the excrescences of trade and commerce, without prejudice to either. And such would be deem'd best that were just sufficient for the purposes they were raised, and for which only they would be employed. But an usurper is a stepfather that builds his own hopes and views on the ruine and destruction of his usurped dominions, and has joy from the fleecing and impoverishing of those under his influence and power. *fol.* 86.

Even his Majesty's enemies allow him great understanding. Nor has any one of them imputed breach of honour to him. His abilities and sense of our situation would move him to interpose in favour of his subjects, and are equal (if human abilities are so) to extricate us out of the various perplexities and intricacies we have been brought into by negotiations for thirty years, for the preservation of the balance of power, to the disappointment of every Briton's hope and the ridicule of all our enemies. *fol.* 87.

30 July If you once think, my brethren, you must repent. If you repent you must make the constitution just reparation; which can only be done by calling in your lawful king, James the Third, who has justice to attempt and wisdom to compleat a thorough reformation in the constitution and to fix it in its pristine happy state; and which, in spite of all chicane and prejudice, without a restoration, will never be done.

fol. 88. I am to declare my happiness in having such a wife and daughter that forgive my involving them in my misfortunes, and having an undeserved share in them. I heartily thank them and wish them both temporal and eternal happiness, and hope that those who are friends to my King will look upon them as the relict and orphan of a fellow-subject that has suffered in the royal cause.

I glory in the honour I have had of seeing his royal highness, Charles, Prince Regent, and of being admitted into his confidence. And I here declare it the greatest happiness I ever knew and the highest satisfaction; and such as even my vainest thoughts could never have suggested to me—an honour to every rational creature that can judge of the many requisite virtues of a prince centred in him truly, tho' so often falsly assign'd to the worst. His character exceeds anything I could have imagined or conceived. An attempt to describe him

fol. 89. would seem gross flattery, and nothing but a plain and naked narrative of his conduct to all persons and in all scenes he is engaged in can properly shew him,—a prince betrayed by the mercy he shewed his enemies, in judging of the dispositions of mankind by the benignity of his own. His fortitude was disarmed by it, and his ungrateful enemies think they have reaped the benefit of it. But let them not rejoice at his misfortunes, since his failure of success will, without the immediate interposition of providence, be absolutely their ruine. What a contrast is there between his royal highness the Prince and the Duke of Cumberland! The first displays his true courage in acts of humanity and mercy; the latter a cruelty in burning, devastation and destruction of the British subjects, their goods and possessions. I would ask, Who is the true heroe?

The report of my having betrayed his royal highness or his

friends is scandalously false. My appeal to the counsel for the 30 July
prosecution on my trial and my suffering death must refute it *fol.* 90.
to all honest men. And I hereby declare I had rather suffer any death the law can inflict. I deem death infinitely preferable to a life of infamy. But the death I suffer for my King gives me vast consolation and honour that I am thought worthy of it.

To conclude, my brethren and fellow-subjects, I must make profession of that religion I was baptized, have continued and shall, through the Divine permission, die in, which is that of the Church of England, and which I hope will stand against the malice, devices and assaults of her enemies, as well those of the Church of Rome as those equally dangerous, the followers of Luther and Calvin, covered under and concealed in the
specious bugbears of Papacy and arbitrary power. This my *fol.* 91.
faith I have fully set forth in a poem of two books, intitled, The Christian Test, or, The Coalition of Faith and Reason, the first of which I have already published, and the latter I have bequeathed to the care of my unfortunate but very dutyful daughter, Mrs. Mary Morgan, to be published by her, since it has pleased God I shall not live to see it. To this poem I refer, which I hope will obviate all cavil to the contrary.

I freely forgive all my enemies, from the Usurper to Weir and Maddox, the infamous witnesses in support of his prosecutions of me. And I must also and do from my heart forgive my Lord Chief Justice[1] for his stupid and inveterate zeal in painting my loyalty to my King with all the reproaches he had genius enough to bestow on it, when he passed sentence on seventeen at once, and which he did without precedent, because it was without concern.

I beg all I have offended that they will forgive me for Jesus *fol.* 92.
Christ sake, my only Mediator and Advocate. To whom with the Father and the Holy Spirit be all adoration, praise, glory, dominion and power for ever. Amen!

DAVID MORGAN.

*Kennington Common, Wednesday, July* 30, 1746.

---

[1] Lee.

## *fol.* 93. THE SPEECH of MR. JAMES BRADESHAW.[1]

1746 28 Nov. IT would be a breach of duty in me to omit the last opportunity of doing justice to those who stood in need of it. I think it incumbent upon me the rather because I am the only Englishman in this part of the world who had the honour to attend his royal highness in Scotland.

When I first joined the King's forces I was induced by a principle of duty only, and I never saw any reason since to convince me that I was in the least mistaken. But, on the contrary, every day's experience has strengthened my opinion that what I did was right and necessary. That duty I discharged to the best of my power; and as I did not seek the reward of my service in this world, I have no doubt of receiving it in the next.

Under an opinion that I could do more good by marching
*fol.* 94. with the army into Scotland than by remaining with the Manchester regiment at Carlisle, I obtained leave to be in my Lord Elcho's corps, for I was willing to be in action.

After the battle of Culloden I had the misfortune to fall into the hands of the most ungenerous enemy that I believe ever assum'd the name of a soldier, I mean the pretended Duke of Cumberland, and those under his command, whose inhumanity exceeded anything I could have imagined in a country where the bare mention of a God is allowed of. I was put into one of the Scotch kirks together with a great number of wounded prisoners who were stript naked and then left to die of their wounds without the least assistance; and tho' we had a surgeon of our own, a prisoner in the same place, yet he was not permitted to dress their wounds, but his instruments
*fol.* 95. were taken from him on purpose to prevent it; and in consequence of this many expired in the utmost agonies. Several of the wounded were put on board the *Jean*, of Leith, and

[1] Bradshaw was a Manchester man, and in the check trade there. Joining the Prince's army he became first a captain in the Manchester regiment, and afterwards entered into the Prince's life-guards, under Lord Elcho, which accounts for his going into Scotland. He was taken prisoner after the battle of Culloden.—'History of the Rebellion,' *Scots' Magazine*, p. 341.

there died in lingering tortures. Our general allowance while we were prisoners there was half a pound of meal a day, which was sometimes increased to a pound, but never exceeded it; and I myself was a eye-witness that great numbers were starved to death. Their barbarity extended so far as not to suffer the men who were put on board the *Jean* to lie down even upon planks, but they were obliged to sit on large stones, by which means their legs swell'd as big almost as their bodies. 28 Nov.

These are some few of the cruelties exercised, which being almost incredible in a Christian country, I am obliged to add an asseveration to the truth of them; and I do assure you upon the word of a dying man, as I hope for mercy at the day *fol.* 96.
of judgment, I assert nothing but what I know to be true.

The injustice of these proceedings is aggravated by the ingratitude of them, for the Elector of Hanover's people had been often obliged by the prince, who ordered his prisoners the same allowance of meal as his own troops, and always made it his particular concern that all the wounded should be carefully dressed and used with the utmost tenderness. His extreme caution to avoid the effusion of blood, even with regard to spies when his own safety made it almost necessary, and his surprizing generosity to all his enemies without distinction certainly demanded different treatment. And I cannot think that an English army under English direction could possibly behave with such unprovoked barbarity.

With regard to the report of his royal highness having ordered that no quarters should be given to the enemy I am *fol.* 97.
persuaded in my conscience it is a wicked malicious lie, raised by the friends of usurpation in hopes of an excuse for the cruelties committed in Scotland, which were many more and greater than I have time to describe. For I firmly believe the Prince would not consent to such orders even if it were to gain the three kingdoms.

I would gladly enter into the particulars of his royal highness's character if I was able; but his qualifications are above description. All I can say is, he is every thing that I could imagine, great and excellent, fully deserving what he was born for—to rule over a free people.

I die a member of the Church of England, which I am satis-

8 Nov. fied would ffourish more under the reign of a Stewart than it fol. 98. does now, or has done for many years. The friends of the House of Hanover say they keep out Popery. But do they not let in Infidelity, which is almost become (if I may so say) the religion established?

I think it every man's business by all lawful means to live as long as he can; and with this view I made a defence upon my trial which I thought might possibly do me service. All that the witnesses swore on my behalf was strictly true, for I would much rather die than be the occasion of perjury. After sentence my friends petitioned for my life, and if it had been granted I should have been thankful for it. But as it otherwise happens I patiently submit, and have confident hopes, that upon the whole, it will be better for me for I suffer for having done my duty.

As I expected, so it happen'd upon my trial, Mr. Maddox perjured himself, and I am afraid he is so immersed in wicked-fol. 99. ness that it would be difficult for him to forbear it. Lieutenant Moore swore he was acquainted with me at Manchester, but I declare I was never in his company before we met at Inverness. I should think it a great reflection upon the honour of any government to encourage officers to lay by their swords and become informers. I forgive both these and all my enemies.

I am convinced that these nations are inevitably ruin'd unless the royal family be restored, which I hope will soon happen. For I love my country, and with my parting breath I pray God to bless it. I also beseech Him to bless and preserve my lawful sovereign, King James the 3d., the Prince of Wales, and Duke of York, to prosper all my friends, and have mercy on me! JAMES BRADESHAW.[1]

*Friday, November 28th, 1746, Upon Kennington Common.*

---

[1] There was a soldier of the name of Enoch Bradshaw in the ranks of Cobham's dragoons in the Duke of Cumberland's army, who also was present at the battle of Culloden and wrote a letter in reference to it to his brother. The contrast in language is strong. But as the letter is not known to have been formerly printed, it is given in the Appendix at Letter A. We are indebted to Mr. C. H. Firth of Oxford for the copy.

The case of Mr. Francis Buchanan of Arnprior is so very singular, and attended with such odd, unaccountable circumstances that an exact narrative of it ought to be preserved, which is as follows: 18 Oct. *fol.* 100.

Arnprior was taken prisoner at his own house some time before the battle of Culloden by Mr. James Dunbar, captain of militia, and eldest son of Sir George Dunbar of Dunbar House or Woodside, and committed to Stirling Castle. As Mr. Buchanan had never been in arms, nor had made any publick appearance whatsomever in the whole affair from first to last, so the ground of his commitment was only *suspicion*. The commanding officer looking upon this to be very thin, and not imagining Arnprior to be in any hazard at all, allow'd him the full liberty of the Castle, to walk up and down as he pleased, without keeping a strict eye over him. When several *fol.* 101. prisoners were ordered from Stirling Castle to Carlisle, Arnprior was appointed to be amongst the number. Captain James Thomson, brother to Charlton, and Lieutenant Archibald Campbell (commonly called Tobie) had the command of the party that guarded the prisoners in their journey. These officers knowing well the case of Mr. Buchanan, and having witness'd the usage he had met with in Stirling Castle, treated him in a quite different manner from the other prisoners. In the forenoon, as if he had been only a fellow-traveller, they would have desir'd him to ride forwards to bespeak dinner at a proper place, and to have it ready for them against the time they should come up. In the afternoon they also desir'd him to ride on to take up night quarters and to order supper for *fol.* 102. them, and all this without any command attending him; so that he had several opportunities every day of making his escape had he dream'd that he ran any risque of his life in the issue of a trial. Besides, the officers wou'd not have indulg'd him such liberties had they imagin'd any danger in his case. When the prisoners came to Carlisle, Arnprior, much to his own surprize and that of the foresaid officers, was immediately ordered into a dungeon and to have irons clapt upon him. Finding himself in a situation he had entertain'd no apprehension of, and dreading the worst from this harsh usage he sent for Captain Thomson, who very readily came to him, and

18 Oct. after some conversation upon the unexpected change of treatment desir'd to know what he could do for him. Mr.
fol. 103. Buchanan beg'd he would wait upon the commanding officer
and let him know his whole case, and the usage he had met
with both in Stirling Castle and in the way to Carlisle, which
he did not doubt would have a good effect for making a
change to the better in his state of confinement. Captain
Thomson frankly undertook to do as he desir'd, and without
loss of time, honestly represented the whole affair to the commanding officer, who said he was heartily sorry for the gentleman, but that it was not in his power to do him any service,
because the Solicitor-General was come to Carlisle, and that
(now he was in the place) his province it was to determine in
these matters. Captain Thomson did not stop here, but like
one of generosity and compassion, went directly to the Solici-
fol. 104. tor-General and laid before him the case of Mr. Buchanan,
requesting him to consider it and to allow the gentleman a
more easy and comfortable confinement. The Solicitor-General
told him he knew there were more Buchanans than one among
the prisoners, and therefore he desired to know what Mr.
Buchanan he meant; and then asked if he knew his Christian
name, and whether or not he had a designation. Captain
Thomson answered that he did not know Mr. Buchanan's
Christian name, that though he was sure he had a designation
he had forgot it. Upon this the Solicitor-General pull'd a
list of names out of his pocket, and after looking it over asked
the Captain if Mr. Francis Buchanan of Arnprior was the person whose case he had been representing. 'That same is the
gentleman,' replied the Captain. 'Then,' says the Solicitor-
fol. 105. General, 'pray, Sir, give yourself no more trouble about that
gentleman. I shall take care of him. I have particular orders
about him, for HE MUST SUFFER!' This unaccountable speech
from such a mouth about one neither convicted nor tried sur-
priz'd the Captain not a little and made him walk off without
insisting any more, to tell Arnprior the result of what had
pass'd, in the softest manner he could.

This narrative was given by Lieutenant Archibald Campbell, after the execution of Arnprior, to several persons in Edinburgh, particularly to the Rev. Mr. Thomas Drummond.

When Arnprior was brought to a trial not a single overt act was prov'd against him. An unsubscrib'd letter was produced in the Court which had been intercepted in going to the Highland army, and several persons, particularly Commissary Finlayson in Stirling, gave their affidavits that it was the handwrit of Mr. Francis Buchanan of Arnprior. Upon this the jury without any hesitation or scruple brought him in guilty. After sentence of death was pronounced against him so little did people imagine that he would suffer that he was prevail'd upon to send off an express to London in order to give a true and exact representation of his case, not doubting but that this would be sufficient to obtain a reprieve from a verdict and sentence pronounced upon such slight grounds, but all to no purpose. To destruction was he destin'd by his enemies, and accordingly suffer'd death at Carlisle in company with the Revd. Mr. Thomas Coppoch, Macdonald of Kinlochmoidart, Major Donald MacDonell, etc., etc., etc.

18 Oct.

*fol.* 106.

Arnprior left no speech behind him, but took an opportunity of declaring that as he was persuaded in his conscience King James the 8th had the sole undoubted right to sit on the throne of these realms, so the only action that stared him most in the face was that he had acted the prudent and over-cautious part in not joining the Prince immediately upon his arrival, and drawing his sword in so glorious a cause, and in not exerting all his endeavours upon those with whom he had any interest to rise in arms for their King and country.

*fol.* 107.

Robert Forbes, A.M.

Arnprior lived at the house of Lenny, near Callender, in Monteith, and Stewart of Glenbucky came from Balquhidder with his men. Arnprior went to see them in Strathyre. There happened some dispute between them about the Majorship of the Perth regiment to which Glenbucky belonged. Arnprior brought Glenbucky home with him to Lenny that night. On the morning of next day he was found dead in his bed with a pistol in his hand.[1]

[1] This paragraph seems to have been inserted here later. It is not in the handwriting of Mr. Forbes.

## *fol.* 108. THE SPEECH of the Right Honourable ARTHUR, LORD BALMERINO, faithfully transcribed from his lordships own handwrit.

1746 18 Aug. I WAS brought up in true loyal Anti-Revolution principles, and I hope the world is convinced that they stick to me.

I must acknowledge I did a very inconsiderate thing, for which I am heartily sorry, in accepting of a company of foot from the Princess Anne, who I knew had no more right to the crown than her predecessor the Prince of Orange, whom I always look upon as a vile, unnatural usurper.

To make amends for what I had done I join'd the King when he was in Scotland, and when all was over I made my escape and liv'd abroad till the year 1734.

In the beginning of that year I got a letter from my father which very much surprized me. It was to let me know that he had got the promise of a remission for me. I did not know what to do. I was then, I think, in the Canton of Bern and had no body to advise with. But next morning I wrote a letter to the King, who was then at Rome, to acquaint his Majesty that this was done without my asking or knowledge, and that I
*fol.* 109. would not accept of without his Majesty's consent. I had in answer to mine a letter written with the King's own hand allowing me to go home, and he told me his banker would give me money for my travelling charges when I came to Paris, which accordingly I got.

When his royal highness came to Edinburgh, as it was my bounden and indispensible duty, I join'd him, though I might easily have excused myself from taking arms on account of my age. But I never could have had peace of conscience if I had stayed at home when that brave Prince was exposing himself to all manner of dangers and fatigue both night and day.

I am at a loss when I come to speak of the Prince; I am not a fit hand to draw his character. I shall leave that to others. But I must beg leave to tell you the incomparable sweetness of his nature, his affability, his compassion, his justice, his temperance, his patience, and his courage are virtues, seldom all to be found in one person. In short, he wants no qualifications requisite to make a great man. 18 Aug.

Pardon me, if I say, wherever I had the command I never suffered any disorders to be committed, as will appear by the Duke of Bucleugh's servants at East Park, by the Earl of Findlater's minister, Mr. Lato, and my Lord's servants at *fol.* 110.
Cullen, by Mr. Rose, minister at Nairn, who was pleased to favour me with a visit when I was an prisoner in Inverness, by Mr. Stewart, principal servant to the Lord President at the house of Culloden, and by several other people. All this gives me great pleasure now that I am looking on the block on which I am ready to lay down my head. And tho' it had not been my own natural inclination to protect every body as far as lay in my power it would have been my interest so to do. For his royal highness abhorred all those who were capable of doing injustice to any of the King, his father's subjects, whatever opinion they were of.

I have heard since I came to this place that there has been a most wicked report spread and mentioned in several of the Newspapers, that his royal highness, the Prince, before the battle of Culloden, had given out in orders that no quarters should be given to the enemy. This is such an unchristian thing and so unlike that gallant Prince that nobody that knows him will believe it. It is very strange if there had been any such orders that neither the Earl of Kilmarnock, who was Colonel of the regiment of *fol.* 111.
Foot-guards, nor I, who was Colonel of the 2d troop of Lifeguards, should never have heard any thing of it, especially since we were both at the head-quarters the morning before the battle. I am convinced that it is a malicious report industriously spread to excuse themselves for the murders they were guilty of in calm blood after the battle.

Ever since my confinement in the Tower, when Major White and Mr. Fowler did me the honour of a visit, their behaviour was always so kind and obliging to me that I cannot find words to express it. But I am sorry I cannot say the same thing of General Williamson. He has treated me barbarously, but not quite so ill as he did the Bishop of Rochester. I forgive him and all my enemies. Had it not been for Mr. Gordon's advice I should have prayed for him as David does, Psalm 109.

18 Aug I hope you will have the charity to believe I die in peace with all men, for yesterday I received the Holy Eucharist from the hands of a clergyman of the Church of England, in whose Communion I die as in union with the Episcopal Church of Scotland.

I shall conclude with a short prayer.

*fol.* 112. O Almighty God! I humbly beseech Thee to bless the King, the prince, and Duke of Yorke, and all the dutiful branches of the royal family! Endue them with thy Holy Spirit, enrich them with thy heavenly grace, prosper them with all happiness and bring them to thine everlasting kingdom! Finally I recommend to thy fatherly goodness all my benefactors and all the faithful adherents to the cause for which I am now about to suffer. God reward them! Make them happy here and in the world to come! This I beg for Christs sake, in whose words, etc. Our Father, etc.

*A List of those who were evidences against my Lord Balmerino taken likewise from his own handwrit.*

William M'Gie, messenger.
Hugh Douglas, drummer to Lord Elcho.
James Barclay.
David Gray.
James Paterson.
} One of these three was servant to the Secretary, and another of them servant to little Black Malcolm.
Roger Macdonald.

*Upon the truly noble Lord Balmerino.*

In this brave Lord, the mirror of mankind
Religion, virtue, loyalty had join'd,
To make him great in ev'ry act of life.
But greater still when he resign'd that life;
With fortitude went through his martyrdom.
No nobler motto can adorn his tomb.
Strictly attached to royal Stewart's race,
For which he died, and by his death gave grace,
To the just cause he bravely did embrace.
Like great Montrose, he fear'd no tyrant rage;
Next to his prince, the hero of the age.

His glorious death to distant climes shall reach, 18 Aug.
And trait'rous minds true loyalty shall teach.
His noble soul to us endears his name,
And future ages shall resound his fame.

*Extempore, upon viewing the scaffold immediately after the execution of Lord Balmerino.*

Lo! where undaunted Balmerino stood,
Firm without canting, seal'd his faith in blood.
In cause of right and truth unmov'd and just,
And as he knew no fear, betray'd no trust.
The amaz'd spectator drop'd the troubled eye,
As more afraid to look than he to die.
Whence sprung this great unparallel'd deport?
God and his conscience were his strong support.

*Upon the death of Lord Balmerino, by a non-jurant clergyman in London in a letter to a friend.* fol. 113.

Short is the term of life, my honour'd friend.
Soon o'er the puny space with rapid speed
The unreturning moments wing their way,
And sweep us from our cradles to the grave.
And yet this puny space is fill'd with toil
And labours in the transitory scene,
To make life wretched, as 'tis frail and fleeting.
Rattles and toys employ and please our childhood.
Wealth, pomp, and pleasure, full as arrant trifles,
Commence the idols of our riper years,
And fill the mind with images as wild;
Absurd, fantastic, as a sick man's dreams,
Disquieting this span of life in vain.

He truly lives and makes the most of life
Who well hath studied its intrinsic worth,
And learnt to lay it down with resignation;
Can like thee, Balmerino! lay it down,
And deem it not his own, when honour claims it.

See the unconquer'd captive (matchless man!),

18 Aug. Collected in his own integrity;
Facing with such a brow the king of terrors,
And treading on the utmost verge of life,
Serene as on a summer's ev'ning walk;
fol. 114. Draws more amazing eyes upon his scaffold
Than ever gaz'd on laurell'd heroes car;
Triumphant in his fall o'er all that crusht him.

Amazement seiz'd the crowded theatre,
Struck with the awful scene; and throb'd a heart
In ev'ry breast but his. The headsman trembl'd
That rais'd the fatal axe. Nor trembl'd he
On whom 'twas falling. Falls the fell edge;
Nor shrinks the mangl'd victim! What are stars and garters?
All titles, dignities, all crowns and sceptres,
Compar'd with such an exit? When these perish
Their owners be as they had never been,
In deep oblivion sunk. This greater name,
As long as any sense of virtue lasts,
Shall live and fragrant smell to after times,
Exhibiting a pattern how to die,
And far the fairest former times have seen.

*Copy of a Letter to a gentleman in Holland, vindicating the character of Arthur, Lord Balmerino, in a certain important point.*

1746 Sept. Dear Sir,—I have not yet been able to answer the cries of the officers for beating orders, and I can conceive no other reason for our Ministry's refusing them than that of the
fol. 115. Young Chevalier's being in Scotland, and that they thought that his escape might have been saved through their means. But now that he is safe arrived in France, I hope that we shall meet with no more difficulties.

I had the honour to be of Lord Balmerino's acquaintance, and it was my misfortune to be pitch'd upon to attend upon him in the Tower at his last moments, and upon the scaffold, where I was witness to a behaviour that even exceeded all that we read of in the heroes of antiquity. His whole behaviour was so composed, so decent that it greatly surprized the sheriffs, the clergymen, his friends and the spectators; and at the same time not a soldier present but was moved by his intrepidity. Sept.

My Lady Balmerino is now at my elbow, and she has desired me to write to your Heer Pensioner that she is greatly offended at a passage in your *Amsterdam Gazette* of Tuesday, September 6th, 1746, where, in giving an account of that Lord's unhappy end, the author is so insolent as to insert so notorious a falsehood that it can in no sort be justified. He has no authority from my lord, from the sheriffs, from the clergymen, nor even from our lying newspapers. The government here had a power over his body, and he has suffered for his rebellion. But neither they nor their agents abroad have any just power over *fol.* 116.
his reputation. 'Tis barbarous to the greatest degree, and lays us under a necessity, let the consequences be what they will, to give you my lord's own words on that point, a point which he had greatly at heart to clear up; and they are as follows:

'I have heard since I came to this place that there has been a most wicked report spread, and mentioned in several of the newspapers that his royal highness, the Prince, before the battle of Culloden, had given out in orders, that no quarters should be given to the enemy. This is such an unchristian thing, and so unlike that gallant Prince that nobody that knows him will believe it. It is very strange if there had been any such orders that neither the Earl of Kilmarnock, who was Colonel of the regiment of foot-guards, nor I, who was Colonel of the 2d troop of life-guards, should never have heard any thing of it, especially since we were both at the head-quarters the morning before the battle. I am convinced that it is a malicious report industriously spread to excuse themselves for the murders they were guilty of in calm blood after the battle.'

I shall take it as a very great favour if you are so kind as to *fol.* 116*a*.
lay the above before the proper person, whose authority it is to take cognizance of it that he may be obliged to retract in the most solemn manner, a falshood, uttered to the prejudice of the reputation of one of the greatest men that ever was

Sept. born, let his principles have been what they will. It is my Lady Balmerino's desire. It is mine, as his friend, and as a friend to truth and justice.

I dare not presume to write to so great a man as the first person of so great a republick. Therefore I beg that you will lay it before him, and you will very much oblige, Dear Sir, your, etc.

*Sic subscribitur*, JOHN WALKINGSHAW.[1]

*London*, $\frac{6}{17}$ *September* 1746.

*P.S.*—The above is writ by the direction of my Lady Balmerino.

## vl. 117. SPEECH of the Rev[d]. Mr. THOMAS COPPACH of Brazenose Colledge, Oxford, commonly (but foolishly) called Bishop of Carlisle.[2]

1746 18 Oct DEAR COUNTRYMEN,—I am now on the brink and confines of eternity, being to suffer a scandalous, ignominious death for my duty to God, my King and country, for taking up arms to restore the royal and illustrious house of Stewart, and to banish from a free, but inslaved people a foreigner, a tyrant, and an usurper. For never was the British nation since the Norman Conquest govern'd more arbitrarily, or enjoyed more precariously. Never was a nation under the canopy of Heaven more grossly abused, more scandalously imposed upon, or more notoriously deceived. Liberty has been banished. Tyranny and oppression, like a deluge, have overflowed the land.

---

[1] Mr. Walkingshaw is frequently mentioned in this collection. He was a London Jacobite, and was able to be of considerable service to the Scottish prisoners there.

[2] He was the son of John Coppoch, or rather Cappoch, a tailor in Manchester, and joined the Prince there, by whom it is said he was appointed chaplain to the Manchester Regiment, and was promised the bishopric of Carlisle. See two pamphlets reprinted by Samuel Jefferson. (1) 'The Trial and Life of Thomas Cappoch (the rebel-bishop of Carlisle),' 1839; and (2) 'An Account of Carlisle during the Rebellion of 1745, to which is added a speech (supposed to have been) delivered by Thomas Cappoch, the rebel-bishop, on his execution at Carlisle,' etc. 18 October 1746 : 1844.

Places of the utmost importance have been taken from the most deserving and given to the illiterate, unexperienced or unqualified. Our fleets and armies, once the terror of Europe, are now the scorn, contempt and derision of all nations. The one, like Æsop's mountain, has brought forth a silly, ridiculous mouse; the other has brought home eternal infamy, shame and disgrace. Such a Ministry and such a Parliament was nation never curs'd with. The former for these thirty years past has exhausted our treasures, drain'd our purses on foolish idle treaties and negotiations to procure us allies and friends; and no friend or ally have we in the world we can trust, rely on or confide in. The latter, vassals, creatures equally despicable, void of honour and conscience, compos'd of pensioners and placemen, have sacrificed their country, their all, to the boundless ambition and insatiable avarice of a beggarly Hanoverian electorate. Estimates, supplies and subsidies have been granted, *nemine contradicente*, though never so illegal, unreasonable and unjustifiable. Such heavy taxes and such a monstrous load of national debt this kingdom never groan'd under since Julius Cæsar's invasion; so that justice may say, never was Parliament (some few members excepted, *rara avis in terris, nigro simillima cygno*) more slavishly devoted or more sottishly infatuated.

18 Oct.

*fol.* 118.

Here it will not be amiss to introduce that worthy honest gentleman, the Elector's Earl of Oxford.[1] When a motion was made by some true patriots to bring him to give an account of his stewardship of the nation's money, did not his Elector solemnly declare that a hair of his head should not be hurt, conscious that he had acted by his direction in sending sums to aggrandize his poor, native, scrubby country, Hanover, —sums to engage the affections of the wavering Dutch, sums to biass the votes at elections?

*fol.* 119.

These are facts the truth of which is too obvious. What soul inspired with the least grain of courage, the smallest spark of honour, or that sympathizes with the sufferings of his fellow-creatures, would tamely sit down or patiently acquiesce under such monstrous and unheard of grievances? When religion and

[1] Robert Harley, Earl of Oxford, the Lord Treasurer.

18 Oct. loyalty, liberty and property call to arms! when a prince adorned with all the gifts of nature, and grace of education, endowed and enriched with every virtue, amiable and commendable (*maugrè* all your vile reports, invidious reflections and slanderous aspersions; *maugrè* all your pulpit harangues, stuff'd with downright falsities, gross calumnies and palpable absurdities), daily amidst the horrid din of war, risks and exposes his precious life to conquer and subdue the Lernæan Hydra, to deliver you from almost Egyptian tyranny, bondage, and slavery:—a prince whose title to the crown is indisputable, whose conduct and courage are inimitable and matchless, and whose virtue, mercy, and goodness none can parallel or equal! *Nil viget simile aut secundum*!

*fol.* 120. Such is your legal *jure-divino*, hereditary and lineally descended Prince, whose father you exiled and excluded, whose grandfather you rebelled against and banished, and whose head, conscious of your own demerits, you have set a price on! Seeing the heir, Come, say you, let us fall upon him and kill him, and the inheritance will be ours. Be not too secure. Your iniquities are almost compleated. The fulness of time is almost at hand, even at the door, when the Almighty I AM, with my Prince under the shadow of his wings, will pour out the vials of his wrath, fury and indignation on that cursed, perjured and abandoned people, on this guilty, perverse, wicked and adulterous generation. For the innocent blood of the righteous cries Vengeance! Vengeance! O my native country! my native soil! What pangs hast thou to endure! What throes to labour with! What misery and desolation is thy lot and portion!

Kind Heaven! Avert all these evils by a speedy and blessed restoration, that Albion may no more be scourged by vultures, storks and logs; may once more see happy days, once more put on its ancient lustre, pristin splendor and glory; that God and Cæsar may enjoy their own just and due right; that
*ol.* 120*a*. tribute may be rendered to whom it is due, custom to whom custom, fear to whom fear, honour to whom honour, and that the supreme powers may receive the sovereign allegiance, obedience and subjection which are really and duly theirs by the laws of God and nature in conjunction.

It is for sentiments and tenets of this kind I am now made a publick spectacle, that my head is publickly to be exposed and my bowels burnt; which I gladly and willingly submit to without the least reluctance. Nay, I should rejoice beyond measure, if this simple head of mine could be fixed on all the Cathedral and parish churches in Christendom to satisfie the whole Christian world of the honesty of my intentions and the integrity of my principles. And could it be engraven on my tombstone:— 18 Oct.

UNDERNEATH ARE DEPOSITED THE ASHES OF THE ONLY ENGLISH PROTESTANT CLERGYMAN WHOSE HONOUR, COURAGE, LOYALTY AND ZEAL ARE CONSPICUOUS IN HIS ROYAL MASTER'S CAUSE. DULCE ET DECORUM EST PRO PATRIA MORI.

I should have been silent about my religion had it not been to satisfie and open the eyes of severals who have been deceived by false representations, which was, I believe, the reason I was spit upon, struck, stoned, insulted and barbarously treated by severals (some of whom are since dead), not only in Carlisle but Kendall and elsewhere, when I was led in a string by Mark *fol.* 121.
Ker's dragoons through all the dirt and nastiness, with my arms pinion'd, from Carlisle to Lancaster Castle, by an express order of the pretended Duke of Cumberland, notwithstanding Baron Clarke's specious harangue to make the jury believe I was not an object worthy of their notice.

I declare then upon the faith of a dying man that I die an unworthy member of that particular church, the Church of England, as she stood before the Revolution, which I firmly believe to be truly primitive, Catholic and Apostolic, free from superstition on the one hand, and Fanaticism and Enthusiasm on the other. May she prosper and flourish! May she, like a house on a rock, withstand all tempests, storms and inundations, till time shall be no more!

And now, God bless my royal, true and undoubted sovereign, King James, his royal highness Charles, Prince of Wales, Henry, Duke of York and Albany! O Jehovah! bless, protect and preserve them! for nothing but fraud and anarchy and confusion; nothing but horrid bloodshed and barbarous murder, villainy, perjury, ambition and cruelty, barbarity within and corruption without, have reigned triumphant in

18 Oct. this island since their banishment. God bless all my enemies,
*fol.* 122. persecutors and slanderers, especially that corrupted judge, Baron Clarke, who put a most malicious construction on every thing said at my trial! God forgive Samuel Pendlebury of Manchester, John Hill, Thomas Joy, an Irishman, John Gardener and Thomas Dennison, both of Carlisle, who all grossly perjur'd themselves at my trial! O Lord God! send them timely repentance and remission of their sins! I freely and voluntarily forgive them; and humbly ask pardon of all I have injured in thought, word or deed. I close with the dying words of my Saviour and Redeemer, and the protomartyr deacon, St. Stephen, 'Father, forgive them, for they know not what they do! Lord, lay not this sin to their charge! Lord Jesus, receive my soul! Amen!'

*At Carlisle upon Saturday, October 18th, the Festival of St. Luke the Evangelist, 1746.*

## SPEECH of ANDREW WOOD, who join'd the PRINCE in ENGLAND.

*Blessed are they who suffer for truth and righteousness sake; for theirs is the kingdom of heaven.*

28 Nov. FRIENDS, COUNTRYMEN AND FELLOW-SUBJECTS,—I was born in
*fol.* 123. Scotland, and brought up in the Established Church (as they call it) of that kingdom. But of late (thanks be to God!) I saw my error and became a member of the Church of England.[1]

I engaged in this just cause, for which I am to suffer, out of the true love and regard I had for my king and country. For I thought it my indispensible duty to join my Prince when I found him in this country endeavouring to restore his father, my lawful sovereign, King James, to his undoubted right. I had the honour to be made a Captain by his royal highness, raised a company out of my own pocket, and served my Prince to the utmost of my power, even beyond what could have been expected of one so little accustomed to military acts as I was.

---

[1] See a full account of how this came about at f. 806.

And for thus faithfully serving my king, and endeavouring to restore him and your ancient liberties, I am to fall a sacrifice to the Usurper and his bloodthirsty son, the pretended Duke of Cumberland. But thy will, O my God! be done! And as Thou art pleased that I suffer for truth and righteousness sake, I resign myself entirely to Thy will! 28 Nov. *fol.* 124.

And now I am in a few moments to launch into eternity, I do solemnly declare, as I must answer at the aweful tribunal of Almighty God, that the order said to be given by his royal highness for giving the Usurper's men no quarters the day of Culloden battle is false, and contrived merely to excuse the barbarities committed by the Duke and his men on all those of our army who fell into their hands; for I myself saw the orders of that day. No. It does not agree with the Prince's former lenity at the battles of Gladesmuir and Falkirk.

I leave the impartial world to judge of this brave Prince's character from his actions, which would require one of the greatest hands to do justice to it.

O my countrymen! Consider the woeful situation you are in. In short, all that ever your forefathers fought for is gone. You have nothing you can depend upon, burthened with debt, ruined with a standing army. Alas! you have no more than the name of Liberty. Rouse you then while it is in your power, and take the first opportunity to restore your lawful *fol.* 125. sovereign, King James, which is the only sure way to make these nations happy. I leave my hearty prayers for concluding the same, and I hope Almighty God will, in His good appointed time, restore my lawful sovereign, King James. And in a particular manner, I beseech Thee, O God! to bless his royal highness, Charles, Prince of Wales, and the Duke of York.

I shall conclude with forgiving all my persecutors, hoping Almighty God will of His infinite mercy, forgive me all my sins, through Jesus Christ, pardon the frailties of my youth, and accept my imperfect repentance.

Into Thy hands I commit my spirit, O Lord, Thou God of mercy and truth! ANDREW WOOD.

*P.S.*—I sent for a Presbyterian minister to have administred

28 Nov. the sacrament to me; but he refused. Lord forgive him; for I do.

*Kennington Common, Friday, November 28th*, 1746.

*fol.* 126. A genuine and full Account of the Battle of Culloden, with what happened the two preceeding days, together with the young Prince's miraculous escape at, from and after the battle, fought on April 16th, 1746; to his return to the continent of Scotland from the Western Islands on the 6th of the succeeding July. Taken from the mouths of the old Laird of MacKinnon, Mr. Malcolm MacLeod, etc., and of Lady Clanronald and Miss Flora MacDonald, by John Walkingshaw of London or Dr. John Burton.

1746 April Upon April 14th (afternoon) the Prince marched from Inverness on foot at the head of his guards to Culloden House, where the clans and others met him, and stayed thereabouts
April under arms. He himself did not go to bed. Vpon the 15th by daybreak he marched the men up to Culloden Muir about a mile south-east of the house, and review'd them drawn up in two lines of battle. About eleven o'clock he ordered them to refresh themselves by sleep or otherwise just in the field, during which time he walked about cajoling the different chiefs, and proposed to all of them separately to march off the men towards the evening and attack the enemy by daybreak; but finding the bulk of them against the proposal (reckoning it rather too desperate an attempt untill they were joined by
*fol.* 127. Keppoch and his men with others that were soon expected), he drop'd the project. About 4 afternoon Keppoch arrived with 200 men. Then it was said Lord George Murray proposed the night march, and undertook to manage the attack, which was agreed to. And when near dark, the men were marched off, the front of the second line following the rear of the first.
April About 2 o'clock of the morning of the 16th the Duke of Perth came galloping up from aside to the front of the second line, and ordered the officers to wheel about and march back to Culloden. They had not gone above one hundred yards back when they met the Prince, who called out himself, 'Where

the devil are the men a-going?' It was answered, 'We are ordered by the Duke of Perth to return to Culloden House.' 16 April
'Where is the Duke of Perth?' says the Prince. 'Call him here.' Instantly the Duke came up, and the Prince, in an angry tone, asked what he meant by ordering the men back. The Duke answered that Lord George with the first line was gone back three-quarters of an hour agoe. 'Good God!' said the Prince, 'what can be the matter? What does he mean? We were equal in number, and would have blown them to the devil. Pray, Perth, can't you call them back yet? Perhaps *fol.* 128.
he is not gone far yet.' Upon which the Duke begg'd to speak with his royal highness. They went aside a very short space. The Prince returned and call'd out, 'There is no help for it, my lads; march back to Culloden House.' Back they marched to Culloden House (the Prince bringing up the rear) where the bulk of them arrived about 6 in the morning. The Prince after ordering and earnestly recommending to everybody to do their utmost to get provisions to his men went into the house, threw himself upon the top of a bed, boots, etc., upon him; but in a few hours, being alarmed with the approach of the enemy he hurried to the field, and endeavoured to put his men in order by drawing them up in two lines. But they, being some fatigued and others dispersed about seeking victuals, could not be all got together; so that when the cannonading began there were not 3000 men in the field, and these not in the best order. At that time the Prince was in the rear of all, ordering some men to replace some others that he had sent from the second line to the left of the first. He immediately sent off an aid-de-camp with orders to the generals in the front *fol.* 129.
to make the attack, and, moving forwards beyond the second line, sent off a second and a third aid-de-camp with positive orders to attack. It seems the first aid-de-camp happened to be killed with a cannon shot just at setting out, which 'tis thought was the reason the attack was not made soon enough.

Upon the right the attack was made with great bravery by the Athol brigade, Stewarts, Camerons, and part of the MacDonalds; but the left was so soon flanked by a great body of the enemy's horse that from the centre to the left they never got up to give their fire. The right broke in upon the enemy,

5 April sword in hand, and did great execution, but were likewise soon flanked and very much galled by the grape-shot. And Lochiel and Keppoch, being both soon wounded in the advancing, were carried off, which their men observing, immediately they fled; which so alarmed all the corps to the left that they gave way in confusion.

Just at this time the Prince called out to stop and he would light from his horse and return to the charge at their head.
*fol.* 130. But a number of his officers got about him, and assured him that it was improbable for them to do any good at present. For since the clans had turned their backs they would not rally, and it was but exposing his person without any probability of success; and therefore intreated he would retire, and really forced him out of the field.

The retreat was made with the utmost regularity. Not above 500 of the Low-country men, having detached themselves from the main body, kept together till they received the Prince's orders to shift for themselves.

*N.B.*—There was a battery of canon that played very smartly for a considerable time just upon the place where the Prince was, and one of his grooms was killed about two hundred yards straight in his rear.

After the forces were entirely defeated he retired to a house of a factor or steward of Lord Lovat, about ten miles from Inverness, where meeting with that lord, he stayed supper.

After supper was over he set out for Fort Augustus (where a musket-bullet was taken out of the counter of his horse), and pursued his journey for Invergary where he proposed to have dined. But finding no victuals he set a boy a fishing, who caught two salmon on which he made a dinner, and con-
*fol.* 131. tinued waiting there for some of his troops, who had promised to rendezvous at that place; and being disappointed he resolved
18 April to proceed to Locharkaig. He arrived there on the 18th at two in the morning and went to sleep, which he had not done for five days and nights, his forces having been under arms, marching and counter-marching without meat for 48 hours before the battle. He remained there till 5 o'clock in the afternoon in hopes of obtaining some intelligence; but gain-

ing none, he set out from thence on foot, and travell'd to the 18 April Glens of Morar, over almost inaccessible mountains, where he arrived on the 19th at 4 in the morning. He set out about noon the same day for Arrisaig, through as bad ways as before, where he arrived at 4 in the afternoon.

He remained there seven days waiting for Captain O'Neil, who joined him on the 27th, and informed him, as did many 27 April others from all quarters, that there were not any hopes of drawing his troops together again in a body. Upon which he resolved to go to Stornway in the Island of Lewis, a town at the head of a loch of that name, in order to hire a ship to go to France. The person employed for this purpose was one *fol.* 132. Donald MacLeod, who had an interest there.

On the 28th he went on board in an eight-oar'd boat, in 28 Apri company with O'Sullivan, O'Neil, and some others, ordering the people to whom the boat belonged to make the best haste they could to Stornway. The night proved very tempestuous, and they all begg'd of him to go back, which he would not do. But seeing the people timorous, he, to keep up their spirits, sung them a Highland song. The weather proving worse and worse, on the 29th, about 7 in the morning they were driven ashore on a point of land called Rushness, in the north-east part of the island of Benbecula, which lies betwixt the islands of North and South Ost or Uist, being about 5 miles long from east to west, and 3 miles broad from north to south, where as soon as they had got on shore, the Prince helped to make a fire to warm the crew, who were almost starved to death with cold.

On the 30th, at 6 in the evening, they set sail again from 30 Ap Stornway, but meeting with another storm were obliged to put into the island Selpa (Scalpa) in the Harris. This island is about one mile long and half a mile broad. There they all *fol.* 13 went ashore to a farmer's house, passing for merchants that were shipwrecked in their voyage to the Orkneys, the Prince and O'Sullivan going by the name of Sinclair, the latter passing for the father, the former for the son.

Thence they thought proper to send Donald MacLeod (who had been with them all the time) to Stornway, with instructions to freight a ship for the Orkneys.

May On the 3d of May they received a message from him that a ship was ready. On the 4th they made the mainland and set out on foot for that place, and arrived on the 5th about noon at the point of Arynish, two miles southeast from Stornway, having travelled 18 hours on the hills without any kind of refreshment, and were misled by their guide, either thro' ignorance or design. There a messinger from Stornway met him, and told him that Donald MacLeod, having got drunk, had told one of his acquaintances for whom he hired the ship; upon which there were soon 200 people in arms at Stornway upon a report that the Prince was landed with 500 men, and was coming to burn the town; so that he and his company were obliged to lie all night on the muir with no other refreshment than bisket and brandy.

May On the sixth they resolved to go in the eight-oar'd boat to
f. 134. the Orkneys, but the crew refused to venture; so that they were obliged to steer south along the coast side, where they met with two English ships which compell'd them to put to a desart island called Seafort or Iffurt, being about half a mile long and near as much broad. There they remained till the 10th, and must have famished, had they not providently found some salt fish upon the island.

May About ten o'clock in the morning that day they embarked
for the Harris, and at break of day on the 11th they were
chased by an English ship, but made their escape among the
rocks. About 4 in the afternoon they arrived at Benbecula,
where they stayed till the 14th, and then set out on foot for
the mountain of Corradell, in South Ost or Uist, being about
16 miles distant. There they stayed till about the 8th of
June June, living upon fish and other kind of game, which the
Prince daily killed himself, and had no other kind of drink
than the water they found there.

The Militia at this time coming to the island of Irsky
(Eriska), (which lies betwixt the island of Barra and South Ost
f. 135. or Uist, is about three miles long and one broad, and is the
very first British ground the Prince landed upon at his coming
on the late expedition); the militia, I say, coming to the
island, obliged the Prince and his company to disperse; and he,
with two or three others, sailed for the island Uia or Ouaya,

lying betwixt South Uist and Benbecula. There he remained three nights, till having intelligence that the militia were coming towards Benbecula, he immediately got into the boat and sailed for Loch Boysdale, but being met by some ships of war he was obliged to return to Loch Karnon, which is about a league and a half west southwest from the island Uia. 11 June

There he remained all day, and at night sailed for Loch Boysdale, which is about 30 miles south of Loch Karnon, and belongs to the MacDonalds. There he arrived safe, and stayed 8 days upon a rock, making a tent of the sail of the boat, and lived upon fish and fowl of his own killing.

There he found himself in the most terrible situation, for having intelligence on June 18th that Captain Caroline Scott had landed at Killbride within less than two miles of them, he was obliged to dismiss the boat's crew, and taking only O'Neil with him, he went to the mountains, where he remained all night, and soon after was informed that General Campbell was at Barnare (an island lying between North Uist and Harris), being about two miles long and one broad. It belongs to the MacLeods. So that now he had forces not far from him on both sides, and was absolutely at a loss to know which way to move, having forces on both the land sides of him, and the sea on the other, without any vessel to venture into securely. 18 June *fol.* 136.

In this perplexity Captain O'Neil accidentally met with Miss Funivella or Flora MacDonald, to whom he proposed assisting the Prince to make his escape, which she at last consented to, on condition the Prince would put on women's cloaths, which he complied with. She then desired they would goe to the mountain of Corradale and stay there till they heard from her, which should be soon.

There they arrived, and accordingly remained two days in great distress, and then hearing nothing from the young lady, the Prince concluded she would not keep her word. But about 5 o'clock in the evening a message came from her desiring to meet her at Rushness, being afraid to pass the Ford, which was the shortest passage, because of the militia. They luckily found a boat which carried them to the other side Uia, where they remained part of the day afraid of being seen of the country people. *fol.* 137.

June In the evening they set out in the same boat for Rushness, and arrived there at 12 o'clock at night, but not finding the young lady, and being alarmed by a boat full of militia they were obliged to return back two miles, where the Prince remained on a muir till O'Neil went to the young lady, and brought her with him to the place appointed about sunset next evening.

About an hour after they had got to the Prince they got an account of General Campbell's arrival at Benbecula, which obliged them to move to another part of the island, where, as the day broke, they discovered four vessels full of armed men close on the shore. They having seen the fire on the land, made directly up to the place where they were,[1] so that there was nothing left for them to do but to throw themselves among
*fol.* 138. the heath, by which means they escaped being found.

When the wherries were gone they resolved to go to Clanranold's house. But when they were within a mile of it they heard that General Campbell was there, which obliged them to retreat again to Rushness; from whence they set out in a little yawl or boat for the isle of Sky about the end of June, and were at sea all night. The next day as they were passing the point of Watternish, in the west corner of Sky, the wind being contrary, and the female frighted at turning back, they thought to have landed there, but found it possess'd by a body of forces; which obliged them immediately to put to sea again after having received several shots from the land.[2]

From hence they went and landed at Killbride, in Troternish in Sky, about twelve miles north from the above mentioned point. There they also found a body of troops within less than two miles of them, whose commanding officer rode as far as Moystod or Mougestot, not far from Sir Alexander MacDonald's seat, near which place they landed. He there enquired of Miss Flora MacDonald who she was, and who was with her, which she answered as she thought proper. [The
*fol.* 139. officer, however, would not be satisfied untill he had searched the boat. In the mean time the Prince was hid on shore, so near as to hear what passed].[3]

---

[1] See f. 528.

[2] See ff. 530-534.

[3] Stated in the sequel to be incorrect.

Immediately after this scene was over the Prince parted with his female guide, and took to the hills, and travelled without rest 15 long miles[1] south south-east in women's cloaths till he came to Mr. MacDonald of Kingsburgh's house, where his female guide met him again, having gone a nearer way.[2] There the Prince got his first refreshment, and stayed till next day, towards the evening; when he set out from Kingsburgh's house, but would not, on any account, let the consequence be what it would, consent to put on women's cloaths again, having found them so cumbersome the day before. He went 15 long miles[1] to a place called Portree or Purtry, where again he met his female preserver, who had gone a different route, and which was the last time they saw each other. June

At Portree the Prince met Young MacLeod of Raaza or Raasa, and with him went directly to the island of Raaza, being about ten (or 6) miles in a small yawl or boat, being the only one to be got at that time. *fol.* 140.

On the 1st of July he landed at a place called Glam, in Raasa, where he remained two nights in a miserable hutt, so low that he could neither sitt nor stand, but was obliged to lie on the bare ground, having only a bundle of heath for his pillow. 1 July

On the 3d of July he proposed going to Troternish, in the Isle of Sky, notwithstanding it blew very hard, and that he had but the small yawl above mentioned, scarce capable of carrying six people. However, he set forward about 7 o'clock in the evening, having with him Mr. Malcolm MacLeod. He had not gone far before the wind blew harder, and the crew, being timorous, begg'd to turn back again. But he refused, and to encourage them sung a merry Highland song. About eleven the same night he landed at a place in the island of Sky called Nicolson's Rock, near Scorobry (Scorobreck), in Troternish, being about ten miles from Glam. He remained there all night without any kind of refreshment, not even so much as a fire to dry his cloathes, being quite wet. In this wet condition he was for the space of 48 hours. 3 July *fol.* 141.

The next day about 7 o'clock in the evening he left this

[1] Should be 7. See f. 144.

[2] See ff. 145, 532, 533.

4 July rock, being accompanied by Mr. Malcolm MacLeod, the latter passing for the master, the former for the man, who always carried the little baggage[1] whenever they saw any person or came near any place. They marched all night through the worst of roads in Europe, and did not halt till they arrived at Ellagol or Ellighuil, near Kilvory or Kilmaree, in Strath, not far from a place in some maps called Ord or Aird, in the Laird of MacIntosh's[2] country, being full 24 miles long.

After two hours rest and some little refreshment the Prince seem'd quite alert and as ready for fatigue as ever, and diverted himself with a young child in the house, carrying him in his arms and singing to him, and said that perhaps that child may be a captain in my service [*or*] might live to be of great use to him hereafter.

5 July At that place the old Laird of MacKinnon came to him, and they set out together that day, being July 5th, for the f. 142. mainland in a small boat, tho' the night was very tempestuous and the coast very bad. The next day, July 6th, they landed safe in Knoidart, which is 30 miles from the place they set out from. At that place he left the Laird of Mackinnon, who was the next day taken prisoner. In their passage they met with a boat in which were some militia, with whom they spoke. As they did not much exceed their own number, they were resolved to make all the head they could, and to fight them in case they had been attack'd.

What method the Prince took to conceal himself on the mainland of Scotland, or what route he took till the 20th of September, being the time he embarked for France, will be made publick at another time.

*Citadel of Leith, Saturday, July* 11*th*, 1747.

1747 11 July Mr. Alexander MacDonald of Kingsburgh and his lady were paying their compliments to my Lady Bruce, when it was proposed to read the above Account or Journal in the hearing of Kingsburgh, that so he might give his

[1] Two shirts, one pair of stockings, one pair of brogs, a bottle of brandy, some scrapes of mouldy bread and cheese, and a three-pint stone bottle for water.—F.

[2] Altered to MacKinnon's. See f. 144.

observations, or rather corrections upon it. He and the whole company (about 14 in number) declared their satisfaction in the proposal. There were present, John Fullarton, senior of Dudwick; James MacDonald, joiner in Leith; Lady Lude, with her eldest son and her daughter; Mrs. Graham and her son; Mrs. Rattray, Mrs. Jean and Rachel Houstons, etc. 11 July

The Account was accordingly read, and Kingsburgh made the following observations: *fol.* 143.

Page[1] 130, near the foot. Instead of Invergar, it should be Invergarry; a place belonging to the Laird of Glengarry.

Page 132, near the foot. Instead of Selpa, it should be Scalpa, commonly called the Island Glass.

Page 134, at the foot. Instead of Irsky, it should be Eriska.

Page 139, at the top. Kingsburgh said it was not fact that the boat was searched, and that the Prince should have heard what passed.

*Ibid.* Instead of 15 long miles south south-east, it should be 7 long miles.

*Ibid.* Kingsburgh was at pains to represent to the Prince the inconveniency and danger of his being in a female dress, particularly from his airs being all so man-like, and told him that he was very bad at acting the part of a dissembler. He advised him therefore to take from him a suite of Highland cloaths with a broadsword in his hand, which would become him much better. But in the meantime that he should go out of his house in the female dress, lest the servants should be making their observations, and stop at the edge of a wood upon the side of a hill, not far from the house, where he and others should come to him with the Highland cloathes, broadsword, etc.

Mrs. MacDonald said that she behoved to employ her daughter as handmaid to the Prince for putting on his womens cloaths, 'For,' said she, 'the deel a preen he could put in.' *fol.* 144. When Miss MacDonald (*alias* Mrs. MacAllastar[2]) was a dressing of him, he was like to fall over with laughing. After the

[1] These pages will be found by the marginal folios.

[2] This is interlined in the manuscript. See f. 216. She married Ronald MacAlister, of the family of Loup.

11 July peeness, gown, hood, mantle, etc., were put on, he said, 'O, Miss, you have forgot my apron. Where is my apron? Pray get me my apron here, for that is a principal part of my dress.'

Kingsburgh and his lady both declared that the Prince behaved not like one that was in danger, but as chearfully and merrily as if he had been putting on women's cloathes merely for a piece of diversion.

Agreeable to Kingsburgh's advice they met at the edge of the wood, where the Prince laid aside his female rags, which were deposited in the heart of a bush till a proper opportunity should offer of taking them up; for these that were present resolved to preserve them all as valuable tokens of distress. After the Prince had got himself equipt in the Highland cloathes with the claymore in his hand, the mournful parting with Kingsburgh ensued. Away he went to struggle through a series of fresh dangers, the faithful MacKechan still attending him.

*Ibid.* Instead of 15 long miles to Portree or Purtry, it should be 7 long miles.

Page 140, line 1. Instead of 10 miles, it should be 6.

*Ibid*, near the foot. Instead of Scorobry, it should be Scorobreck.

Page 141. Kingsburgh said that MacIntosh's country there named behoved to be an error in the writer, for that MacIntosh had no property in Sky, and it ought to be named MacKinnon's country.

*fol.* 145. Page 142. Kingsburgh said that he thought the Prince with old MacKinnon had landed in Moror and not in Knoidart; but he own'd MacKinnon behov'd to know best. He said he was pretty sure that old MacKinnon was made prisoner in Moror, which might happen after his coming from Knoidart.

When all the Journal was read over, Kingsburgh observed that the persons from whose mouths it had been taken had not medled with his part of the story; 'and,' said he, 'they were indeed right, for they know very little about it.'

Then particular questions were put to him with respect to that pamphlet called 'ALEXIS, Part 1st.' To give some instances, it was asked him, Whether or not it was true that he took along with him out of Sir Alexander MacDonald's house a bottle of wine and some bread in his pocket for the refreshment of the Prince; that he had great difficulty to find him, and that it was owing to the accidental running of a flock of sheep that at last he found him sitting upon a rock? He answered, 'All these things are exactly true as related in that small pamphlet.' Then it was asked, Whether or not the Prince made briskly up to him with a thick short cudgel in his hand, and asked, If he was Mr. MacDonald of Kingsburgh? He said, 'It was really so, and that the Prince very pleasantly said, Then all is well; come, let us be jogging on;' but that he told him he had brought some refreshment along with him, which he behoved to take before they set out; which accordingly was done, they sitting upon the top of the rock. 11 July *fol.* 146.

Asked further. If it was true that the Prince lifted the petticoats too high in wading the rivulet when going to Kingsburgh, and that honest MacKechan[1] hastily called to him to beware? He said, 'It is fact; and that MacKechan cried, "For God's sake, Sir, take care what you are doing, for you will certainly discover yourself;" and that the Prince laughed heartily, and thanked him kindly for his great concern.'

Asked further. If the cursing and blasphemous speech of the Duke of Cumberland was such as represented in 'ALEXIS, Part 1st.' 'Exactly so,' said he, for I had it almost in the very same words from the mouth of Sir Alexander MacDonald, who was witness to the Duke's expressing himself in that rough way. 'Whom,' added he, 'I indeed never saw in the face.' Then he said that 'ALEXIS' was exactly and literally true in every ace (not only as to facts but even circumstances) that concerned his management of and conversation with the Prince, the *brogs* not excepted, and that he looked upon the recovery

---

[1] Neil MacEachan or MacKechan, the attendant of Flora MacDonald, was a descendant of the MacDonalds of Howbeag in South Uist. He followed the Prince to France, and settled there. One of his sons was Marshal MacDonald, Duke of Tarentum, one of Napoleon's most distinguished generals.—MacGregor's *Flora MacDonald*, p. 64.

11 July of Cœlestius[1] as a great blunder, for that he had reason to think that he fell (as design'd) in the attempt. 'This is not to say,' added he, 'that I know anything certain of that affair, as if I had been an eye-witness or conversed with those that had seen the fact. But when I was prisoner in Fort Augustus, an officer came to me and very seriously asked if I would know
*fol.* 147. the head of the young Pretender if I saw it. I told him I would know the head very well, provided it were upon the body. But the officer said, What, if the head be not upon the body? Do you think you could know it in that case? To which I replied, In that case, Sir, I will not pretend to know anything about it.' Kingsburgh told the company that he was resolved if any head should have been brought before him that he would not have made them a whit the wiser, even though he should have known it. But he owned no head was brought to him. He left it to the company to draw what inferences they pleased from this conversation betwixt him and the officer.[2]

Kingsburgh informed us that when at Fort Augustus, he happened to be released one evening in mistake for another man of the same name. When the irons were taken off him he went to Sir Alexander MacDonald's lodgings to ask his commands for Sky. Sir Alexander happened to be abroad, but when he came in he was quite amazed when he saw Kingsburgh, and said, 'Sanders, what has brought you here?' 'Why, Sir,' said he, 'I am released.' 'Released,' says Sir Alexander, 'how has this come about? I have heard nothing of the matter. I do not understand it.' 'As little do I know,' says Kingsburgh, 'how it has come about. But so it is that I have got free.' Then Sir Alexander ordered a bed to be made
*fol.* 148. up for Kingsburgh in the same room with himself, and when Kingsburgh (about 11 o'clock) was beginning to undress in order to go to bed an officer came to the door of the room, and asked if MacDonald of Kingsburgh was there. 'Yes, Sir,' said Kingsburgh, 'I am here. What want you with me?'

---

[1] This was Roderick Mackenzie, who was killed by Cumberland's soldiers near Fort Augustus, and in dying tried to put an end to the pursuit of the Prince by pretending that it was he whom they had slain. See ff. 482, 1800.

[2] There is a printed copy of 'ALEXIS, Part 1st,' bound up in the end of volume eighth of this collection.

'Why,' replied the officer, 'you must goe with me to Lord Albemarle, who wants to speak with you.' 'Then,' said Kingsburgh, 'I began to think within myself all was wrong with me. I begged that I might be allowed to take my rest all night in the place where I then was, and that in the morning I should wait upon Lord Albemarle as soon as he pleased; and that I would give my word of honour to do as I promised; and besides, that Sir Alexander would engage for me.' 'No, no,' said the officer, 'that will not do, Sir. These are not my orders. You must come along with me quickly.' When Kingsburgh came to the door and saw ten or 12 sogers with screwed bayonets waiting to receive him, he did not like that piece of ceremony at all. They had not gone many paces from Sir Alexander's lodgings till they met Lord Albemarle running himself out of breath, foaming at the mouth, and crying out, 'Have ye got the villain? Have ye got the villain?' Kingsburgh mildly answered, 'O why all this hurry? Where is the man that will refuse freedom when it is offered him? I am here, my Lord, at your service. I had no intention of being in a haste to leave the place, and though I had left it you would have easily found me again, for I would have gone to my own house. I had no fear about any thing.' 'However,' says Albemarle, still in a passion, 'it is well, Sir, you are not gone; I had rather by G—— have given anything before this mistake had happened.' 'Go,' added he, 'and throw the dog into irons.' Instantly the orders were obeyed. But to do Albemarle justice, Kingsburgh said that in a day or two he ordered him into a better place and the irons to be taken away from him; and every day after this that his lordship sent to him at dinner time, three dish of meat from his own table, with two bottles of wine. By this time the Duke of Cumberland had left Fort Augustus in great haste to London.

11 July

*fol.* 149.

It was represented to Kingsburgh that his lady during his confinement had been telling some folks that upon conversing with him (her husband) about the pamphlet 'ALEXIS,' he should have said that he knew no body who could be the author of it but Neil MacKechan, so pointed and exact it was in giving the narrative. Kingsburgh, looking to his lady, said, 'Goodwife, you may remember, I said that I knew nobody who could be the

11 July author of that pamphlet but either Neil MacKechan or myself.' When it was suggested that Neil MacKechan (a low man) could not be thought capable of drawing up any thing of that sort, Kingsburgh and his lady informed the company that MacKechan had been educated in the Scots College in Paris with the view of commencing clergyman, but that after
fol. 150. getting his education he had dropt the design; that therefore he was capable enough, and that he had proved a great comfort to the Prince in his wanderings by talking to him in the French language about matters of importance in their difficulties, when perhaps it was not so prudent or convenient that those who were present should know what they were conversing about. They told likewise that they had never been so much afraid of any person's conduct as that of MacKechan, because he was a good-natured man and very timorous in his temper. But they frankly owned they had done him great injustice by entertaining any suspicion about him; for that he had behaved to admiration, and had got abroad with the Prince, the great wish of his soul; for he could never think of parting with him at any time but upon condition of meeting again, which MacKechan was so lucky as frequently to accomplish even when at parting they could scarce condescend upon a time or place when and where to meet.

Kingsburgh said that he asked particularly at the Prince about Lord George Murray, whether or not he could lay treachery or any such thing to his charge. The Prince answered that he never would allow anything of treachery or villainy to be laid to the charge of Lord George Murray. But he could not help owning that he had much to bear of him from his temper.

fol. 151. The Prince asked Kingsburgh if he could inform him anything about the heads of the clans, what they were doing in the present confusion. Kingsburgh answered that MacDonald of Glencoe had surrendred himself, and that Cameron of Dungallan had done the same. The Prince made no remark at all upon Glencoe; but as to the other, said: 'Cameron of Dungallan! Is not that Lochiel's major?' 'Yes,' said Kingsburgh, 'he is the same.' 'Why,' replied the Prince, 'I always looked upon Dungallan to be a man of sense.'

When the Prince was going out of Kingsburgh's house he turned about and said, 'Can none of you give me a snuff?' Upon which Mrs. MacDonald made up to him and offered him a snuff out of a little silver-mill with two hands clasped together upon the lid of it, and the common motto, Rob Gib. Kingsburgh begged the Prince to put the mill into his pocket, and, said Kingsburgh, 'He accordingly put it into a woman's muckle poutch he had hanging by his side.' After the Prince had met with Malcolm MacLeod, Kingsburgh said he had heard that the Prince spying the carving and the motto asked MacLeod what it meant. 'Why,' said MacLeod, 'that is the emblem we use in Scotland to represent a firm and strong friendship, and the common saying is Rob Gib's contract, stark love and kindness.' 'Well, MacLeod,' says the Prince, 'for that very same cause shall I endeavour to keep the mill all my life.'

11 July

*fol.* 152.

'All the female rags and bucklings,' said Kingsburgh and his lady, 'that were left in the heart of the bush, were taken up and carried to our house in order to be carefully preserved. But when we had got notice that the troops had such exact intelligence about the Prince that they particularized the several bucklings of women's cloathes he had upon him, even to the nicety of specifying colours, etc., (and Kingsburgh and Miss MacDonald being by this time made prisoners) word was sent to Mrs. MacDonald and her daughter to throw all the female dress into the flames to prevent any discovery in case of a search.' When the rags were a destroying the daughter insisted upon preserving the gown (which was stamped linen with a purple sprig), saying that 'They might easily keep it safe, and give out that it belonged to one of the family.' The gown was accordingly preserved, and Kingsburgh and his lady promised to send a swatch of it to Mr. Stewart Carmichael at Bonnyhaugh as a pattern to stamp other gowns from.

Kingsburgh rose from his seat, and coming about to one of the company whispered in his ear, 'Sir, since you seem to know a good deal of these affairs, pray will you inform me what you know of Barrisdales case?'[1] What do you think

*fol.* 153.

[1] For some interesting particulars about the MacDonalds of Barrisdale, see the *Scottish Antiquary*, vol. viii. p. 163, and vol. ix. p. 30.

11 July of that point?' It was answered, 'It is certain enough that Barrisdale entred into terms with the Duke of Cumberland, that he received a protection for a certain limited time, and that he touched money; but whether or not he was sincere in the design of seizing the Prince, or if he intended to make use of these stratagems for consulting the safety and preservation of the Prince, was what that person could not pretend to determine. But one thing was constantly affirmed by all the accounts from abroad that Barrisdale was still in some sort of confinement in France, *i.e.* a prisoner at large.' Kingsburgh shook his head and said, 'I am sorry to hear that he is a prisoner in any shape, for that says ill for him.' When Kingsburgh was seated again this subject happened to be spoken of publickly in the company, and all agreed that they had heard that Barrisdale still continued to be in some sort of confinement in France. Kingsburgh insisted upon its being a very bad sign, and again declared his concern to have such an account of him.

*fol.* 154. When some of the company happened to be talking of Major Lockheart's cruelties in the Highlands, particularly that of his having thrust his sword through the body of a child aged four years, in at the belly and out at the back, Kingsburgh's lady said, 'That was no rarity among them, for that several old men, women, and children had been butchered by them in the Highlands.'

Dudwick was exceedingly much delighted with the interview, and said he had never before entertained any notion of that little thing 'ALEXIS'; but that now it should be a favourite of his, as he well knew the veracity of it, and what to say in its behalf.

*N.B.*—After a confinement of twelve long months for one night's hospitality, Kingsburgh was at last set at liberty upon Saturday, July 4th, 1747, upon his preferring a petition to the Justiciary Lords, wherein he pled the benefit of the Indemnity. Before transcribing the above conversation into this book I went to Edinburgh upon Tuesday's morning, July 14th, 1747, and read my *prima cura* in the hearing of Dudwick, in order to know of him if I had been exact enough. He told me it was very right, and exactly written according to the terms of the conversation. That day Kingsburgh and his lady had left Edinburgh, so that I could not have the opportunity of reading it over in their hearing. 14 July

ROBERT FORBES, A.M.

## Journal by Mr. JOHN CAMERON, Presbyterian Preacher and Chaplain at Fort-William. *fol.* 155.

The retreat from Stirling was made with the utmost hurry 1746
and confusion. The evening before, Mr. O'Sullivan wrote 1 Feb.
from Bannockburn to Lord John Drummond ordering him to leave Stirling and cross the Forth by break of day, which order his lordship obeyed, and by 5 in the morning marched. This surprized the Highlanders, to whose officers it appears these orders were not communicate, and made them believe the enemy was near them, which occasioned such an universal consternation that they went from Stirling as every one was ready, and left most of their baggage, all the cloaths they brought from Glasgow, and some of their arms.

Lochiel, who had been wounded at Falkirk, not being able to ride or walk, went in a chaise with Mrs. Murray, and was driving through St. Ninian's when the church blew up. Some of the stones came very near them. The horses startled and threw Mrs. Murray on the street, where she lay speechless till she was taken up by some of the men. Had there been any intention to blow up the church, doubtless Lochiel, one of their principal officers, and the Secretary's lady had been apprized of it and put on their guard to avoid danger.

When the Prince join'd the body of the army a Council of War was held, in which it was debated whether the army should march in a body to Inverness by Aberdeen or take the Highland road, by which the chiefs could, with the greater ease, get such of their men to rejoin them as had gone home with plunder after the battle of Falkirk, which would considerably *fol.* 156
increase their army. The low-country men were of the former opinion, the Highlanders of the latter. It was put to the vote,

and the latter carried it by a great majority. However, the Prince was positive for the Aberdeen road, with which Lochiel complied. But Cluny, going out, met Mr. Murray, and told him it was surprizing the Prince should be so positive in a thing contrary to reason and his own interest, especially when a great majority of the Council of War were of another opinion. His expressing himself with a little warmth made Mr. Murray speak to Sir Thomas Sheridan, who went to the Prince and prevailed upon him to agree with what had been the opinion of the Council of War. He marched with the Highlanders the Highland road by Ruthven in Badenoch, to Inverness, where it was resolved to attack Fort Augustus and Fort William. Of either I can give no distinct account, but that the first was taken and the siege of the other deserted.

Earl Cromertie and others were sent to different countries to cover the rising of some and to prevent that of others. This weakened the army, and tho' many joined the day before the battle of Culloden, a great number did not. Earl of Cromertie, tho' many expresses were sent to order his returning to Inverness, in place of doing as commanded, was surprized and taken prisoner, and these that did join were much fatigued. None had got pay after they left Tay bridge in their march north, and they were straitned in provisions for some days before the battle. Cumberland's army was not opposed in passing the Spey, tho' a considerable force had been sent there[1] for that end. The Prince was in danger of being taken at MacIntosh's
*fol. 157.* house, and his safety was chiefly owing to a mistake of Earl of Loudon's men.

14 April On Monday, April 14th, Lochiel in his return from Fort William (from whence he had been called on Cumberland's crossing the Spey) marched through Inverness. His men were mustered at the Bridge-end, and being but two hours in town when informed that Cumberland's army was at Nairn, 12 miles from Inverness, he immediately marched to Culloden, tho' his men and he were much fatigued, having marched from Fort William in little more than two days, being 50 long miles. He arrived in the evening, and then his regiment, with a few

[1] Not fact, as Donald Roy, who was there, told me.—F.

of Glengarie's, were ordered to mount guard upon the Prince. They got a few sacks of meal, of which some baked bread. The body of the army lay on the hill above the house.

Next morning the whole army was drawn up in order of battle a little nearer Nairn than where the battle was fought, much in the same order as on the day following. In this situation they continued all day without meat or drink, only a biscuet to each man at 12 o'clock. About 7 at night they encamped on a dry hill without tents, being cold and hungry. Great numbers being dispersed through the country, many of them did not return. That night, betwixt 8 and 9, orders were given for their marching, with an intention to surprize the enemy in their camp. The word was King James. The attack was to be made with sword and pistol. They marched in one column, by which the rear was near a mile from the front, each rank consisting of 33 men only. Many were so much fatigued that they slept on the march. Others to a great number wandered, and by the time they came within three miles of Nairn, a person of distinction,[1] observing the state of the army, and fearing all there would be cut off, told Lord George Murray the condition the army was in, and to prevent the loss of so many gallant men wished he would retreat in time. Lord George Murray was of his opinion, but, for reasons he gave him, desired he might inform the Prince of their situation, and bring him orders, which he undertook. But before he could return with the Prince's orders, Lord George Murray, observing day coming on, began to retreat, which occasioned some reflections, and confirmed several in their opinion formerly of him, though, I believe, without any just foundation. We came to Culloden about 9 next morning, being April 16th. The provisions being all spent, the Prince ordered each colonel to send some of their officers to Inverness with money to buy such as could be got, and sent orders to the inhabitants to send provisions to the army, otherwise he would burn the town.

*15 April* · *fol. 158.* · *16 April*

Before the Prince left Inverness, on certain intelligence that Cumberland had passed the Spey, Major Kennedy went to Mr. John Hay who, in Mr. Murray's absence, officiated as Secretary,

[1] No doubt Lochiel. See ff. 441, 616.—F.

16 April and told him that as the enemy was on their march towards
them it was more than probable there would be a battle; and
as the event was very uncertain, it was prudent to guard against
the worst. They might get the better or be defeated. In this
situation he wish'd he would propose to the Prince his sending
a large quantity of provisions then in Inverness to some dis-
*fol.* 159. tance that, in case of the worst, scattered troops might join
and have wherewithal to subsist them till rejoin'd by such as
had not returned from their commands they had been out
upon. If this was not done all must disperse, the cause must
be given up, and the Prince behov'd to be in danger; for the
neighbourhood of that country could not supply the smallest
number of men for one week. Mr. Hay said nothing, nor do
I believe he ever mentioned it to the Prince. But to return.

The Prince intended to give the army an hearty meal and a
day's rest, and to fight next morning. But being inform'd that
Cumberland's army was within half a mile, he resolved to fight
that day. Lord George Murray and the chiefs of the clans,
especially Lochiel, were against it. However they complied,
though it was their opinion to keep the ground they were on
and receive Cumberland, if he attack'd them, which they were
still in doubt of. Our army came to the height of the muir
before Cumberland came in view. The Prince ordered the
men to be immediately formed in order of battle, but Lord
George Murray begged to have a little time to view the ground
and observe the motions of the enemy. Cumberland soon
appear'd and was forming his men, on which ours began to
form by the Prince's orders, who all the while stood with
Lochiel and Mr. Sullivan, frequently complaining they were long
in forming. A little after they were formed we observed the
*fol.* 160. horse and the Argileshire men on the left of the enemy drawing
to a distance from the main body and inclining to our right,
on which the Athol and Cameron officers were afraid to be
flanked. This made Lochiel send to Lord George Murray,
then on the left with the Duke of Perth, to tell him of the
danger. Lord George Murray (whom I heard formerly say
that the park would be of great service to prevent our being
flanked) on this took a narrower view of it, and sent three
gentlemen, viz., Colonel Sullivan, John Roy Stewart, and Ker

of Grydan to view it down to the Water of Nairn. At their return they said it was impossible for any horse to come by that way. The men still believed they might be flanked, and some proposed lining the park wall. The Duke of Perth, who came from the left, was of their opinion. But Lord George Murray, thinking otherwise, ordered Lord Ogilvie's regiment to cover the flank, told there was no danger, and to Lord Ogilvie said, he hoped and doubted not but he would acquit himself as usual. 16 April

The Prince, who with a body of horse was in the rear of the French, sent 8 or 10 times to Lord George Murray to begin the attack on the right; but that was not obeyed. He sent Sir John MacDonald to the Duke of Perth, who moved immediately with the left. The right, observing this, without orders from Lord George Murray, followed their example. Lord George behaved himself with great gallantry, lost his horse, his periwig and bonnet, was amongst the last that left the field, had several cutts with broadswords in his coat, and was covered with blood and dirt.

The Prince was in the heat of the action, had one of his grooms killed close by him, the horse he rode on killed by a musket bullet[1] which struck him within an inch of the Prince's leg. Some of the Camerons on the right gave way, being flanked, as they expected, from the park wall, which the Argyleshire men had broke down. Lochiel endeavoured to rally them but could not. On which under the greatest concern he returned to the action and was wounded by a flank shot. Thus did some of his men desert their chief and the cause they fought for, who at the battle of Gladesmuir and Falkirk behaved with so much intrepidity and courage. I more than once heard Major Kennedy tell that after the Highlanders were broke and the French engaged, he went to the Prince and told him they could not hold it long, that some dragoons had gone from the right and left of the enemy probably to surround the hill and prevent his escape, and begged he would retire. In this request he was joined by others. The Prince complied with great reluctance, retired in good order and in no hurry. *fol.* 161.

[1] Not true. See ff. 1161, 1162.—F.

6 April As the action was near over, as has been told, Lochiel was wounded in both his legs. He was carried out of the field by four of his men who brought him to a little barn. As they were taking off his cloaths to disguise him the barn was surrounded by a party of dragoons, but as they were entring
ol. 162. the barn they were called off, which prevented his being taken. The dragoons were no sooner out of sight but his four men carried him out, put him on a horse, and brought him to Clunie's house in Badenoch, where he continued till next morning, and then went to Lochabar. When he left the barn he dismist two of the four men, the other two supported him on the horse.

At a meeting held at Murlagan, near the head of Loch Arkaig (present Lord Lovat, Lochiel, Mr. Murray, Major Kennedy, Glenbuicket, Colonel John Roy Stewart, Clanranald, Barrisdale, Lochgarie, Mr. Alexander MacLeod, Sir Stewart Threpland, Keppoch's nephew, and Barrisdale's son), it was agreed that they, viz., Lochiel, Lochgary, Clanranald, and Barrisdale, should assemble their men at Glenmallie and cross Lochie, where Clunie and Keppoch's men should join them. Lochiel got a body of 3 or 400 men, Barrisdale and Lochgerrie came with about 150 men each; but so soon as Lochgerrie got pay for his men, he went away, promising to return in a few days and at the same time to observe the Earl of Loudon's motions. But neither of these was done, for the Earl marched thro' Glengarry and had taken Lochiel but for some of his scouts as shall be told. Barrisdale, before Lord Loudon came to Achnecarie, told Lochiel he would go and bring more men, and left his son with a few. Early in the morning a body of men appear'd marching over a hill, whom Lochiel believed to be Barrisdale's men; but he was soon undeceived by some out-scouts he had placed at proper distances who told him these men were certainly Loudon's, for they saw red crosses in their bonnets. On this Lochiel dispersed
ol. 163. his men and crossed the loch in a boat which he kept to prevent his being surprized. It prov'd as he had been told, and he owed his escape more to the red crosses than Barrisdale's honesty.

Lord Lovat and others took different routes. Mr. Murray continued with Lochiel till they came to Lochleven near

Glencoe, and after being there some time Mr. Murray went from thence to Glenlion. Sir David Murray, Dr. Cameron, and I went with him. We continued there 12 or 14 days. From that we went to Glenochie, where he (Murray) was taken very ill. He desired we should return. Sir David Murray went south, and we to Lochiel. He bid us tell him that he would continue about Glenlion till he recovered, and if he could not in safety get south to provide a ship he would return to him. But we were soon informed that in 2 or 3 days after we parted from him he went south. Captain MacNab went with him to the Braes of Balquidder, and provided him in an horse and cloaths. I return to the battle.

As to the left of our army I can give no particular account but that the officers, nobility and gentry, behaved with great gallantry, in which all there did agree. The Duke of Athol had been ill at the time the Prince was at Inverness, and so was not in the action, but before Cumberland came there he left it. I was told by one that was with him that a little after the battle he met with John Hay and enquired what was become of the Prince. To which he replied he was gone off and desired none to follow him. On which the Duke took the road to Ruthven of Badenoch, where he met severals of the unfortunate, who took different roads for their safety.

The Prince, as I have already told, being prevailed on to retire after the action, went to Invergary, Glengary's house; *fol. 164.*
but that gentleman and his lady were not at home. However, he continued there that night without meat, drink, fire or candle except some firr-sticks and a salmon he brought, which he ate with gridiron bannocks. He was made believe his loss was much greater than it was; that Lochiel, Keppoch, and other leading men of the Highlanders were killed, and was advised by Sullivan, O'Neil, and John Hay to dismiss all that were then with him for greater security of his person, as in that situation he could trust none. Accordingly he dismissed all but the above three; but whether Sir Thomas Sheridan was then with him I have not been inform'd. Many would have followed him after the battle, but were forbid, as the Duke of Athol was.

From Invergary, where he was but one night, the Prince went by the head of Locharkeig to the west coast, where he

9 April embarked for the Island of Uist. How long he continued there at that time I know not. But from thence he went in an open boat to the Lewis in order to get a ship to carry him off. But being in that disappointed he returned to Uist, where he skulked, till he was informed that Major General Campbell, and a body of Argyleshire men and others were come to that island. To avoid them he went to Clanronald's house, continued there no longer than to dress himself in woman's cloaths, and
fol. 165. with Miss MacDonald went in an open boat to the Isle of Sky. In his passage he met with a boat in which were some of the Argyleshire men, who seeing a small boat with two men and two women took no notice of them. On his landing in Sky he sent Miss MacDonald to Lady Margaret MacDonald, Sir Alexander's lady, to tell her of his being there and to know if he would be safe in her house if but for one night, as he was the day following to leave the island. What reception Miss had, or what return was made, I cannot say with any certainty (it being told in so many different ways), but certain it is the Prince went that night to Mr. MacDonald's of Kingsburgh, where he slept very well, and next day in an open boat left the island with the Laird of Mackinnon and another. He landed in Moidart, went to Angus MacDonald's house in Boradale, returned MacKinnon to Sky, changed his own dress, and sent for Glenaladale of Clanranald's family.

After the battle of Culloden many of the wounded who were not able to leave the field were that and the next day killed upon the spot, and few were made prisoners. Cumberland came to Inverness, where such as had been prisoners were released. The clans who were at the action dispersed, and such as were only coming on their march to join the Prince returned. Earl Cromerty and others were taken prisoners in Sutherland, and sometime after brought to Inverness. The French surrendred prisoners; and different parties were sent to take up the stragglers. After Cumberland had been sometime in Inverness he ordered Earl Loudon with a good body of men to Lochabar to prevent our coming to a body and receive such as would come and deliver up their arms to him. He met with no
fol. 166. opposition, received a great number of arms, and gave protections. When he was encamped at Moy, three miles from

Achnacarry (Lochiel's house), where he (Lochiel) had been, and six miles from Fort-William, Monroe of Culcairn was sent by Cumberland with a body of men to Earl Loudon with orders to him to burn Lochiel's house. On receiving these orders he told Culcairn that as he was to march from thence, he (Culcairn) might burn it. To which he answered he had done that already. The Earl, tho' as an officer he with exactness discharged his duty, yet behav'd with great humanity to the unfortunate, which I believe made Culcairn execute what he had no orders for.

At this time or soon after a line was formed from Inverness to Fort Augustus, from thence to Fort William to prevent the Prince or any others to escape ; as also a line was formed from the head of Locharkaig to prevent coming in or going out of Lochabar.

While Cumberland was at Fort Augustus great liberties were taken by some officers sent on different commands, particularly Colonel Cornwallis, Major Lockheart, Monroe of Culcairn, Captain Caroline Scott, and Captain Grant, son to Grant of Knockando and Strathspey. Culcairn, after he had burnt and plundered from Moy to the head of Locharkeig, marched from thence to Kintale. Captain Grant, above mentioned, with about 200 men of Loudon's regiment, marched into Lochabar, stripped men, women, and children without distinction of condition or sex. He burnt Cameron of Cluns's house, took a few cows he had bought after Culcairn had formerly plundered him of all, stript his wife and some others naked as they came into *fol. 167.*
the world.[1] Thus was this unfortunate gentleman made partner in the miseries of his wife and children and deprived of all means of subsistence except five milk goats. From thence he marched by the wood of Tervalt to Locharkeig. He told he was going to carry off Barrisdale's cattle who had undertaken to apprehend the Prince, but had deceived them ; which was owing more to its not being in his power than want of inclination. He burnt and plunder'd as he marched. The day he left Cluns he apprehended one Alexander Cameron, on the side of Locharkeig, who had a gun on his shoulder. This man, tho' he discovered

[1] See f. 1685.

the party at a distance made no attempt to run from them but came and delivered his arms. Being asked how he came not to deliver his arms sooner, he answered he saw these who had submitted to the King's mercy plundered as well as those who did not; that he had gone with his wife and children and cattle to a remote wilderness, which was the reason he had not delivered up his arms before that time. This to any but Captain Grant would have been a sufficient excuse, but so void was he of the least humanity that he ordered him immediately to be tied to a tree and shot dead by the highway in the wood of Muick. This party was joined in Knoidart by Monroe of Culcairn, who commanded 200 men and had been in Kintail. About eight days after, as they were returning with Barrisdale's cattle and some belonging to others, Culcairn was shot from a
*fol. 168.* bush, not a gun-shot length or distance from that spot where Cameron had been (it may be said) murdered by Captain Grant.[1] Evan MacHoule or Cameron, tho' he never had been out of the country or join'd the Prince's army or any part of it, came to deliver his arms to the first party that came to Lochabar then at the head of Locharkeig. He was desired to tell where arms were hid. He declared he knew not where any were hid with asseverations and oaths. But these did not save him, for he was immediately shot. I do not remember who commanded the party, but I believe it was Colonel Cornwallis. Archibald MacLauchlan, brother to John MacLauchlan of Greenhall, was an officer in that command. William Dow MacHoule and his brother going to a sheeling in Glenkengie were taken up on suspicion that one of the black horses was in their custody, and for this aggravating circumstance, viz., that a gun was found in one of their houses, were both immediately shot.[2] The last that encamped in the Braes of Locharkeig, seeing what they believed to be a boat on the side of the loch, sent a party. But it proved to be no other than a large black stone. But that they might not return without some gallant action, on meeting a poor old man about sixty, begging, they shot him. Much about the same time meeting a poor old woman, blind of an eye, a beggar for several years before, they desired her to tell where Lochiel

[1] See f. 558.

[2] See f. 1684.

was; and for not telling what she did not know she was immediately shot. This is certain; but what is reported to have been done to her before she was dead I incline not to *fol. 169.*
repeat—things shocking to human nature. Colonel Cornwallis, when sent with a large body of men to the head of Locharkeig, in his march thro' Grant of Glenmoriston's country spied two men leading dung to their land. They were ordered to come to the party, but happening to turn their backs upon it they were instantly shot dead. John Cameron, brother to Lochiel, never join'd him or any of his servants. On the contrary when the Prince came to Glenfinan or before it, he went to his father-in-law, John Campbell's house in Broadalbin, where he continued till the Prince marched out of Lochabar, and so soon as he returned he waited upon Captain Campbell, deputy governor of Fort William, continued some days with him and ever behaved himself peaceably, keeping at home. But that could not save his effects; for Captain Caroline Scott, the last that plundered that unfortunate country, took from him an hundred of his cows and all his small and young cattle. An order being given to apprehend, on suspicion, Peter MacLauchlan, taxman of a farm in Mull, belonging to the Duke of Argyle, he came within the time limited in Cumberland's proclamation, at least as soon as he was informed of it and surrendred himself and arms to Major General Campbell. But how soon the general went to the Isles, Captain Millar of Guise's regiment, *fol. 170.*
formerly a prize-fighter, was sent with a party to Mull, as is believed by orders of Captain Caroline Scott, to burn and plunder some few tenants in MacKinnon's lands; which being done with great severity, he went to Peter MacLauchlan's house, burnt it, plundered everything that he had, horses, cows, and sheep, except a lame cow that could not travell.

Captain Caroline Scott came to Stewart of Ardsheill's house in Appin and took from his lady a few cows General Campbell had bought from the soldiers and made a present of to her. All Ardsheil's cattle being taken by the soldiers, the Captain desired she would give him her keys, which she did. He then demanded what he called her small keys which she had no sooner delivered than he offered her his hand, led her out of the house, and told her she had no more to do in it. She desired to know

where she was to go. He replied to Appin's house. She then told him she could not leave her young children to starve, as he had taken all her provisions from her. On which he ordered her one boll of meal of her own to be given her. The Captain, after he had rummaged the house, took great care to have the slates and sarking taken from the roof. He gutted the house and office-houses of all the timber in them with the least damage possible even to the drawing of the nails. He then had all the walls cast down, the free stone, lintels, rabats, etc., laid by themselves, all which he sold with the planting, which chiefly
*fol. 171.* consisted of many large ash trees. It was this Captain Caroline who hanged three men near Glenevis, that when some others were pursued, came and delivered their arms, expecting to get protection. In place of which the Captain told them, as others had not done the same they were to be hang'd. The poor men said it would be hard to punish them for the fault of others; and so little did they think he intended any such thing, but that he threatened to fright them, they were laughing when the soldiers were putting the ropes about their necks. But they were mistaken; for instantly they were hang'd and had not so much time as to beg God to have mercy upon their souls.

The same Captain, when he went to the island of Barra with a party to search for arms, he apprehended a man, being informed that he had been in arms, and ordered him immediately to be hang'd. The poor man begg'd he might delay for a few hours that he would prove by 50 he had never been out of the country or under arms in it. But this was not granted, tho' Captain Millar of Guise's regiment begged he might consider what he was doing—for tho' he (Scott) was an older Captain, yet he had served much longer. To which the other replied he knew very well what he was doing, which was not without orders. What made this the more surprizing is that tho' in the islands belonging to Barra there will be about 4 or 500 souls there is but one gentleman and 7 or 8 common people that are Protestants, of whom this poor unfortunate man was one.

I have hitherto confin'd myself to facts; but in this place must observe that all those who were hang'd or shot were Pro-
*fol. 172.* testants; that in plundering the cattle, burning, etc., the

Roman Catholick's countries, Braes of Lochabar, Glengary, Knoidart, Moidart, Arisaig, and Morar suffer'd little by burning or taking of cattle, and not one that I know of was hang'd or shot who was a Papist. How loud would the clamour have been had such burning and murders, etc., been committed by the Prince's army, or the like indulgence shown to Popish countries and Papists!

I have been told Major Lockheart came not short of Captain Caroline in many of the like actions. But as I was not then in that country, I leave it to others better informed. What I have told of the above plunderings, burnings, and killing may be absolutely depended on; and have left off to put them together, lest, if mention'd in their proper places, it might interrupt what more particularly concern'd the Prince, to which I return.

Glenaladale, as I have related, being sent for, came; and the Prince being better inform'd as to Lochiel, Keppoch, and others, that his loss had not been as Sullivan and O'Neil told him, proposed going to Lochabar where he believed Lochiel was. But as all the passes were then guarded, this was represented to be impracticable. He continued a few days in that country and was advised to go to the Braes of Glenmoriston, and there and in Lord Lovat's country to continue till the passes were opened. Accordingly he went attended by Glenaladale, his brother, and a son of Angus MacDonald's, two young boys. They sent for Donald Cameron of Glenpean to be their guide to the Braes of Locharkeig. He came, and in the night conducted the Prince safe thro' the guards that were on the pass so close to their tents as to hear every word they spoke.[1] When they came to Glenmoriston they got six stout trusty men, but spoke not a word of English, with whom and Glenaladale the Prince continued betwixt the Braes of Glen- *fol.* 173.
moriston and Glen Strathferrar till the guards were removed and all the passes opened.

About the begining of August he went to Lochabar with the above retinue, came to Achnasual on the side of Locharkeig, two miles from Achnacarie. They had no provisions,

[1] See an addition to the narrative at this point, at f. 569.

1 Aug. but expected to be supplied in that country, in which they were disappointed, it having been plundered, and all the people were fled to the mountains to save their lives. In this situation the Prince was in danger of being starved, when one of the Glenmoriston men discovered a large fine hart and shot him. The day following the Prince was inform'd that Lochgarie, Cluns, and Achnasual were in the neighbouring mountains, and sent for them, and dispatched one to inform Lochiel, then about 20 miles distant, of his being in that country. But Lochiel, some days before, hearing a surmise of the Prince's being come to the continent had sent his brother (the doctor) and me by different roads to get all the intelligence we could of the Prince. The person who was sent to Lochiel met the Doctor within a few miles of the place where Lochiel was, who was obliged to return with two French officers that were likewise in quest of the Prince.[1]

This faithful person would not own he knew anything about the Prince, his orders being only to tell Lochiel. However, he said he had business of the utmost consequence. The Doctor brought him and the two officers to his brother. The next day Lochiel sent the Doctor to the Prince, and the officers to the care of one of his friends with whom they were to continue till further orders. In the mean time, after travelling and searching several days to no purpose, I met the Doctor at Achnacarie as he was going to the Prince. He had four servants with him, who, as the river was not passable, raised a
*fol.* 174. boat Culcairn had sunk after his searching the Isle of Locharkeig, where from former experience he expected to get a great deal of plunder.

When Culcairn was in this island he discovered some newraised earth, and believing money or arms to be hid there had it dug up, and only discovered the corpse of a man without a coffin, which had not been many days buried. On the corps there was a good Holland shirt, which made him believe it to be Lochiel, and sent an express to Cumberland to tell that he had found Lochiel's corps, who had died of his wounds. From this it was put in the newspapers. This was the corps

[1] See f. 1546.

of John Cameron, brother to Allan Cameron of Callart, who was taken at Culloden and sent prisoner to London. The shirt was taken from the corps and it left to be food for the birds of prey, etc. August

The Prince at this time was in a small hutt built for the purpose in the wood betwixt Achnasual and the end of Lochar-keig. Observing some men in arms by the water side, we sent two of Cluns' children to know who they were. We soon discovered them to belong to Cluns, sent the boat for them, and dismist the four servants on pretence we were going to skulk in the wood for some days; and that keeping such a number together might be dangerous. We cross'd the river and went to the hutt. The Prince with Achnasual had gone a little from it; but being informed what we were, came immediately to us. He was then bare-footed, had an old black kilt coat on, a plaid, philabeg and waistcoat, a dirty shirt and a long red beard, a gun in his hand, a pistol and durk by his side. He was very cheerful and in good health, and, in my opinion, fatter than when he was at Inverness.

When we told him what we were and from whence we came, and that Lochiel was well and recovered of his wounds,[1] he thanked God thrice for it, and expressed an uncommon satis- *fol. 175.* faction. They had kill'd a cow the day before, and the servants were roasting some of it with speets. The Prince knew their names, spoke in a familiar way to them and some Erse. He ate very heartily of the roasted beef and some bread we had got from Fort Augustus, and no man could sleep sounder in the night than he. He proposed going immediately where Lochiel was. But we knew by the newspapers the Government had been inform'd some time before that he had pass'd Corierag with Lochiel and 30 men,which probably might occasion a search in those parts. This made him resolve to continue for some time where he was. Some days after Lochgary and the Doctor were sent to Lochiel and Glenaladale, and the faithful Glenmoriston men were dismist. The Prince continued in the hutt with Cluns's children. Captain MacRaw

[1] See f. 1479.

of Glengary's regiment, one or two servants, and I had the honour to add one to the number.

June The two officers who, I told, went to Lochiel with the Doctor, came from Dunkirk in a small vessel with sixty other young gentlemen, who had formed themselves in a company of volunteers under the command of the foresaid two officers, some time before they could hear of the battle of Culloden. They came in June to Polliew in Seaforth's country, where four of them landed to deliver their dispatches, of whom two were taken; and the other two wandered in Seaforth's country till Lochgarie, hearing they had letters for the Prince, sent
*fol.* 176. Captain MacRaw and his own servant for them, that they might be sent to Lochiel, since the Prince was not to be found.
July This happen'd about the middle of July. When they came to Lochiel they told him they had left their papers with Mr. Alexander MacLeod, one of the Prince's aid de camps, then skulking in Seaforth's country. Tho' this prov'd true, yet as they themselves had not told it to Lochgary or any other, made him (Lochiel) suspect them to be Government spies. The Prince wanted much to see them. But we told him what Lochiel and we were afraid of, which made him resolve to act in this with greater caution. He said it was surprizing that two men, strangers, and without one word of Earse, could escape from the troops, who were always in motion in quest of him and his followers. But to see them in safety, he wrote a letter to them himself to this purpose,—that to avoid falling into the hands of his enemies he was under a necessity to retire to a remote country where he had none with him but one, Captain Drummond, and a servant, and as he could not remove from where he was without danger to himself and them, he had sent Captain Drummond with this letter; and as he could repose entire confidence in him, desired whatever message they had to him, to tell it to the bearer, Captain Drummond, and take his advice as to their conduct. This letter he proposed to deliver to them himself under the name of Captain Drummond, for both of them told Lochiel they had never seen the Prince. They were sent for, and when they came, were introduced to the Prince under his borrowed name. He delivered the letter to them with which they were very well pleased, and told him

everything they had to say, which he afterwards said was of no great consequence as his affairs then stood. They continued two days with us, asked the fictitious Captain Drummond several questions about the Prince's health and manner of living. His answers they heard with the utmost surprize. The Prince, believing the pacquet left with Mr. Alexander MacLeod might be of use to him, sent for it; but as it was cyphers and directed to the French ambassador, he could make nothing of it. August *fol. 177.*

We continued in this wood and that over against Achnacarie (having three hutts in different places to which we removed by turns) till I think about the 10th of August, on which day Cluns's son and I went to the Strath of Cluns for intelligence. We were not half an hour in the hut, which Cluns had built for his family (after his house was burnt), when a child of six years old went out and returned in haste to tell that she saw a great body of soldiers. This we did not believe, as Lochgary had promised to Lochiel to have a guard betwixt Fort Augustus and this place to give intelligence. We went out to know the truth and it proved as the girl had said. Cluns skulked to observe the motions of the party. His son and I went to inform the Prince. He was that day in one of the hutts on the other side of the Water Kiaig a short mile from Cluns. Crossing the ford of that water under cover of the wood, and coming within pistol shot of the hutt, I observed the party advancing. The Prince was then asleep, being about 8 in the morning. I wakened him and desired him not to be surprized, for that a body of the enemy were in sight. He with the utmost composure got up, called for his gun, sent for Captain MacRaw and Sandy, Cluns's son, who with a servant were doing the duty of sentries about the wood. We concluded by our having no intelligence of the party marching from Fort Augustus, as had been promised, there was treachery in it and that we were surrounded. Cluns came soon up to where we were. However tho' but eight in number we were determined, rather than to yield, to be butchered by our merciless enemies to sell our lives dear and in defence of our Prince to die like men of honour. We left the hut and marched to a small hill above the wood from whence we could see a great way up 10 Aug. *fol. 178.*

11 Aug. Glenkingie and not be discovered. We got there unobserved, which was owing to the cover of the wood. The Prince examined all our guns, which were in pretty good order, and said he hoped we would do some execution before we were killed. For his part he was bred a fowler, and could charge quick, was a tolerable marksman, and would be sure of one, at least. He said little more, but sent Cluns and me to take a narrow view of the party, and resolved that night to goe to the top of Mullantagart, a very high mountain in the Braes of Glenkengie, and to send one to us to know what we discover'd or were informed of. When we came to the Strath of Cluns the women told us that the party was of Lord Loudon's regiment, consisting of about 200 men, commanded by one Captain Grant, son to Grant of Knockando in Strathspey; that they had carried away ten milk cows which Cluns had bought after he was plundered, and found out the hutt we had in the wood of Tervalt, and that they gave it out that they were going to bring Barrisdale's cattle to the camp, who had promised to apprehend the Prince but had deceived them. I have told you
fol. 179. already how this Captain Grant, I may say, barbarously murdered Alexander Cameron on the side of Locharkeig. In the evening Cluns' son came to us from the Prince, with whom we returned, told him as we were informed, and brought some whiskie, bread, and cheese. This was about 12 at night. He was on the side of the mountain without fire or any covering. We persuaded him to take a hearty dram and made a fire, which we durst not keep above half an hour lest it should be seen by the people in the neighbourhood. By daylight we
13 Aug. went to the top of the mountain, where we continued till eight in the evening without the least cover, and durst not rise out of our seats. The Prince slept all the forenoon in his plaid and wet hose, altho' it was an excessive cold day, made more so by several showers of hail. From thence we went that night to the Strath of Glenkengie, killed a cow and lived merrily for some days. From that we went to the Braes of Achnacarie. The Water of Arkeg in crossing came up to our haunches. The Prince in that condition lay that night and next day in open air, and though his cloaths were wet he did not suffer the least in his health.

In a day or two after Lochgary and Dr. Cameron return'd from Lochiel (to whom they had been sent) and told it was Lochiel's opinion and theirs that the Prince would be safe where he (Lochiel) was skulking. This pleased him much and the next night he set out with Lochgary, the Doctor and Sandy (Cluns's son), myself and three servants. We travell'd in the night and slept all day, till we came to Lochiel, who was then in the hills betwixt the Braes of Badenoch and Athol. The Doctor and I went by another road on a message to Badenoch. I return'd about September 13th and the next day was sent south. The Prince by moving from place to place and but few with him had hitherto escaped the narrow and strict search of the troops. But as the like good fortune might not always continue he ordered Lochiel to send south to have a ship freighted to bring him and others off by the East Coast. The ship was provided, and one sent to inform the Prince of it, who with Lochiel and others was to come where the ship lay. But before this messenger came to where the Prince had been, two of Lochiel's friends that had orders to watch on the West Coast came and told that two French ships were arrived at Moidart. Upon this, the night following, the Prince set out from where they were, and at the same time sent to inform others skulking in different places. Some arrived in time; but others by some accident or other had not that good fortune.

30 Aug.

13 Sept.

*fol.* 180.

I have told you what I was witness to or informed of by such as I could absolutely depend upon. I shall only add that the Prince submitted with patience to his adverse fortune, was chearful, and frequently desired those that were with him to be so. He was cautious when in the greatest danger, never at a loss in resolving what to do, with uncommon fortitude. He regretted more the distress of those who suffered for adhering to his interest than the hardships and dangers he was hourly exposed to. To conclude, he possesses all the virtues that form the character of a HERO and GREAT PRINCE.

fol. 181. ## CAPTAIN O'NEIL'S JOURNAL of the Prince's Retreat and Escape after April 16th, 1746.[1]

15 April APRIL 15th.—The Prince marched his army in three columns from Culloden Muir to surprize the Duke of Cumberland in his camp at Nairn, ordering at the same time 2000 men to pass the river Nairn and post themselves between Elgin and the camp of the enemy. To deceive the ships in Inverness Road, we made several fires on the mountain, where we drew up in battle order, and at 8 o'clock at night we began our march.

16 April About 2 o'clock next morning (April 16th) within a mile of the enemy our van halted. The Prince, who marched in the centre, dispatched an aid de camp to know the motive of the halt. Colonel O'Sullivan, who marched in the van, immediately hasted to the Prince, and told him. Lord George Murray and some others of the chiftains, as they wanted some of their men, did not think themselves sufficiently strong to attack the enemy, and, upon a strong belief that the Duke of Cumberland was apprized of their design, refused to advance, maugrè the instances he (Sullivan) made use of to engage them to the contrary. Upon this the Prince advanced to the head of the column, where, assembling the chiefs, in the most pathetic manner and strongest terms he demonstrated to them the visible and real advantages they had of an enemy who thought themselves secure of any such attempt; and descending from his horse, drew his sword and told them, he would head them to an enemy they had as often defeated as seen. But deaf to his example and intreaties the greater part declined, which so sensibly shocked the Prince that, remounting his horse, he told them, with tears in his eyes, that he did not so much regret his own loss as their inevitable ruine. We immediately march'd back to our camp at Culloden where we arriv'd at 5 in the
fol. 182. morning. At ten o'clock we were inform'd that the Duke of Cumberland was in full march towards us. The Prince on this report gave the necessary orders for the attack, riding from

[1] See observations on this document by Donald MacLeod, f. 270. There is another *attested* copy of this Journal given at f. 670.

rank to rank, encouraging his troops and exhorting them to 16 April behave as formerly at Prestonpans and Falkirk; and between 12 and one we began the attack and engaged the enemy, the Prince commanding the centre. Our right wing immediately broke the left of the enemy; but their flank being exposed to nine squadrons of horse, who attacked them when in pursuit of the foot, put them into so much confusion that they instantly dispersed. The Prince, galloping to the right and endeavouring to rally them, but to no purpose, had his horse shot under him.[1] The left followed the example of the right which drew on an entire flight, maugrè all the Prince could do to animate or rather rally them. He remain'd on the field of battle till there were no more hopes left, and then scarce could be persuaded to retire, ordering the French picquets and Fitz-James's horse to make a stand in order to favour the retreat of the Highlanders, which was happily effected.

Previous to the battle the Prince ordered the chiftains in case of a defeat, as the Highlanders could not retreat as regular troops, to assemble their men near Fort Augustus. In consequence of which immediately after the battle the Prince dispatched me to Inverness to repeat his orders to such of his troops as were there. That night the Prince retired six miles from the field of battle, and next day arrived at Fort Augustus, where he remained all that day in expectation his troops would *fol.* 183. have join'd him. But seeing no appearance of it he went to the house of Invergary and ordered me to remain there to direct such as passed by that way the road his royal highness took. I remained there two days and did the Prince's orders to such as I met; but to no effect, every one taking his own road. I then followed the Prince, who was so far from making a precipitate retreat that he retired by six and six miles, and arrived the 26th of April at Knoidart, where I join'd him next 26 April day and gave him an account of the little appearance there was of assembling his troops. Upon which he wrote circuler letters to all the Chiftains, enjoining them by the obedience they owed him to join him immediately with such of their clans as possibly they could gather together; at the same

[1] Not true. See f. 1161.—F.

27 April time representing the imminent danger they were in if they neglected it.

After remaining there some days in hopes his orders would have been obeyed, and seeing not one person resort to him, the extreme danger of his person was remonstrated to him, being within 7 miles of Lord Loudoun, Sir Alexander MacDonald and the MacLeods; and to evade this it was proposed to retreat to one of the islands near the continent. After repeated instances of the like nature he reluctantly assented, leaving Mr. John Hay behind to transmit him the answers of his letters with an account of what passed; and departed for the Isles in an open fishing boat at 8 o'clock that night, accompanied by Colonel O'Sullivan and me. About an hour
*fol.* 184. after we set out a violent storm arose, which drove us ninety miles from our intended port; and next day running for shelter into the island of North Uist, we struck upon a rock, the boat staved to pieces, and with the greatest difficulty we saved our lives. At our landing we were in the most melancholy situation, knowing nobody and wanting the common necessaries of life. After much search we found a little hut uninhabited and took shelter there, and with great difficulty made a fire to dry our cloaths. Here we remained two days, having no other provisions but a few biscuit we had saved out of the boat, which were entirely spoiled with the salt water. As this island belonged to Sir Alexander MacDonald, and not judging ourselves safe, we determined on going elsewhere; and by the greatest good fortune one of our boatmen discovered a boat stranded on the coast, and having with great difficulty launched her in the water we embarked for the Harris. In our passage we unfortunately met with another storm, which obliged us to put into an island near Stornoway. Next day the Prince dispatched me for the Harris to look out for a ship, ordering me to embark on board the first I could get, and to make the most diligent haste after my landing on the continent to the Court of France, enjoining me to give a most exact account to his most Christian Majesty of his disasters, and of his resolution never to abandon the country untill he knew the final result of France; and if possible once more to assemble his faithful Highlanders. Unluckily the person his

royal highness sent with me getting drunk told the master of May
the ship somewhat that induced him to refuse taking me on *fol.* 185.
board, and immediately alarm'd the country, which obliged me to retreat and join the Prince, who, when I told him, resolved for the continent by way of Seaforth's country. But the boatmen absolutely refused to comply, which made us take the road we came; and meeting with three ships of war we were constrain'd to retire to a desart island, where we remained eight days in the greatest misery, having no sustenance but
dried fish Providence threw in on the island.[1] When the ships 10 May
disappeared we put out to sea, and next morning we met with another, just coming out of one of the lochs who pursued us near an hour; but the wind rising we made our escape. In the afternoon we arrived at the island of Benbicula, and one of the boatmen being acquaint with a herd of the island, we all went to his house, where passing for friends of the boatman we remain'd four days, and then the Prince sent the boat to the continent with an Highland gentleman whom he charged with letters to the chiefs, Secretary Murray and John Hay, requiring an exact account how affairs stood. Not thinking ourselves secure in the cottage, by the advice of a friend we retired to the mountain of Corradale to wait the return of the gentleman, where we remained 22 days, when the gentleman returned with a letter from Secretary Murray importing that almost all the clans had delivered up themselves and arms, and consequently they were no more to be depended upon. He
likewise acquainted the Prince of two French ships which had *fol.* 186.
arrived at the continent with money and arms, and in which the Duke of Perth and his brother, Sir Thomas Sheridan and John Hay had embark'd for France. Here we remained for some days longer till the Duke of Cumberland, having intelligence the Prince was concealed in the Long Island, ordered the militia of the Isle of Sky and the independent companies to go in search of him. As soon as we had notice of their landing we retreated to an island about twelve miles distance, called Hoya, where we remained till we found they had followed us. We then went for Loch Boysdale and staid there

[1] See ff. 292-297.

June for eight days, where Captain Caroline Scott landed within a mile of us, which obliged us to separate, the Prince and I taking to the mountains, and Sullivan remaining with the boatmen. At fall of night we marched towards Benbicula, being inform'd Scott had ordered the militia to come and join him. At midnight we came to a hutt where by good fortune we met with Miss Flora MacDonald, whom I formerly knew. I quitted the Prince at some distance from the hut, and went myself with a design of being inform'd if the independent companies were to pass that way next day as we had been informed. The young lady answered in the negative, saying they would not pass till the day after. I then told her I brought a friend to see her. She with some emotion asked if it was the Prince. I answered in the affirmative and instantly brought him in. We then consulted on the immediate danger the Prince was in, and could think of no more proper or safe
*fol. 187.* place or expedient than to propose to Miss Flora to convey him to the Isle of Sky, where her mother lived. This seem'd the more feasable, as the young lady's father being captain of an independent company would afford her a pass for herself and servant to go visit her mother. The Prince assented and immediately proposed it to the young lady, to which she answered with the greatest respect and loyalty but declined, saying, Sir Alexander MacDonald was too much her friend to be the instrument of his ruine. I endeavoured to obviate this by assuring her Sir Alexander was not in the country, and that she could with the greatest facility convey the Prince to her mother's house, as she lived close by the water side.

I then remonstrated to her the honour and immortality that would redound to her by such a glorious action; and she at length acquiesced, after the Prince had told her the sense he would always retain of so conspicuous a service. She promised to acquaint us next day when things were ripe for execution, and we parted for the mountain of Corradale. Next day at 4 in the afternoon we received a message from our protectrix telling us all was well. We determined joining her immediately, but the messenger told us we could not pass any of the fords that separated the island we were in from Benbicula, as they were both guarded. In this dilemma a man of the country tendred his boat to us, which we readily accepted of; and next day landed at Benbicula, and immediately marched for Rushness, the place of rendezvous, where we arrived at midnight, and instead of our protectrix found a guard of the enemy. We were constrain'd to retreat four miles, having eat nothing for 34 hours before. The Prince ordered me to go to the lady and know the reason she did not keep her appointment. She told me she had engaged a cousin of hers in North Uist to receive him into his house, where she was sure he would be more safe than in the Isle of Sky.[1] I immediately dispatched a boy with these news to the Prince and mentioned to him the place of appointment, whither his royal highness came. But the gentleman absolutely refused to receive us, alleging for a motive he was a vassal to Sir Alexander MacDonald. In this unexpected exigence, being within a small half mile of a captain and 50 men, we hasted for Rushness, being apprized the enemy had just abandoned it. The Prince sent me to acquaint Miss Flora of our disappointment, and to intreat her to keep by her promise as there was no time to be lost. She faithfully promised next day. I remained with her that night, the Prince remaining at Rushness attended by a little herd boy. Next day I accompanied Miss Flora to the place of rendezvous, where we had not long been when we had an account that General Campbell was just landed with 1500 men. We now were apprehensive we were betrayed and instantly got to our boat and put to another place, where we arrived at daybreak. We then dispatched a person to Clanronald's house to learn what news, who brought us word that General Campbell was there with Captain Ferguson, and that he saw Captain Scott's detachment coming to join them, and that they amounted in all to 2300 men.

June

*fol.* 188.

*fol.* 189.

The Prince intreated the young lady that I should accompany him, but she absolutely refused it, having a pass but for one servant. His royal highness was so generous as to decline going unless I attended him, untill I told him that if he made the least demur I would instantly go about my business, as I was extremely indifferent what became of myself, provided his

[1] See ff. 526, 589.

person was safe. He at length embarked, attended only by Miss Flora MacDonald, etc.

1747 20 July

## REMARKS, etc., and PARTICULAR SAYINGS of some who were concerned in the PRINCE'S PRESERVATION. Leith, Citadel, July 20, 1747.

'Tis pity that Captain O'Neil has not been more particular in his journal, for he has not so much as mentioned the necessity the Prince was in to disguise himself in a female dress, which serves to explain his distress and danger as much as any thing can do. Besides by studying too much brevity he has altogether omitted several remarkable particulars which he minutely described to those he conversed familiarly with both in the Castle of Edinburgh,[1] and after he was set at liberty. He used to tell that when he was along with the Prince they happen'd to be twice within a gun-shot of parties of the enemy,
fol. 190. that he quite despair'd of being any longer kept out of their clutches, and that he failed not to represent to the Prince the impossibility of not falling into the enemy's hands. 'The Prince,' said he, 'always reproved me for my desponding thoughts, and endeavoured to encourage me in times of the greatest danger by saying, "O'Neil, is this all the faith and trust you have in God? Let us only take care to have enough of faith and trust in his providence and there is no fear of us at all. Pull up your spirits, man. Never despair."' O'Neil frankly own'd that in place of his being useful to the Prince by endeavouring to comfort and support him when dangers thicken'd upon them, the Prince had the like good offices to perform to him, and that he frequently exerted himself in different shapes to raise his spirits. One time having nothing to eat for about two days but some mouldy dirty crumbs in O'Neil's pocket, they luckily happened at last to come to a very mean cottage where they found only an old poor woman who received them kindly, and gave each of them two eggs and a piece of bear-bannocks, but having not so much in her

---

[1] See f. 529.

hut as a cup of cold water to give them to put down their morsel, she told them that some lasses had lately gone up the hill to milk the goats, etc., and that if they would follow them, probably they might have a drink of milk from them. The advice was very seasonable, and away they went, the honest old woman directing them the way they should go. The Prince skipped so speedily up the hill that O'Neil could not keep up with him. The lasses gave them plenty of milk, and poor O'Neil lay along among the grass, being quite undone with fatigue and fear. The Prince did all he could to rouse him up both by arguing and joking with him; but all to no purpose. At last the Prince turning from him, said, 'Come, my lasses, what would you think to dance a Highland reel with me? We cannot have a bag-pipe just now, but I shall sing you a Strathspey reel.' The dance went merrily on, and the Prince skipped so nimbly, knacking his thumbs and clapping his hands that O'Neil was soon surprized out of his thoughtful mood, being ashamed to remain any longer in the dumps when his Prince had been at so much pains to divert his melancholy. He was sure he said that the Prince entred into this frolick merely upon his account, for that there could be no dancing at his heart, seeing at that time they knew not where to move one foot. The Captain used to say he believed there was not such another man in all the world as the Prince.

20 July

*fol.* 191.

It is worth noticing too that O'Neil has not mentioned his going on board with O'Sullivan after parting with the Prince, and how he was taken prisoner upon his coming ashore again about something they wanted to have, how he was very roughly used, particularly by some of the Campbells, who took from him his gold and watch, and every valuable thing about him, and how he was stript naked and threatened (if he would not tell where the Prince was to be found) with being put into that racking machine which Barisdale invented and made use of to extort confession from thieves, and in which one could not live above one hour.[1] But perhaps the Captain reserves these and some other points to be the subject-matter of another Journal when he comes to a country where he can make a

*fol.* 192.

[1] See ff. 528, 529, 688-690.

20 July plain declaration of all that he knows with freedom and safety.

Captain O'Neil had very great difficulty to prevail upon Miss MacDonald to undertake being guardian to the Prince. She was not only frighten'd at the hazards and dangers attending such a bold enterprize, but likewise insisted upon the risque she would run of losing her character in a malicious and ill-natured world. The Captain was at some pains to represent to her the glory and honour she would acquire by such a worthy and heroic action, and he hoped God would make her successful in it. 'You need not fear your character,' said he, 'for by
l. 193. this you will gain yourself an immortal character. But if you will still entertain fears about your character, I shall (by an oath) marry you directly, if you please.' After she had consented O'Neil then thought it a proper time to say something for himself, and earnestly begged that he himself might have the happiness of being taken under her tuition. But she positively refused to grant his request. At last he became so pressing in his suit that he fell down upon his knees and prayed her to consider his case and the desire he had to share in the Prince's fate whatever it should be. She steadily resisted all his importunities and judiciously remarked to him that the safety of the Prince depended much upon few being in company, that she could more easily undertake the preservation of one than of two or more; and therefore she desired that he might not insist upon that point, for if he should she resolv'd not to embark in the affair at all. He found himself obliged to desist, and owned afterwards upon reflection the wisdom of her resolution.

Her step-father (Hugh MacDonald of Armadale in Sky) did really serve her with a passport, although at that time he was captain of militia, and had a command of Sir Alexander's men in South Uist in order to prevent the Prince's escape. He
l. 194. is reckoned the strongest man of all the name of MacDonald, as I have more than once heard Kingsburgh declare, and his strength of mind seems to bear proportion to the strength of his body. He was obliged for some time to keep out of the way till the suspicion of the passport began to be forgot. But every one would not have been desirous of the task to lay hands

on him; for he never quit with his arms when he was skulking, and the people in Sky stood in awe of him. Before they went to the boat the Prince renewed the request about O'Neil's going along; but Miss wisely persisted in her former resolution and would not hear of the proposal, though the Prince pressed the matter with great earnestness. 20 July

In the Journal taken from the mouths of the Laird of MacKinnon, Malcolm MacLeod, etc., Miss MacDonald has omitted several things which she particularly mentioned to those who conversed with her when she was lying in the Road of Leith on board the *Eltham* and the *Bridgewater* ships of war. She told that when the Prince put on women's cloaths he proposed carrying a pistol under one of his petticoats for making some small defence in case of an attack. But Miss declared against it, alleging that if any person should happen to search them the pistol would only serve to make a discovery. *fol.* 195.
To which the Prince replied merrily: 'Indeed, Miss, if we shall happen to meet with any that will go so narrowly to work in searching as what you mean they will certainly discover me at any rate.' But Miss would not hear of any arms at all, and therefore the Prince was obliged to content himself with only a short heavy cudgel, with which he design'd to do his best to knock down any single person that should attack him.

She us'd likewise to tell that in their passage to the Isle of Sky a heavy rain fell upon them, which with former fatigues distressed her much. To divert her the Prince sung several pretty songs. She fell asleep, and to keep her so, the Prince still continued to sing. Happening to awake with some little bustle in the boat she found the Prince leaning over her with his hands spread about her head. She asked what was the matter? The Prince told her that one of the rowers being obliged to do somewhat about the sail behoved to step over her body (the boat was so small), and lest he should have done her hurt either by stumbling or trampling upon her in the dark (for it was night) he had been doing his best to preserve his *fol.* 196.
guardian from harm. When Miss MacDonald was telling this particular part of the adventure to some ladies that were paying their respects to her on board the *Bridgewater* in Leith

20 July Road, some of them with raptures cried out: 'O Miss, what a happy creature are you who had that dear Prince to lull you asleep, and to take such care of you with his hands spread about your head, when you was sleeping! You are surely the happiest woman in the world!' 'I could,' says one of them,[1] 'wipe your shoes with pleasure, and think it my honour so to do, when I reflect that you had the honour to have the Prince for your handmaid. We all envy you greatly.' Much about the same time a lady of rank and dignity,[2] being on board with Miss MacDonald in the foresaid ship, a brisk gale began to blow and make the sea rough, and not so easy for a small boat to row to Leith. The lady whispered to Miss MacDonald that she would with pleasure stay on board all night that she might have it to say that she had the honour of lying in the same bed with that person who had been so happy as to be
*fol.* 197. guardian to her Prince. Accordingly they did sleep in one bed that night. Several ladies[3] made valuable presents to Miss MacDonald, viz., gowns, skirts, headsutes, shoes, stockings, etc., etc. Commodore Smith made her a present when she was in Leith Road of a handsome sute of riding-cloaths, with plain mounting, and some fine linen for riding shirts, as also a gown to her woman (Kate MacDonal) and some linen to be shirts for poor Kate, who could not talk one word of English, being a native of Sky, and who generously offered herself to Miss MacDonald when she could get not one that would venture to go with her.

The Prince gave to Miss MacDonald the garters he wore with the woman's cloaths, which were French, of blue velvet covered upon one side with white silk, and fastened with buckles. Miss MacDonald's brother (son of honest Armadale) coming south to find a passage for Holland, where he was to enter into the Dutch service, brought these garters along with him, and deposited them in the hands of a friend[4] in Leith,

---

[1] Miss Mary Clerk.

[2] Lady Mary Cochran.

[3] My Lady Bruce, Lady Mary Cochran, Mrs. Rattray, Mrs. Cheap, Miss Peggie Forbes, Miss Susie Graham, Miss Magdalen Clerk, Miss Mary Clerk, Miss Rachie Houston, Miss Peggie Callander.

[4] My Lady Bruce of Kinross.

to be kept for his sister till she should be so happy as to return from London. He said his sister had writ from the Road of Leith to Sky concerning the garters, intreating they might be carefully preserved, for that she put a great value upon them. 20 July

When Miss MacDonald was a prisoner she happened in coursing about from place to place to fall in luckily with *fol.* 198. Captain O'Neil, then a prisoner likewise, to whom she made up, and giving him a gentle slap upon the cheek with the loof of her hand, said, 'To that black face do I owe all my misfortune.' The captain with a smile replied, 'Why, Madam, what you call your misfortune is truly your greatest honour. And if you be careful to demean yourself agreeably to the character you have already acquired, you will in the event find it to be your happiness.' She told him she was much afraid they designed to carry her to London, which she could not think of but with the utmost uneasiness, not knowing what might turn out to be the consequence. Upon this O'Neil told her that he would take upon him to commence prophet in the case, and to foretell what would happen to her. 'For,' said he, 'if you are carried to London I can venture to assure you it will be for your interest and happiness; and instead of being afraid of this you ought to wish for it. There you will meet with much respect and very good and great friends for what you have done. Only be careful to make all your conduct of a piece. Be not frighten'd by the thoughts of your present circumstances either to say or do anything that may in the least tend to contradict or sully the character you are now[1] *fol.* 199. mistress of, and which you can never be robbed of but by yourself. Never once pretend (through an ill-judg'd excess of caution and prudence) to repent or be ashamed of what you have done, and I dare take upon me to answer for the rest. I do not think (added he) that the Government can be so very barbarous and cruel as to bring you to a trial for your life, and

[1] Here begins vol. ii. of Bishop Forbes's Manuscript Collection. It is entitled: 'THE LYON IN MOURNING, or a Collection (as exactly made as the iniquity of the times would permit) of Speeches, Letters, Journals, etc. relative to the affairs, but more particularly, the dangers and distresses of. . . . Vol. 2d. 1747.'

*'Qui modo* SCOTORUM *leges sceptrumque gerebat;*
*Proh dolor! externi Principis orat opem.'*

10 July therefore I hope you have nothing to fear, and that things will happen to you as I have said.'

Captain O'Neil was wont to tell those who visited him in the Castle of Edinburgh that he had been at the same pains as a parent would be with a child to lay down rules to Miss MacDonald for her future behaviour under the misfortune of being a prisoner, and that it gave him infinite pleasure to find that things had happened to her hitherto according to his words, and to hear by all the accounts he could learn that she had sacredly observed the advices he had given her. He frequently expressed his heartiest wishes that she might get free of all her troubles, and arrive at that which so justly she deserved.

When Miss MacDonald was on board the *Bridgewater* in Leith Road, accounts had come that the Prince was taken prisoner, and one of the officers had brought the news of this report on board. She got an opportunity of talking privately to some who were then visiting her, and said with tears in her eyes, 'Alas, I am afraid that now all is in vain that I have
I. 200. done. The Prince at last is in the hands of his enemies.' Though at that time great fear was entertained about the truth of this account, yet those that were with Miss MacDonald endeavoured all they could to chear her up, and to dissuade her from believing any such thing. But still fears haunted her mind till the matter was cleared up and the contrary appeared.

Miss MacDonald is Protestant, and is descended of the family of Clanranald by her father, and of an Episcopal clergyman by her mother. She is daughter of the deceast Ranald MacDonald of Milton in South Uist, in which island (when the Prince was skulking thereabouts) she happened to be visiting her brother-german who had a little before taken up house at Milton. She was not many days there till she was engaged in the hazardous enterprize; and when she returned to her mother in Sky, the honest old woman was surprized to see her, and asked the reason why she had made such a short stay with her brother. Miss replied that things being in a hurry and confusion in South Uist, with such a number of military folks, she was uneasy till she got out of it; but she never once hinted at the adventure she had so successfully managed, of which the mother knew nothing at all till a party came to take the daughter prisoner, although Miss had been with her mother eight or ten days before she was seized. Immediately Miss Flora was hurried on board of a sloop of war without being allowed the priviledge of taking leave of her mother, or telling her anything of the matter, or taking along with herself one stitch to change another. The sloop called the *Greyhound*, or rather the *Furnace*, was commanded by John Ferguson of Aberdeenshire,[1] a man remarkably rigid and severe in his way, but one of too much greedy sense to have butchered the Prince if he had fallen into his hands. For when he was asked by a friend of his own[2] in Edinburgh what he would have done with the Prince had he got him into his clutches, whether or not he would have dispatched him, he answered, 'No (by G——), I would have been so far from doing any such thing that I would have preserved him as the apple of mine eye, for I would not take any man's word, no, not the Duke of Cumberland's for £30,000 Sterling, though I knew many to be such fools as to do it.' Ferguson was more than once (as he thought) within an hour of catching the Prince, so closely he pursued the royal wanderer, and such an anxiety he had to touch the price of blood.

20 July.

*fol.* 201.

*fol.* 202.

It was Miss MacDonald's good fortune to be soon removed out of the hands of Ferguson into those of the polite and generous Commodore Smith, who, in the coursing about, obtained leave of General Campbell to allow Miss to go ashore to visit her mother and to seek a servant to attend her in the state of confinement. Then it was that poor Kate MacDonal generously made an offer to run all risques with the captive lady, who gladly accepted.

One day in the Road of Leith a lady[3] asking Miss if she had any books on board, she said she had only a prayer book, but regreted much the want of a bible, which that lady soon furnished her with in a present in two pretty pocket volumes, handsomely bound. That she might have some innocent and useful employment for her time, care was taken by a lady[4] to

[1] See ff. 216-218, 690, 873, 922.

[2] Mrs. Ferguson of Pitfour.

[3] Miss Rachie Houston.

[4] My Lady Bruce.

20 July send her a thimble, needles, white thread of different sorts, etc., with some linen and cambrick cut and shaped according
p. 203. to the newest fashions. This piece of friendship Miss Flora admired as much as any instance of kindness and regard that had been shown her, because all the time she had been in custody she was quite idle, having no work to do, and thereby time pass'd very dully on.

While she was in the Road of Leith, from the beginning of September to the 7th of November, she never was allowed to set her foot once on shore, though in other respects the officers were extremely civil and complaisant to her, and took it exceedingly well when any persons came to visit her. Sometimes they were so obliging as to come ashore for good company to attend her, and frequently declared that if they knew any person to come on board out of curiosity and not out of respect for Miss MacDonald, that person should not have access to her. This genteel behaviour makes it to be presumed that their orders were so exceedingly strict that they could not dare to bring her ashore. Commodore Smith (Commander of the *Eltham*) behaved like a father to her, and tendered her many good advices as to her behaviour in her ticklish situation; and Captain Knowler of the *Bridgewater* used her with the utmost decency and politeness. When company came to visit her she was indulged the privilege by both these humane and well-bred gentlemen to call for anything on board as if
p. 204. she had been at her own fireside, and the servants of the cabin were obliged to give her all manner of attendance; and she had the liberty to invite any of her friends to dine with her when she pleased. Her behaviour in company was so easy, modest, and well-adjusted that every visitant was much surprized; for she had never been out of the islands of South Uist and Sky till about a year before the Prince's arrival that she had been in the family of MacDonald of Largie in Argyllshire for the space of ten or eleven months; and during her confinement she had been all along on board a ship of war till she went to London.

Some that went on board to pay their respects to her, used to take a dance in the cabin, and to press her much to share with them in the diversion. But with all their importunity

they could not prevail with her to take a trip. She told them 20 July
that at present her dancing days were done, and she would not readily entertain a thought of that diversion till she should be assured of her Prince's safety, and perhaps not till she should be bless'd with the happiness of seeing him again. Although she was easy and chearful, yet she had a certain mixture of gravity in all her behaviour which became her situation exceedingly well, and set her of to great advantage. She is *fol.* 205
of a low stature, of a fair complexion and well enough shap'd. One could not discern by her conversation that she had spent all her former days in the Highlands; for she talks English (or rather Scots) easily, and not at all through the Earse tone. She has a sweet voice and sings well; and no lady, Edinburgh bred, can acquit herself better at the tea-table than what she did when in Leith Road. Her wise conduct in one of the most perplexing scenes that can happen in life, her fortitude and good sense, are memorable instances of the strength of a female mind, even in those years that are tender and unexperienced. She is the delight of her friends and the envy of her enemies.

When the Prince came to Kingsburgh's house (Sunday, 1746
June 29th) it was between ten and eleven at night; and Mrs. 29 June
MacDonald, not expecting to see her husband that night was making ready to go to bed. One of her servant maids came and told her that Kingsburgh was come home and had brought some company with him. 'What company?' says Mrs. MacDonald. 'Milton's daughter, I believe,' says the maid, 'and some company with her.' 'Milton's daughter,' replies Mrs. MacDonald, 'is very welcome to come here with any company she pleases to bring. But you'll give my service to her, and *fol.* 206
tell her to make free with anything in the house; for I am very sleepy and cannot see her this night.' In a little her own daughter came and told her in a surprize, 'O mother, my father has brought in a very odd, muckle, ill-shaken-up wife as ever I saw! I never saw the like of her, and he has gone into the hall with her.' She had scarce done with telling her tale when Kingsburgh came and desired his lady to fasten on her bucklings again, and to get some supper for him and the company he had brought with him. 'Pray, goodman,' says she, 'what company is this you have brought with you?' 'Why,

9 June goodwife,' said he, 'you shall know that in due time; only
make haste and get some supper in the meantime.' Mrs. Mac-
Donald desired her daughter to go and fetch her the keys she
had left in the hall. When the daughter came to the door of
the hall, she started back, ran to her mother and told her she
could not go in for the keys, for the muckle woman was walking up and down in the hall, and she was so frighted at seeing
her that she could not have the courage to enter. Mrs. Mac-
Donald went herself to get the keys, and I heard her more
than once declare that upon looking in at the door she had
fol. 207. not the courage to go forward. 'For,' said she, 'I saw such
an odd muckle trallup of a carlin, making lang wide steps
through the hall that I could not like her appearance at all.'
Mrs. MacDonald called Kingsburgh, and very seriously begged
to know what a lang, odd hussie was this he had brought to
the house; for that she was so frighted at the sight of her
that she could not go into the hall for her keys. 'Did you
never see a woman before,' said he, 'goodwife? What frights
you at seeing a woman? Pray, make haste, and get us some
supper.' Kingsburgh would not go for the keys, and therefore
his lady behov'd to go for them. When she entered the hall,
the Prince happen'd to be sitting; but immediately he arose,
went forward and saluted Mrs. MacDonald, who, feeling a long
stiff beard, trembled to think that this behoved to be some
distressed nobleman or gentleman in disguise, for she never
dream'd it to be the Prince, though all along she had been
seized with a dread she could not account for from the moment
she had heard that Kingsburgh had brought company with
him. She very soon made out of the hall with her keys, never
saying one word. Immediately she importun'd Kingsburgh to
tell her who the person was, for that she was sure by the salute
that it was some distressed gentleman. Kingsburgh smiled at
fol. 208. the mention of the bearded kiss, and said: 'Why, my dear, it
is the Prince. You have the honour to have him in your
house.' 'The Prince,' cried she. 'O Lord, we are a' ruin'd
and undone for ever! We will a' be hang'd now!' 'Hout,
goodwife,' says the honest stout soul, 'we will die but ance;
and if we are hanged for this, I am sure we die in a good
cause. Pray, make no delay; go, get some supper. Fetch

what is readiest. You have eggs and butter and cheese in the house, get them as quickly as possible.' 'Eggs and butter and cheese!' says Mrs. MacDonald, 'what a supper is that for a Prince?' 'O goodwife,' said he, 'little do you know how this good Prince has been living for some time past. These, I can assure you, will be a feast to him. Besides, it would be unwise to be dressing a formal supper, because this would serve to raise the curiosity of the servants, and they would be making their observations. The less ceremony and work the better. Make haste and see that you come to supper.' 'I come to supper!' says Mrs. MacDonald; 'how can I come to supper? I know not how to behave before Majesty.' 'You must come,' says Kingsburgh, 'for he will not eat a bit till he see you at the table; and you will find it no difficult matter to behave before him, so obliging and easy is he is in his conversation.' 29 Jun fol. 209

The Prince ate of our roasted eggs, some collops, plenty of bread and butter, etc., and (to use the words of Mrs. MacDonald) 'the deel a drap did he want in 's weam of twa bottles of sma beer. God do him good o't; for, well I wat, he had my blessing to gae down wi't.' After he had made a plentiful supper, he called for a dram; and when the bottle of brandy was brought, he said he would fill the glass for himself; 'for,' said he, 'I have learn'd in my skulking to take a hearty dram.' He filled up a bumper and drank it off to the happiness and prosperity of his landlord and landlady. Then taking a crack'd and broken pipe out of his poutch, wrapt about with thread, he asked Kingsburgh if he could furnish him with some tobacco; for that he had learn'd likewise to smoke in his wanderings. Kingsburgh took from him the broken pipe and laid it carefully up with the brogs, and gave him a new clean pipe and plenty of tobacco.

The Prince and Kingsburgh turn'd very familiar and merry together, and when the Prince spoke to Kingsburgh, he for the most part laid his hand upon Kingsburgh's knee and used several kind and obliging expressions in his conversation with the happy landlord. Kingsburgh remarked what a lucky thing it was that he happened to be at Mougstot (Sir Alexander MacDonald's house), and that it was all a matter of chance fol. 210

9 June that he was there, for he had no design of being there that day. And then he asked the Prince what he would have done if he had not been at Mougstot. The Prince replied, 'Why, sir, you could not avoid being at Mougstot this day; for Providence ordered you to be there upon my account.' Kingsburgh became so merry and jocose that putting up his hand to the Prince's face, he turned off his head-dress which was a very odd clout of a mutch or toy; upon which Mrs. MacDonald hasted out of the room and brought a clean nightcap for him.

Both Kingsburgh and his lady said that the Prince's face and hands were very much sun-burnt. But they declared he had not a spot of the itch upon him, though a silly report had been raised by his malicious enemies that he was scabbed to the eye-holes. His legs, they said, were hacked in some parts, which was occasioned by his walking and sleeping so often in
*l.* 211. wet hose. Mrs. MacDonald used the freedom to put up the sleeve of his gown and of his shirt (a very coarse dud), 'and there,' said she, 'I saw a bonny, clean, white skin indeed. The deel a lady in a' the land has a whiter and purer skin than he has.'

10 June Next morning Mrs. MacDonald went to Miss Flora's bedside before she got up and asked of her an account of the adventure. Miss (among other things) told her that there was not any other probable way of saving the Prince but that single one which had been used, and that it had the appearance of a desperate attempt at best: that Lady Clanronald provided them with women's cloathes for the disguise, and that she had contributed all in her power for preserving the Prince out of the hands of his enemies. Mrs. MacDonald desired to know what was become of the boat and the rowers. 'They returned directly,' said Miss Flora, 'to South Uist.' Mrs. MacDonald declared great concern to hear that, because upon their return they would immediately be seized by the military and harshly used to tell what they knew. 'I wish,' said Mrs. MacDonald, 'you had sunk the boat and kept the boatmen in Sky where they could have been concealed, and then we would have known
*ol.* 212. the better what to have done with the Prince, because his enemies by this means would have lost scent of him. But all will be wrong by their returning to South Uist.' 'I hope not,'

said Miss, 'for we took care to depone them before they parted *30 Jun* from us.' 'Alas!' replied Mrs. MacDonald, 'your deponing of them will not signifie a farthing. For if once the military get hold of them they will terrifie them out of their senses and make them forget their oath.'

As Mrs. MacDonald said, so it happened. The boatmen were made prisoners instantly upon their landing in South Uist and threatened with tortures if they did not declare everything they knew, which (to avoid pain, and perhaps death itself) they complied with. From their declaration no doubt it happen'd that his enemies could specifie the particular parts of the dress the Prince was disguised in, even to the nicety of telling the colour of the gown.

After Miss Flora had got up, Mrs. MacDonald told her that she wanted much to have a lock of the Prince's hair, and that she behoved to go into his room and get it for her. Miss Flora refused to do as she desired, because the Prince was not yet out of bed. 'What then,' said Mrs. MacDonald, 'no harm will happen to you. He is too good to harm you or any *fol. 213* person. You must instantly go in and get me the lock.' Mrs. MacDonald, taking hold of Miss with one hand, knocked at the door of the room with the other. The Prince called, 'Who is there?' Mrs. MacDonald, opening the door, said, 'Sir, it is I, and I am importuneing Miss Flora to come in and get a lock of your hair to me, and she refuses to do it.' 'Pray,' said the Prince, 'desire Miss MacDonald to come in. What should make her afraid to come where I am?' When Miss came in he begged her to sit down on a chair at the bedside, then laying his arms about her waist, and his head upon her lap, he desired her to cut out the lock with her own hands in token of future and more substantial favours. The one half of the lock Miss gave to Mrs. MacDonald and the other she kept to herself. I heard Mrs. MacDonald say that when Miss Flora at any time happened to come into the room where the Prince was, he always rose from his seat, paid her the same respects as if she had been a queen, and made her sit on his right hand.

Kingsburgh visited the Prince before he got out of bed and asked how he had rested all night. 'Never better,' replied he, 'for I have rested exceedingly well, having slept, I believe, nine *fol. 214*

30 June or ten hours without interruption. Then it was that the conversation happened about Lord George Murray and the landing of the French, etc.[1]

When the Prince had got himself dress'd in the Highland cloaths at the side of the wood, he embraced Kingsburgh in his arms and bad him a long and a happy adieu, most affectionately thanking him for all his services, and assuring him he would never forget them. Then the Prince wept, and some drops of blood fell from his nose. Kingsburgh could not refrain from weeping too, and when he saw the blood, expressed his concern, dreading the Prince not to be in health with the fatigues, fastings, etc., he was obliged to undergo. The Prince assured him he was in very good health, and that this was no extraordinary thing with him at all. 'This,' said he, 'is only the effect of parting with a dear friend, and ordinarily it happens to me in such a case. Alas! Kingsburgh, I am afraid I shall not meet with another MacDonald in my difficulties.'[2] When Kingsburgh returned to his own house he told his lady that after the Prince had got on the Highland dress and the claymore in his hand he was a soger-like man indeed.

*fol.* 215. I heard Mrs. MacDonald of Kingsburgh say that she had the following particular from Malcolm MacLeod's own mouth before

4 July he was made prisoner. Malcolm went with the Prince and MacKinnon to the shore to see them fairly boated for the continent. When he was about to take leave of the Prince he spied some ships coming in sight and hovering about the coast. He intreated the Prince not to go on board for some time, but to wait till he should see how these ships steer'd their course; 'For just now,' said he, 'the wind blows so as to fetch them this way and to hinder your passing to the continent.' The Prince replied, 'Never fear, MacLeod, I'll go on board directly. The wind will change immediately and make these ships steer a contrary course. Providence will take care of me, and it will not be in the power of these ships to look near me at this time.' Malcolm MacLeod declared that the Prince's words made him astonished and determin'd him to sit down upon the shore to see what would happen. He said the Prince and his small

---

[1] See ff. 150, 236.

[2] See ff. 538, 600.

retinue had not rowed many yards from the shore till the wind changed to a point directly opposite to what it had been, and blowing pretty briskly made the ships steer so as to be soon out of sight. Mr. MacLeod affirm'd that in all the course of his life he had never known any man that had such a firm trust and well-grounded confidence as the Prince was remarkably endued with. 4 July *fol.* 216.

Captain John Ferguson searched Sir Alexander MacDonald's house for the Prince, and in quest of him he came to Kingsburgh, where he examined Kingsburgh and his lady and their daughter, Miss Nanie MacDonald, *alias* Mrs. MacAllaster, for she is married. Kingsburgh told his lady that Captain Ferguson was come to examine her about some lodgers she had lately in her house, and desired her to be distinct in her answers. Mrs. MacDonald looking Ferguson broad in the face said, 'If Captain Ferguson is to be my judge, then God have mercy upon my soul.' Ferguson asked for what reason she spoke such words. 'Why, Sir,' said she, 'the world belies you if you be not a very cruel, hard-hearted man; and indeed I do not like to come through your hands.' Ferguson had nothing else to say for himself but the common saying, viz., That people should not believe all that the world says.

When Ferguson asked Kingsburgh where Miss MacDonald and the person along with her in woman's cloaths lay all night in his house, he answered, 'I know in what room Miss MacDonald herself lay, but where servants are laid when in my house, I know nothing of that matter, I never enquire anything about it. My wife is the properest person to inform you about that.' Then he had the impertinence to ask Mrs. MacDonald, Whether or not she had laid the young Pretender and Miss MacDonald in one bed? To which she answered, 'Sir, whom you mean by the young Pretender I shall not pretend to guess; but I can assure you it is not the fashion in the Isle of Sky to lay the mistress and the maid in the same bed together.' Then Ferguson desired to see the different rooms where their late lodgers had slept; and after seeing them he said, it was pretty remarkable that the room in which the maid had slept seem'd to look better than the one where the mistress had been laid; and this behoved to confirm him in the *fol.* 217.

20 July belief that it was the young Pretender in women's cloaths who had been along with Miss MacDonald. Kingsburgh's daughter said it could not be the person he meant in women's
fol. 218. cloaths, for that she had heard that person ask something (a bottle of water) from Miss MacDonald in Erse. 'This,' says Ferguson, 'confirms me more and more in my opinion, for I have often heard that a fellow went to Rome some years agoe on purpose to teach the young Pretender the Erse language.' This, by the bye, is a gross mistake in Ferguson; for the Prince could not speak a word of Erse till he arriv'd in Scotland, and he knew but very little of it till he was forced to commence wanderer for the preservation of his life, and then he learned to speak it pretty well, which prov'd of very great use to him.

When Kingsburgh and Miss MacDonald were made prisoners and brought before General Campbell (which happened at different times) both of them honestly own'd the parts they had acted, and, if I rightly remember, declarations were written from their own mouths and they subscribed them.

*N.B.*—Miss Flora MacDonald called her disguised handmaid Bettie Bourk, or Burk, an Irish name, and made the dress of a piece with the proposed character, being a hood with a long mantle almost down to the heel.[1]

Robert Forbes, A.M.

## fol. 219. Mr. Cameron of Glenevis[2] gave the following Narrative to several persons in Edinburgh after his liberation out of the Castle of Edinburgh, which happened some time in the beginning of July 1747. He said—

August 1646 Lord George Sackville with a command of 400 men was ordered from Fort Augustus to gather up the gleanings of the

[1] See ff. 525, 595.

[2] Alexander Cameron of Glenevis personally took no part in the Rebellion, but was imprisoned for nearly a year on suspicion of befriending his relatives who

cattle that might happen to be left in the countries that had been plundered and pillaged. When he was at Locharkaig the Prince and his small retinue had been thirty or forty hours without any meat. One evening they spied Lord George and his command driving away the cattle they had pick'd up here and there. They were then consulting with one another what was fittest to be done to procure themselves some provisions in this extremity, and it was proposed that they should go to a place at the distance of sixteen miles from them. The Prince objected against this measure alleging that the journey was too long for them in their present distressed condition, and that perhaps they might be disappointed of their intention when they should come to the place spoken of. 'What would ye think, gentlemen,' said he, 'of lifting some of the cattle we spied under a command this evening? They are not far from us, and I hope we will succeed in the design, for the gloom of the night will favour us in the attempt.' His companions looked upon the enterprize as too hazardous, and could not think at all of running such a risque. But the Prince still insisted upon it as the best expedient they could pitch upon in the present difficulty, and said, 'If the dangers attending this expedition be all that can be said against it, I myself will be one of the number that will made the attempt.' Upon this four of the company declared they would gladly go along with him and try what they could do. Away they went, and (as the Prince had suggested) by the favour of the dark night they brought off six cows without being in the least discovered—a most lucky and plentiful supply in such necessitous circumstances.

August

*fol.* 220.

*N.B.*—Though Glenevis had never join'd the Prince, but had lived peaceably at home, and though no overt act could be proved against him, yet his conduct could not screen him from cruel treatment. All his effects were plundered and pillaged, his houses burnt down to the ground, and he himself

---

did. He was released on 7th July 1747. His lady and family suffered considerably at the hands of the government troops, and his house was burned. See f. 552.

July suffered imprisonment for eleven or twelve months, and was
*fol. 221.* not released till by a petition presented before the lords of justiciary he pled the benefit of the indemnity.

*N.B.*—Among the several remarkable and lesser circumstances of Kingsburgh's history I have forgot to mention some which are well worth remarking, and are as follows :—

When Kingsburgh came to Fort Augustus he was immediately ordered into the provo's guard, where the common fellows took the buckles out of his shoes, the garters from his legs, and his watch and money out of his pockets, a ceremony, it seems, preparatory to one's being taken out to be hang'd; at least Kingsburgh looked upon it as such. 'For,' said he, 'I expected every moment to be ordered out to end my life on a gibbet, and I laid my account with it.' After staying there for some hours he was then ordered to be thrown into a dungeon with heavy irons upon him, which he looked upon as a change to the better by reason of the insults, the opprobrious and blasphemous language, he behoved to endure from the common fellows.

When Kingsburgh was removed from Fort Augustus he was brought to Edinburgh under a guard of Kingston's Light horse, who entered the city with sound of trumpet and beat of kettledrums, a circumstance very much noticed by everybody as a
*fol. 222.* form of procession quite unusual for the bringing a prisoner into a metropolis. The command halted a considerable time upon the street of Edinburgh till further orders should be got, when the mob came flocking about them, and some of them said, 'What can be the matter with this honest-like, well-looking man that he is brought here a prisoner? Show your face, honest man, to the world, for, faith, you may be seen as well as the best of them all.' Then Kingsburgh was put into the same room of the Castle with Major MacDonell, George Moir, the Laird of Leckie, Mr. Thomas Ogilvie, etc., where he thought himself very happy indeed; but that happiness did not last long.

One day when I was visiting him and his fellow-prisoners, one of them happened to be complaining of the hardships of their situation, saying, 'Is not this a dull and uncomfortable state to be pacing up and down this room, waiting the freak and humour of an officer to let us out when he thinks fit to walk for an hour or so within the narrow bounds of the Half-moon?' Kingsburgh gently check'd him for his complaining, and said, 'Do not complain, Sir, for there are many situations far worse than ours. Had you been only in my condition at Fort Augustus you would have experienc'd a very great odds. When I was taken out of the provo's guard and put into the dungeon with irons upon me, I thought myself happy; but when I was removed to a room and the irons taken off me, though I was not allowed to step over the threshold, I thought myself in a kind of paradise. And now that I am here and in exceeding good campany (a happiness I had not before) I think myself still more and more in a paradise. I am really content. I am quite satisfied with my condition, if they will only allow me to stay with this good company. And what do you think, Sir, of the liberty of walking upon the Half-moon, tho' it were but for an hour or two at a time? I do assure you this is no small happiness in a state of confinement. What would I have given for such a liberty at Fort Augustus?' Kingsburgh was not allowed to make a long abode with his agreeable companions, for he was soon removed to a room by himself under a strict and close confinement, not having the liberty to step over the threshold of his door, and no person being allowed to come near him but the officer upon guard, the serjeant, and the keeper that was appointed to attend him as a servant. July *fol.* 223.

When his lady came to Edinburgh she was not allowed access to him, but only to stand upon the parade and see her husband looking down to her through the grate of a window, the officers and sogers witnessing their enquiring about ane another's welfare. At last Kingsburgh fell so ill in his health that a physician and surgeon behoved to have access to him, but always in presence of an officer. Then his lady after many and earnest solicitations obtain'd the privilege of being with him throughout the day, but was obliged to leave him upon the approach of the evening. When he was recovering he was allowed to step out, only once or twice a week, with an officer attending him, to take a walk in the garden or any other by-place of the Castle, not being indulged the pleasure of seeing *fol.* 224.

July the other prisoners or of walking on the same spot with them; till some short time before his releasement that he was permitted now and then to be on the Half-moon with them. All the reason that ever could be discovered for this severity and strictness upon Kingsburgh was this. When he was in the same room with Major MacDonell, Leckie, etc., many persons came to pay their respects to him, and to hear his story, which he very plainly and honestly gave, at the same time never
*fol. 225.* failing to give an exact account of the Prince's adventures and chearful conduct in the course of his wanderings, as far as he had got any intelligence about them, This reaching the ears of those in power it proved not a little disgusting to them to hear such things as served to form a great and glorious character of the Prince, and therefore Kingsburgh behoved to suffer for narrating some stubborn, ill-manner'd truths, and to feel the effects of being a plain, honest man. Truth, tho' never so glaring, when it runs cross to the partial notions and inclinations of poor frail mortals, grates very hard and becomes a very uneasy and painful thing.

One day a gentleman happening to visit the lady prisoners upon the same stair where Kingsburgh endured his strict and close confinement, and spying Kingsburgh's room door to be open, he made a stop. Upon this the sentry, knowing the gentleman, whispered to him that as the keeper was employed in bringing some things to Kingsburgh the door would be open for some short time, and that he would allow him to step in and ask Kingsburgh about his welfare, provided that he would not sit down, but come
*fol. 226.* out as quickly as possible. Accordingly the gentleman went in and embracing Kingsburgh regreted this change in his condition. Kingsburgh smiled, and said, 'The Government little knows what pleasure this treatment gives me; for they are doing me much honour without designing it. They are at much pains to make me a considerable person. Little did I ever think that I was a man of such consequence that a whole Government should be so much taken up about me. If I am so lucky as to keep my health, this change shall give me no uneasiness.' Then he desired the gentleman to inform his companions in the other room that he was in very good health,

and that he kept up his heart in his solitary state, and to forbid them to be any way uneasy about his solitary condition.

When the Prince was in Kingsburgh's house talking about the difficulties and dangers attending his situation, and consulting with him what might be the best and fittest expedient for the safety of his person, he suggested going to the Laird of MacLeod's house as by far the properest place that could be pitched upon, because it was not liable to any suspicion or jealousy upon the part of the Government, and therefore would not be searched for him. If he could only get there without discovery, he said, he thought he would be in absolute safety. Kingsburgh told him that he would not take upon him positively to oppose any measure the Prince was pleased to condescend upon for the preservation of his own person; but then, if his opinion could be of any use in the present case, he behoved to declare that he should never have his advice or approbation for going to the Laird of MacLeod's house at any rate.[1] The Prince in a surprize clapped his hand to his breast and said, 'What! Kingsburgh! Do you think that MacLeod to his other doings would add that of thirsting after my blood? Do you really think he would go the length of giving me up into the hands of my enemies?' Kingsburgh would not pretend to assign particular reasons for its not being advisable that the Prince should go to MacLeod's house; but still he assured him, it should never be with his consent. The Prince insisted no more upon this project, and dropt it altogether. This I had from Kingsburgh's own mouth, and his narrating of it consists with the knowledge of several others, particularly his fellow-prisoners.

29 June

*fol. 227.*

Robert Forbes, A.M.

---

[1] See ff. 263-265, 472,477.

fol. 228. LEITH, Friday's Evening, 6 o'clock, August 7th, 1747, in the house of JAMES MACDONALD, joiner, who and STEWART CARMICHAEL of Bonnyhaugh, were present, CAPTAIN MALCOLM MACLEOD,[1] second cousin to MALCOLM MACLEOD (Laird of Raaza), gave the following Account or Journal.[2]

30 June 1746. BY appointment the said Captain Malcolm MacLeod and Murdoch MacLeod, Raaza's third son, met the Prince at Pourttree, a publick house in the isle of Sky, upon Monday's night, June 30th, 1746. After taking leave of Kingsburgh at the side of a wood, the Prince[3] had set out directly for this place, where Miss Flora MacDonald (taking a different road) met him once more and bad farewel to him. Captain Malcolm MacLeod said he would not positively affirm whether it was Monday's night or Tuesday's morning when they met; 'But,' said he, 'it was dark.' Raaza's third son had been in the Prince's service, and had received a musket-shot through his shoulder at the battle of Culloden.[4]

Before these two gentlemen had set out from the island of Raaza in order to meet the Prince at Pourttree, the young fol. 229. Laird of Raaza, John MacLeod, came to the Captain and told him what a great anxiety he had to see that young man, the Prince. Malcolm MacLeod begged him to consider well what he was doing, that as he had not been out, he ought to run no risque for satisfying his desire, which at present could be of no real use or service, and therefore he suggested to him to act in this affair with the utmost prudence and caution. Meantime Malcolm could not help owning frankly that he himself heartily wished that his friend might see the Prince,

---

[1] See ff. 1714-1730.

[2] This narrative, at least as far as f. 248, is printed in the *Jacobite Memoirs*, pp. 468-487.

[3] Attended by Neil MacKechan and a boy to show them the way. Neil MacKechan went with Miss MacDonald to Slate.—F. See f. 537.

[4] See f. 879.

provided he could do it with safety. But then he would leave it altogether to himself to determine on which side he should think fit to chuse. After thinking a while, young Raaza positively declared he was resolved to see the Prince if it should cost him the estate and the head, and accordingly accompanied his brother and the Captain to Pourttree[1] in a small boat that would contain only six or seven men with difficulty. Upon meeting with the Prince they spent very little time at Pourttree, but attended him soon to the same small boat; and the Captain did not introduce young Raaza to the Prince till they were in the boat.[2] Early in the morning, July 1st, they arrived at Glam, in Raaza, where they remained two days in a mean, low hut; and young Raaza was the person that brought provisions to them, viz., a lamb and a kid in the nook of his plaid. 1 July

At that time there happened to be in Raaza a fellow who had come into the island upon pretence of selling a roll of tobacco; but after he had sold off his tobacco he continued strolling up *fol.* 230. and down the island in an idle way without anything to do, for no less than twelve or fourteen days, which made the people of the island suspect him to be a spy. When the Prince and his friends were in the hut, Malcolm MacLeod happened to see this stroller coming towards the hut, which he took notice of to the Prince, and told him withal what kind of a fellow he was suspected to be. The Prince not liking the thing so well, Malcolm said he should take care that the fellow should not go back again, for that he would immediately go out and shoot him through the head. 'O, no,' said the Prince, 'God forbid that any poor man should suffer for us, if we can but keep ourselves anyway safe.' And he would not allow the Captain to stir, though their apprehensions behov'd to be the greater that the hut was not upon any road. But the fellow happened to pass by it without looking into it.

The Prince began to be anxious to be out of Raaza, alleging the island to be too narrow and confin'd in its bounds for his purpose, and proposed setting out for Troternish in Sky.

---

[1] Or Portree, *i.e.* The King's Port.

[2] See f. 862.

1 July But his companions told him that they thought him in safety where he was, and did not like that he should change his place so soon. The Prince pressed so much for going to the place he had mentioned, pretending he had a tryst there with a
fol. 231. gentleman,[1] which he would not break for any thing, that his friends yielded to his importunity.

2 July July 2d. About 7 o'clock at night he went on board the above mentioned small boat, attended by the young Laird of Raaza (who could not think of parting from him soon) and his brother Murdoch, Captain MacLeod and the two boatmen, John MacKenzie and Donald MacFrier, who had been both out in his service, the one a sergeant and the other a private man. They had not well left the shore till the wind blew a hard gale, and the sea became so very rough and tempestuous that all on board begged he would return; for the waves were beating over and over them, the men tugging hard at the oars, and Captain MacLeod laving the water out of the little boat. The Prince would by no means hear of returning, and to divert the men from thinking on the danger he sung them a merry Highland song. About nine or ten o'clock the same night they landed at a place in Sky called Nicolson's Rock, near Scorobreck, in Troternish. In rowing along they found the coast very bad and dangerous, and when they came to the Rock the Prince was the third man that jump'd out among the water and cried out, 'Take care of the boat, and hawl her up to dry ground,' which was immediately done, he himself assisting as much as any one of them.[2] The Prince had upon him a large big coat, which was become very heavy and
fol. 232. cumbersome by the waves beating so much upon it, for it was wet through and through. Captain MacLeod proposed taking the big coat to carry it, for the rock was steep and of a very uneasy ascent. But the Prince would not part with the coat, wet as it was, alleging he was as able to carry it as the Captain was.[3] They went forwards to a cow-byre on the rock, about two miles from Scorobreck, a gentleman's house. In this byre the Prince took up his quarters, the whole company still

---

1 Captain Donald Roy MacDonald.

2 See ff. 1564, 1565.

3 See f. 757.

attending him. Here they took some little refreshment of 2 July
bread and cheese they had along with them, the cakes being
moulded down into very small crumbs.

Captain MacLeod intreated the Prince to put on a dry shirt
and to take some sleep; but he continued sitting in his wet
cloaths, and did not then incline to sleep. However, at last
he began to nap a little, and would frequently start in his
sleep, look briskly up, and stare boldly in the face of every one
of them as if he had been to fight them. Upon his waking he 3 July
would sometimes cry out, 'O Poor England! O Poor England!'
The Prince desired the Captain to take some rest, but he did
not chuse to sleep at that time. However, when the Prince
began to importune him, the Captain thought perhaps the
Prince wants a private opportunity to say something to Raaza's *fol.* 233.
son, and therefore he stept aside a little. The two brothers[1]
and the boatmen parted from the Prince at the byre. He
promised to meet the youngest brother again at Camistinawagg,
another place in the same island.[2]

The Prince said he expected Donald MacDonald *alias*
Donald Roy to come to him; but he not coming, the Prince
asked Captain MacLeod if he was a stout walker? and if he
could walk bare-footed? The Captain replied he was pretty
good at walking, and that he could travell bare-footed very
well. The Prince told him by bare-footed he meant, if he
could walk in his shoes without stockings, 'for,' said he, 'that
is the way I used to walk at my diversions in Italy.' The
Captain said he could not really tell if he could do that or not,
for that he had never tried it.

About six or seven o'clock at night the Prince, taking the little
baggage in his hand, stept out of the byre, and desired the
Captain to follow him. The Captain came up to him and
said, 'Give me that,' taking hold of the little baggage, which
he gave him, and then the Captain followed him without
speaking one word till they were out of sight of the cow-byre,
when the Prince happening to turn such a way as the Captain
did not think so safe, he made up to him and said: 'Your *fol.* 234.

---

[1] Wrong, for one of them, young Rasay, had gone to find out Donald Roy MacDonald.—F. See ff. 764, 867. [2] See ff. 1564, 1565.

3 July royal highness will pardon me to ask where you are going, for that I dread you may chance to fall into the hands of some party or another, if you do not take exceeding good care, as there are many small parties dispersed up and down the country.' The Prince then said: 'Why, MacLeod, I now throw myself entirely into your hands, and leave you to do with me what you please. Only I want to go to Strath, MacKinnon's country. I hope you will accompany me, an you think you can lead me safe enough into Strath.' The Captain declared he would go with him where he pleased, and said he could undertake to bring him into MacKinnon's country safe enough, provided he would go by sea, which he might easily do, for that he really did not think it so safe for him to go by land by reason of the several parties that were searching the country. The Prince said he would go by land, for that there was no doing anything in their situation without running risques, and proposed directing their course immediately for the place intended, alleging that he himself knew the way very well. 'I am sure,' says the Captain, 'I must know it much
fol. 235. better, and I must tell you that we have a long journey to make, no less than 24 or 30 long miles. For I dare not lead you the direct road, but take you byways, and go here and there cross the country to keep as free as we can of the parties scattered up and down.' Then the Captain hinted that he thought it not so convenient to set out when night was coming on lest they should fall into dangers and inconveniences for want of knowing well where they were. But the Prince insisted upon setting out immediately; and accordingly away they went along the ridges of high hills, and through wild muirs and glens. All the time from first to last of this adventure the Captain was exceedingly afraid of what might happen, lest bad things should be imputed to him, in case of any harm befalling the Prince.

The Prince proposed to pass for the Captain's servant, the better to conceal him, which was agreed to, and that he should be named Lewie Caw,[1] there being of that name a young surgeon lad (who had been in the Prince's service) skulking at

---

[1] See f. 1715.

that time in Sky, where he had some relations. The Captain 4 July
advised the Prince, since he had proposed being his servant, to walk at some distance behind him; and if at any time he happened to meet with any persons and to converse with them, *fol.* 236.
as he was well known in the island, that the Prince should show no concern at all in his face, but sit down at a small distance, when he should happen to talk with any folks. The Prince assured him that no appearance of concern should be seen about him, and that he should be careful to observe the proper distance of a servant, and to do the duty of one by carrying the baggage, which very often he would not part with to the Captain when he desired it of him, and even pressed to have it.

The conversation happening to turn upon Lord George Murray, the Prince said that Lord George Murray (whether out of ignorance, or with a view to betray him he would not say) did not behave well at all with respect to obeying of orders; and that particularly for two or three days before the battle of Culloden Lord George did scarce any one thing he desired him to do.[1]

When the Captain was informing the Prince about the many cruelties and barbarities committed after Culloden battle, the Prince was amazed, and said, 'Surely that man who calls himself the Duke, and pretends to be so great a general, cannot be guilty of such cruelties, I cannot believe them.'

The Captain, happening to see the Prince uneasy and fidging, took him to the back of a know, and opening his breast, saw him troubled with lice for want of clean linen, and by reason *fol.* 237.
of the coarse odd way he behoved to live in, both as to sustenance and sleep. He said, he believed, he took fourscore off him.[2] This serves to show that he was reduced to the very lowest ebb of misery and distress, and is a certain indication of that greatness of soul which could rise above all misfortunes, and bear up with a chearfulness, not to be equall'd in history, under all the scenes of woe that could happen. He used to say that the fatigues and distresses he underwent signified nothing at all, because he was only a single person; but when

[1] See ff. 150, 667, 668.

[2] See f. 1675.

July he reflected upon the many brave fellows who suffered in his cause, that, he behoved to own, did strike him to the heart, and did sink very deep with him.

The Prince, even when warm and sweating, used to drink a great deal of water in his wandering from place to place, and the Captain was always sure to desire him to take a dram above the water to qualifie it. The Captain intreated him not to drink water when he was sweating lest he should thereby injure his health. 'No, no,' said the Prince, 'that will never hurt me in the least. If you happen to drink any cold thing when you are warm, only remember, MacLeod, to piss after drinking, and it will do you no harm at all. This advice I had from a friend abroad.' The Captain said the Prince was always sure to observe this direction.

When the Captain was asked if the Prince was really in good
238. health when he happened to be with him he said, it was not possible he could be altogether in good health considering the many fatigues and distresses he was obliged to undergo, and that (as he had heard) he had been seized with a bloody flux before he left South Uist. But then, he said, the Prince would never own himself to be in any bad state of health at all, and always bore up with a surprizing stock of spirits. It was never in the power of any person to discover an appearance of bad health about him. He walked very quickly, and had a good appetite.

At last the brandy bottle began to come near the bottom, when the Prince pressed the Captain to take a dram lest he should faint with the excessive fatigue. But he refused to take it, and desired the Prince himself to drink it off. The kind contest ran so high that the Prince told him: The devil a drop of it he would drink, and therefore he should make an end of it. The Captain behoved to empty the bottle, which the Prince proposed to throw away and to break it. 'No, no,' said the Captain, 'I will be so far from breaking it that I will do my best to preserve it as a curious piece. It may come to drink many a cask of whiskie to me yet.' He then hid the bottle in the heart of a thick bush of heath, and as he knows the ground well, he hopes to find it upon his return to Sky, if the cattle have not trampled it to pieces. He said he hoped the bottle would make a figure in Westminster yet. He has likewise the big coat, which the Prince wore wet and heavy. He took it to London with him, and gave orders to send it after him when he set out for Scotland. 4 July *fol.* 239.

As they were marching along and talking of the fatigues the Prince was obliged to undergoe, he said: 'MacLeod, do you not think that God Almighty has made this person of mine for doing some good yet? When I was in Italy, and dining at the king's table, very often the sweat would have been coming through my coat with the heat of the climate; and now that I am in a cold country, of a more piercing and trying climate, and exposed to different kinds of fatigues, I really find I agree equally with both. I have had this philibeg on now for some days, and I find I do as well with it as any the best breeches I ever put on. I hope in God, MacLeod, to walk the streets of London with it yet.' Then he remarked that the waistcoat he had upon him was too fine for a servant, being a scarlet tartan with a gold twist button, and proposed to the master to change with him, the better to carry on the disguise, which accordingly was done, the master's vest not being so fine as the servant's. When the Prince was making the exchange he said, 'I hope, MacLeod, to give you a much better vest for this yet.'

The Captain remarked it was proper they should pass the road that leads to the Laird of MacLeod's country in the night time for fear of parties spying them; which accordingly they did by break of day. And the Prince looking about him, and seeing nothing but hills all around them said, 'I am sure, the Devil cannot find us out now.' *fol.* 240.

As they were coming near Strath, MacKinnon's country, the Captain suggested to the Prince that now he was coming to a country where he would be known and consequently liable to be discovered in every corner of it, as MacKinnon and his men had been out in his service, and therefore some shift behoved to be faln upon to disguise him more and more still. The Prince proposed blacking his face with some one thing or another. But the Captain was against that proposal as what would serve rather to discover him all at once than to conceal him. The Prince then pulling off the periwig and putting it into his pocket took out a dirty white napkin and desired the

4 July Captain to tye that about his head, and to bring it down upon his eyes and nose. He put the bonnet on above the napkin and said, 'I think I will now pass well enough for your servant, and that I am sick with the much fatigue I have undergone. Look at me, MacLeod, and tell me what you think. How will it do?' MacLeod told him—this would not do yet, for that those who had ever seen him before would still discover his face for all the disguise he was in. The Prince said, 'This is an odd remarkable face I have got that nothing
*fol.* 241. can disguise it.' I heard Mr. MacLeod declare more than once that the Prince could do any thing or turn himself into any shape, but that of dissembling his air.' That he could never disguise with all the arts he could use. 'There is not a person,' he said, 'that knows what the air of a noble or great man is, but upon seeing the Prince in any disguise he could put on would see something about him that was not ordinary, something of the stately and the grand.

They were no sooner come into Strath than they met two of MacKinnon's men who had been out in the expedition. Immediately they stared upon the Prince, and with hands lifted up, wept bitterly to see him in such a pickle. Malcolm begged them to take care what they were doing and to compose themselves, for that they might do harm by showing any concern. He took them back with him so far, and cautioning them not to take any notice of this meeting, took an oath of them, not to discover at any rate that they had seen the Prince in disguise or in that corner of the country, and then dismist them. The men accordingly proved true to their trust.

When they were near the place the Captain designed to set up at, he told the Prince that he had a sister that dwelt there who was married to John MacKinnon, a captain, lately under
*fol.* 242. the Laird of MacKinnon, and that he judged it advisable to go to his sister's house, advising the Prince in the meantime to sit at a little distance from the house till he should enquire at John MacKinnon or his wife if any party was near the place, and if he (Malcolm MacLeod) could be safe there; and likewise telling the Prince that he was still to pass for his servant, Lewie Caw. Mr. MacLeod accordingly went to the house where he found his sister, but her husband was not at home. After

the usual compliments he told his sister that he had come there perhaps to pass some little time, provided that no party was near them, and that he was in safety to stay. She assured him that no party she knew of was in that corner, and that he was very welcome, and she hoped he would be in safety enough. He told her that he had no body along with him but one Lewie Caw (son of Mr. Caw, surgeon in Crief) who had been out in the late affair, and consequently in the same condemnation with himself; and that he was with him as his servant. Upon this Lewie Caw was called upon to come into the house, the place being called Ellagol, or Ellighuil, near Kilvory or Kilmaree (*i.e.* a chapel, or rather a burying place, dedicate to the Virgin Mary) in Strath. When Lewie entered the house with the baggage on his back and the napkin about his head he took off his bonnet, made a low bow and sat at a distance from his master. The Captain's sister said there was something about that lad that she liked unco well, and she could not help admiring his looks. When meat and drink, viz., bread and cheese, milk, etc. were set down before the master he said to his servant that he might come in by and take a share, for that there were no strangers in the house. The sick Lewie made it shy and refused to eat with his master, and alledged he knew better manners. But the master ordering him to come and take a share he obeyed, still keeping off the bonnet.

4 July

*fol.* 243.

In their way to this place the Prince in the night time happened to fall into a bogue almost to the top of the thighs and MacLeod behoved to pull him out by the armpits and thereby was bogued himself. The Captain desired the servant lass, who could talk nothing but Erse, to bring some water for his feet, which she did; and being much fatigued he desired her to wash his feet and legs. When she was washing them he said, 'You see that poor sick man there, I hope you 'll wash his feet too. It will be great charity, for he has as much need as I have.' 'No such thing,' said she, 'although I wash the master's feet, I am not obliged to wash the servant's. What! he 's but a low countrywoman's son. I will not wash his feet indeed. However, with much intreaty Malcolm prevailed upon the maid to stoop so low as to wash poor Lewie's feet.

*fol.* 244.

4 July While she was washing them she happened to use him right roughly, and the Prince said to Malcolm, 'O MacLeod, if you would desire the girl not to go so far up.'

Malcolm importuned the Prince to go to bed and take some rest. The Prince then asked who would keep guard for fear of an alarm? Malcolm said he would do it himself. The Prince at last was prevailed upon to throw himself upon a bed, but would not strip. Malcolm desired his sister to go out, and sit upon the top of a knowe near the house and keep watch while he and his servant Lewie should take some sleep, which she accordingly did.

The Captain hearing that the landlord was coming towards home went out to meet him. After saluting him he asked if he saw these ships of war (pointing to them) that were hovering about upon the coast. Mr. MacKinnon said he saw them very well. 'What,' said MacLeod, 'if our Prince be on board one of them?' 'God forbid,' replied MacKinnon, 'I would
*fol.* 245. not wish that for anything.' 'What!' said Malcolm, 'if we had him here, John? Do you think he would be in safety enough?' 'I wish with all my heart we had him here,' replied John, 'for he would be safe enough.' 'Well then,' said MacLeod, 'he is here already. He is just now in your house. But when you go in you must be careful to take no notice of him at all. He passes for one Lewie Caw, my servant.' John faithfully promised to observe the direction, and thought he could perform it well enough. But he was no sooner entred the house than he could not hold his eyes from staring upon Lewie, and very soon he was forced to turn his face away from the Prince and to weep. In this house the Prince diverted himself with a young child, Neil MacKinnon,[1] carrying him in his arms and singing to him, and said, 'I hope this child may be a captain in my service yet.'

The Prince and Malcolm began to deliberate about going to the continent, and the proper measures to be taken for that purpose. They both agreed not to let the old Laird of MacKinnon know anything of their being in that country, because though he be a mighty honest, stout, good man, yet

---

1 Son of said John.

through his old age, and the infirmities attending it, they 4 July
thought he was not so well cut out for the difficulties of the Prince's present situation, and therefore they judged it advisable to desire John MacKinnon to hire a boat under a pretence of Malcolm MacLeod's only sailing to the continent, taking his promise in the meantime that he should not communicate any- *fol.* 246.
thing of the matter at all to the old Laird if he should chance to see him. Accordingly John went to hire the boat, and meeting with the old chiftain he could not keep the matter from him. The Laird told John that he should get a right boat and manage that matter well enough, and that he would instantly come to the place where the Prince was. John returned to the Prince and told him what he had done, and that old MacKinnon was coming to wait upon him. Upon this Malcolm represented to the Prince that seeing they were upon the bounds of the old Laird and that he had taken the matter in hand, he behoved to order and direct everything, for that if he should take upon him to give his opinion or contradict honest MacKinnon in anything he should propose, a difference might arise that would not be so convenient in the present juncture. And therefore suggested it as a wise thing that he should leave the Prince altogether to the management of old MacKinnon, who he was persuaded would be very careful of him, and exceedingly true and firm to the trust. The Prince did not savour this proposal at all, for he conld not think of parting with his trusty friend. But the Captain insisted upon it as advisable upon other accounts. He told the Prince that now he behoved to be amissing among his own friends and acquaintances, and ten to one but parties would be employed in search of him, which, if they should still keep together, might end in making a discovery of them both; and that therefore he would chuse rather to return to the *fol.* 247.
place from whence he came, though he should happen to have the misfortune of being made a prisoner, which was very like to be the case. 'And no matter for that at all,' said he, 'if it can tend to promote your safety, which it cannot readily fail to do.' With much reluctancy the Prince at last agreed to the proposal, and upon old MacKinnon's coming to them they went directly to the boat, John MacKinnon going with

4 July them, who likewise accompanied the Prince and old MacKinnon to the continent.

When the Prince was about stepping into the boat, about 8 or 9 at night, he turned to Malcolm and said, 'Don't you remember that I promised to meet Murdoch MacLeod at such a place?'[1] 'No matter,' said Malcolm, 'I shall make your apology.' 'That's not enough,' said the Prince. 'Have you paper, pen and ink upon you, MacLeod? I'll write him a few lines. I'm obliged so to do in good manners.' Accordingly he wrote him in the following words:

'Sir,—I thank God I am in good health, and have got off as design'd. Remember me to all friends, and thank them for the trouble they have been at.—I am, Sir, Your humble servant, JAMES THOMSON.

Elliguil, July 4th, 1746.'[2]

The Prince delivered the letter into the Captain's hands, and then asked him if he could light him a pipe, for he wanted

*fol.* 248. to smoke in the passage. The Captain desir'd him to have the cutty ready in his cheek, and that he should fall upon a method to light it. Malcolm took some tow out of his pocket, and snapping one of the guns held the tow to the pan and kindled it. Then putting it to the mouth of the pipe he blew and the Prince smok'd. But the cuttie being exceedingly short, Malcolm scarred the Prince's cheek with the tow.

At parting the Prince presented the Captain with a silver stock-buckle, which among all his difficulties he has still got preserv'd; and embracing him in his arms saluted him twice, and bad God bless him, putting ten guineas into his hand. Malcolm positively refused to accept of the gold, because the Prince behoved to have great use for money in his wandering from place to place; and he said he believed he had not much about him at that time. The Prince pressed it upon him and would have no refusal, wishing it had been much more for his sake, and that he could have gone to the continent with him.

Captain MacLeod took care to have one of the cutties the Prince had used and carried it to London with him, where

---

[1] See ff. 233, 765, 871, 1564.

[2] See ff. 262, 1714.

meeting with one, Dr. Burton of York, a prisoner, and chancing to tell the story of the cuttie the Doctor begged as a great favour to have the cuttie, which Malcolm gave him. The Doctor has made a fine shagreen case for it, and preserves it as a valuable rarity. This Dr. Burton was made prisoner upon a suspicion of his having crossed England with an intention to kiss the Prince's hands. Malcolm in coming down from London made a stop at York for a day or two, and visited the Doctor and his cuttie. July *fol.* 249.

Captain MacLeod,[1] after taking leave of the Prince made the best of his way back again to Raaza, and on his way visited Mrs. MacDonald of Kingsburgh, to whom he told the whole adventure, particularly the story of the motto and carving upon the silver-mill she had given to the Prince; and how the Prince said that the wind would soon change and set the ships of war off from the coast, which Malcolm said accordingly happened.

After Malcolm had returned to Raaza, parties landed upon the island to rummage it. One day a party of red-coats happened to be pretty near him before he spied them. He and a servant he had with him took to their heels and ran for it. The party did not fire but called upon them to stop. Endeavouring to get clear of this party, he had almost run himself into the hands of Captain Caroline Scott, upon the head of fifty or sixty men. Scott ordered his party to fire at Malcolm and his servant, and to run after them.[2] They catched the poor servant, and would have him to tell if yon was the Pretender that had got off from them; and because he would not not say it was the Pretender, they tortured him so that they left him for dead upon the spot. But whether or not the poor man (Donald Nicolson) recovered was what Malcolm had never yet discovered. Malcolm ran to the clift of a rock upon the sea-shore, where he said no person would ever run but in the greatest necessity, so difficult it was of access. There he remained three days and three nights, having only some crumbs of bread and cheese in his pocket. But being like *fol.* 250.

---

[1] He is only 34 years of age. See ff. 1714, *et seq.*

[2] See ff. 875, 1718.

July to starve of hunger and thirst, he left his cliff and came once more upon the island. One day happening to take a nap in a house, an alarm came that a party of MacLeods from Sky was near, and before he could get out at the door the party was hard at hand. Once more he ran to the old clift, the party firing at him and crying after him to stop; but he continued running with all speed, and they endeavoured to outrun him but could not. In his way to the clift he happened to meet with a boy whom he took along with him, lest he should have fallen into the hands of the party, and perhaps have discovered which way he saw him running. He remained in the clift three days more. The boy growing weary of the cold and hungry quarters, frequently pressed to be gone. But the Captain could not well think of that, for fear of a discovery. However, at last he allowed the boy to go, taking his promise that he would fetch him some provisions and intelligence, and that he would not discover where he had left him. The poor
*fol.* 251. boy soon fell into the hands of the same party, who by threats forced him to tell what he knew. Malcolm rising up to look about him a little, spied six MacLeods creeping in about to the clift with their muskets cock'd. He had no way left him to escape; but having some gold upon him he offered them every farthing of it, provided they would let him go and shift for himself, which they refused to do, even though they were his own blood-relations, and the party commanded by his friend, John MacLeod of Talisker. They carried him prisoner to a command of fusiliers at Pourtree in Sky. From thence he was guarded by a party to the sloop, commanded by that cruel, barbarous man, John Ferguson of Aberdeenshire.[1]

When he was to go on board his wife and some other friends came flocking about him, weeping bitterly and lamenting his fate. He very pleasantly desired them to dry up their tears, for that he hoped to return yet from London in coach. This merry saying of his prov'd not amiss, for he came from London in a post-chaise with Miss Flora MacDonald, passing for one Mr. Robertson, and Miss, for his sister; they not chusing to discover themselves upon the road, lest the mob might insult

---

[1] See f. 1728.

them and use them ill. They arrived in Edinburgh upon Sunday's evening, August 2nd, 1747. Aug. 2.

Though Ferguson could not fail to know Captain MacLeod to be a gentleman both from his manner and the cloaths he had upon him (for he was very genteelly dress'd in scarlet cloath and fine tartan), yet he was never pleased to vouch- *fol.* 252.
safe him one single look but in the way of surliness and ill-nature. He was oblig'd to retire every evening by eight o'clock with the other prisoners to the place assigned them under deck, where they had their choice of lying upon cable ropes, boards, or stones, without any covering, and had only half-men's allowance given them of very coarse indifferent fare.

Before the Captain got to London his cloaths were so wore that the skin began to appear through them, and by that time he had not one shirt to change another. Though he had been an officer in the Prince's service under his chiftain, the Laird of Raaza, yet he had the good luck to get off by a mistake, for he was thought when brought to London to be Raaza himself, both whose feet turn inwards; and when Malcolm's feet were examined by order, the return given was 'that they were both straight and stout.' However, his name being much talked of and growing somewhat famous over all London, the Government had a mind once more to be at him, and sent the evidences to visit him to see if they knew him, and if they did not know him, to endeavour to fish something out of him by entangling him in his talk. Particularly one, Urquhart, came to him in a very kind and familiar manner, and inquiring about his welfare. Captain MacLeod told him that he had the advantage of him, for that he was at a loss to know who it *fol.* 253.
was that favoured him with such a kind visit, not remembring he had ever seen the face before. 'O Mr. MacLeod,' said Urquhart, 'don't you remember to have seen me at Edinburgh at such a time?' It happened very luckily for Malcolm that he had never been in Edinburgh before that time, and therefore he assured Urquhart that he behoved to take him for some other person. Raaza and his men had come only to Perth sometime before Falkirk battle. Urquhart still insisted that he was sure he had seen him before, particularly at Inver-

4 July. ness at such a time. The Captain still kept him off with long weapons and discreet returns; so that neither Urquhart nor none of his kidney could gain any ground upon him at all. There being no evidence to be found against him, he had the benefit of the indemnity. Accordingly he was liberate out of the messengers hands upon July 4th, 1747, together with Clanranald, senior, and his lady, Boisdale, John MacKinnon, my Lady Stewart, etc. Miss Flora MacDonald was not liberate till some few days after.

1745 [Se]ptember Captain MacLeod gave likewise the following remarkable narrative:[1] After the battle of Gladesmuir, a Glenelg man came over to Sky to give the accounts of it. Upon this Sir Alexander MacDonald, the Laird of Raaza, Kingsburgh and
*fol.* 254. Captain MacLeod had a meeting some time in the end of September, 1745, at Sconsary, a publick house in the Isle of Sky. When Sir Alexander came to the place, he desired that none might be present but friends. The company assured him that the Glenelg man was a very honest fellow; but Sir Alexander would not hear of his witnessing what passed among them, and therefore he was not admitted.

Sir Alexander said that this was certainly a most remarkable and surprizing victory the Prince had obtained; that he doubted not now of the Prince's succeeding in the attempt; and that therefore every one should raise his men to assist him in the design. Then directing his discourse to Raaza, he said, 'Raaza, tis true you cannot raise many men; but the men you have are good. You can easily raise an hundred, and I resolve to raise nine hundred, which will make out a thousand good stout fellows betwixt us: for I am not for having boys or superannuate men amongst them. These I would divide into two battalions, 500 in each; and as you are a man that one can confide in, I resolve to make you Colonel of one of the battalions.' Raaza most cheerfully accepted of the offer, and heartily thanked Sir Alexander for the command he designed to honour him with. Then the marching off the men was laid down by Sir Alexander himself,—that Raaza should go off with his battalion first, and that Sir Alexander should follow

[1] See f. 1829.

at the distance of a day's march; and the particular places for quartering on the march were condescended upon. They likewise agreed upon what number of cattle they should drive along with each battalion for provisions till they should come to the low country, where they would get plenty. In a word, all matters were most amicably and frankly resolved upon for joining the Prince's standard without loss of time, and the company were highly delighted with the interview. Sir Alexander stayed all that night in the same house, making very merry, and taking a hearty glass with the gentlemen. *fol.* 255. September

Next day the post brought letters to Sir Alexander from President Forbes and the Laird of MacLeod, then at Culloden, which were delivered to him in presence of the company. He stept aside to a window and read the letters by himself, not allowing the company to know anything of the contents. Immediately he left his former chearfulness and frank way, and was quite upon the grave and thoughtful. He spoke not one word more of the matter, and left the company soon like one in confusion. To the importunities of the President and MacLeod had Sir Alexander in an instant yielded himself up entirely, and dropt the declared resolution of his own mind.

Just as Sir Alexander went away, Malcolm MacLeod asked at Kingsburgh what was become of yesternight's resolution, *fol.* 256. for that he was much surprized at Sir Alexander's leaving them so abruptly and dryly. Kingsburgh said he knew as little what was become of that affair as Mr. MacLeod did, but he was afraid that there would be no more of it. When Captain MacLeod was asked whether or not he thought that Lady Margaret MacDonald had any influence upon Sir Alexander to make him change his resolution; his answer was, that from all he knew of that matter he could not discover any reason to believe that Lady Margaret had any influence at all in the affair upon Sir Alexander.

After giving this narrative, Malcolm likewise told that *c.* June. before the Prince's arrival Sir Alexander MacDonald had been with Boisdale, brother of the Laird of Clanranald, and who lives in South Uist, with whom he had a conference about the Prince's designing to come over; insinuating that he intended to land first in some part of the Long Isle, and perhaps might

:. June send for Boisdale; adding withal that if he should happen to come without a backing, he could wish he would return to France. To this purpose Sir Alexander left a message with Boisdale to the Prince, importuning him, if he arrived without a following to return and wait for a more favourable oppor-
ol. 257. tunity, and till he should get matters in better order for the attempt.

When Boisdale came to the Prince upon his first landing he delivered the message to him, and did all he could to support the purport of it. The Prince asked Boisdale if he thought that he would get a hundred men to join him. 'No doubt,' said Boisdale, 'you'll get more than a hundred. But what then, though you get 500? what will that do?' 'Well then,' said the Prince, 'if I can get only a hundred good stout honest-hearted fellows to join me, I'll make a trial what I can do.' Although Boisdale spoke to the Prince in a very discouraging way, and after the standard was set up kept back all Clanranald's men that lived in South Uist and the other Isles to the number of four or five hundred good men (for he had more to say with them than either Clanranald himself or his son), yet to do Boisdale justice, he was of great use to the Prince when wandering up and down through South Uist, Benbicula, and other parts of the Long Isle, and exerted his utmost endeavours (with the assistance of honest Armadale) to keep him out of the hands of his enemies.

As to the several parts of the above sentence particular questions were asked at Malcolm MacLeod, and in his answers he gave a plain account of Boisdale's conduct, both before and after the Prince's distress, and particularly mentioned what number of men Clanranald might be reckoned to have in the Isles. Both the Captain and James MacDonald, joiner (in
ol. 258. whose house this Journal was given), agreed in affirming that Clanranald had in the Isles four or five hundred good men, and upon the continent three hundred. These upon the continent were the only men that followed young Clanranald in the Prince's service.

Captain MacLeod likewise gave the following account of the great danger the Prince was in of being taken prisoner in the retreat from Sterling to Inverness:—

The Prince, one night, quartering in the Laird of MacIntosh's house, had not many about him for a guard, and these too dispersed up and down for proper quarters, there being no apprehension at all of any danger. Lord Loudon, then at Inverness, got intelligence that the Prince was that night to sleep in MacIntosh's house with no great guard about him. When it was dark, orders were given the men to be in readiness upon a minute's warning, and accordingly Lord Loudon marched off with about seventeen hundred men.[1] When the Prince was about going to rest, or rather when it became dark, Lady MacIntosh ordered one Frazer, a blacksmith (who happened to be there by chance, having a desire to see the Prince), and four servants to get loaded muskets, and to go away privately beyond all the guards and sentries without allowing them to know anything about them or their design, and to walk on the fields all night, and to keep a good look-out. Thereby she said they would prove a check upon the guards, and would be ready to discover approaching danger, if any should happen before the sentries could know anything of the matter. All this proceeded merely from Lady MacIntosh's great care and anxiety about the Prince. The blacksmith and his faithful four accordingly went pretty far beyond all the sentries, and walked up and down upon a muir, at the distance, Captain MacLeod said he believed, of two miles from MacIntosh's house. At last they spied betwixt them and the sky a great body of men moving towards them, and not at a great distance. The blacksmith fired his musket and killed one of Loudon's men, some say, the piper; but Captain MacLeod said he could not positively affirm anything about that particular.[2] The four servants followed the blacksmith's example, and it is thought they too did some execution. Upon this the blacksmith huzzaed and cried aloud, 'Advance, Advance, my lads, Advance! (naming some particular regiments) I think we have the dogs now.' This so struck Lord Loudon's men with horrour that instantly they wheel'd about, after firing some shots, and in great confusion ran back with speed to Inverness. It is thought that Lord Loudon's men

16 Feb.

*fol.* 259.

[1] See ff. 648, 989, 1207, 1256.

[2] See f. 380.

17 Feb. who fired wounded some of their own companions. An express had been sent off privately to Lady MacIntosh by some friend in Inverness to warn her of the danger. He came to the house much about the time that the trusty five discovered
*fol. 260.* the body of men advancing towards them. Lady MacIntosh ran directly to the room where the Prince was fast asleep and gave him notice of Lord Loudon's design. Instantly he jumped out of bed and would have been going down stairs directly, but Lady MacIntosh importuned him to stay in the room till she should get him further notice and try what could be done. They were soon put out of any apprehension of danger. Some of Lord Loudon's men, through the darkness of the night mistaking their way, fell into the hands of the guard, and told that when they were ordered to march from Inverness they were not allowed to know where they were going, and that Lord Loudon upon the firing should have said, 'There's an end to this; we are certainly discovered.' He was the prettiest fellow that could make Inverness first. The firing of the five alarmed the guard, and quickly put them and others in motion. But Loudon and his men were far out of reach before they could come to the ground where the firing happen'd. Clanranald's men were that night keeping guard upon the Prince, and Captain MacLeod, being in the neighbourhood, was amongst the number of those that were alarm'd with the firing and made haste to come up.

Among other subjects the Prince and Captain MacLeod in their wanderings happen'd to talk of the above remarkable incident when the Prince was pleased to inform him that the
*fol. 261.* Laird of MacIntosh himself (in Lord Loudon's command) was the kind friend that had sent off the express from Inverness to give notice of the danger. The Prince said he had a very good opinion of that gentleman.

After the hurry of the alarm was over, the Prince ordered all the men to be got together and to march directly for Inverness; and when they were approaching that town he drew them up in order of battle, expecting, as was given out, that Lord Loudon was to march out of the town to fight. For a considerable way they marched in order of battle, and when they came near Inverness they saw Lord Loudon and his men making all the haste they could out of it, betaking themselves to ships and boats to carry them off. The Prince and his army entred the town without opposition or violence of any kind.[1] 17 Feb.

*N.B.*—Upon Thursday, August 13th, 1747, Captain Malcolm MacLeod and James MacDonald, joiner, dined with my Lady Bruce in the Citadel of Leith. After dinner they were so kind as to retire to my room, where they staid till between six and seven at night. The Captain was but poorly provided for in money matters, and therefore a contribution was set on foot for him in and about Edinburgh. I was so happy[2] as to make among my acquaintances six guineas and a crown, which I delivered into his own hand. I then told him the freedom I had taken in writing down from my memory the conversation he had honoured me with, Friday last, in presence of Stewart Carmichael and James MacDonald, but that I still wanted to have an additional favour of him, which was, that he would be so good as to allow me to read my *prima cura* in his hearing, in order to get his observations and amendments upon it. He frankly granted my request, and said he was glad to embrace the opportunity of so much exactness, which had never been used with him in any one of the many conversations he had formerly given. He was pleased to declare his being much satisfied with what I had written and said, he would now tell me some things he had not mentioned before, which accordingly I writ in his own words, always reading over every sentence to him for the greater certainty of the facts being exactly and circumstantially narrated. I have been carefull to insert these particulars in their proper places in the above transcript. There was one thing I had some difficulty rightly to adjust with Captain MacLeod, which was the day of the month when he parted with the Prince after seeing him in the boat with old Mac- 1747 13 Aug. *fol.* 262.

[1] See ff. 273, 993, 1258.

[2] lucky *interlined.*

13 Aug. Kinnon. When I asked him about this, he said it was upon July 4th.[1] I told him that would not answer at all with the days formerly mentioned by him, and that it behoved to be July 5th. He was still positive that
fol. 263. it was the 4th, 'For,' said he, 'I remember nothing better than that I set it down upon a piece of paper lest I should forget it. [The difficulty was still like to remain unresolved, he being equally positive both as to the days formerly mentioned by him, and the particular day upon which he parted with the Prince, till it luckily came into my mind to ask him how many days he reckoned in June? He answered, Thirty-one, which mistake served to clear up this point.[2]] Captain MacLeod said he expected his brother-in-law, John MacKinnon, soon down from London, and then suggested to James MacDonald that if John should happen to come by the way of Edinburgh, he should be at pains to procure a meeting betwixt the said Mr. MacKinnon and me, and that (considering the exactness I observed) James MacDonald should lay himself out to get me a meeting with Donald MacLeod, Miss Flora MacDonald, and any others if they came in his reach that could be useful in making a discovery of facts and men. To which Mr. MacDonald answered, he would do all that lay in his power.

I then took occasion to acquaint Captain MacLeod about a report that had passed currently in Kingsburgh's name after he had set out from Edinburgh in his return to Sky. The report was this, that Kings-
fol. 264. burgh should have declared to several persons that the Laird of MacLeod should have writ him a letter, desiring him to deliver up the Prince, if he should happen to come in his way, and representing to him what a service he would thereby do to his country; and that the said Laird should have come to Kingsburgh (as the

---

[1] See ff. 767, 879.

[2] The passage within brackets is scored through as delete by Bishop Forbes. [Ed.]

story gave out) either at Fort Augustus or in the Castle of Edinburgh, desiring to have that letter up from him again, which Kingsburgh refused to comply with. Several persons (knowing that I had frequently and familiarly conversed with Kingsburgh) had come to me enquiring about the above report if I knew anything of the matter. My answer always was, that as Kingsburgh had never so much as made the most distant hint to me about any letter whatsomever from the Laird of MacLeod, I could say nothing either as to the truth or the falshood of that report. 13 Aug.

After informing Captain MacLeod about this story as above, I told him what a desire I had to have this particular cleared up, that if the report was false and calumnious it might be contradicted, and if true, it might be recorded *in futuram rei memoriam*; and then asked him if he would be so good as to take from me a memorandum to Kingsburgh about this matter. He said he would with all his heart, and that he would likewise lay himself out to expiscate facts and transmit exact accounts of them to me by any sure private hand that should come in his way. Here follows an exact *fol.* 265. copy of the

MEMORANDUM, etc.

To ask particularly at Kingsburgh if ever the Laird of MacLeod sent him a letter about delivering up the Prince; and whether or not he should have at any time desired to have that letter up from him again. If such a letter be in Kingsburgh's hands, it could be wished he would be so good as to give a copy of it.[1]

Thursday, August 13th, 1747.

Upon Saturday, August 22nd, I met once more with Captain MacLeod about 3 o'clock afternoon in the house of James MacDonald, joiner, when the Cap- 22 Aug.

[1] See ff. 701, 793, 851, 1056, 1631.

22 Aug. tain was making ready to pass over to Kinghorn, which accordingly he did that night. I put him in mind of the above Memorandum, and asked the favour of him to take John MacKinnon's account from his own mouth and transmit it to me, as I had heard that Mr. MacKinnon had taken the opportunity of a ship bound for Inverness from some part of the coast of England, and therefore I could not expect to have a meeting with him. Then I begged him to try if Armadale would vouchsafe me a written account of his part of the management, and to exert his endeavours to pick up for me an exact narrative of all the cruelties, barbarities, etc., he could get any right intelligence about. The Captain was pleased to come under a promise that
*fol. 266.* he would do his utmost to comply with my desires as to all these particulars.

ROBERT FORBES, A.M.

## JOURNAL of DONALD MACLEOD,[1] etc.

17 Aug. 1747 Citadel of Leith, Monday, August 17th, betwixt six and seven at night, 1747, Deacon William Clerk, taylor, came to see me, and did me the favour of bringing along with him Donald MacLeod (tenant at Gualtergill, in the Isle of Sky, under the Laird of MacLeod), the honest and faithful steersman of the eight-oar'd boat from the continent to the Isles of Benbicula, South Uist, Lewis, etc. etc. etc., and who had the Prince among his hands, and was employed in going upon his errands for nine or ten weeks after the battle of Culloden.

After the usual compliments and some little chit-chat, I took occasion to inform Donald anent the favour I had obtained of Malcolm MacLeod, and how easily and chearfully he had granted my request, begging in the meantime to have the like favour from him, as his history, taking in so much time, behoved to be very interesting. Honest Donald modestly

[1] There are frequent references in *The Lyon in Mourning* to Donald MacLeod. See ff. 460 and 1384, where his death is noticed.

said he would very willingly grant my desire for all that he had to say would take up no great time—it would easily be contained in a quarter of a sheet of paper. But then he said, as he had heard that I had been employing myself in collecting these things, he behoved to hear all the accounts I had gathered together, particularly O'Neil's Journal, before he would give me one word. I begged leave to tell him that I was persuaded his account would take up much more than a quarter of a sheet, considering the length of time he happened to be with the Prince in his greatest distresses, and that I would willingly read to him all that I had collected, but that it consisted of so many sheets that I was afraid it would take up too much of our time, which I would chuse much rather to spend in taking his account in writing from his own mouth. However, I said I could easily gratify him in reading O'Neil's Journal, as it happened not to be of any great length. He said he would content himself with O'Neil's Journal only, as he had been along with him in company all the time he had attended the Prince after the battle of Culloden. For this made him the more anxious to know what O'Neil advanced in his journal, as he himself could judge where O'Neil was in the right and where in the wrong. 17 Aug. *fol.* 267.

I then represented to him that if he would indulge me the freedom of asking questions at him (without which, from experience, I could assure him there was no taking of journals from one with any tolerable exactness), he would soon see that his journal behoved to take up much more paper than he imagined. He said he would allow me to ask any questions I should think fit to propose. I asked him where he was to be that night. He told me he resolved to sleep in James MacDonald's house. I desired to attend him and to spend the evening with him, which was agreed to. *fol.* 268.

When we were in James's house I began to ask some questions, to which Donald gave plain answers. After asking several questions, Donald, looking at James MacDonald with a smiling countenance, spoke in Erse to him; and James laughing very heartily, said to me, 'Do you know, Sir, what Donald was saying just now? He says you are the uncoest cheel he ever met wi'; for if you go on in asking questions so

7 Aug. particularly, and if he shall tell you all the nig-nacs o't, he believes indeed his account will take up much more time and paper than be imagined.'

Upon this I told him it was not enough to inform me that the Prince and his small retinue were in this or the other place such a day, and that they did breakfast, dine, or sup here or there, which I acknowledge to be the foundation of the Journal. But then there were many other things that ought to be care-
*ol.* 269. fully remarked and taken notice of, otherwise the Journal would turn out to be only a very dull, insipid thing. I therefore earnestly begged he would be at pains to recollect himself as much as possible, and inform me exactly what particular dangers and distresses they met with, how the Prince bore up under them, what passed in conversation among them, and more especially that he would endeavour to call to mind the sayings of the Prince upon any subject, etc. Then a particular day was fixed (Thursday, August 20th) for meeting together in the same house at nine o'clock in the morning, in order to write the Journal from Donald's own mouth.

o Aug. Betwixt 9 and 10 of the said day, I was sent for and found with Donald, Deacon William Clerk, taylor, and one Mr. Finlayson, mathematical instrument-maker, and late engineer in the Prince's army. I had no sooner entred the room than Donald asked me if I had been as good as my word,—if I had brought along with me O'Neil's Journal? for that, he said, the deel a word would he gie me till he should hear O'Neil's Journal, which he was afraid was far from being right. And this he said he had reason to think from what he had heard about it already in conversation. I then read O'Neil's Journal
*ol.* 270. to him, in which he found fault with several things, particularly as to the staving of the boat to pieces, which he said was not fact. 'For,' said he, 'if the boat had stayed to pieces, where O'Neil mentions, the world could not have saved one life that was on board. We would certainly have all perished in the sea; that place is so very rocky and dangerous. Besides, I have reason to think that the boat is still to the fore, and that I may get her into my custody when I go home, if I please to seek after her.' He likewise quarrell'd O'Neil's asserting that he went with him (Donald) to Stornway, which

he said was not fact, but that he (O'Neil) remained with the Prince, while he himself was employed about the message upon which he was dispatched to Stornway, where he was well known. He also blamed O'Neil for not taking any notice of the Prince's being under a necessity to disguise himself in women's cloaths, which consisted with O'Neil's knowledge, and served as much as anything to represent the great danger the Prince was in of being discovered and seized; and for taking (as Donald said) too much of the praise to himself. Here Donald had a remarkable expression which I cannot fail to set down in his own words, and they are these: 'What a deel could O'Neil do for the preservation and safety o' the Prince in a Highland country, where he knew not a foot of ground, and had not the language o' the people. And sic far'd o' him, for he was no sooner frae the Prince than he was tane prisoner. I own he was as faithful and trusty a friend as the Prince or any man could have, and made an excellent companion to him. But then he could have done nothing for his preservation if there had not been some Highland body like mysell wi' them. Faith he taks ower mickell to himsell; and he is not blate to mind himsell sae mickle and to forget others that behoved to do much more than he could do in sic a case.'

20 Aug.

*fol.* 271.

Donald found fault with some other instances in O'Neil's Journal, which it is needless to particularize; for the above particulars are sufficient for a specimen. In general he said the Journal was not at all just and exact.

Mr. Finlayson too found fault with O'Neil's account of the battle of Culloden, and said that in that matter he was far from being right.

After reading O'Neil's Journal, Deacon Clerk and Mr. Finlayson went off. But luckily Malcolm MacLeod came to us, to whom I resumed what had passed upon O'Neil's Journal. Malcolm said he had reason to think that O'Neil's account was not just in several things, for that it consisted with his knowledge that O'Neil had advanced several things in London that would not stand the test. He said he could not have a good opinion of O'Neil when he was not at the pains to call for Donald MacLeod, his companion in distress, whom he could not fail to know to be in London at the very same time he himself was

*fol.* 272.

20 Aug. in it, and to whom he could have had easy access at any time he pleased. Mean time Malcolm joined with Donald in asserting that he believed O'Neil was most faithful and trusty to the Prince, and would do any thing or run any risque to promote his interest. But then he could not help observing that it was impossible for O'Neil to do anything for the safety of the Prince in a country where he was altogether a stranger, and behoved to be at a very great loss for want of the language.

When I was beginning to take down Donald's account in writing, he told me it was not in his power (as I had asked him) to remember particularly the days of the month in such a long time; but he would do his best to call to mind how many days and nights they had been in this and the other
*fol. 273.* place, and from that I might if I pleased at my own leisure afterwards make out the days of the month so as to agree with April 20th or 21st, the day on which he met with the Prince in the wood, and undertook to pilot him to the Isles; and to make his parting with the Prince to come within three or four days of the time when the Prince and Miss MacDonald went off together to the Isle of Sky; which, he said, was exactly the case. He desired me to fix their setting out from the Continent on board the eight-oar'd boat to the 26th of April, and then he said I might make out the other days of the month at my own leisure.

1746 February. Donald MacLeod[1] coming to Inverness (when Lord Loudon and his men were lying in and about that town) with a view of taking in a cargoe of meal for the inhabitants of Sky, happened to make a much longer stay there than at first he had proposed, the weather having proved very stormy and cross. When the Prince and his army were marching towards Inverness, Lord Loudon and his men gave out that they were resolved to fight them, and accordingly (as they pretended) made ready for battle, the pipes playing and the drums beating to arms; when in an instant, instead of fighting they wheel'd about and made off with speed, some to the old citadel

[1] From this point to f. 316 of the manuscript, this narrative is printed in *Jacobite Memoirs*, ff. 373-411.

(called Cromwell's Fort), and others to the bridge, in order to get on board of ships and boats, the better to make their escape.[1] Donald, walking along the bridge to see what course they were to take, chanced to fall in with his own chiftain, the Laird of MacLeod, who asked him how he was to dispose of himself now. Donald said he was to go back to Inverness for a horse he had there, for that he thought it foolish for him to lose his horse whatever might happen. The Laird forbad him to do any such thing, assuring him he would certainly be made a prisoner by the rebels if he returned into the town. Donald replied he was very indifferent whether he was made a prisoner or not, being confident that they would not do any harm to him that was nothing but a poor auld man. The Laird walked back with him as if he had been wanting some thing out of the town till they came near the gate next to the bridge, where they began to hear the pipes of the Prince's army playing very briskly; and then the Laird thought fit to turn tail and run with speed. Donald never ance fashed himself, but went into the town at his own leisure, where he had not been long till he fell in with the MacDonalds of Glencoe, who took him prisoner, and would have him to give up his broadsword, 'which,' said Donald, 'I was unco unwilling to part wi', for it was a piece of very good stuff.' But luckily for him the old Laird of MacKinnon came up, who, taking him by the hand and asking very kindly about his welfare, assured the party that Donald was an honest man, and that he would be bail for him. Upon which they allowed Donald to keep the claymore and to go along with MacKinnon. After this Donald had no great inclination to leave Inverness, but saunter'd about among his good friends and acquaintances in the army.

17 Feb. *fol.* 274. *fol.* 275.

About the beginning of April 1746, Æneas MacDonald (one of Kinlochmoidart's brothers, and a banker at Paris) sent for Donald MacLeod and told him that he heard that he (Donald) knew the coast well, and likewise the course to the different Isles, and that as he was upon going to the island of Barra for a small sum of money that was lying there, only

April.

[1] See ff. 261, 649, 1258.

April. about £380 Sterling, he was desirous to have him for his pilot and guide. Donald MacLeod very frankly agreed to do that, or anything else in his power to promote the Prince's interest. On board they go, and though the sea was swarming with sloops of war, boats and yawls full of militia, viz., the Campbells, the MacLeods, and MacDonalds of Sky, etc., yet they had the good luck to get safe to Barra, where they got the money. But they behoved to remove from place to place for *fol. 276.* fear of being discovered and taken, when Æneas and Donald were in Barra. John Ferguson (captain of the *Furnace* sloop) came upon the coast of the Island, and sent a letter to MacDonald of Boisdale (in whose house Æneas and Donald had been) by a yawl full of the MacLeods, desiring Boisdale to come on board and speak with him. When the MacLeods returned to the sloop, they informed Captain Ferguson that they had seen Donald MacLeod upon shore; and they were persuaded he was about no good. He behoved to be about some mischief or another, for well did they know him, and what way he would be employed. After this Æneas and Donald were obliged to be more wary and cautious than ever, and were much put to it how to get off, as the sloops, boats, etc., were cruizing in great numbers about all the places of the Long Isle. At last they got off with the cash to the island of Cana, at the distance of ten leagues from South Uist towards the mainland. From thence they sailed to the island of Egg, twelve miles from Cana; and from Egg they steered their course to the mainland, where they arrived at Kinlochmoidart's house, which is about six or seven leagues from Egg.

About four or five days after they came to Kinlochmoidart they were thinking of setting out for Inverness, when Æneas MacDonald received a letter from the Prince containing the *fol. 277.* accounts of the battle of Culloden. Æneas said to Donald that he had very bad news to give him, and then told him that the Prince and his army had been totally routed near Culloden house. In this letter Æneas was ordered to meet the Prince at Boradale, and immediately upon receipt of the letter he set out, and returned that same night to Kinlochmoidart. About two days after this, Lord Elcho and Captain O'Neil came to Kinlochmoidart.

In one day three several messages (for the greater security lest any one of them should happen to miscarry or come by any misfortune) came to Donald MacLeod desiring him forthwith to go to the Prince at Boradale, which order he obeyed directly. When Donald came to Boradale, the first man he met with was the Prince in a wood, all alone. This was about four or five days after the battle. April 20th or 21st. 20 April

[It is to be remarked here when Donald spoke to the Prince he always used these terms, May it please your Majesty, or May it please your excellency.]

The Prince, making towards Donald, asked, 'Are you Donald MacLeod of Guatergill in Sky?' 'Yes,' said Donald, 'I am the same man, may it please your Majesty, at your service. What is your pleasure wi' me?' 'Then,' said the Prince, 'You see, Donald, I am in distress. I therefore throw myself into your bosom, and let you do with me what you like. I hear you are an honest man, and fit to be trusted.'

When Donald was giving me this part of the narrative he *fol.* 278. grat sare, the tears came running down his cheeks; and he said, 'Wha deel could help greeting when speaking on sic a sad subject?' Donald made this return to the Prince. 'Alas, may it please your excellency, what can I do for you? for I am but a poor auld man, and can do very little for mysell.' 'Why,' said the Prince, 'the service I am to put you upon I know you can perform very well. It is that you may go with letters from me to Sir Alexander MacDonald and the Laird of MacLeod. I desire therefore to know if you will undertake this piece of service; for I am really convinced that these gentlemen for all that they have done, will do all in their power to protect me.' Upon hearing this Donald was struck with surprize, and plainly told the Prince he would do anything but that. It was a task he would not undertake if he should hang him for refusing. 'What,' said Donald, 'does not your excellency know that these men have played the rogue to you altogether, and will you trust them for a' that? Na, you mauna do 't.' Then Donald informed the Prince that Sir Alexander MacDonald and the Laird of MacLeod were then, with forces along with them, in search of him not above the distance of ten or twelve miles by sea from him, but a

20 April much greater distance by land; and therefore the sooner he left that place the better, not knowing how soon they might come up to it, especially if they should happen to take their
*fol.* 279. course by sea. Donald still repeated his dislike of the measure in sending any message to Sir Alexander MacDonald and the Laird of MacLeod, and said he would not risque upon going any message to these gentlemen from the Prince at any rate (in the present circumstances) for more reasons than one.

At this time, very luckily for the Prince, Cumberland and his army entertain'd the notion that he had set sail from the continent for St. Kilda, being a place so remote that no suspicion would be readily entertained of his being there. Upon this General Campbell was dispatched with such a considerable force as took up all the fleet that was upon the coast, but to no purpose. When General Campbell appeared upon the coast of St. Kilda, the greater part of the poor inhabitants ran off to the clifts of their rocks to hide themselves, being frighted out of their wits at seeing such an appearance coming towards their island. Such of the forces as landed enquired at the inhabitants they met with about the young Pretender. The poor creatures were quite amazed, and declared they knew nothing of that man, for they had never
*fol.* 280. heard of him before. They said they had heard a report that their Laird, MacLeod, had lately had war with a great woman abroad, but that he had got the better of her, and that was all they knew of the disturbances in the world. Upon this the General and his command (not a small one) returned with their finger in their cheek, when in the meantime they thought they had been sure to catch the much-coveted price of blood.

When Donald MacLeod had absolutely refused to go any message whatsomever to Sir Alexander MacDonald and the Laird of MacLeod, the Prince said to him. 'I hear, Donald, you are a good pilot; that you know all this coast well, and therefore I hope you can carry me safely through the islands where I may look for more safety than I can do here.' Donald answered he would do anything in the world for him; he would run any risque except only that which he had formerly mentioned; and that he most willingly undertook to do his best in the service he now proposed. For this purpose Donald procured a stout eight-oar'd boat, the property of John MacDonald, son of Æneas or Angus MacDonald of Boradale. Both Donald MacLeod and Malcolm MacLeod said that this John MacDonald was either killed at the battle of Culloden or butchered next day in cold blood (which was the fate of many), for that he had never been heard of since that time. Donald took care to buy a pot for boyling pottage or the like when they should happen to come to land, and a poor firlot of meal was all the provision he could make out to take with them. April *fol.* 281.

April 26th. They go on board in the twilight of the evening in Lochnannua, at Boradale, being the very spot of ground where the Prince landed at first upon the continent; and Boradale's house was the first roof he was under when he arrived upon the continent. There were in the boat the Prince, Captain O'Sullivan, Captain O'Neil, Allan MacDonald, commonly called Captain MacDonald (of the family of Clanranald), and a clergyman of the Church of Rome; and Donald MacLeod for pilot managing the helm, and betwixt whose feet the Prince took his seat. The names of the boatmen are: Rhoderick MacDonald, Lauchlan MacMurrich, Rhoderick MacCaskgill, John MacDonald, Murdoch MacLeod (son of the pilot), Duncan Roy, Alexander MacDonald, and Edward Bourk or Burk, a common chairman in Edinburgh. 26 April

The above Murdoch MacLeod was then a lad only of 15 years of age, a scholar in the Grammar School of Inverness. When he heard of the appearance of a battle, having got himself provided in a claymore, durk, and pistol, he ran off from the school, and took his chance in the field of Culloden battle. After the defeat he found means to trace out the road the Prince had taken, and followed him from place to place; 'and this was the way,' said Donald, 'that I met wi' my poor boy.' *fol.* 282.

As to Ned Bourk, I asked if Bourk was not an Irish name, and where Ned was born. Both Donald and Malcolm joined in saying that Bourk indeed was originally an Irish name, but that there had been some of that name for three or four generations past in and about the Isle of Sky, where, or rather in North Uist, Ned was born. They likewise told me that

26 April Ned from the beginning of the expedition had been servant to Mr. Alexander MacLeod (son of Mr. John MacLeod, Advocate), one of the Prince's aid-de-camps; that Ned knew all Scotland well, and a great part of England, having been servant to several gentlemen; and that he was *the man* that led the Prince off the field of battle, and guided him all the way to Boradale. They spoke excellent things of poor Ned; and James MacDonald, the landlord, supported them in what they said, for he knows Ned very well.

When the Prince and his small retinue were thinking of going on board the eight-oar'd boat, Donald MacLeod begged
*fol.* 283. the Prince not to set out that night, for that it would certainly be a storm, and he could not think of his exposing himself. The Prince asked how Donald came to think it would be a storm. 'Why, sir,' said Donald, 'I see it coming already.' However, the Prince, anxious to be out of the continent where parties were then dispersed in search of him, was positive to set out directly without loss of time. They had not rowed far from the shore till a most violent tempest arose, greater than any Donald MacLeod had ever been trysted with before, though all his lifetime a seafaring man, upon the coast of Scotland. To this they had the additional distress of thunder and lightning and a heavy pour-down of rain, which continued all the time they were at sea. When the Prince saw the storm increasing still more and more he wanted much to be at land again, and desired Donald to steer directly for the rock, which runs no less than three miles along one side of the loch. 'For,' said the Prince, 'I had rather face canons and muskets than be in such a storm as this.' But Donald would not hear of that proposal at all, assuring the Prince that it was impossible for them to return to the land again, because the squall was against them, and that if they should steer for the rock the boat would undoubtedly stave to pieces and all of them behoved to be drowned, for there was no
*fol.* 284. possibility of saving any one life amongst them upon such a dangerous rock, where the sea was dashing with the utmost violence. The Prince then asked Donald what he had a mind to do. 'Why,' replied Donald, 'since we are here we have nothing for it, but, under God, to set out to sea directly. Is

it not as good for us to be drown'd in clean water as to be dashed in pieces upon a rock and to be drowned too?' 27 Apri

After this all was hush and silence; not one word more amongst them, expecting every moment to be overwhelmed with the violence of the waves, and to sink down to the bottom. To make the case still worse they had neither pump nor compass nor lantern with them, and the night turned so pitch dark that they knew not where they were for the most of the course. This made them afraid of being tossed upon some coast (such as the Isle of Sky) where the militia were in arms to prevent the Prince's escape. 'But,' to use Donald's words, 'as God would have it, by peep of day we discovered ourselves to be on the coast of the Long Isle, and we made directly to the nearest land, which was Rushness in the Island Benbecula. With great difficulty we got on shore, and saved the boat, hawling her up to dry land, in the morning of April 27th.

I asked how long the course might be that they made in the violent storm. Donald declared that they had run at least thirty-two leagues in eight hours. About this Malcom Mac- *fol.* 285.
Leod made some doubt, alleging the course not to be so long, and they reasoned the matter betwixt them. James MacDonald supported Donald in what he had advanced, and after some debate Malcolm acknowledged that Donald was in the right, and that the course they had been driven was rather more than thirty-two leagues. The storm lasted 4 hours after landing.

Then I asked Donald if the Prince was in health all the time he was with him. Donald said that the Prince would never own he was in bad health, though he and all that were with him had reason to think that during the whole time the Prince was more or less under a bloody flux; but that he bore up most surprizingly, and never wanted spirits. Donald added, that the Prince, for all the fatigue he underwent, never slept above three or four hours at most at a time, and that when he awaked in the morning he was always sure to call for a chopin of water, which he never failed to drink off at a draught; and that he had a little bottle in his poutch out of which he used to take so many drops every morning and throughout the day, saying if anything should ail him he hoped he should cure him-

27 April self, for that he was something of a doctor. 'And faith,' said Donald, 'he was indeed a bit of a doctor, for Ned Bourk happening ance to be unco ill of a cholick, the Prince said, 'Let him alane, I hope to cure him of that,' and accordingly
*fol.* 286. he did so, for he gae him sae mony draps out o' the little bottlie and Ned soon was as well as ever he had been.'

When they landed at Rushness in Benbecula, they came to an uninhabited hut where they made a fire to dry their cloaths, for all of them were wet through and through in to the skin, and an old sail was spread upon the bare ground, which served for a bed to the Prince, who was very well pleased with it, and slept soundly. Here they kill'd a cow, and the pot which Donald had brought served them in good stead for boyling bits of the beef. In this poor hut they remained two days and two nights.

29 April April 29th. In the evening they set sail from Benbecula on board the same eight-oar'd boat for the island Scalpay, commonly called the Island Glass, where they landed safely about two hours before daylight next day, the Prince and O'Sullivan going under the name of Sinclair, the latter passing for the father, and the former for the son. Betwixt Benbecula and Scalpay there is the distance of thirteen or fifteen leagues. In this island Donald MacLeod had an acquaintance, Donald Campbell, to whose house he brought the Prince and his
30 April small retinue before break of day, April 30th. Being all cold and hungry, Donald MacLeod desired immediately to have a good fire, which was instantly got for them. Donald MacLeod was here only one night, but the Prince remained four nights, and was most kindly entertained by his hospitable landlord, Donald Campbell, whose civility and compassion the Prince entertained a most grateful sense of.[1]

*fol.* 287. May 1st. Donald MacLeod was dispatched by the Prince to
1 May Stornway in the island of Lewis in order to hire a vessel under a pretence of sailing to the Orkneys to take in meal for the Isle of Sky, as Donald used to deal in that way formerly. Here Donald once more affirmed that O'Neil did not go with him to Stornway, and desired me to remark his assertion

[1] See ff. 926-928.

accordingly. Donald left the eight-oar'd boat at Scalpay, and got another boat from his friend, Mr. Campbell, in which he sailed for Stornway, where he remained some time without making out the design on which he was sent. But at last he succeeded, and then dispatched an express to the Prince in Scalpay (between which and Stornway thirty miles by land) to inform him that he had got a vessel to his mind. 1 May

May 4th. The Prince (leaving Allan MacDonald, the Popish clergyman in Scalpay, who afterwards returned to South Uist), set out on foot for Stornoway, attended by O'Sullivan and O'Neil, taking a guide along to direct them the right road. This guide, in going to the Harris (between which and Scalpay there is a ferry of only a quarter of a mile) took them eight miles out of the way. In coming from Harris to the Lewis they fell under night, and a very stormy and rainy night it was, which fatigued them very much, their journey, by the mistake of their guide, being no less than thirty-eight long Highland miles. 4 May

May 5th. When in sight of Stornway the Prince sent the guide to Donald MacLeod to inform him that he and the two captains were at such a place, desiring withal that he would forthwith send them a bottle of brandy and some bread and cheese, for that they stood much in need of a little refreshment. Donald immediately obeyed the summons and came to the Prince, bringing along with him the demanded provisions. He found the Prince and his two attendants upon a muir all wet to the skin, and wearied enough with such a long journey through the worst of roads in the world. Donald told the Prince that he knew of a faithful and true friend to take care of him till things should be got ready for the intended voyage. This was the Lady Killdun[1] at Arynish, to whose house Donald conducted the Prince and his two attendants. Here the Prince was obliged to throw off his shirt, which one of the company did wring upon the hearth-stone, and did spread it upon a chair before the fire to have it dried. *fol.* 288. 5 May

The same day, May 5th, Donald was sent back to Stornway to get things in readiness. But when he came there, to his

[1] Of the family of MacKenzie.

5 May great surprize he found no less than two or three hundred men in arms. The Lewis is inhabited by the MacKenzies, and belongs to the Earl of Seaforth. Donald could not understand
fol. 289. at all what was the matter that occasioned such a sudden rising of men, and therefore, without fear or dread, he went directly into the room where the gentlemen were that had taken upon themselves the rank of officers, and asked them what was the matter. Every one of them immediately cursed him bitterly, and gave him very abusive language, affirming that he had brought this plague upon them; for that they were well assured the Prince was already upon the Lewis, and not far from Stornway, with five hundred men. This they said exposed them to the hazard of losing both their cattle and their lives, as they heard the Prince was come with a full resolution to force a vessel from Stornway. Donald very gravely asked, How sorrow such a notion could ever enter into their heads? 'Where, I pray you,' said he, 'could the Prince in his present condition get 500 or one hundred men together? I believe the men are mad. Has the devil possessed you altogether?' They replied that Mr. John MacAulay, Presbyterian preacher in South Uist, had writ these accounts to his
fol. 290. father in the Harris, and that the said father had transmitted the same to Mr. Colin MacKenzie, Presbyterian teacher in the Lewis. Donald saned these blades, the informers, very heartily, and spared not to give them their proper epithets in strong terms. 'Well then,' said Donald, 'since you know already that the Prince is upon your island, I acknowledge the truth of it; but then he is so far from having any number of men with him that he has only but two companions with him, and when I am there I make the third. And yet let me tell you farther, gentlemen, if Seaforth himself were here, by G—— he durst not put a hand to the Prince's breast.'

Here Donald desired me to remark particularly for the honour of the honest MacKenzies in the Lewis (notwithstanding the vile abusive language they had given him) that they declared they had no intention to do the Prince the smallest hurt, or to meddle with him at present in any shape. But then they were mighty desirous he might leave them and go to the continent, or anywhere else he should think convenient. The

wind being quite fair for the continent Donald desired they 5 May
would give him a pilot, but they absolutely refused to give him one. Donald offered any money for one, but he said he believed he would not have got one though he should have offered £500 sterling, such was the terror and dread the people were struck with. Donald then returned to the Prince and *fol.* 291.
gave him an honest account how matters stood, which made them all at a loss to know what course to take, all choices having but a bad aspect.

At this time the Prince, O'Sullivan and O'Neill had but six shirts amongst them, and frequently when they stript to dry those that were upon them they found those that they were to put on as wet as the ones they had thrown off.

In this great difficulty the Prince declared, let the consequence be what it would, he could not think of stirring anywhere that night till he should sleep a little, so much was he fatigued with the late tedious journey. And the two captains were no less wearied, being quite undone. To make their case still worse, two of the boatmen had run away from Stornway, being frighted out of their wits at the rising of the men in arms.

May 6th. About eight o'clock in the morning the Prince, 6 May
O'Sullivan, O'Neil, Donald MacLeod and the six boatmen (two whereof were Donald's own son and honest Ned Bourk), went on board Donald Campbell's boat, which they had got at Scalpa, and sailed for the Island Euirn, twelve miles from Stornway, and landed safely. This Euirn is a desert island *fol.* 292.
round which the people of the Lewis use to go a fishing, and upon which they frequently land to spread their fish upon the rocks of it for drying. The fishermen were then at Stornway, but not one of them could be prevailed upon to accompany the Prince to the uninhabited island, for the wind was contrary, and it blew a very hard gale.

When they were in Lady Killdun's house they had killed a cow, for which the Prince desired payment to be made; but the landlady refused to accept of it. However, Donald said, before they left the house he obliged her to take the price of the cow. 'For,' said Donald, 'so long as there was any money among us, I was positive that the deel a man or woman should have it to say that the Prince ate their meat for nought.'

6 May They took the head and some pieces of the cow along with them in the boat, as also two pecks of meal and plenty of brandy and sugar. They had all along a wooden plate for making their dough for bread, and they made use of stones for birsling their bannocks before the fire. When they were parting with Lady Killdun she called Ned Bourk aside and (as Donald said) gave him a junt of butter betwixt two fardles of
*fol.* 293. bread, which Ned put into a wallet they had for carrying some little baggage.

Upon the desart island they found plenty of good dry fish, of which they were resolved to make the best fare they could without any butter, not knowing of the junt that Ned had in his wallet. As they had plenty of brandy and sugar along with them, and found very good springs upon the island, they wanted much to have a little warm punch to chear their hearts in this cold remote place. They luckily found a earthen pitcher which the fishers had left upon the island, and this served their purpose very well for heating the punch. But the second night the pitcher by some accident or another was broke to pieces, so that they could have no more warm punch.

When Donald was asked if ever the Prince used to give any particular toast when they were taking a cup of cold water, whiskie, or the like, he said that the Prince very often drank to the Black Eye, 'by which,' said Donald, 'he meant the second daughter of France; and I never heard him name any particular health but that alone.[1] When he spoke of that lady, which he did frequently, he appeared to be more than ordinary well pleased.' When Donald was asked if ever he heard the Prince mention that he had any trust to put in the King of France
*fol.* 294. for assistance, he answered that the Prince when he spoke of the King of France mentioned him with great affection, and declared that he firmly believed the King of France had his cause much at heart, and would (he hoped) do all in his power to promote it. When the Prince at any time was talking upon this subject, Donald said he used to add these words: 'But, gentlemen, I can assure you, a King and his Council are two very different things.'

---

[1] See f. 1686.

Ned Bourk stood cook and baxter; but Donald said, the Prince was the best cook of them all. One day upon the desart island the Prince and Ned were employed in making out a dish of fish, while all the rest were asleep. Ned, not minding that he had the junt of butter, began to complain that the fish would make but a very sarless morsel without butter. The Prince said the fish would do very well in their present condition, and that they behoved to take the fish till the butter should come. Ned, at last reflecting, told the Prince that he had got a junt of butter from Lady Killdun, which he laid up betwixt two fardles of bread in the wallet, which was then lying in the boat. The Prince said that would do exceedingly well, for it would serve to compleat their cookery, and desired Ned to go fetch it immediately. When Ned came to take out the butter the bread was all crumbled into pieces, so that it made a very ugly appearance. Ned returned and told the Prince the butter would not serve the purpose at all, for that it was far from being clean, the bread being crumbled into pieces and wrought in amongst it, and therefore he thought shame to present it. 'What,' said the Prince, 'was not the butter clean when it was put there?' 'Yes,' answered Ned, 'it was clean enough.' 'Then,' replied the Prince, 'you are a child, Ned. The butter will do exceedingly well. The bread can never file it. Go, fetch it immediately.' When the fish were sufficiently boyled they awakened the rest of the company to share in the entertainment. Donald MacLeod, looking at the butter, said the deel a drap of that butter he would take, for it was neither good nor clean. But the Prince told him he was very nice indeed, for that the butter would serve the turn very well at present, and he caused it to be served up. They made a very hearty meal of the fish and the crumbs of bread swimming among the butter.

6 May

*fol.* 295.

At another time, when Ned was preparing to bake some bannocks, the Prince said he would have a cake of his own contriving, which was to take the brains of the cow and mingle them well in amongst the meal, when making the dough, and this he said they would find to be very wholesome meat. His directions were obeyed, and, said Donald, 'he gave orders to *fol.* 296. 6 May birsle the bannock well, or else it would not do at all.' When the cake was fully fired the Prince divided it into so many pieces, giving every gentleman a bit of it; and Donald said, 'it made very good bread indeed.'

Here I asked if the boatmen did eat in common with the Prince and the gentlemen? 'Na, good faith, they!' said Donald, 'set them up wi' that indeed, the fallows! to eat wi' the Prince and the shentlemen! We even kept up the port of the Prince upon the desart island itself and kept twa tables, one for the Prince and the shentlemen, and the other for the boatmen. We sat upon the bare ground, having a big stone in the middle of us for a table, and sometimes we ate off our knee or the bare ground as it happened.'

Upon this uninhabited island they remained four days and four nights in a low, pityful hut, which the fishers had made up for themselves; but it was so ill-roofed that they were obliged to spread the sail of the boat over the top of it. They found heath and turf enough to make a fire of; but had nothing but the bare ground to lie along upon when disposed to take a nap, without any covering upon them at all.

When they were consulting about taking their departure from this barren island, the Prince ordered two dozen of the fish to be put on board the boat whatever might happen to *fol.* 297. them, and said he would leave money for them, placing the cash upon a fish, that so the people, when they missed of the number of their fish might find the value of what they wanted. But O'Sullivan or O'Neil told him it was needless to leave any money, lest vagrants should happen to land upon the island and take the money which did not belong to them. These two prevailed upon him to allow the money to be taken up again.

10 May May 10th. They set sail from the uninhabited island, when the Prince told his retinue he was determined to return to Scalpay or the Island Glass, in order to pay his respects to honest Donald Campbell for the remarkable civilities he had shown him; and then he ordered to steer the course directly to that island. When they arrived at Scalpay, Donald Campbell was not at home, having gone a skulking for fear of being laid up, an account or rumour having passed from hand to

hand that the Prince had been in his house, and that the landlord had entertained him kindly. The Prince was sorry at missing his hospitable friend, and set sail directly from Scalpa the same day, May 10th. Here Donald said the Prince would not part with Campbell's boat, because it was such a fine, light, swift-sailing thing. In coursing along they happened to spy a ship at Finisbery, in the Harris, within two musket-shot, before they observed her. They were on the windward of the ship at the mouth of the said bay, and made all the haste they could along the coast to Benbicula. In this course they spied another ship in Lochmaddy, in North Uist, which occasioned them to make all the sail and rowing they could to get free of the mouth of the loch and out of sight of the ship. 10 May *fol.* 298

May 11th. Being still upon the sea they fell short of bread; but having some meal on board and the men turning very hungry and thirsty, they began to make Dramach (in Erse *Stappack*) with salt water, and to lick it up. The Prince said that was a kind of meat he had never seen before, and therefore he behoved to try it how it would go down. Donald said the Prince ate of it very heartily, and much more than he could do for his life. Never any meat or drink came wrong to him, for he could take a share of every thing, be it good, bad, or indifferent, and was always chearful and contented in every condition. 11 May

May 11th. They arrived at Lochwiskaway, in Benbicula, and had scarce got ashore when the wind proved quite contrary to what it had been, blowing a hard gale, which served to make the ships they had spied steer an opposite course. A heavy rain likewise came on at the same time. It happened then to be low water; and one of the boatmen went in among the rocks where he catched a large partan, and taking it up in his hand he wagged it at the Prince, who was at some distance from him. The Prince then took up a cog in his hand, and running towards the lad desired to share in his game.[1]

. . . . . . .

[1] There is a hiatus here, a leaf of the original having apparently been lost, viz., ff. 299, 300.

*fol.* 301. June dispatched Donald MacLeod in Campbell's boat to the continent with letters to Lochiel and John Murray of Broughton, in order to know how affairs stood, and that Donald might bring along with him some cash and brandy. Donald met with Lochiel and Murray at the head of Locharkaig; but got no money at all from Murray, who said he had none to give, having only about sixty louis d'ores to himself, which was not worth the while to send. Donald received letters from Lochiel and Murray to the Prince, and found means without much ado to purchase two anchors of brandy at a guinea per anchor. Here Donald observed that the Prince had a very good opinion of Murray, looking upon him as one of the honestest, firmest men in the whole world.

Donald was absent from the Prince eighteen days or thereabouts, and upon his return he found the Prince where he left him upon Coradale. During his abode on this mountain he lived in a tenant's house, only a hut better than ordinary, diverting and maintaining himself with hunting and fishing; for he used frequently to go down to the foot of the hill upon the shore, and there go on board a small boat, which continued rowing along, and he catched with hand-lines fishes called lyths, somewhat like young cod.

14 June June 14th. From the foot of Coradale they set sail in
*fol.* 302. Campbell's boat still towards Loch Boisdale, but spying three sail within canon-shot of the shore about break of day, this obliged them to put back to a place called Cilistiela in South
15 June Uist.[1] Next morning, June 15th, once more they set sail for Loch Boisdale, where they arrived safely. Here they got accounts that Boisdale was made a prisoner, which was a thing not looked for at all, as he had all along lived peaceably at home, and had kept back all Clanranald's men upon the Isles from following their young chiftain. These accounts of Boisdale's being a prisoner distressed the Prince and his small retinue exceedingly much, as Boisdale was the person principally concerned in the preservation of the Prince; and all along had been most careful to consult the safety of the Prince in his dangers upon and about the Isles. Malcolm MacLeod and

[1] See f. 460, for some additions here.

Donald MacLeod both agreed in affirming that had not Boisdale been made a prisoner the Prince needed not to have left the Long Isle for all the searches (and very strict ones they were) that were made after him by the troops and militia; so well did Boisdale know all the different places of concealment throughout the Long Isle that were fittest for the Prince to be in, and so exact he was in sending timeous notice to the Prince by proper hands, if he could not with safety wait upon him in person, to be here or there, in this or the other place, at such and such times as he thought convenient to point out to him. Boisdale's confinement therefore behoved to be an inexpressible hardship and distress upon the Prince, and make him quite at a loss what to do or what corner to turn himself to. 15 June *fol.* 303.

Lady Boisdale sent four bottles of brandy to the Prince, and every other thing she could procure that was useful for him and his attendants. In and about Loch Boisdale the Prince continued for eight or ten days, till June 24th, that the woeful parting behoved to ensue betwixt the Prince and Donald MacLeod, etc.[1] 24 June

One day coursing up and down upon Loch Boisdale Donald MacLeod asked the Prince if he were once come to his own what he would do with Sir Alexander MacDonald and the Laird of MacLeod for their behaviour. 'O Donald,' said the Prince, 'what would you have me to do with them? Are they not our own people still, let them do what they will? It is not their fault for what they have done. It is altogether owing to the power that President Forbes had over their judgment in these matters. Besides, if the king were restored, we would be as sure of them for friends as any other men whatsomever.' The Prince blamed the young Laird of MacLeod much more than the father; for that, he said, the son had been introduced to him in France, where he kissed his hands, and solemnly promised him all the service that lay in his power to promote his cause; but that when put to the trial he did not keep to his engagements at all.

Here Malcolm MacLeod remarked that the Prince spoke likewise to him about the Laird of MacLeod and his son; and *fol.* 304.

[1] See f. 462.

20 Aug. he said when the Prince was talking about them, he could not fail observing with what wariness and caution the Prince (knowing he was talking to a MacLeod) ordered his words, not being sure likewise in his then circumstances whom to trust, or how easily people might be offended at any observations he might happen to make upon those who had not dealt so fairly by him.

Both Donald and Malcolm agreed in giving it as their opinion that the Prince had an excess of mercy and goodness about him at all times.

They likewise agreed in saying they had good reason to believe that honest Hugh MacDonald of Armadale in Sky (stepfather of Miss MacDonald) had a meeting with the Prince at Rushness in Benbecula, that he got the Prince's pistols in keeping, and that he had them still in his custody.[1] They added further, they were persuaded he would sooner part with his life than with these pistols, unless they were to be given to the proper owner; and that he was the grand contriver in laying and executing the scheme for the Prince's escape in women's cloaths from the Long Isle to the Isle of Sky. They said they had often heard that Armadale sent a letter by Miss Flora to his wife, wherein he used some such expression as this, 'that he had found out an Irish girl, Bettie Bourk, very fit for

*fol.* 305. being a servant to her, and that among her other good qualifications she had this one, that *well could she spin*, which, he knew, she liked well.'[2]

They also agreed in telling me that the whole Island of Raaza had been plundered and pillaged to the utmost degree of severity, every house and hut being levelled with the ground; and there was not left in the whole island a four-footed beast, a hen or a chicken.[3] As there is plenty of free stone and marble in Raaza, the Laird had built of these materials a very neat genteel house for himself, which was razed out at the foundation. But in destroying it they had carefully preserved the windows (all of oak), and put them on board of a ship of war for sale. When the ship came to the Road of Leith, James MacDonald, joiner, and a kinsman of Raaza's, went on

[1] See ff. 770, 805.

[2] See ff. 525, 769, 805.

[3] See f. 873.

board, and bought the windows, which were all done with crown glass, chusing rather they should fall into his hands than into those of any indifferent person, because he could account for them to the owner when a proper opportunity should offer. I saw the windows in James MacDonald's house. 20 Aug.

Donald MacLeod said the Prince used to smoak a great deal of tobacco; and as in his wanderings from place to place the pipes behoved to break and turn into short cutties, he used to take quills, and putting one into another, and all, said Donald, 'into the end of the cuttie, this served to make it long enough, *fol.* 306. and the tobacco to smoak cool.' Donald added that he never knew, in all his life, any one better at finding out a shift than the Prince was when he happened to be at a pinch; and that the Prince would sometimes sing them a song to keep up their hearts.

They expected that Boisdale would get free at Barra. But 1746 one came and told the Prince (to his great sorrow) that Boisdale 24 June was still to be detained a prisoner, and that there was no appearance of his being set at liberty. This, with other distresses that were still increasing upon him, made the Prince resolve upon parting from his attendants for the greater safety. There were at that time two ships of war in the mouth of Loch Boisdale, for whom they durst not make out of the loch to the sea. Besides there was a command of above five hundred red-coats and militia within a mile and a half of them. All choices were bad, but (under God) they behoved to remove from the place where they then were, and to do their best.

The Prince called for the boatmen, and ordered O'Sullivan to pay every one of them a shilling sterling a day, besides their maintenance. He gave a draught of sixty pistols to Donald MacLeod to be paid by Mr. John Hay of Restalrig, if he should happen to be so lucky as to meet with him upon the continent. But as Donald never met with Mr. Hay the draught remains *fol.* 307. yet unpaid. Donald could not help saying here that he did not despair of the payment, for that he hoped for (as old as he was) to see the draught paid to him with interest.

When Donald came to talk of the parting he grat sare and said, It was a woeful parting indeed, but still insists that he hopes to see him yet 'for a' that's come and gane.'

24 June June 24th. They parted with a resolution to meet again at a certain place by different roads; Donald MacLeod, O'Sullivan, and the boatmen walking away and leaving O'Neil only with the Prince. Donald MacLeod went south about, but all the men left him, one only excepted; upon which he was obliged to sink the boat, and to do the best he could to shift for himself. But it was not possible for an old man like him to keep himself any considerable time out of grips, especially as the troops and militia at last became so very numerous upon the different parts of the Long Isle. The militia were the worst of all, because they knew the country so well. Donald and Malcolm MacLeod were positive that the red-coats could have done but little, particularly in taking those that were *fol.* 308. skulking, had it not been for the militia, viz., Campbells, Monroes, Grants, etc., etc., who served to scour the hills and woods, and were as so many guides for the red-coats to discover to them the several corners of the country, both upon the continent and on the islands.

5 July July 5th. Donald MacLeod had the misfortune to be taken prisoner in Benbecula by Allan MacDonald of Knock, in Slate in Sky, a lieutenant. The same day Mr. Allan MacDonald,[1] of the family of Glenaladale, and Mr. Forrest, clergyman of the Church of Rome, were made prisoners by the said Knock, but not at the same time of day nor upon the same spot with Donald MacLeod. Mr. MacDonald, one of the clergymen, commonly called Captain MacDonald, had sixty guineas in his pocket, which Knock took from him, though he was his blood relation, and would not give him one single shilling to purchase necessaries with.

From Benbecula the two priests and honest Donald were brought to Barra, in order (as was given out) to appear before General Campbell; but they did not see him there. From Barra they were carried to Loch Brachandale in Sky, and from Loch Brachandale to Portree in Sky, where Donald had the mortification of being neglected and disregarded by some of his own relations, who saw him, but soon turned their backs upon him, and would not vouchsafe to speak one word to him. This

---

1 At last banished. See f. 281.

affected Donald's honest heart very much. 'But,' said Donald, 'the rogues will be fain to speak to me now when I go back to Sky, where indeed I thought never to return any more. But I shall make them understand themselves.' *fol.* 309. July

At Portree Donald MacLeod and Malcolm MacLeod met as fellow-prisoners, and from that were carried to Applecross Bay towards the continent, and there they were put on board the sloop commanded by the noted John Ferguson so often mentioned. Donald MacLeod was immediately brought into the cabin before General Campbell, who examined him most exactly and circumstantially. The General asked if he had been along with the young Pretender? 'Yes,' said Donald, 'I was along with that young gentleman, and I winna deny it.' 'Do you know,' said the General, 'what money was upon that man's head? no less a sum than *thirty thousand pounds sterling*, which would have made you and all your children after you happy for ever.' Donald's answer to this is so very good that the beauty of it would be quite spoil'd if I did not give it in his own words, which are these. 'What then? *thirty thousand pounds!* Though I had gotten 't I could not have enjoyed it eight and forty hours. Conscience would have gotten up upon me. That money could not have kept it down. And tho' I could have gotten all England and Scotland for my pains I would not allowed a hair of his body to be touch'd if I could help it.' Here Donald desired me particularly to remark for *fol.* 310. the honour of General Campbell, and to do him justice, that he spoke these words, 'I will not say that you are in the wrong.' Then the General said, 'But now you are in the king's mercy, and if you will not declare every thing you know of this matter, here is a machine (pointing to it) that will force you to declare.' Donald replied that 'Many a prettier fellow than he was now in his mercy, and that he would tell anything he knew without any machine whatsoever.' This was Boisdale's machine in which he used to torture thieves to make them confess.[1]

Such particular questions were then asked that Donald behoved to give an account of the violent storm they were engaged in when sailing from the continent to the Isles, what

[1] See ff. 192, 690.

July persons were on board at that time and what their characters were. When the General heard of a Popish priest in the case he asked, Seeing it was a very tempestuous night they set out in from the continent, whether or not the priest was not very busy in praying heartily for the young Pretender, as he was in danger of drowning? 'Na, good faith he, Sir,' replied Donald, 'for if he prayed for himsell, he thought he did well enough. And had you been there, Sir, you would have thought you did well enough too if you prayed for yoursell. Every one of us was minding himsell then.' Then a written declaration was taken from Donald's own mouth and he subscribed it.

*fol.* 311. Donald said he could easily give all his own part of the adventure without doing the smallest harm to the Prince as he then knew that the Prince had set out some time before from Sky to the Continent, and was out of the reach of General Campbell and his command.

Here Malcolm MacLeod informed me that he likewise gave a written declaration, but did not subscribe it.

They both concurred in affirming the Ferguson behaved very roughly and barbarously to them. When they were in health they and the other prisoners were brought upon the quarter-deck betwixt 9 and 10 in the morning, and were allowed to walk among two dozen or so of sheep with sentries placed on each side of them. So long as Ferguson was cruizing upon the Highland coast he took care to have great plenty of fresh victuals of all sorts, the sweet fruits of plundering and pillaging. The prisoners got only half-mans allowance in every respect. For one day of the week they had pease; but the common fellows of the ship behoved to be served first before the gentlemen got any at all; and if the pease happened to fall short, the fellows would have mixed them up with salt-water. The victuals were brought to the prisoners in foul nasty buckets, wherein the fellows used to piss for a piece of ill-natured diversion. They were assigned their quarters in a dark place of the ship, where
*fol.* 312. they were not allowed the light of a candle of any kind, 'from the 1st of August 1746 to the day,' said Donald and Malcolm, 'upon which Lord Lovat suffered, being April 9th (Thursday) 1747. When they were brought opposite to Tilbury Fort upon the Thames, they were turned over from Ferguson to another

ship, where they lay for months together in a most deplorable state of misery, their cloaths wearing so off them that many at last had not a single rag to cover their nakedness with. Here they were treated with the utmost barbarity and cruelty, with a view (as they suppose) to pine away their lives, and by piece-meal to destroy every single man of them. And indeed the design had too great success, for many of them died. Donald MacLeod said he had reason to think that no less than four hundred men died on board three ships opposite to Tilbury Fort,[1] among which sixty or seventy Grants of Glenmoriston, who by the persuasion of the laird of Grant had surrendred themselves and delivered up their arms at Inverness, when Cumberland was there not long after the battle of Culloden. Donald and Malcolm declared that finer and stouter men never drew a sword then what these Glenmoriston men were; and none of them survived the miserable situation and returned to their own country, but only one or two. They likewise joined in laying great blame to the door of the Laird of Grant, who, they said, could not fail to know what would turn out to be the fate of those men if they should be prevailed upon to surrender. In a word they looked upon him as the instrument of the misery of these brave fellows, and spoke no good things of him at all, affirming that he entertained a hatred at the Grants of Glenmoriston.[2]

April

*fol.* 313

Here Donald and Malcolm had a remark very much to the purpose. They said, It was most lucky that a greater number had not surrendered at the same time, for that the treatment of the Glenmoriston men became a warning to others not to follow their example. And indeed their fate did prevent many surrendries that otherwise would have happened.

Donald MacLeod affirmed that they lived at least for two days upon horse flesh. Here Malcolm did not fully agree with him, and after some little debate betwixt them Malcolm qualified the expression and told me I might write down that the beef they got was so very bad and black that they could not take it for anything else but horse flesh or carrion. Upon this Donald smiled and said, 'Well, Malcolm, how much have

[1] See f. 1967.

[2] See ff. 1329, 1489, 1660.

April you mended the matter?' When Donald was asked how such beef went down with them, he replied, 'O what is it that will not go down wi' a hungry stomack? I can assure you we made no scruple to eat anything that came in our way.'

f. 314. Almost all those that were in the same ship with Donald and Malcolm were once so sick that they could scarce stretch out their hands to one another. Old MacKinnon, one of their companions, held out wonderfully, although a man upwards of 70. He was only about eight days in such a way that he needed one to help him up in the morning; while others much younger, and to all appearances stronger too, were dying by pairs, as at last there was a general sickness that raged among all the prisoners on board the different ships, which could not fail to be the case when (as both Donald and Malcolm positively affirmed) they were sometimes fed with the beeves that had died of the disease which was then raging amongst the horned cattle in England.

When Donald and Malcolm were talking of the barbarous usage they themselves and others met with, they used to say, 'God forgie them; but God lat them never die till we have them in the same condition they had us, and we are sure we would not treat them as they treated us. We would show them the difference between a good and a bad cause.'

Donald MacLeod spoke very much good of Mr. James Falconar, a Scots non-jurant clergyman, and Charles Allan, son of Hary Allan in Leith. He said that Charles Allan behaved exceedingly well in his distress, and had very much of
f. 315. the gentleman about him, and that he was in a state of sickness for some time. He said that Mr. Falconar was scarce ever any way ill in his health, that he bore up better than any one of them, having a great fund of spirits, being always chearful, and never wanting something to say to divert them in their state of darkness and misery. He added that he did not know a better man, or one of greater courage and resolution in distress.

Donald desired me to take notice that he was set at liberty (out of a messenger's house in London, where he had been but a short time) upon a most happy day, the 10th of June 1747.[1]

[1] The birthday of the Old Chevalier.

Donald has got in a present a large silver snuff-box prettily chessed, from his good friend, Mr. John Walkingshaw of London, which serves as an excellent medal of his history, as it has engraven upon it the interesting adventure, with proper mottos, etc. The box is an octagon oval of three inches and three quarters in length, three inches in breadth, and an inch and a quarter in depth, and the inside of it is doubly gilt. Upon the lid is raised the eight-oar'd boat, with Donald at the helm, and the four under his care, together with the eight rowers distinctly represented. The sea is made to appear very rough and tempestuous. Upon one of the extremities of the lid there is a landskip of the Long Isle, and the boat is just steering into Rushness, the point of Benbicula where they landed. Upon the other extremity of the lid there is a landskip of the end of the Isle of Sky, as it appears opposite to the Long Isle. Upon this representation of Sky are marked these two places, viz., Dunvegan and Gualtergill. Above the boat the clouds are represented heavy and lowring, and the rain is falling from them. The motto above the clouds, *i.e.* round the edge of the lid by the hinge, is this—OLIM HÆC MEMINISSE JUVABIT—APRILIS 26$^{to}$ 1746. The inscription under the sea, *i.e.* round the edge of the lid by the opening, is this—QUID, NEPTUNE, PARAS? FATIS AGITAMUR INIQUIS. Upon the bottom of the box are carved the following words—DONALD MACLEOD OF GUALTERGILL, in the Isle of Sky, THE FAITHFULL PALINURUS, Æt. 68, 1746. Below these words there is very prettily engraved a dove, with an olive branch in her bill. June fol. 316.

When Donald came first to see me, along with Deacon Clark, I asked him why he had not snuff in the pretty box? 'Sneeshin in that box!' said Donald. 'Na, the deel a pickle sneeshin shall ever go into it till the K—— be restored, and then (I trust in God) I'll go to London, and then will I put sneeshin in the box and go to the Prince, and say, "Sir, will you tak a sneeshin out o' my box?"' fol. 317.

*N.B.*—Donald MacLeod, in giving his Journal, chused rather to express himself in Erse than in Scots (as indeed he does not much like at any time to speak in Scots), and Malcolm MacLeod and James MacDonald explained to me. I was always sure to read over every sentence, in order to know 20 Aug.

0 Aug. of them all if I was exactly right. Malcolm MacLeod and James MacDonald were exceedingly useful to me in prompting Donald, particularly the former, who having heard Donald tell his story so often before in company, put him in mind of several incidents that he was like to pass over. Donald desired Malcolm to refresh his memory where he thought he stood in need, for that it was not possible for him to mind every thing exactly in such a long tract of time, considering how many different shapes and dangers they had gone through in that time.

August 20th. When I was writing Donald's journal from his own mouth, I did not part with him till betwixt 10 and 11 o'clock at night, and before we parted, our company increased to 16 or 17 in number.

Some days after this Donald MacLeod and James MacDonald
i. 318. coming to dine with my Lady Bruce, I made an appointment with Donald to meet James MacDonald and me upon Monday, September 7th, with a view to dine with Mr. David Anderson, senior, in the Links of Leith, who was very desirous to see Donald, and to converse with him for some time. Upon the
7 Sept. day appointed Donald came down from Edinburgh, and brought along with him Ned Bourk, to shew him Mr. Anderson's house. When Ned was known to be the person that was along with Donald, he was desired to come into the house and get his dinner. I went out from the company a little to converse with Ned, who put into my hand a paper, telling me that this was his account of the matter. When I returned to the company, I told them what I had got from Ned, and they were all desirous to know the contents of it. After dinner, when I was reading Ned's Journal, Donald MacLeod frowned, and was not pleased with his account of things, and therefore would needs have Ned brought into the room to answer for himself. Accordingly Ned was called in, and after a pretty long and warm debate betwixt them in Erse, we found that Donald's finding fault amounted to no more than that Ned had omitted to mention several things, which Ned acknowledged to be the case, confessing that his memory did not serve him as to many particulars.

The Journal had been taken from Ned's own mouth in a
i. 319. very confused, unconnected way, as indeed it requires no small

attention and pains to come at Ned's[1] meaning in what he narrates, because he speaks the Scots exceedingly ill. I therefore desired Ned to be with me in my own room upon Wednesday's afternoon, September 9th, that I might have the opportunity of going through his Journal with him at leisure, and likewise of having an account from his own mouth how he happen'd to be so lucky as to escape being made a prisoner, when so many were catched upon the Long Isle, where he skulked for some time. Ned kept his appointment, as will hereafter appear. 9 Sept.

Though Donald MacLeod's history be most extraordinary in all the several instances of it (especially considering his advanced age), yet when he arrived at Leith, he had not wherewith to bear his charges to Sky, where he has a wife and children, from whom he had been absent for at least one year and an half. There was therefore a contribution set on foot for him in and about Edinburgh; and I own I had a great anxiety for my own share to make out for honest Palinurus (if possible) a pound sterling for every week he had served the Prince in distress; and (I thank God) I was so happy as to accomplish my design exactly. Donald MacLeod and James *fol.* 320. MacDonald came from the Links of Leith to my room, as they were to sup that night with my Lady Bruce upon invitation. I then delivered into Donald's own hand, in lieu of wages for his services of ten weeks,

| | £ | s. | d. | |
|---|---|---|---|---|
| his services of ten weeks, . . | £10 | 0 | 0 | Sterling. |
| *Vide* page *hujus* 261, . . | 6 | 11 | 0 | |
| *Vide* vol. i. page 73, . . | 37 | 1 | 6 | |
| In all, | £53 | 12 | 6 | |

The above sum went through my hands in the compass of about thirteen months and an half. Meantime I have not reckoned up a guinea, half a guinea, or a crown, which I had from time to time from my Lady Bruce, as a necessitous sufferer happened to come in the way.

God Almighty bless and reward all those who liberally contributed for the support of the indigent and the deserving in times of the greatest necessity and danger, for Jesus Christ's sake. Amen and Amen.

---

[1] Near thirty years old before he could speak English at all.—F.

10 Aug. At the same time above mentioned, I gave Donald MacLeod the trouble of two letters, copies whereof follow.

## Copy of a Letter to Mr. ALEXANDER MACDONALD of Kingsburgh in Sky.

7 Sept. DEAR SIR,—I could not think of honest Palinurus's setting out upon his return to Sky, without giving you the trouble of some few lines, to wish you and Mrs. MacDonald much joy
ol. 321. and happiness in being at your own fireside again. You and all your concerns are frequently made mention of here with very much respect; and so long as a spark of honesty remains, the name of MACDONALD OF KINGSBURGH will ever have a mark of veneration put upon it.

You know very well how I employ much of my time in a certain affair. I have already made up a collection of between twenty-four and thirty sheets of paper, and I would fain flatter myself with the hopes of still increasing the number till the collection be made compleat, by your assistance and that of other worthies who prefer truth to falshoods, and honesty to trick and deceit. Now is the time or never to make a discovery of facts and men; and it is pity to omit any expedient that may tend to accomplish the good design.

I gave Captain Malcolm MacLeod the trouble of a written Memorandum, which I hope you will honour with a plain and distinct return; and hereby I assure you no other use shall be made of it but to preserve it for posterity; it being my intention not so much as to speak of it, and to make a wise and discreet use of every discovery I am favoured with.

ol. 322. I wish the worthy Armadale would be so good as to give his part of the management from his own mouth. But as I have writ fully by the same hand to the faithful Captain Malcolm MacLeod upon this and some other particulars, to his letter I refer you, and I hope you will join your endeavours with him in serving the cause of truth and justice.

For my own part I am resolved to leave no stone unturn'd to expiscate facts and characters, that so *the honest man* may be known and revered, and those of the opposite stamp may have their due. 7 Sept.

That God Almighty may ever have you, Mrs. MacDonald, and all your concerns in His holy care and protection, is the hearty and earnest prayer of, my dear Sir, your most affectionate friend and very humble servant,

Robert Forbes.

*Citadel of Leith, September 7th*, 1747.

*P.S.*—Palinurus has promised to drop me a line by post to inform me of his safe arrival, and about your welfare, and that of other friends. Pray keep him in mind of his promise, and let him not mention any other thing in his letter. Is it possible to get Boisdale's part from himself? I would gladly have it. You see I am exceedingly greedy. Adieu.[1]

## Copy of a Letter to Captain Malcolm MacLeod of Castle in Raaza. fol. 323

Dear Sir,—This comes by honest Palinurus to congratulate you upon your safe return to your own place; I wish I could say to your own fireside. But I hope that and all other losses will be made up to you with interest in due time. A mind free from the sting of bitter reflections is a continual feast, and will serve to inspire a man with spirits in a low and suffering state of life, made easy by contentment, whilst others are miserable under a load of riches and power, and must betake themselves to a crowd of company to keep them from thinking.

I hope you are happy in meeting with Mrs. MacLeod in good health. Long may ye live together, and may your happiness increase.

I need not put you in mind of my Memorandum to Kingsburgh, and of your promise to procure me an exact account from the mouth of your brother-in-law, Mr. MacKinnon, as to his particular concern in the adventure, for you have too much honour to neglect anything committed to your trust.

I heartily wish that honest Armadale could be prevailed

[1] See ff. 701, 792, 837.

7 Sept. upon to give a full and plain account of his part of the manage-
f. 324. ment in a certain affair which is very much wanted. If he intends to visit Miss Flora while in Edinburgh, I then can have the happiness of conversing with that truly valuable man, and of getting his history from his own mouth. But if he comes not to this country soon, I earnestly beg you 'll employ your good offices with him to allow you to write it down in his own words. Though I have not the honour of that worthy gentleman's acquaintance, please make him an offer of my best wishes to him and his family in the kindest manner, and tell him that he has a most amiable character amongst the honest folks in and about this place. May God Almighty multiply his blessings upon him, and all his concerns both here and hereafter.

If I rightly remember I desired the favour of you to lay yourself out in procuring me an exact account of all the cruelties and barbarities, the pillagings and burnings, you can get any right intelligence about, which will be an infinite service done to truth. In doing of this be so good as to be very careful in finding out the names of persons and places as much as possible. But where the names cannot be discovered, still let the facts themselves be particularly set down.

Though I have not the honour of being known to the worthy
f. 325. family of Raaza, I beg my most respectful compliments may be presented to them.

I need not mention to you that regard which is entertained for you by the worthy person, the protection of whose roof I enjoy; for I dare say you cannot fail to be sensible with what respect you and all such are made mention of here.

That God Almighty may bless you and Mrs. MacLeod with health and happiness and give you your hearts desire is the hearty and earnest prayer of, my dear Sir, Your most affectionate friend and very humble servant,

Robert Forbes.

*Citadel of Leith, September 7th*, 1747.

*P.S.*—By the same hand I have sent a letter to that valuable and faithful gentleman, Kingsburgh, with whom you may compare notes.[1]

---

[1] See f. 856.

*September 7th.*—Donald MacLeod when at supper spoke much in commendation of Ned Burk as being an honest, faithful, trusty fellow.[1] He said in the event of a R[evoluti]on Ned would carry a chair no more; for he was persuaded the Prince would settle an hundred pounds sterling a year upon Ned during life. And he could affirm it for a truth that not any man whatsomever deserved it better. Meantime Donald added that Ned, though true as steel, was the rough man, and that he used great freedoms; for he had seen him frequently at ***Deel speed the leers*** with the Prince, who humour'd the joke so well that they would have ***flitten together like twa kail wives***, which made the company to laugh and be merry when otherwise they would have been very dull. 7 Sept. *fol.* 326

Robert Forbes, A.M.

*Wednesdays afternoon, September 9th*, 1747.

At the hour appointed (4 o'clock) Ned Bourk came to my room, when I went through his Journal with him at great leisure, and from his own mouth made those passages plain and intelligible that were written in confused, indistinct terms. 9 Sept.

A Short but Genuine Account of Prince Charlie's Wanderings from Culloden to his meeting with Miss MacDonald, by Edward Bourk.[2]

Upon the 16th of April 1746 we marched from the field of Culloden to attack the enemy in their camp at Nairn, but orders were given by a false[3] general to retreat to the place from whence we had come, and to take billets in the several parts where we had quartered formerly. The men being all much fatigued, some of them were dispersed here and there in order to get some refreshment for themselves, whilst the greater part of them went to rest. But soon after, the enemy appearing behind us, about four thousand of our men were with difficulty 1746 16 Apr

[1] See f. 281.

[2] This Journal as far as f. 338 is printed in the *Jacobite Memoirs*, pp. 362-373. Burke died in Edinburgh on 23rd November 1757. See f. 1706.

[3] This epithet is not to be regarded.—F. See f. 667.

6 April got together and advanced, and the rest were awakened by the
ol. 327. noise of the canon, which surely put them in confusion. After engaging briskly there came up between six and seven hundred Frazers commanded by Colonel Charles Frazer, younger, of Inverallachie, who were attacked before they could form in line of battle, and had the misfortune of having their Colonel wounded, who next day was murdered in cold blood, the fate of many others.

Our small, hungry, and fatigued army being put into confusion and overpowered by numbers, was forced to retreat. Then it was that Edward Bourk fell in with the Prince, having no right guide and very few along with him. The enemy kept such a close fire that the Prince had his horse shot under him;[1] who, calling for another, was immediately served with one by a groom or footman, who that moment was killed by a canon bullet. In the hurry, the Prince's bonnet happening to fall off, he was served with a hat by one of the life-guards. Edward Bourk, being well acquainted with all them bounds, undertook to be the Prince's guide and brought him off with Lord Elcho, Sir Thomas Sheridan, Mr. Alexander MacLeod, aid-de-camp, and Peter MacDermit, one of the Prince's footmen. Afterwards they met with O'Sullivan, when they were but in very bad circumstances. The Prince was pleased to say to Ned, if you be a true friend, pray endeavour to lead us safe off. Which honour Ned was not a little fond of, and promised
ol. 328. to do his best. Then the Prince rode off from the way of the enemy to the Water of Nairn, where, after advising, he dismist all the men that were with him, being about sixty of Fitz-James's horse that had followed him. After which Edward Bourk said, 'Sir, if you please, follow me. I'll do my endeavour to make you safe.' The Prince accordingly followed him, and with Lord Elcho, Sir Thomas Sheridan, O'Sullivan, and Mr. Alexander MacLeod, aid-de-camp, marched to Tordarroch, where they got no access, and from Tordarroch through Aberarder, where likewise they got no access; from Aberarder to Faroline, and from Faroline to Gortuleg, where they met with Lord Lovat, and drank three glasses of wine with him.

---

[1] See f. 1161.

About 2 o'clock next morning with great hardships we arrived at the Castle of Glengary, called Invergary, where the guide (Ned Burk) spying a fishing-net set, pulled it to him and found two salmonds, which the guide made ready in the best manner he could, and the meat was reckoned very savoury and acceptable. After taking some refreshment the Prince wanted to be quit of the cloathing he had on, and Ned gave him his own coat. At 3 o'clock afternoon, the Prince, O'Sullivan, another private gentleman, and the guide set out and came to the house of one Cameron of Glenpean, and stayed there all night. In this road we had got ourselves all nastied, and when we were come to our quarters, the guide happening to be untying the Prince's spatter dashes, there fell out seven guineas. They being alone together, the Prince said to the guide, 'Thou art a trusty friend and shall continue to be my servant.' April *fol.* 329.

From Glenpean we marched to Mewboll, where we stayed one night, and were well entertained. Next morning we went to Glenbiasdale, stayed there four nights or thereabouts, and from that we took boat for the Island of South Uist, about six nights before the 1st of May, where we arrived safely but with great difficulty. There we stayed three days or so, and then we boated for the Island Scalpa, or Glass, and arrived at Donald Campbell's house.

When I asked at Ned to whom Scalpay belonged, he answered, To the Laird of MacLeod. I asked likewise, what this Donald Campbell was? Ned told me that he was only a tenant, but one of the best, honestest fellows that ever drew breath; and that his forefathers (from father to son) had been in Scalpa for several generations past. Ned said he believed they were of the Campbells of Lochniel.

In Scalpa we stayed about three days, sending from thence our barge to Stornway to hire a vessel. By a letter from Donald MacLeod we came to Loch Seaforth, and coming there by a false guide, we travelled seven hours, if not more, under cloud of night, having gone six or eight miles out of our way. This guide was sent to Stornway to know if the vessel was hired. Either by him or some other enemy it was divulged that the Prince was at Kildun's house (MacKenzie) in Arynish, upon which a drum beat in Stornway, and upwards of *fol.* 330.

May an hundred men conveened to apprehend us. However the MacKenzies proved very favourable and easy, for they could have taken us if they had pleased. We were then only four in number besides the Prince, and we had four hired men for rowing the barge. Upon the alarm Ned Burk advised they should take to the mountains; but the Prince said, 'How long is it, Ned, since you turned cowardly? I shall be sure of the best of them ere taken, which I hope shall never be in life.' That night he stood opposite to the men that were gathered together, when two of our boatmen ran away and left us. The rogue that made the discovery was one MacAulay, skipper of the vessel that was hired, who next morning went off to Duke William with information. In the morning we had killed a quey of little value, and about 12 o'clock at night our little barge appeared to us, whereof we were very glad. We put some pieces of the quey in the barge and then went on board. We rowed stoutly; but spying four men of war at the point of the Isle of Keaback we steered to a little desart island where were some fishermen who had little huts of houses like swine's
*fol.* 331. huts where it seems they stayed and made ready their meat while at the fishing. They were frighted at seeing our barge sailing towards the island, and apprehending we had been a press boat from the men-of-war they fled and left all their fish.

When landed Edward Burk began to dress some of the fish, but said he had no butter. The Prince said, 'We will take the fish till the butter come.' Ned, minding there was some butter in the barges laid up among bread, went to the barge and brought it; but it did not look so very clean, the bread being all broke in pieces amongst the butter; and therefore Ned said he thought shame to present it. The Prince asked if the butter was clean when put amongst the bread. Ned answered it was. 'Then,' said the Prince, 'it will do very well. The bread is no poison; it can never file the butter.'

Ned having forgot here to mention the cake which the Prince contrived with the cow's brains I asked him about it; and he acknowledged the truth of it. I likewise asked him if he knew the name of the desart island; but he frankly

owned that he did not know it, assuring me in the mean time April.
that Donald MacLeod knew it well.[1]

Upon the desart island we stayed four nights, and on the 5th set to sea and arrived at the Island Glass, where we were *fol.* 332.
to enquire about the hire of Donald Campbell's boat. Here four men appeared coming towards them, upon which Ned Burk went out of the boat to view them, and giving a whistle, cried back to his neighbours, being at some distance, to take good care of the boat. Ned not liking these men at all, thought fit to return with speed to the boat, and putting his hand to the gunnel jumped aboard and stayed not to converse with the four men.

From Glass, having no wind, we rowed off with vigour. About break of day, the wind rising, we hoisted sail; and all of us being faint for lake of food, and having some meal, we began to make drammach (in Erse, stappack) with salt water, whereof the Prince took a share, calling it no bad food, and all the rest followed his example. The Prince called for a bottle of spirits, and gave every one of us a dram. Then we passed by Finsbay, in the Isle of Harris, where we spied a man-of-war, commanded by one Captain Ferguson, under full sail, and our little sail was full too. He pursued us for three leagues; but we escaped by plying our oars heartily, they being better to us than arms could have been at that time. The water failing the man-of-war, he was not in a condition to pursue farther. We steered upon a point called Rondill, *fol.* 333.
when the Prince expressed himself as formerly that he should never be taken in life. After this the said Captain Ferguson, being anxious to know what we were, endeavoured to make up with us a second time, but to no purpose, the water being at ebb, and we continuing still to row in amongst the creeks. Seeing this he turned to the main sea, when we sailed to Lochmaddy to the south of the Isle of Uist, thence to Lochuiskibay, thence to an island in said loch, where we came to a poor grasskeeper's bothy or hut, which had so laigh a door that we digged below the door and put heather below the Prince's knees, he being tall, to let him go the easier into the

[1] See f. 291.

May. poor hut. We stayed there about three nights, and provided ourselves very well in victuals by fowling and fishing, and drest them in the best shapes we could, and thought them very savoury meat. Thence we went to the mountain of Coradale, in South Uist, and stayed there about three weeks, where the Prince one day, seeing a deer, run straight towards him, and firing offhand killed him. Edward Burk brought home the deer, and making ready some collops, there comes a poor boy,
*fol.* 334. who, without asking questions, put his hand among the meat, which the cook (Edward Burk) seeing, gave him a whip with the back of his hand. The Prince observing this, said, 'O man, you don't remember the Scripture which commands to feed the hungry and cleed the naked, etc. You ought rather to give him meat than a strip.' The Prince then ordered some rags of cloaths for the boy, and said he would pay for them, which was done accordingly. The Prince added more, saying, 'I cannot see a Christian perish for want of food and raiment had I the power to support them.' Then he prayed that God might support the poor and needy, etc.

There was one Donald MacLeod of Gualtergill, a trusty friend, who went to Moidart and brought us news and brandy, for which the Prince thanked him heartily, calling him a trusty servant.

The foresaid boy after [being] fed and cloathed, hearing of the enemy's approaching in search of the Prince, (like Judas) thought fit to go privately to them, being fifteen hundred of Campbells, MacLeods, and MacDonalds, to inform them where the Prince was, which some of the enemy hearing, ridiculed the boy, and said he deserved to be thrown into the sea, for what he advanced was entirely false and all lies.

Now, the enemy coming from the Isle of Barra, who were well known in these places, and we being utter strangers, with
*fol.* 335. the disadvantage too of some men-of-war lying before, we had no way to escape. But committing ourselves to Providence, the Prince, O'Sullivan, O'Neil (who had come on an errand from France), Donald MacLeod, Edward Burk, and the boatmen went on board the barge, to be sure melancholy enough, having none to trust in but the Providence of God only, we escaped narrowly by Ouia Island to Benbicula, in Clanronald's

country. We stayed there for about two nights; but the May. enemy came to that country likewise in search of the Prince, where one Hamar MacLeod landed near our quarters; which the Prince being informed of, asked at Edward Burk, 'Is this a friend or a foe?' To which Ned answered, 'He never was a friend to your family.' But by good providence Hamar happened to go off without making any search, and we did not think proper to go the same way with him, not knowing what the event may have been.

Immediately after this the Prince with O'Neil only went to the wilderness, desiring we might stay behind with this design that if any enquiry was made about him, our answer should be that we knew nothing about him at all further than that by that time we believed he had made his escape. We all resolved to suffer than that the Prince should be exposed. Mean- *fol.* 336. time Providence ordered it otherwise, for without trouble we escaped also, and afterwards met with the Prince, and that night boated in our little barge and sailed by Ouia, above the island of Benbicula, where from the point of a rock a young seal (a whelp) swimmed directly to the barge as if it had been frighted; and Edward Burk leaning over the side of the boat, pulled the seal into the boat; but it died soon after. The same night we rowed and sailed with vigour, when we spied two men-of-war with one Captain Scott, not knowing the names of any of the rest.[1] We then steered with all speed to a shore at Aikersideallach, in South Uist, where coming to a creek of a rock above the water, and finding some ashes and the place very private, we kindled up a fire; and the Prince lay that night in a clift of the rock, drawing his bonnet over his eyes for preserving them. Ned Burk, as he was turning himself, the place being exceedingly narrow, and he not adverting to that, fell backwards over the rock about six yards high, and narrowly escaped being bruised, by falling among sand.

Afterwards we took boat and rowed to the south part of South Uist for Loch Boisdale, when we perceived fifteen sail, and a number of the enemy being upon the land, we knew not what to do. All that day we were obliged to keep in a narrow *fol.* 337.

---

[1] See f. 461.

June. creek till night that we got into Loch Boisdale. Afterwards coming ashore very much fatigued, we came to an old tower in the mouth of the island, where we kindled fire, put on our pot in order to make ready some provisions; and Ned Burk went out to pull some heath for the Prince's bed. Meantime Donald MacLeod of Gualtergill said there were two French ships of war appearing; but to our great surprize they proved to be Englishmen. The Prince with three others took to the mountains, and the rowers went to the barge lying in the creek and steered up the loch.

The men-of-war steered to the main. At night we all met again at our barge, wherein we had still some small provisions. We stayed in the open fields two nights, having only the sails of the boat for covers. On the third night we went farther into the loch, and rested thereabouts for other two nights. When the enemy (viz., redcoats and Campbells) appeared, then we passed to the north side of the loch.

The Prince, finding himself so invironed by the enemy, took
*fol.* 338. two shirts under his arm and went off, allowing none to follow him but O'Neil. After parting from the rest the Prince on the other side of the mountain met with one Neil MacDonald, who conveyed him that night near to one Lauchlan MacDonald, a falsified friend, who designed to have betrayed both the Prince and his country. But Neil MacDonald, finding out his design, conveyed the Prince to Benbicula, a place then called Rushness, where he met with one Florence MacDonald, stepdaughter to MacDonald of Armadale, who pretended to cross the sea to visit her mother in Sky, when the Prince went along with her, having disguised himself in women's cloaths, and changing his name to Bettie Burk, the sirname of his first guide.

Now, gentlemen and ladies, who read this, believe it to be a true and genuine short account of hardships that happened and what the author saw. But for brevity's sake I have not made mention of many wants the Prince suffered, the many ill-drest diets he got, the many bad beds he lay in, the many cold and wet beds in the open fields, etc., with all which he chearfully and patiently put up; and this any well-thinking person may easily consider from what is above set down.

## September 9th, 1747. After going thro' the Journal with Ned I writ from his own mouth the following Account, etc. *fol.* 339. 9 Sept. 1747

Edward Burk, after parting with the Prince, went over North Strand to North Uist, where he skulked in a hill called Eval for about seven weeks, twenty days of which he had not any other meat than dilse and lammocks, a kind of shell fish, for much about this time a paper had been read in all the kirks strictly forbidding all persons to give so much as a mouthful of meat to a rebel, otherwise they should be destroyed. Upon this Oliver Burk, a married man, and brother to Ned, would not give poor Ned a bit of bread, or any countenance whatsomever, being frighted out of his wits. But Ned resolved to take amends of him for his cruel cowardice, and went to a place where Oliver had a flock of sheep feeding. Ned took the head off one of them, and throwing the body over his shoulder, carried it to a place where he could order it at his conveniency. But Jacob Burk, an unmarried man, and brother to Ned, did as much as could lie in his power, and gave Ned everything he could purchase, and did not fear at all. *fol.* 340.
God bless poor Jacob. One night, Ned being in great misery, went to steal a boat in order to take the sea. But some fishers being near by, and hearing a noise, came out with a force, thinking this to be an enemy. Ned was obliged to leave the boat and take to his heels, for he had far rather have been killed or drowned than to be taken prisoner, because by that time it was well known that he had been the Prince's servant, and therefore he was afraid, if taken, they would put him to the torture to make him tell all that he knew, and he could not bear the thoughts of doing hurt to anybody.

A near relation of his own (Peter MacDonald) put him to much trouble, having gone to Captain John MacDonald, son of Tutor MacDonald in North Uist, in order to put Ned out, and get a party to catch him. But Captain John broke a staff over the fellow's head and told him he had other uses for his men than to send them upon false errands. At that time Ned

9 Sept. went to Lochmaddy in North Uist, where one of the Independent Company (commanded by the said John MacDonald) came to him and desired him to follow him. Ned asked to what place was he to follow him? 'Farther into the country,' said the fellow. 'Friend,' said Ned, 'have you got any more
*fol.* 341. help than yourself?' 'No,' replied the fellow. 'And, Sir, you are one of the Prince's servants?' Ned answered, 'Many a prettier fellow had been his servant.' The fellow added that he knew Ned's face. Upon which Ned owned his name, and said he would not deny it, and immediately drew his pistol, which frighted the fellow so that he ran off with himself. But soon after he brought a party to the same spot to seize Ned, but he had got himself hid in a private place.

This made Ned more careful and timorous, especially as Donald MacDonald (a son of Clanranald, and one of Ned's good friends) was under a necessity to deliver himself up, which put him in no danger, as he was a French officer. After this Ned was obliged to betake himself to a cave in North Uist, being so hard beset. A shoemaker's wife, when neither one friend nor another durst be seen with him, came under cloud of night and brought him a little food.

A little before this Ned had gone one day to buy a pair of shoes at Clatachcaranish, when General Campbell, Captain Ferguson and their whole force came to the place. Ned was
*fol.* 342. then in a sad perplexity, and did not well know what to do. Spying an old black coat and a pair of old breeches in the house, he put them on, hiding his own cloaths under a chest, and went out at the door unconcerned. He stood a while among the men and conversed easily with them, then slipping by degrees out amongst them, he got to the hills to his old cave. Jacob Burk and the shoemaker's wife got his cloaths (a highland dress) and brought them to him.

At last Ned resolved, right or wrong, to get out of these hardships, and, making his way to Lochmaddy, found there a vessel ready to ferry some cattle over to Sky. Ned gave a false token to the skipper in place of a pass, and got on board. When he arrived in Sky he came to a gentleman's house of the name of MacLeod, near which place MacDonald of Knock coming with a command of 36 men, Ned made off, not chusing to have his quarters near any place where Knock was. That night Ned went to an old kiln-cogie and took his rest, and the gentleman, MacLeod (in whose house he had been) sent him meat privately. Next morning, before daylight, he made off and went to Talisker MacLeod, whom he had served several years before that, and gave himself up to him. Talisker made him welcome, and took care of him. Ned, being desirous to be upon the mainland, took the opportunity of a boat sailing for Seaforth's country where he met with his master, Mr. Alexander MacLeod, aid-de-camp, and stayed with him till the indemnity came out, when he left his master and returned to Edinburgh, where he follows his old business. 9 Sept. *fol.* 343.

Ned told me that Donald MacLeod, all the time he was with the Prince, sat at the helm and steered the course, and that they had neither compass, lamp, nor pump in the great storm from the mainland to Benbicula, not knowing, through the darkness and tempest, where they were, or what land they might make; and therefore they behoved to let the boat drive and trust all to Providence, for they could do nothing for themselves. By peep of day, he said, they observed Benbicula and made to it with great difficulty, the storm continuing no less than twelve hours after they landed. Ned assured me that O'Neil's saying that the boat staved to pieces was a downright falshood; and moreover, he did not doubt but the eight-oar'd boat was still entire upon the island Scalpa or Glass.

When I spoke to Ned about the priest's leaving them at Scalpa, Ned said, 'Faith, I have reason to think that the Prince is not a great Papist, for he never gree'd well wi' the priest at all, and was very easy about his company.' *fol.* 344.

Ned owned the truth of what Donald MacLeod had said about his using such freedoms with the Prince, and added that he used to play antiques and monkey tricks to divert the Prince and his small retinue.

One of the soles of Ned's shoes happening to come off, Ned cursed the day upon which he should be forced to go without shoes. The Prince hearing him, called to him and said, 'Ned, look at me;' 'when,' said Ned, 'I saw him holding up one of his feet to me where there was deel a sole upon the shoe;

9 Sept. and then I said, 'O my dear, I have nothing more to say. You have stopt my mouth indeed.'

When Ned was talking of seeing the Prince again he spoke these words: 'If the Prince do not come and see me soon, good faith, I will go and see my daughter (Bettie Burk) and crave her. For she has not yet paid her christening money, and as little has she paid the coat I gae her in her greatest need.' ROBERT FORBES, A.M.

N.B.—Donald MacLeod is much more to be depended upon than Ned Burk in the account of things, because Ned
Vol. 345. can neither write nor read, and was near thirty years of age before he could speak one word of English. Ned had a great difficulty to put things together in any tolerable way, as he is one of these honest, low men that are intent for the present upon doing their duty with fidelity without minding anything else. Such honest, plain persons as these allow the world to rub on as it pleases, and never once trouble their heads about making observations and remarks upon the occurrences of life as they pass along. If they jog on from day to day they ask no more, and are very much strangers to the exercises of the memory. Besides, honest, plain, rough Ned had never entertained a notion that any journal or account would ever be asked of him, or else perhaps he would have stored his memory with a more plentiful stock, as he had abundance of materials to work upon. Honest Ned is not (by his own confession) much above forty years of age, and is both stout and sturdy for all he has gone through.[1]

ROBERT FORBES, A.M.

---

[1] See p. 1706.

## JOURNAL of the Prince's imbarkation and arrival, etc., the greatest part of which was taken from DUNCAN CAMERON at several different conversations I had with him.[1] *fol.* 346.

After the battle of Fontenoy and taking of Tournay, among other regiments the one commanded by Lord John Drummond was garrisoned in Tournay, in which corps Duncan Cameron (some time servant to old Lochiel at Boulogne in France) served. When Duncan was in Tournay he received a letter from Mr. Æneas MacDonald, banker in Paris, desiring him forthwith to repair to Amiens, and if possible to post it without sleeping, where he should receive orders about what he was to do. Accordingly Duncan set out, and in a very short time posted to Amiens, from whence Æneas, etc., had set out, but had left a letter for Duncan ordering him to follow them to Nantes, to which place he set out without taking any rest, where he found the Prince and his small retinue, consisting of seven only, besides servants. June.

The seven were the Duke of Athol, Sir Thomas Sheridan, Sir John MacDonald, Colonel Strickland, Captain O'Sullivan, Mr. George Kelly (a nonjurant clergyman), and Æneas MacDonald, banker at Paris, brother to Kinlochmoidart.

As Duncan Cameron had been brought up in the island of Barra, and knew the coast of the Long Isle well, in some *fol.* 347.
part of which the Prince intended to land first, so Duncan's business was to descry to them the Long Isle.

At Nantes the Prince and his few attendants waited about fifteen days before the *Elizabeth* ship of war came, which was to be their convoy in the expedition. To cover the design the better, Sir Thomas Sheridan[2] passed for the father, and the Prince for the son, for none knew the Prince to be in company

---

[1] Of this journal there is printed in the *Jacobite Memoirs* (pp. 1-27), from ff. 348-360, in combination with that of Æneas MacDonald, which occurs at f. 490 *et seq.*

[2] See f. 496.

July. but the seven, some few others, and Mr. Welch (an Irishman, a very rich merchant in Nantes), who was to command the frigate of sixteen guns,[1] on board of which the Prince and the few faithful friends with the servants were to imbark.

After the Prince was on board he dispatched letters to his father, and the King of France, and the King of Spain, advising them of his design, and no doubt desiring assistance.

The Prince when in Scotland, used to say that the 10th of June was the day on which he stole off, and that he did not mind it to be his father's birth-day till night was far spent. From whence some have affirmed that to have been the day of the embarkation, and others to have been the day when he left Paris and began to be incog.

9 July. They had not been above five or six days at sea, till one
*fol.* 348. evening the *Lyon* ship of war appeared, and came pretty near them, and then disappeared. Next morning she came again in view and disappeared. She continued to do so three or four times, and the last time of her appearing she came within a mile or so of them; when the captain of the *Elizabeth* (a Frenchman) came on board the frigate, and told Mr. Welch if he would assist him by keeping one side of the *Lyon* in play at a distance, he would immediately put all things in order for the attack. Mr. Welch, well knowing the trust he had on board, answered him civilly, and told him it was what he could not think of doing, and withal remarked to him it was his humble opinion that he should not think of fighting unless he should happen to be attacked, because his business was to be convoy to the frigate in the voyage. However, he said, as he pretended not to any command over him, he might do as he thought proper.

The French captain to all this replied, that from the *Lion's* appearing and disappearing so often, it seemed as if she were looking out for another ship to assist her, and if she should happen to be joined by any other, they no doubt would instantly fall upon the *Elizabeth* and the frigate, and devour them both; and therefore he behoved to think it the wisest course to fight the *Lion* when single, because the *Elizabeth* in

[1] Called the *Doutelle*.

that case was fit enough for the engagement, and would bid 9 July. fair enough to give a good account of the *Lion*. Upon this *fol.* 349. the French captain drew his sword, took leave of Mr. Welch and his company, went on board the *Elizabeth* with his sword still drawn in his hand, and gave the necessary orders for the attack.

Immediately the *Elizabeth* bore down upon the *Lion* (each of them consisting of about sixty guns, and therefore equally matched), and began the attack with great briskness. The fight continued for five or six hours, when the *Lion* was obliged to sheer off like a tub upon the water.

About the time when the captain came on board the frigate, the Prince was making ready to go on board the *Elizabeth* for more air and greater conveniency every way, the frigate being crowded with the gentlemen, the servants, and the crew. His friends reckoned it very lucky that he had not gone on board.

The frigate all the time of the engagement lay at such a small distance, that (as the Prince observed to several friends in Scotland) the *Lion* might have sunk her with the greatest ease. But he said it was their good fortune that the *Lion* had despised them, and thought not the frigate worth the while. Besides, *fol.* 350. the *Lion* found enough of employment for all her hands in playing her part against the *Elizabeth*.

During the time of the fight the Prince several times observed to Mr. Welch what a small assistance would serve to give the *Elizabeth* the possession of the *Lion*, and importuned him to engage in the quarrel. But Mr. Welch positively refused, and at last behoved to desire the Prince not to insist any more, otherwise he would order him down to the cabin.

After the fight was all over, Mr. Welch sailed round the *Elizabeth*, and enquired particularly how matters stood with the captain and the crew. A lieutenant came upon deck from the captain, who was wounded in his cabin, and told Mr. Welch that between thirty and forty officers and gentlemen (besides common men) were killed and wounded, and that if Mr. Welch could supply him with a mainmast and some rigging, he would still make out the voyage with him.

Mr. Welch replied that he could not furnish him with either mainmast or rigging, and that although he should have hap-

July. pened to be capable to serve him in these things, yet he would
f. 351. not have made it his choice to lose so much time as it would require to put the *Elizabeth* in some better order. He desired to tell the captain it was his opinion that he should without loss of time return to France, and that he himself would do his best to make out the intended voyage. The *Elizabeth* accordingly returned to France, and the frigate continued her course to the coast of Scotland. She had not been long parted from the *Elizabeth* till the crew descried two ships of war at some distance, which they could not have well got off from; but that a mist luckily interveened, and brought them out of sight.

Two or three hours before landing, an eagle came hovering over the frigate, and continued so to do till they were all safe on shore. Before dinner the Duke of Athol had spied the eagle; but (as he told several friends in Scotland) he did not chuse then to take any notice of it, lest they should have called it a Highland freit in him. When he came upon deck after dinner, he saw the eagle still hovering about in the same manner, and following the frigate in her course, and then he could not help remarking it to the Prince and his small retinue,
f. 352. which they looked upon with pleasure. His grace, turning to the Prince said, 'Sir, I hope this is an excellent omen, and promises good things to us. The king of birds is come to welcome your royal highness upon your arrival in Scotland.'

When they were near the shore of the Long Isle, Duncan Cameron was set out in the long boat to fetch them a proper pilot. When he landed he accidentally met with Barra's piper, who was his old acquaintance, and brought him on board. The piper piloted them safely into Erisca (about July
July. 21st), a small island lying between Barra and South Uist. 'At this time,' said Duncan Cameron, 'there was *a devil of a minister* that happened to be in the island of Barra, who did us a' the mischief that lay in his power. For when he had got any inkling about us, he dispatched away expresses with informations against us. But as the good luck was, he was not well believed, or else we would have been a' tane by the neck.'

When Duncan spoke these words, '*a devil of a minister*,' he bowed low, and said to me, 'Sir, I ask you ten thousand pardons for saying so in your presence. But, good faith, I can assure you, sir (asking your pardon), he was nothing else but the *devil of a minister*.' 23 July

When they landed in Eriska, they could not find a grain of meal or one inch of bread. But they catched some flounders, which they roasted upon the bare coals in a mean low hut they had gone into near the shore, and Duncan Cameron stood cook. The Prince sat at the cheek of the little ingle, upon a fail sunk, and laughed heartily at Duncan's cookery, for he himself owned he played his part awkwardly enough.[1] fol. 35

Next day the Prince sent for young Clanranald's uncle (Alexander MacDonald of Boisdale), who lived in South Uist, and discovered himself to him. This gentleman spoke in a very discouraging manner to the Prince, and advised him to return home. To which it is said the Prince replied, 'I am come home, sir, and I will entertain no notion at all of returning to that place from whence I came; for that I am persuaded my faithful Highlanders will stand by me.' Mr. MacDonald told him he was afraid he would find the contrary. The Prince condescended upon Sir Alexander MacDonald and the Laird of MacLeod as persons he might confide in. Mr. MacDonald begged leave to tell him that he had pitched upon the wrong persons; for from his own certain knowledge he could assure him these gentlemen would not adhere to his interest; on the contrary, they might chance to act an opposite part. And seeing the Prince had been pleased to mention Sir Alexander MacDonald's name, Boisdale desired he might run off an express to him, and let his return be the test of what he had advanced. He added withal, that if Sir Alexander MacDonald and the Laird of MacLeod declared for him, it was his opinion he might then land on the continent, for that he doubted not but he would succeed in the attempt. But if they should happen to refuse their assistance (which he still insisted would be the case), then their example would prove of bad consequence, and would tend only to make others backward and to keep at home. And in that event he still thought it advisable to suggest his returning back to where he came from. 22 July. fol. 35

According to this advice the Prince did send a message to

[1] See ff. 256, 302, 507.

Sir Alexander MacDonald, intimating his arrival, and demanding assistance. Before the messenger could return, Æneas MacDonald (anxious to have the honour of seeing the Prince in the house of his brother, the Laird of Kinlochmoidart) prevailed upon the Prince to set out for the continent, and
fol. 355. they arrived at Boradale in Moidart, or rather Arisaig, upon
25 July. July 25th, St. James's day, 1745.[1] When the messenger returned to the Prince he brought no answer with him, for Sir Alexander refused to give any.

It is worth remarking here that though MacDonald of Boisdale had played the game of the government by doing all he could to dissuade the Prince from making the attempt; and after the standard was set up, by keeping back all Clanranald's men (to the number of four or five hundred good stout fellows) that lived in South Uist and the other isles, yet his conduct could not screen him from rough and severe treatment. For after the battle of Culloden he suffered in his effects as well as others, and had the misfortune to be made a prisoner and to be carried to London by sea, in which expedition he had the additional affliction of having his brother, the Laird of Clanranald, senior (who had never stirred from his own fireside), and his lady to bear him company, and none of them were released till the 4th of July 1747. However, to do Boisdale justice, he was of very great use to the Prince (as Donald MacLeod and Malcolm have both declared) when wandering up and down
fol. 356. through South Uist, Benbicula, and other parts of the Long Isle, and exerted his utmost power to keep him out of the hands of his enemies.[2]

After the Prince's arrival upon the continent, some friends met to consult what was to be done, and I have heard it affirmed by good authority that Keppoch honestly and bravely gave it as his opinion that since the Prince had risqued his person and generously thrown himself into the hands of his friends, therefore it was their duty to raise their men instantly merely for the protection of his person, let the consequence be what it would. Certain it is that if Keppoch, Lochiel, young Clanranald, etc., had not joined him, he would either have

---

[1] See f. 640.

[2] See ff. 257, 302, 462.

fallen into the hands of his enemies or been forced immediately to cross the seas again.[1]

The royal standard was set up at Glenfinnan (August 19th), 19 Au
the property of Clanranald, at the head of Lochshiel, which marches with Lochiel's ground, and lies about ten miles west from Fort William. The Prince had been a full week before this, viz., from Sunday the 11th, at Kinlochmoydart's house, and Lochiel had been raising his men who came up with them just as the standard was setting up.

The Prince stayed where the standard was set up two days,
and I have heard Major MacDonell frequently say in the Castle *fol.* 35
of Edinburgh, that he had never seen the Prince more chearful at any time, and in higher spirits than when he had got together four or five hundred men about the standard. Major MacDonell presented the Prince with the first good horse he mounted in Scotland, which the Major had taken from Captain Scott, son of Scotstarvet.

On Friday, August 23d, the Prince lodged in Fassafern, 23 Au
three miles down the Loch Eil, and about five miles from Fort William. On sight of a warship which lay opposite to the garrison, the Prince crossed a hill and went to Moy or Moidh, a village on the river Lochy belonging to Lochiel. There he stayed till Monday, August 26th, waiting intelligence about General Cope; and that day he crossed the river Lochy, and lodged in a village called Leterfinla, on the side of Loch Lochy. At 12 o'clock at night, being very stormy and boisterous, he learned that General Cope was at Garvaimor, whereupon the men stood to arms all night. But the General had altered his route, and by forced marches was making the best of his way for Inverness, which (as was given out) happened by an express from President Forbes advising the General not to attempt
going up the country to attack the Highlanders at the Pass of *fol.* 35
Corierag (very strong ground) where they had posted themselves, but to make all the haste he could to Inverness, where he might expect the Monroes, etc., to join him, whereby he would be considerably reinforced.

Upon notice that the General was marching towards Inver-

---

See f. 643.

23 Aug. ness, about six hundred of the Highlanders urged the being allowed to follow him under cloud of night and promised to come up with him and to give a good account of him and his command. But the Prince would not hear of such an attempt, and desired them to wait for a more favourable opportunity. It was with much difficulty that they could be prevailed upon to lay aside the thoughts of any such enterprize. This I had from the brave Major MacDonell.

When the Prince was coming down the Highlands to meet General Cope (as was supposed) he walked sixteen miles in boots, and one of the heels happening to come off, the Highlanders said they were unco glad to hear it, for they hoped the want of the heel would make him march at more leisure. So speedily he marched that he was like to fatigue them all.

*fol.* 359. August 27th. The Prince slept at Glengary's house, and next
27 Aug. night lay at Aberchallader, a village belonging to Glengary.[1]

30 Aug. August 30th. The Prince and his army were at Dalnacardoch, a publick house in Wade's road, as appears from a letter writ by the Duke of Athol to a lady[2] desiring her to repair to Blair Castle to put it in some order, and to do the honours of that house when the Prince should happen to come there, which he did the day following, August 31st. I saw the letter and took the date of it.

31 Aug. When the Prince was at Blair he went into the garden, and taking a walk upon the bowling-green, he said he had never seen a bowling-green before. Upon which the above lady called for some bowls that he might see them; but he told her that he had got a present of some bowls sent him as a curiosity to Rome from England.

2 Sept. September 2d. He left Blair and went to the house of Lude, where he was very chearful and took his share in several dances, such as minuets, Highland reels (the first reel the Prince called for was, 'This is not mine ain house,' etc.), and a Strathspey minuet.

3 Sept. September 3d. He was at Dunkeld, and next day he dined
*fol.* 360. at Nairn House, where some of the company happening to observe what a thoughtful state his father would now be in

[1] See f. 643.

[2] Mrs. Robertson of Lude, a daughter of Nairn.

from the consideration of those dangers and difficulties he had to encounter with, and that upon this account he was much to be pitied, because his mind behoved to be much upon the rack—the Prince replied that he did not half so much pity his father as his brother. 'For,' said he, 'the king has been inured to disappointments and distresses, and has learnt to bear up easily under the misfortunes of life. But poor Hary! his young and tender years make him much to be pitied, for few brothers love as we do.' 3 Sept.

September 4th. In the evening he made his entrance into Perth upon the horse that Major MacDonell had presented him with. 4 Sept.

September 11th. Early in the morning he went on foot attended by few and took a view of the house of Scoon; and leaving Perth that day, he took a second breakfast at Gask, dined at Tullibardine, and that night went towards Dumblain and next day to Down. 11 Sept.

September 14th. In the morning the Prince, after refreshing himself and his army at the Laird of Leckie's house, marched by Stirling Castle and through St. Ninians. From Stirling Castle a six-pounder was discharged four times at him, which determined Lord Nairn, who was bringing up the second division *fol.* 361. of the army, to go farther up the country in order to be out of the reach of the canon of the Castle. When the Prince was in St. Ninians with the first division, Mr. Christie, provost of Stirling, sent out to them from Stirling a quantity of bread, cheese, and ale in abundance, an order having come before by little Andrew Symmer desiring such a refreshment. Colonel Gardiner and his dragoons had galloped off towards Edinburgh from their camp near Stirling Castle the night before, or rather the same morning, when it was dark, September 14th, without beat of drum. 14 Sept.

September 16th. The Prince and his army were at Gray's Mill upon the Water of Leith, when he sent a summons to the Provost and Town Council of Edinburgh to receive him quietly and peaceably into the city. Two several deputations were sent from Edinburgh to the Prince begging a delay till they should deliberate upon what was fittest to be done. Meantime eight or nine hundred Highlanders under the command of 16 Sept.

16 Sept. Keppoch, young Lochiel, and O'Sullivan, marched in between the Long Dykes without a hush of noise, under the favour of a dark night, and lurked at the head of the Canongate about the
fol. 362. Nether Bow Port till they should find a favourable opportunity for their design, which soon happened. The hackney coach that brought back the second deputation, entred at the West Port, and after setting down the deputies at their proper place upon the street, drove down the street towards the Canongate, and when the Nether Bow Port was made open to let out the coach, the lurking Highlanders rushed in (it being then peep of day) and made themselves masters of the city without any opposition, or the smallest noise.

Robert Forbes, A.M.

*N.B.*—When the Prince was marching his army towards England, Duncan Cameron was ordered to attend the Prince's baggage, and had got a young horse to ride upon that had not been accustomed to noise, and therefore threw Duncan upon hearing the pipes and the drums. Duncan was so bruised with the fall that he behoved to be left behind, and accordingly was carried to the house in which Lady Orbiston was then living in the neighbourhood of Dalkeith. Soon an information was given that the Highlanders had left one behind them at such a place, and he was said to be Colonel Strickland in his wounds,
fol. 363. upon which a party of dragoons was dispatched to take the Colonel prisoner. But they found only plain Duncan, whom they brought into Edinburgh. He was committed to the city jayl, where he was so lucky as to be overlooked, either through sickness or want of evidence, when others were sent off to England to stand trial. At last he was released, nothing appearing against him, some time before the indemnity came out, and got a protection for going to his own country in the Highlands. However Duncan had no mind to make use of that protection, being resolved to return to France. He luckily fell in with Mrs. Fothringham, who was going over to France to her husband, late governor of Dundee. This lady was allowed a pass and protection for herself, a child, a man-servant, and a maid-servant, to sail for Holland. She wanted much to have Duncan Cameron along with her, because, having

the French language well, he would prove an excellent guide for her to France. Duncan on the other hand was fond of having it in his power to oblige such a lady, and glad to go into any scheme whereby he could safely make his way to Holland, and therefore he agreed to pass for Mrs. Fothringham's servant, and accordingly he was insert in the pass under the name of Duncan Campbell, an Argyleshire man. They sailed from Leith Road on board of one *Sibbald*, upon Friday, June 19th, and arrived in Holland the 23d, 1747. June. *fol.* 364.

It was most lucky for Duncan Cameron that it was never known to any in the government that he was one of those who came over in the same frigate with the Prince. The most distant suspicion was never entertained about this, otherwise his fate would have turned out in quite another shape.

Robert Forbes, A.M.

## Copy of a letter from the Prince to his father after the Battle of Gladesmuir. *fol.* 365.

*Pinkay House, near Edinburgh,*
*September 21st*, 1745.

Sir,—Since my last from Perth it hath pleased God to prosper your Majesty's arms under my command with a success that has even surprized my wishes. On the 17th we entred Edinburgh, sword in hand, and got possession of that town without being obliged to shed one drop of blood, or to do any violence. And this morning I have gained a most signal victory with little or no loss. If I had a squadron or two of horse to pursue the flying enemy there would not one man of them have escaped; as it is they have hardly saved any but a few dragoons who, by a most precipitate flight will, I believe, get into Berwick. If I had obtained this victory over foreigners my joy would have been compleat. But as it is over Englishman, it has thrown a damp upon it that I little imagined. The men I have defeated were your Majesty's enemies, it is true, but they might have become your friends and dutiful subjects when they had got their eyes 21 Sept. 1745 fol. 366. 21 Sept. opened to see the true interest of their country which I am come to save, not to destroy. For this reason I have discharged all publick rejoicing. I do not care to enter into the particulars of the action, and chuse rather that your Majesty would hear it from another than from myself. I send you this by Stewart, to whom you may give entire credit. He is a faithful, honest fellow, and thoroughly instructed in everything that has happened to this day. I shall have a loss in him; but I hope it will be soon made up by his speedy return with the most agreeable news I can receive, I mean that of your majesty's and my dearest brother's health.

I have seen two or three Gazettes filled with addresses and mandates from the bishops to the clergy. The addresses are such as I expected, and can impose on none but the weak and credulous. The mandates are of the same sort, but were artfully drawn. They order their clergy to make the people sensible of the great blessings they enjoy under the present family that governs them, particularly of the strict administration of justice, of the sacred regard that is paid to the laws, and the great security of their religion and property. This sounds all very well, and may impose upon the unthinking.
fol. 367. But one who reads with a little care will easily see the fallacy. What occasion has a Prince who has learnt the secret of corrupting the fountain of all laws to disturb the ordinary course of justice? Would not this be to give the alarm, and amount to telling them that he was not come to protect as he pretended, but really to betray them? When they talk of the security of their religion, they take care not to mention one word of the dreadful growth of atheism and infidelity which (I am extremely sorry to hear from very sensible, sober men) have within these few years got to a flaming height; even so far that I am assured many of their most fashionable men are ashamed to own themselves Christians; and many of the lower sort act as if they were conversing upon this melancholy subject.

I was let into a thing which I never understood rightly before, which is that those men who are loudest in the cry of the growth of Popery, and the danger of the Protestant religion, are not really Protestants, but a set of profligate men, of good parts, with some learning, and void of all principles, but pretending to be republicans. 21 Sept.

I asked those who told me this what should make these men so zealous about preferring the Protestant religion, seeing they *fol.* 368. are not Christians? And was answered that it is in order to recommend themselves to the ministry, which (if they can write pamphlets for them, or get themselves chosen members of Parliament), will be sure to provide amply for them. And the motive to this extraordinary zeal is that they thereby procure to themselves the connivance at least, if not the protection of the Government, while they are propagating their impiety and infidelity.

I hope in God Christianity is not at so low an ebb in this country as this account I have had represents it to be. Yet if I compare what I have formerly seen and heard at Rome, with something I have observed since I have been here, I am afraid there is too much truth in it.

The bishops are as unfair and partial in representing the security of their property as that of their religion, for when they mention it they do not say a word of the vast load of debt (that increases yearly) under which the nation is groaning, and which must be paid (if ever they intend to pay it) out of their property. It is true all this debt has not been contracted under the prince of this family, but a great part of *fol.* 369. it has, and the whole might have been cleared by a frugal administration during these thirty years of a profound peace which the nation has enjoyed, had it not been for the immense sums that have been squandered away in corrupting Parliaments and supporting foreign interest that can never be of any service to these kingdoms. I am afraid I have taken up too much of your majesty's time about these sorry mandates, but having mentioned them I was willing to give your majesty my sense of them.

I remember Dr. Wagstaff (with whom I wish I had conversed more frequently, for he always told me truth) once said to me that I must not judge of the clergy of the Church of England by the bishops, who were not preferred for their piety and learning, but for very different talents: for writing pamphlets, for being active at elections, and for voting in Parliament as

11 Sept. the ministry directed them. After I have won another battle they will write for me, and answer their own letters.

There is another set of men amongst whom I am inclined to
fol. 370. believe the lowest are the honestest, as well as among the clergy, I mean the army. For never was there a finer body of men to look at than those I fought with this morning, yet they did not behave so well as I expected. I thought I could plainly see that the common men did not like the cause they were engaged in. Had they been fighting against Frenchmen come to invade their country I am convinced they would have made a better defence. The poor men's pay and their low prospects are not sufficient to corrupt their natural principles of justice and honesty, which is not the case with their officers, who, incited by their own ambition and false notions of honour, fought more desperately. I asked one of them, who is my prisoner (a gallant man) why he would fight against his lawful prince, and one who was come to rescue his country from a foreign yoke. He said he was a man of honour, and would be true to the Prince, whose bread he ate, and whose commission he bore. I told him it was a noble principle, but ill applied, and asked him if he was not a Whig? He replied that he was. 'Well then,' said I, 'how come you to look on the commission you bear, and the bread you eat to be the
fol. 371. Prince's and not your country's which raised you, and pays you to serve and defend it against foreigners, who came not now to defend but to enslave it, for that I have always understood to be the true principle of a Whig. Have you not heard how your countrymen have been carried abroad to be insulted and maltreated by those defenders, and to be butchered, fighting in a quarrel in which your country has little or no concern, only to aggrandize Hanover?' To this he made no answer, but looked sullen and hung down his head. The truth is there are few good officers among them. They are brave, because an Englishman cannot be otherwise, but they have generally little knowledge in their business, are corrupt in their morals, and have few restraints from religion, though they would have you believe they are fighting for it. As to their honour they talk so much of, I shall soon have occasion to try it, for, having no strong places to put any

prisoners in, I shall be obliged to release them upon their parole. If they do not keep it I wish they may not fall into my hands again, for in that case it will not be in my power to protect them from the resentment of my Highlanders, who would be apt to kill them in cold blood, which (as I take no pleasure in revenge) would be extremely shocking to me. My haughty foe thinks it beneath him, I suppose, to settle a cartel. I wish for it as much for the sake of his men as my own. I hope ere long I shall make him glad to sue for it. 21 Sept. *fol.* 372.

I hear there are six thousand Dutch troops arrived, and ten battalions of the English sent for. I wish they were all Dutch that I might not have the pain of shedding English blood. I hope I shall soon oblige them to bring over the rest, which in all events will be one piece of service done to my country in helping it out of a ruinous foreign war.

It is hard my victory should put me under new difficulties that I did not feel before, and yet this is the case. I am now charged with the care both of my friends and enemies. Those, who should bury the dead, are run away as if it was no business of theirs. My Highlanders think it beneath them to do it, and the country people are fled away. However, I am resolved to try if I can get people for money to undertake it, for I cannot bear the thoughts of suffering Englishmen to rot above ground. *fol.* 373.

I am in great difficulty how I shall dispose of my wounded prisoners. If I make an hospital of the church it will be looked upon as a great profanation, as having violated my manifesto in which I promised to violate no man's property. If the magistrates would act they would help me out of this difficulty. Come what will I am resolved I will not suffer the poor wounded men to lie in the streets, and if I can do no better I will make an hospital of the palace, and leave it to them.

I am so distracted with these cares, joined to those of my own people, that I have only time to add that I am, Sir, your Majesty's most dutiful son, and obedient servant,

CHARLES.

## f. 374. Edinburgh, Tuesday, August 25th, in the forenoon,
## ; Aug. 1747. 1747. I visited Mrs. Cameron, Dr. Archibald Cameron's lady,[1] who told me

That it was a common practice amongst the red-coats after Culloden battle, dispersed up and down the Highlands, to raise the bodies of man, woman, and child out of the graves for greed of the linen, or whatever was wrapped about them, and after they had taken that off them to leave the bodies above ground. She herself had two children that died at that time, and she was advised to bury them privately in some remote heathy brae, to prevent their being taken up again; but she could not think of burying them in any other place than where their forefathers were laid, and therefore she was obliged to bribe a serjeant to keep the fellows from digging up the bodies again.

She and her poor children behoved to take to the hills, no houses being left in the whole country about them. Mrs.
f. 375. Cameron said she never saw the Prince in his skulking, nor knew not where he was.

Robert Forbes, A.M.

## ; Aug. 1747 Tuesday's Afternoon, August 25th, 1747, in Edinburgh, I had the favour of being introduced by Miss Cameron (daughter of Allan Cameron, who died at Rome) to Mrs. Robertson, Lady Inches, who gave me the following particulars:

Some time before, and at the time of the battle, Lady Inches was living with her family in Inverness, her husband being in a dying condition, who was laid in his grave just as the

[1] This lady was Jean Cameron, daughter of Archibald Cameron of Dungallon. See other narratives by her at ff. 547 and 566. An account of her husband's death is given at f. 1734 *et seq.*

cannonading began upon Drummossie Muir. On Friday after the battle, April 18th, she went home to her house called the Lees, within a mile or so of the field of battle. Upon the road as she went along she saw heaps of dead bodies stript naked and lying above ground. When she came to the Lees she found sixteen dead bodies in the Closs and about the house, which as soon as possible she caused bury. When she came into the Closs some of the sogers came about her, calling her a rebel-bitch, and swearing, that certainly she behoved to be such, or else so many of these damned villains would not have come to get shelter about her house. Then pulling her by the sleeve they desired her to come along with them, and they would shew her a rare sight, which was two dead bodies lying in the Closs with a curtain laid over them. They took off the curtain and made her look upon the bodies, whose faces were so cut and mangled that they could not be discerned to be faces. They told her that the party who had been formerly there had cut and mangled these villains, and had left them in the house in their wounds; but when they themselves came there they could not endure to hear their cries and groans, and therefore they had dragged them out to the Closs and given them a fire to their hinder-end. 'For,' said they, 'we roasted and smoked them to death, and have cast this curtain taken down from the side of one of your rooms over them, to keep us from seeing the nauseous sight.' Lady Inches said she saw the ashes and remains of the extinguished fire.

18 April.

*fol.* 376.

The house of the Lees was all pillaged, the doors of the rooms and closets, the outer doors, the windows, and all the liming being broke down to pieces. The charter-chest was broke open, and the papers were scattered up and down the house; all her horses and cattle were taken away, though Inches was not in the least concerned in the affair, save only that he was a great Whig, and had a son out with the Duke of Cumberland.

*fol.* 377.

When she complained to David Bruce, he told her to go through the camp and see if she could spy out any of her furniture or goods among the sogers; and if she did, the fellows should be seized upon, and she should have the satisfaction of having them hanged. But seeing she could have no

April. reparation of damages she did not chuse to follow Mr. Bruce's advice, and she declared she had never received one farthing for the losses sustained.

On the day of the battle when the chace happened, one of
Inches's tenants and his son, who lived at the gate of the Lees,
f. 378. stept out at the door to see what was the fray, and were shot
by the red-coats, and fell down in one another's arms, the son dying upon the spot; but the father did not die till the Friday, the 18th, when Lady Inches went to see him, and he was then expiring. Much about the same place they came into a house where a poor beggar woman was spinning, and they shot her dead upon the spot. In a word, Lady Inches said they were really mad; they were furious, and no check was given them in the least.[1]

Upon the day of the battle, about nineteen wounded men (but so as with proper care they might have been all cured) got into a barn. Upon the Thursday (the day after the battle) orders were issued out to put them to death. They were accordingly taken out, and set up at a park wall as so many marks to be sported with, and were shot dead upon the spot. In the barn there was one of the name of Shaw, whom a Presbyterian minister was going forwards to intercede for, because
f. 379. he was his particular acquaintance. But seeing the fury and
madness of the sogers, he thought fit to draw back lest he had been set up amongst the poor wounded men as a mark to be sported with in this scene of cruelty. Lady Inches said she had forgot the minister's name, but she believed he was settled at Castle Stewart; but she would not be positive about the place of his abode, though she had got the particular story from a sister of that minister, a married woman in Inverness.[2]

To confirm this the more, it is to be remarked that when Provost Frazer and the other magistrates of Inverness (attended by Mr. Hossack, the late provost) went to pay their levee to Cumberland and his generals, the generals were employed in giving orders about slaying the foresaid men and other wounded persons. Mr. Hossack (the Sir Robert Walpole of the place, under the direction of President Forbes,

---

[1] See ff. 421, 707, 1087, 1323, 1376. [2] See f. 1485.

and a man of humanity) could not witness such a prodigy of intended wickedness without saying something, and therefore making a low bow to General Hawley or General Husk, he said, 'I hope your excellency will be so good as to mingle mercy with judgment.' Upon this Hawley or Husk cried out in a rage, 'Damn the rebel-dog. Kick him down stairs and throw him in prison directly.[1] The orders were literally and instantly obeyed, and those who were most firmly attached to the Government were put in prison at the same time. *fol.* 380 April.

The country people durst not venture upon burying the dead, lest they should have been made to bear them company till particular orders should have been given for that purpose.

The meeting-house at Inverness [and all the bibles and prayer-books in it were][2] was burnt to ashes.

Lady Inches said it was really Loudon's piper that the stout blacksmith killed, and that MacIntosh's house is seven or eight miles from Inverness. When Lady MacIntosh was to be brought a prisoner into Inverness, a great body of men, consisting of several regiments, were sent upon the command, and when she was leaving her own house the dead-beat was used by the drummers. In the commands[3] marching from and to *fol.* 381. Inverness the horses trode many corpses under foot, and the generous-hearted Lady MacIntosh behoved to have the mortification of viewing this shocking scene.

ROBERT FORBES, A.M.

---

[1] See ff. 259, 1320, 1378.

[2] The passage in brackets is scored through as delete [ED.]

[3] Here begins volume third of Bishop Forbes's Manuscript Collection. It is entitled: 'THE LYON IN MOURNING, or a Collection (as exactly made as the iniquity of the times would permit) of Speeches, Letters, Journals, etc. relative to the affairs, but more particularly, the dangers and distresses of. . . . Vol. 3d. 1747.

*Cui modo parebat subjecta Britannia Regi,*
*Jactatus terris, orbe vagatur inops!*

On the inside of the front board of volume 3d are adhibited—1. Piece of the Prince's garter-ribbon. 2. Piece of red velvet, anent which on back of title-page is as follows: (by Mr. Robert Chambers) The small piece of red velvet on the inside of the board was part of the ornaments of the Prince's sword-hilt. While on his march to England he rested on a bank at Faladam, near Blackshiels, where the young ladies of Whitburgh, sisters to his adherent, Robert Anderson, presented some refreshments to him and his men. On being requested by one of these gentlewomen for some keepsake, he took out his pen-

19 July 1746

## Copy of a Letter from Mr. Deacon to his father.[1]

Honoured Sir,—Before you receive this I hope to be in Paradise. Not that I have the least right to expect it from any merits of my own, or the goodness of my past life, but merely through the intercession of my Saviour and Redeemer, a sincere and hearty repentance of all my sins, and the variety of punishments I have suffered since I saw you, and the death which I shall die to-morrow, and which I trust in God will be some small atonement for my transgressions; and to which I think I am almost confident I shall submit with all the resignation and chearfulness a truly pious Christian and a brave souldier can wish.

I hope you will do my character so much justice (and, if you
f. 382. think proper, make use of this) as absolutely to contradict the false and malicious reports, spread only by your enemies, in hopes it might be of prejudice to you and your family, that I was persuaded and compelled by you to engage, contrary to my own inclinations. I send my tenderest love to all the dear children, and beg Almighty God to bless you and them in this world, and grant us all a happy meeting in that to come. I

---

knife and cut a portion of velvet and buff leather from the hilt of his sword, which he gave to her with his usual courtesy, and which is still (1836) preserved at Whitburgh. The above piece was cut from the larger fragment, and presented to me by Miss Anderson of Whitburgh.—R. C. 3. Piece of Bettie Burk's gown, sent by Mrs. MacDonald of Kingsburgh, according to promise, f. 152. 4. Piece of apron-string, received from Miss Flora MacDonald. R. F. saw the apron on that occasion and had it on him. On the inside of the backboard of volume 3d are 5. Pieces of tartan, explained as under: The above are pieces of the outside and inside of that identical waistcoat which MacDonald of Kingsburgh gave to the Prince, when he laid aside the women's cloaths at the edge of a wood, f. 1434. The said waistcoat being too fine for a servant, the Prince exchanged it with Malcolm MacLeod, f. 239. Malcolm MacLeod, after parting with the Prince and finding himself in danger of being seized, did hide the waistcoat in a clift of a rock, where (upon his returning home in the beginning of September 1747) he found it all rotten to bits, except only as much as would serve to cover little more than one's loof, and two buttons, all which he was pleased to send to me, f. 472. The waistcoat had lain more than a full year *in* the clift of the rock, for Malcolm MacLeod was made prisoner some time in July 1746, ff. 251, 309.—Robert Forbes, A.M.

[1] See f. 37.

shall leave directions with Charles to send them some trifle whereby to remember me. Pray my excuse naming any particular friends, for there is no end. But give my hearty service and best wishes to all in general. 29 July.

Mr. Syddal is very well, and sends his sincere compliments, but does not chuse to write. He behaves as well as his best friends can wish. My uncle has behaved to me in such a manner as cannot be paralell'd but by yourself. I know I shall have your prayers, which I am satisfied will be of infinite service to, dear father, your dying but contented and truly affectionate son,

THOMAS THEODORE DEACON.

*July 29th*, 1746.

## Copy of some Paragraphs of a Letter to Mr. DEACON's Father, said to be written by the non-jurant clergyman that used to visit Mr. DEACON, etc. *fol.* 283

Their behaviour at divine worship was always with great reverence, attention, and piety. But had you, sir, been present the last day I attended them, your soul would have been ravished by the fervour of their devotion.

From the time of their condemnation a decent chearfulness constantly appeared in their countenances and behaviour, and I believe it may truly be said that no men ever suffered in a righteous cause with greater magnanimity and more Christian fortitude. For the appearance of a violent death, armed with the utmost terrour of pain and torments, made no impression or dread upon their minds. In a word, great is the honour they have done to the Church, the K[ing], and you, and themselves, and may their example be imitated by all that suffer in the same cause.

This short but faithful account of our martyred friends will, I hope, sir, yield great consolation to you and poor Mrs. Syddal. Poor, dear Charles bears in a commendable manner his great loss and other afflictions, and behaves like a man and *fol.* 284
a Christian in all his actions.

## Copy of a Letter from Sir Archibald Primrose of Dunipace,[1] to his sister, etc.

v°. My dear Sister,—I have endeavoured to take some small time, from a much more immediate concern, to offer you a few lines, and to let you know that this day I am to suffer, I think, for my religion, my prince, and my country. For each of these I wish I had a thousand lives to spend. The shortness of the intimation will not allow me much time to write to you so fully in my vindication for what I did that I know concerns you. But I heartily repent of the bad advice I got even from men of judgment and sense. And what I did by their advice in my own opinion was no more than acknowledging I bore arms against the present government, for my lawful, undoubted prince, my religion, and country; and I thought by my plea to procure some time longer life only to do service to my poor
*fol.* 385. family, not doubting but yet in a short time that glorious cause will succeed, which God of His infinite mercy grant.

I repent most heartily for what I did, and I merit this death as my punishment, and I trust in the Almighty for mercy to my poor soul. As I am very soon to leave this world, I pray God to forgive all my enemies, particularly Mr. Gray,[2] who did me all the injury he could by suborning witnesses, and threatening some which was my terror. Particularly there is one poor man[3] to suffer with me that had an offer of his life to be an evidence against me, which he rejected.

Much more I could say, but as my time is short, I now bid my last adieu to my dear mother and you, my dear sister, and I intreat you'll be kind to my dear wife and children; and

---

[1] He was son of George Foulis of the Ravelston family, who, on inheriting the estate of Dunipace from his grandfather, assumed the name of Primrose in terms of the entail. Taken in the north of Scotland he was first imprisoned in Aberdeen, thence sent to Carlisle, where he was tried, and pleading guilty, was sentenced to death, and executed there on 15th November 1746.

[2] William Gray, commonly called Duntie Gray, foremanto Lord Shualton.—(F.)

[3] Patrick Kier, late wright at Moultrie Hill, near Edinburgh.—(F.)

may all the blessings of Heaven attend you all. Live together comfortably and you may expect God's favour. My grateful acknowledgments for all your favours done and designed. Novr.

Remember me kindly to my Lady Caithness,[1] Sauchie, and his sisters, and all my friends and acquaintances. May the Almighty grant you all happiness here, and eternal bliss hereafter, to which bliss, I trust, in His mercy soon to retire; and am for ever, dear sister, your affectionate brother, A. P. *fol.* 386.

*P.S.*—My blessing to your dear boy, my son.

## Copy of a Letter to the same Lady, which served as a cover to the above, from Mr. JAMES WRIGHT, Writer in Edinburgh.

MADAM,—Your brother, who is no more, delivered me this immediately before he suffered. His behaviour was becoming a humble Christian. I waited on him to the last, and with some other friends witnessed his interment in St. Cuthbert's Churchyard. He lies on the north side of the Church, within four yards of the second window from the steeple. Mr. Gordon of Tersperse,[2] and Patrick Murray,[3] goldsmith, lie just by him. God Almghty support his disconsolate widow and all his relations. I trust in His mercy He will provide for the fatherless and the widow. I am just now going to wait upon poor Lady Mary.[4] I am, Madam, yours, etc., J. W. 15 Nov. 1746 *fol.* 387.

*Carlisle*, 15*th November* 1746.
4 *o'clock afternoon.*

*SONG to the tune of 'A Cobler there was,' etc.*

1.

As the devil was walking o'er Britain's fair isle,
George spied in his phiz a particular smile,
And said, My old friend, if you have leisure to tarry,
Let 's have an account what makes you so merry.
Derry, etc.

---

[1] Lady Margaret Primrose, second daughter of Archibald, first Earl of Rosebery. [2] See f. 425. [3] Commonly called Cowley Murray.
[4] Lady Mary Primrose, Sir Archibald's widow.

2.

Old Beelzebub turn'd at a voice he well knew,
And stopping, cried, O Brother George, is it you?
Was my business of consequence ever so great,
I always find time on my friends for to wait.
Derry, etc.

3.

This morning at 7 I set out of Rome,
Most fully intending ere this to've been home.
Pray stay, stay (says George), and took hold of his hand,
You know that St. James's is at your command.
Derry, etc.

4.

And what says the Pope? our monarch began,
And what does he think of our enemy's son?
Why, first, when I came there (Old Satan replied)
He seem'd to have very great hope of his side.
Derry, etc.

5.

But soon from the north arriv'd an express
With papers that gave me great joy, I confess,
Defeated was Charles, and his forces all gone,
I thought, on my soul, I should 've leapt over the moon.
Derry, etc.

*fol.* 388 6.

Of Charles's descendants I 'm only afraid
Against my dominions their projects are laid;
Was a Stewart to govern England again,
Religion and honesty there soon might reign.
Derry, etc.

7.

I oftentimes travel thro' France and thro' Spain
To visit my princes and see how they reign.
But of all my good servants, north, south, east and west,
I speak it sincerely, George! thou art the best.
Derry, etc.

8.

Our monarch replied, looking wise as an ass,
Pray, none of your compliments—Take up your glass.
Tho' the trouble I gave you e'nt much, I must own,
But as for religion, you know I have none.
Derry, etc.

9.

Then, as to my offspring, there 's Feckie, my son,
Whom you wish and I wish may sit on the throne.
For by all men of wisdom and sense 'tis allow'd
If he there does no harm, he 'll there do no good.
Derry, etc.

10.

There 's Billy, my darling, my best belov'd boy,
Can ravish, can murder, can burn, can destroy—
Just a tool for you—'tis his nat'ral delight,
And likes it as well ev'ry whit as to fight.
Derry, etc.

11.

They shook hands at parting, and each bid adieu;
Old Beelzebub mutter'd these words as he flew—
'May thou and thy offspring for ever reign on,
For the devil can't find such a race when you 're gone.'
Derry, etc.

FINIS.

*fol. 389.* *ON A LATE DEFEAT*, 1746, *said to have been composed by a Scots gentleman, an officer in the Dutch service.*

Canst thou, my muse, such desolation view—
Such dreadful havoc 'mong the loyal few;
Vile murders, robbery, consuming fire;
Mothers, with tender infants, starv'd, expire;
Daggers and death in ev'ry hideous face
Threat'ning destruction to the northern race;
Villains contending with a dev'lish joy
Who first shall plunder, or who first destroy;
Successful tyranny and laurell'd vice,
The gods assisting him, who Heav'n defies;
Seeming to spurn the good, th' illustrious youth,
Renown'd for mercy, piety, and truth;
Reluctant fighting passage to a crown
Which none but bigot-whigs deny his own?
Can'st thou behold, and still thy grief suppress,
Our prince and country in so deep distress?
Nor, fir'd with indignation, aid my pen
To lash the cruel deeds of guilty men?

Rouze, rouze, my muse, and curse the hated cause
Of lost religion, liberty, and laws!
Thy freedom, Scotland! in one fatal hour
Is sacrific'd, alas! to lawless pow'r.
All, all is lost! No spark of hope remains;
Death only now, or banishment and chains.
Hard fate of war! How hast thou chang'd the scene!
What just, what glorious enterprize made vain!
Pale Nature trembles; general decay
Succeeds the horrors of th' unlucky day.
*fol. 390.* The good, the brave, in sympathy unite,
Amaz'd that Heav'n did not maintain the fight.
Despairing beauty languishes to see
Such virtue vanquish'd in a righteous plea.

Has godlike Charles (such matchless glories past!)
Conquered so oft to be subdued at last?
These valiant chiefs, whom native courage fir'd,
Then exil'd king's and country's wrongs inspir'd,

T' assert the rights each one enjoy'd before,
And king and country's liberties restore;
Failing in that, with just contempt of life,
Resolv'd to perish 'midst the glorious strife;
Must these true heroes, these great patriots yield
And the usurper's forces keep the field?
A bloody, perjur'd, mercenary crew,
Who fled but lately whom they now pursue
Like fiends of hell, by worse than demon led,
They *kill the wounded* and they rob the dead.
O! Act of horror! more than savage rage
Unparallel'd in any former age!
Curst be the barb'rous executing hand,
And doubly curst who gave the dire command.
A deed so monstrous, shocking ev'n to name,
To all eternity 'twill damn their fame.

Ah! why, just Heaven! (But Heav'n ordain'd it so)
Are impious men allow'd to rule below?
Why does misfortune still attend the best,
Whilst those with life's supreme delights are blest?
Perplexing mistery to human sense;
The wonderful decree of Providence.
But virtue, happy in her self can bear *fol.* 391.
(The ills of life most seemingly severe)
Whatever fate the gods allot us here;
Convinc'd that earthly happiness is vain
And most of pleasure 's only rest from pain.
No shocks of fortune can her peace destroy,
Deserving bliss, indiff'rent to enjoy.
Calm and serene amidst the wrecks of fate,
As ne'er exalted in a prosp'rous state,
She bears adversity with stedfast mind,
To Heavn's decrees religiously resign'd.

Some time, perhaps, fair virtue will take place,
Shining conspicuous in the royal race,
To bless the land with liberty and peace.
Tyrants subdu'd shall tremble at her nod
And learn that virtue is the cause of God.

## *A PARAPHRASE UPON PSALM* 137.

*(As it is said) by Willie Hamilton.*

1.

On Gallia's shore we sat and wept
  When Scotland we thought on,
Rob'd of her bravest sons and all
  Her ancient spirit gone.

2.

Revenge, the sons of Gallia said,
  Revenge your native land.
Already your insulting foes
  Crowd the Batavian strand.

3.

How shall the sons of freedom e'er
  For foreign conquest fight?
*fol. 392.* For pow'r how wield the sword, depriv'd
  Of Liberty and right?

4.

If thee, O Scotland! I forget
  Ev'n to my latest breath,
May foul dishonour stain my name
  And bring a coward's death.

5.

May sad remorse of fancy'd guilt
  My future days employ!
If all thy sacred rights are not
  Above my chiefest joy.

6.

Remember England's children, Lord!
  Who, on Drummossie day,
Deaf to the voice of kindred love,
  Raze, raze it quite, did say.

7.

And thou, proud Gallia! faithless friend,
  Whose ruin is not far,
Just Heav'n on thy devoted head
  Pour all the woes of war!

8.

When thou thy slaughter'd little ones
  And ravish'd dames shalt see,
Such help, such pity may'st thou have
  As Scotland had from thee.

## *ODE ON THE 20TH OF DECEMBER* 1746.[1]

*Hic dies, anno redeunte, festus, etc.* *fol.* 393.

1.

A while forget the scenes of woe,
Forbid a while the tears to flow,
  The pitying sigh to rise.
Turn from the ax the thought away;
'Tis Charles that bids us crown the day,
  And end the night in joys.

2.

So when bleak clouds and beating rain
With storms the face of Nature stain,
  And all in gloom appears.
If Phœbus deign a short-liv'd smile,
The face of Nature charms a while,
  A while the prospect cheers.

3.

Come then, and while we largely pour
Libations to the genial hour,
  That gave our hero birth;
Let us invite the tuneful nine
To sing a theme, like them, divine,
  To paint our hero's worth.

[1] Charles Edward is generally said to have been born on 31st December; but 20th December is the date in the Manuscript, being old style.

4.

How on his tender infant years,
The cheerful hand of Heav'n appears
To watch its chosen care.
Estrang'd to ev'ry foe to truth
Virtuous affliction nurs'd his youth,
Instructive tho' severe.

5.

fol. 394. No sinful court its poison lent
With early bane his mind to taint,
And blast his young renown.
His father's virtues fir'd his heart,
His father's sufferings truths impart,
That form'd him for a throne.

6.

How at an age when pleasure charms,
Allures the stripling to her arms,
He plann'd the great design:
T' assert his injur'd father's cause,
Restore his suffering country's laws,
And prove his right divine.

7.

How when on Scotia's beach he stood
The wond'ring throng around him crowd
To bend th' obedient knee.
Then thinking on their country chain'd,
They wept such worth so long detain'd
By Heav'n's severe decree.

8.

Where'er he mov'd, in sweet amaze,
All ranks with transport on him gaze,
Ev'n grief forgets to pine.
The wisest sage, the chastest fair,
Applaud his sense and praise his air
Thus form'd with grace divine.

9. *fol.* 395.

How great in all the soldier's art,
With judgment calm, with fire of heart,
He bade the battle glow:
Yet greater on the conquer'd plain
He felt each wounded captive's pain,
More like a friend than foe.

10.

By good unmov'd, in ill resign'd,
No change of fortune chang'd his mind,
Tenacious of his aim.
In vain the gales propitious blew,
Affliction's darts as vainly flew,
His soul was still the same.

11.

Check'd in his glory's full career,
He felt no weak desponding fear
Amid distresses great.
By ev'ry want and danger prest,
No care possest his manly breast,
But for his country's fate.

12.

For oh! the woes, by Britons felt,
Had not aton'd for Britain's guilt.
So will'd offended Heav'n;
That yet a while th' usurping hand
With iron rod should rule the land,
The rod, for vengeance giv'n.

13. *fol.* 396.

But in its vengeance Heav'n is just,
And soon Britannia from the dust
Shall rear her head again.
Soon shall give way th' usurper's claim,
And peace and plenty soon proclaim
Again a Stewart's reign.

14.

What joys for happy Britain wait
When Charles shall rule the British state,
Her sullied fame restore:
When in full tides of transport tost,
Ev'n mem'ry of her wrongs is lost,
Nor Germans thought of more.

15.

The nations round with wondering eyes
Shall see old England aweful rise
As oft she did of yore.
And when she holds the ballanc'd scale,
Oppression shall no more prevail,
But fly her happy shore.

16.

Corruption, vice on ev'ry hand,
No more shall lord it o'er the land,
With their protectors fled.
Old English virtues in their place,
With all their hospitable race,
Shall rear their decent head.

*fol.* 397.

17.

In peaceful shades the happy swain,
With open heart and honest strain,
Shall sing his long-wish'd lord.
Nor chuse a tale so fit to move
His list'ning fair one's heart to move,
As that of Charles restor'd.

18.

Tho' distant, let the prospect charm,
And ev'ry gallant bosom warm,
Forbear each tear and sigh.
Turn from the ax the thought away,
'Tis Charles that bids us crown the day
And end the night in joy.

## *UPON THE TENTH OF JUNE*, 1747.[1]

Let universal mirth now rear its head,
And joy, exulting, o'er the nation spread.
Let all this day forget each anxious fear,
And cease to mourn the ills which Britons bear—
This day, which once auspicious to our Isle,
Did all its long expecting hopes fulfil,
Gave to the world Great Britain's glorious heir,
Th' accomplishment of vows and ardent pray'r.

The hero now in good old age appears,
By Heav'n propitious, brought to sixty years;
While all th' admiring world do justly own
Their present wonder, fix'd on him alone—
Him whom no pow'r can force, no art persuade *fol.* 398.
To shake that basis so securely laid
On inborn virtue, which maintains its reign
While all the storms of fortune rage in vain.
He thro' the dusky gloom more bright does shine,
And in the ambient cloud appears divine.
Remove the cloud, kind Heav'n, and shew that ray
Sparkling in brightest splendour of the day!
Content with trials of misfortunes past,
Allow deserved honours at the last!

Had I been born with Homer's fertil vein,
Or softer genius of the Mantuan swain,
To 've rais'd an Iliad in my sov'reign's praise,
And sing his fame in never-dying lays,
The world had first admir'd his manly state,
And wonder'd how he strove with adverse fate.
The future glories of our monarch now
Had swell'd my song, and made my numbers grow.
But tho' my muse does no such fire impart,
The mind is faithful and sincere the heart.

---

[1] The birthday of the Prince's father, the Old Chevalier, or as the Jacobites called him, King James the Eighth.

Then while in humble notes our joy we sing,
Paying our private homage to the king,
Bright Phœbus, gild each corner of the sky,
And with new lustre feed our dazled eye,
T' inspire our mirth and animate our joy.
But see, the face of Heav'n begins to frown,
*fol.* 399. The sullen, heavy day goes low'ring on.
The sun in mists and vapours hides his head,
And gloomy darkness o'er the world is spread.
Hear, Heav'n's hoarse voice runs murmuring thro' the sky,
And pales of horrid thunder dreadful fly.
Flashes of lightning thro' the air do gleam,
And Æther seems but one continued flame;
Clouds dash'd on clouds with utmost fury rend,
And on the drowned earth their watery ruines send.

Kind Heav'n! is this the pomp that thou dost raise?
This thy rejoicing on festival days?
To hear thy angry threats proclaim aloud
Thy dismal vengeance on the guilty crowd,
We kiss the hand from whence these terrors come,
And own our well-deserv'd and fatal doom.
We take the omen which thou 'rt pleased to give.
Our errors we repent. Then let us live.
Thou spurn'st to see this day neglected lie,
Another shining with vain pageantry.
Since then in anger once thou hast declar'd
That vice no more shall triumph with regard.
Let all the plagues of murder now be flung
On these curst bratts from whom our mischief sprung.

There 's ruffling work abroad, and hence must flow
Mutations here, th' usurper's overthrow.
Tho' at some distance, yet methinks I hear
Most pleasant news—the Restoration 's near.
Receive the off'rings which we humbly make;
Appease thy fury ere thy vengeance break.
Accept our penitence, and let us see
Our monarch glorious and our country free.

### *SOLILOQUY, September 29th*, 1746.

*fol.* 400.

29 Sept. 1746

This prop and that successively decays.
Strokes thicken ; each alarm my heart dismays,
Widow'd of ev'ry earthly flatt'ring joy.
Sorrows on sorrows roll without alloy.
My country bleeds, and in its ruines lie
Thousands. My all 's perhaps condemned to die.
Amaz'd, o'erwhelmed, without one cheering ray,
From those dread scenes, when shall I wing my way ?
To Thee, great God, I lift my fainting soul,
Who fierce, devouring passions canst controul.
Nature, convulsive, wrapt in furious forms,
Calms at thy word. Contend shall mortal worms ?
If partial ill promotes the gen'ral good,
'Tho' nature shrinks, I kiss the angry rod.
This, this alone, my spirits can sustain,
That thou supreme o'er all the world dost reign.
When I or mine, howe'er decreed to fall,
Shall turn to dust, be our eternal all.
Meanwhile, inspire with fortitude divine ;
In prisons and in death, thy face make shine.
Thy smiles, O God ! each trial can unsting,
And out of gall itself can sweetness bring.

O Liberty ! O Virtue ! O my Country !
Tell me, ye wise, now sunk in deep despair,
Where grows the med'cine for oppressive care ?
Where grows it not ? th' ingenious Pope replies ;
' To make the happy, friend, be good, be wise ;
Add only competence to health and peace,
You need no more to perfect happiness.'

O strangers to the sorrows of the mind, *fol.* 401.
The load of ills that oft afflicts mankind !
One chain of woes another still succeeds.
Our friends are martyr'd, and our country bleeds.

29 Sept. Humanity 's too weak these ills to bear;
Too plain a proof no happiness is here.
Must we, content, slavery's curse endure,
Nor bravely wish, nor once attempt a cure?
Will rebel-murderers from blood refrain?
Will corrupt statesmen liberty maintain?
Will Britain clear her long-contracted scores
On armies, fleets, for Hanover and whores?
Will justice flourish, will our trade increase,
Our fame grow greater, or our taxes less?

Bid things impossible in our natures rise!
Bid knaves turn honest, nay, bid fools turn wise!
Bid France keep faith! Bid England show her zeal,
And fight as well as wish to turn the scale!
Bid sympathy forsake my joyless breast,
Or miracles revive to give me rest!

In private life may happiness be found
With those who only live, or who abound?
Mark all estates, and shew me if you can,
What 's more precarious than the bliss of man.
Amidst his joys, uncertain to possess,
The fear of losing makes the pleasure less.
Thus one 's tormented with foreboding pain,
Another 's wretched thro' desire of gain.
Some who enjoy health, peace, and competence,
Are still unhappy; they 've but common sense.
*fol. 402.* The man of genius, brighter far and great,
Would gladly change for a genteel estate.

In ev'ry station discontent we see;
Each thinks his neighbour happier than he.
Search the world o'er, 'tis doubtful if you find
One man's condition fitted to his mind.
Alternate real or imagin'd woes
Disturb our life and all our joys oppose.

Nor can my muse the mournful tale avoid, 29 Sept.
What numbers zeal and brav'ry have destroy'd,
The gen'rous, faithful, uncorrupted band,
Design'd deliv'rers of a sinking land.
Tho' good, unfortunate; oppress'd, tho' brave;
See spiteful foes pursue them to the grave.
Unshaken loyalty is all their crime,
And struggling with their chains a second time.
For this they suffer worse than traitor's fate,
Condemned by knaves and furies of the state,
In loathsome dungeons close confin'd they lie,
To feel a thousand deaths before they die.
At last these heroes must resign their breath,
And close the scene with ignominious death.
Thus ev'n the best their virtue has undone,
And fix'd the slav'ry which they sought to shun.

How then shall man attain the state of bliss?
In t' other world he may, but not in this.
Unjustly, therefore, some we happy call. *fol. 403.*
More or less wretched is the fate of all.

*Upon the different Accounts of the behaviour of the two executed lords (Kilmarnock and Balmerino), taken out of an English Newspaper.*

If Ford and Foster haply disagree,
What is a trivial circumstance to me.
But this of their two heroes I remark,
Howe'er the historians leave us in the dark,
OLD ROUGH AND TUGGED much outmann'd the Earl,
And tho' mistaken was a steady carl.
The Earl's conversion is an obvious thing,
If not to Christ, at least to George our king.

*Arthurus, Dominus de Balmerino, decollatus* 18 *die Augusti* 1746, *ætatis suæ* 58. *By a Lady.*

Here lies the man, to Scotland ever dear,
Whose honest breast ne'er felt a guilty fear.

By principle, not mean self int'rest, sway'd,
The victor left to bring the vanquish'd aid;
His courage manly, but his words were few,
Content in poverty, and own'd it too.
In life's last scene with dignity appears,
Not for himself, but for his country, fears;
Pities the graceful partner of his fall,
And nobly wishes he might die for all.
*fol.* 404. Ev'n enemies, convinc'd, his worth approv'd:
He fell admir'd, lamented, and belov'd.

*The above turned into the form of an Inscription.*

Here lies Arthur, Lord Balmerino,
Whose memory will be ever dear to his country.
Religiously strict and judicious in the choice
Of his principles and maxims of life,
With an inflexible constancy was he attached to them.
He left the service of George, in which he bore some rank,
To join the sinking cause of the injured James,
After the woeful defeat at Dumblane.
He was a man of great personal courage
And remarkable modesty
In a corrupted age, asham'd of nothing but want.
He bore unmerited poverty with a Roman greatness of soul.
In the closing scene of life
He behaved with surprizing dignity,
Expressing a warm regard for his unhappy country
And vindicating his own honour and that of the injured Charles P.
Feelingly he express'd a generous concern for his companion,
And nobly wish'd he alone might suffer for the cause.
He triumphed over calumny, silenced his enemies
Struck with admiration at his uncommon intrepidity,
And fell admired, lamented, esteemed by all.

*Upon the same.*

Here Arthur lies, the rest forbear;
There may be treason in a tear.

Yet this bold soger may find room
Where scepter'd tyrants dare not come.

*Upon the death of Sir Alexander MacDonald,*[1] *etc.* *fol.* 405.

If Heav'n be pleas'd when sinners cease to sin;
If Hell be pleas'd when sinners enter in;
If earth be pleas'd to lose a truckling knave;
Then all are pleas'd—MacDonald 's in his grave.

*Spoken extempore on Lovat's Execution, by a lover of all those who will and dare be honest in the worst of times.*

None but the hangman, Murray,[2] or some tool,
Could from his heart say Lovat was a fool.
Yet ev'ry coxcomb will explain and teach
The chain of causes that surpass his reach.
When soft Kilmarnock,[3] trembling, came to bleed,
He fell a traitor and a wretch indeed.
His coward soul the canting preacher awes,
He weeps and dies a rebel to the cause.
'Twas hope of pardon; 'twas fanatick fear;
And none but Hanoverians dropt a tear.

Brave Balmerino, whom no words can paint,
Embrac'd his martyrdom and died a saint.
He sprang triumphant to a better state,
By all confest, superiour to his fate.

If Ratcliffe's[4] youthful crimes receiv'd their due, *fol.* 406.
Ratcliffe was steady, bold and loyal too.

---

[1] See f. 1829, where these lines are repeated.

[2] John Murray of Broughton (see f. 411 *et seq.*) became an evidence against his former associates, especially against Simon, Lord Lovat, who was executed at London on 9th April 1747, in his eightieth year, for being implicated in the Rebellion.

[3] William, fourth Earl of Kilmarnock, taken prisoner at Culloden and beheaded on Tower Hill, 18th August 1746.

[4] Charles Ratcliffe, brother of James, third Earl of Derwentwater, who was executed on 24th February 1716 for his share in the rebellion of 1715. At that time Charles had also been taken and condemned, but he escaped out of Newgate and went to France. In November 1745 he was recaptured on board the

This much be said, to palliate his offence,
Howe'er he liv'd, he died a man of sense.

But Frazer was a man by Heav'n decreed
Not quite so legible for fools to read.
Him in his manly labyrinth they mistook,
And partial to their wit the clue forsook.
He has no policy when none they find,
And is not visible when they are blind.
As the sun's course thro' various scenes does wind
From one great principle to one great end;
So did his actions, words and deeds combine
To perfect and accomplish one design.
For this alone he labours to be great;
For this he courts his honours and estate;
For this in secret he his faith conceals;
For this invents a plot and then reveals;
For this holds combat with domestick strife,
And seizes, like old Rome, a Sabine wife;
Wins confidence from artful foes by art,
And on the statesman plays the statesman's part.
The making one great stake, and that his last,
He ventures all on the important cast
On which the whole of 's happiness depends,
His life, his fortune, family and friends.
All, all 's too litttle for the glorious cause.
If he had won (for there the diff'rence lies),
That very crowd his triumph would attend
Who lately came, to view his noble end.

---

*Esperance* on his way to Scotland with other French officers to take part in the Rebellion, and after identification, he was condemned to suffer the sentence formerly passed upon him. He was accordingly executed on Tower Hill on 8th December 1746. He was a grandson of King Charles the Second, his mother being Mary Tudor, a natural daughter of that king.

*Upon a young lady, who died on seeing her lover,*[1] *Mr Dawson,*[2] *executed on the 30th of July* 1746. *fol.* 407.

As the fair martyr her dear lover saw
Lie the pale victim of inhuman law,
His gen'rous blood distilling all around,
And life, swift ebbing, thro' each crimson wound;
It seemed as if from mortal passion freed
She blest his death, for honour doom'd to bleed.
But when, high-raised, she saw the panting heart,
Now let thy handmaid, Heav'n! she cried, depart.
Be Judge, O Thou, whose ballance sways above!
Receive our souls to pardon and to love!
At once she burst the feeble bonds of clay,
And her free soul, exulting, springs away.
To endless bliss, they issue, out of pain.
One moment separates, and joins again.

*The Contrast set in its proper light. Said to be done by a lady.*

Fam'd were the bards of old untainted days,
When only merit felt the breath of praise.
When Heav'n-born muses taught the tuneful lay,
The brave to honour and the good display,
Virtue's fair form, tho' hid in rags, to sing,
And loath the baneful court and sinful king.

But now (sad change!) no more the poet's theme
Tastes thy chaste waters, Hippocrenè's stream.
His breast no more the sacred sisters urge, *fol.* 408.
Of truth the patrons and of vice the scourge.

[1] Not fact, for Mr. Dawson never saw her before she had come to glut herself with the bloody scene.—F.

[2] James Dawson, a young Lancashire man. He was being educated at St. John's College, Cambridge; but having misbehaved, and fearing expulsion, ran away. Dreading his father's displeasure, he, on falling in with the Manchester regiment, joined it and was taken at Carlisle. He was tried at London and executed on Kennington Common. The day before his death his father visited him, and took his farewell of him in a most pathetic scene. ['History of the Rebellion,' *Scots Magazine*, pp. 294, 297.]

Venal, he seeks the court, and shuns the lawn,
On pride to flatter and on pow'r to fawn;
Pour forth his incense at the country's shrine,
And raise th' usurping race to race divine.
He who would toil in Honour's ard'ous tract
Must virtue seek alone for virtue's sake,
For now to merit are unwonted things
The breath of poets and the smiles of kings.

See where the rhiming throng on William wait,
And patch up ev'ry worth to make him great;
Sing how he triumph'd on fair Clifton's Green,
And how his mind is lovely as his mien;
Call ancient heroes from their seat of joy,
To see their fame outshadow'd by a boy;
Rob ev'ry urn and ev'ry page explore,
And tell now Cæsar's deeds are deeds no more;
No more shall guide the war, nor fire the song,
But William be the theme of ev'ry tongue,
While Brunswick-kings Britannia's throne shall grace,
And George's virtues live in George's race.

Such is the theme the flatt'ring songsters chuse,
And oh, how worthy of the theme the muse!
While, lo! a youth arises in the north
Of royal virtues as of royal birth;
Of worth, which in the dawn of ages, shewn
Without the claim of birth, had gain'd a throne.
Tho' in him ev'ry grace and glory join
To add new lustre to the Stewart's line;
*fol. 409.* Tho' Vict'ry makes the youthful Charles her care,
No bard attends on his triumphal car.
On firmer base he builds his sure applause,
Recover'd freedom and protected laws.

Say, Scotland, say, for thou must surely know;
You felt the rapture, and you feel the woe.
Say, when he trode upon the kindly earth,
The genial soil which gave his fathers birth,

Did not his outstretched hand with bounty spread
Paternal blessings on thy children's heads ;
Hush them to peace amidst the din of war,
And still the matron's sigh and virgin's fear?
Bid peaceful plenty wave along the plain
The untouch'd harvest of the golden grain?
Did not the youth, enliven'd with his flame,
Glow for the fight and ardent pant for fame?
Strove not each rev'rend sage and hoary sire
His worth to honour and his sense admire?
Did not his form, with ev'ry beauty grac'd,
Raise a chaste rapture in each virgin's breast?
But when he quits the scene of soft delight,
The graceful measure for the deathful fight,
Say, saw thy plains (where many a deathless name,
Where Bruce, where Wallace, fought their way to fame,
Where Douglas, race heroick, nobly rose,
Secur'd thy freedom and expell'd thy foes)—
Saw they e'er one amongst the chieftain throng,
So ripe in glory and in years so young;
Whose pride not more to vanquish than to save,
In conquest gentle as in action brave?
Like Philip's son, victorious in the course
With skill superiour and inferiour force;
Like Xenophon, secure midst hostil bands, *fol.* 410.
He led his glorious few from distant lands,
And join'd to sense of head the fire of heart,
Of one the courage, and of one the art.

While virtue lives, while honour has a name,
While acts heroic fill the rolls of fame,
First in the list shall Gladesmuir have a place,
And Falkirk-plain, mark, Hawley! thy disgrace.
Now change the scene and show the sad reverse,
Where winter blasts th' autumnal smiles disperse;
Where the fierce Hanover directs the storm
And Hawley joys his mandates to perform.
To whom compar'd an Alva's name is sweet,
Brave in the field tho' cruel in the State.

See thro' the land how hostil fury burns
And peopled vales to rueful deserts turns!
See how the smoking country round thee groans,
Invokes in vain thy desolated towns!
See age unrev'renc'd, dragg'd from peaceful ease
And join'd in dreary jayls to loath'd disease!
Before their sires see ravished maids complain,
And raise their beaut'ous eyes to Heav'n in vain.
Oh! more than savage, who pursue their rage
On bloom of beauty and the hoar of age!

And what exploits exalt this hero's praise?
Where spring the laurels which your poets raise?
Spring they from conquest o'er the village tame,
The sire enfeebled and the aged dame.

*fol.* 411. View well this sketch and say of which the face
Presents the royal mark of Scotland's race.
He who would save thee from destruction's blast,
Or he who lays thy beauties in the dust?

So judg'd of old the good King David's heir
With nice discernment the deserving fair;
Repuls'd the dame who cruel would destroy,
And blest the feeling mother with her boy.

## *A CATCH*, 1746.

Here's a health to the King, the Prince and the Duke.
May all loyal subjects say—God bless the three!
Come weal or come woe, to my master I'll go,
And follow his standard, wherever it be.
I'll chear up my heart with a health to my master,
In hopes of another Dundee or Montrose.
I'm heartily griev'd for my Prince's disaster.
God save him, and send him the heart of his foes!

## To Mr. Secretary Murray, on his turning evidence. By the Rev. Mr. Thomas Drummond, Edinburgh, 1747.

*Quantum mutatus ab illo.*

To all that Virtue's holy ties can boast,
To truth and honour and to manhood lost,
How hast thou wand'red from the sacred road,
The paths of honesty, the pole to God?
O fallen! fallen from the high degree
Of spotless fame and pure integrity!
Where all that gallantry that fill'd your breast, *fol.* 412.
The pride of sentiment, the thought profest,
Th' unbiass'd principle, the gen'rous strain
That warm'd your blood, and beat in ev'ry vein?
All! all are fled! Once honest, steady, brave,
How great the change—to coward, traitor, knave!
O! hateful love of life that prompts the mind,
The godlike, great and good, to leave behind;
From wisdom's laws, from honour's glorious plan,
From all on earth that dignifies the man,
With steps unhallow'd wickedly to stray
And trust and friendship's holy bands betray.
Curs'd fear of death, whose bugbear terrors fright
Th' unmanly breast from suff'ring in the right
That strikes the man from th' elevated state,
From ev'ry character and name of great,
And throws him down beneath the vile degree
Of galley'd slaves, or dungeon villainy.

O Murray! Murray! once of truth approv'd,
Your Prince's darling, by his party lov'd;
When all were fond your worth and fame to raise,
And expectation spoke your future praise.
How could you sell that Prince, that cause, that fame,
For life enchain'd to infamy and shame?

See gallant ARTHUR,[1] whose undaunted soul
No dangers frighten, and no fears controul;
With unconcern the ax and block surveys,
And smiles at all the dreadful scene displays;
While undisturb'd his thoughts so steddy keep
He goes to death, as others go to sleep.
*fol.* 413. Gay midst their gibbets and devouring fire
What numbers hardy in the cause expire!
But what are these to thee? examples vain.
Yet see, and blush, if still the pow'r remain.
Behold the menial hand,[2] that broke your bread,
That wiped your shoes, and with your crumbs was fed;
When life and riches proffer'd to his view
Before his eyes the strong temptation threw,
Rather than quit integrity of heart,
Or act like you the unmanly traitor's part,
Disdains the purchase of a worthless life,
And bares his bosom to the butch'ring knife;
Each mean compliance gallantly denies,
And in mute honesty is brave and dies.
While you, tho' tutor'd from your early youth
To all the principles of steddy truth;
Tho' station, birth, and character conspire
To kindle in your breast the manly fire;
Friends, reputation, conscience, all disclaim.
To glory lost, and sunk in endless shame,
For the dull privilege to breathe the air,
For everlasting infamy declare,
And down to late posterity record
A name that's curs'd, abandon'd, and abhorr'd.

---

[1] Lord Balmerino.

[2] John MacNaughton, one of Murray's servants who, when he was upon the sledge, was offered his life and £30 or £40 sterling *per annum* during life, provided he would turn evidence. He answered that they had done him much honour in ranking him with gentlemen, and he hoped to let the world see he would suffer like a gentleman. He suffered at Carlisle, October 18th, 1746, in company with the Rev. Mr. Coppoch, Arnprior, Kinlochmoidart, Major MacDonell, etc. ROBERT FORBES, A.M.

Go, wretch! enjoy the purchase you have gain'd. *fol. 414.*
Scorn and reproach your ev'ry step attend.
By all mankind neglected and forgot
Retire to solitude, retire and rot.
But whither? whither can the guilty fly
From the devouring worms that never die;
Those inward stings that rack the villain's breast,
Haunt his lone hours and break his tortur'd rest?
Midst caves, midst rocks and deserts you may find
A safe retreat for all the human kind.
But to what foreign region can you run,
Your greatest enemy, yourself, to shun?
Where'er thou go'st, wild anguish and despair
And black remorse attend with hideous stare;
Tear your distracted soul with torments fell,
Your passions devils, and your bosom hell.

Thus may you drag your heavy chain along,
Some minutes more inglorious life prolong.
And when the fates shall cut a coward's breath,
Weary of being, yet afraid of death;
If crimes like thine hereafter are forgiv'n,
Judas and Murray both may go to Heav'n.

## Satan transformed into an Angel of Light, or copy of a Letter from Mr. Evidence Murray, to his nephew, Sir David Murray, of seventeen or eighteen years of age, in jayl in the city of York, 1747. *fol. 415.*

The pleasure it gave me to hear that the king had been graciously pleased to grant you a reprieve, was far greater than the world could perhaps be willing to imagine for one in my situation, as mankind is most apt to be concerned about their own misfortunes. As I look upon it as my duty to give you the best advice in my power, I would not fail to lay hold on the liberty granted me to observe some few things which I hope may be of service to you, when I may not have an opportunity to advise you by word of mouth.

I must first observe that the grace shown you must have proceeded entirely from a greatness of soul and a compassion of your youth, as it was not in the least in your power to atone for the offence. I know that you are brave, and I have no doubt but you are generous, the latter being ever looked upon as a concomitant of the former. Gratitude has always
*fol.* 416. been esteemed one of the greatest virtues, and its opposite regarded in so vile a light that the antient Spartans punished it with death. Don't allow yourself to be too much elevated, but consider coolly on the uneasiness you have felt, and thereby judge of the favour you have received.

I hear there are zealots in the world who would willingly make mankind believe that they act from principle alone, and even would wish to die martyrs for their cause; and their lofty notions are ready to gain even on those of riper years. But be assured that at the bottom it is self-interest prevails. They only intend to promote their own ambitious views without the least regard to the welfare and happiness of others. Pull off their mask and they appear in their native dress. Some such you may meet with. But always remember the story of the cat and the monkey; for depend upon it, when your hands are
*fol.* 417. in the fire they will hug themselves on being safe. That there ever have been such men is past dispute, and had there been none such, that you and I would not have been in our present situation is as undeniable. I shall now say a little to what I know is a tender point, but nevertheless may be gently touch'd.[1]

There are a certain set of men who can confine salvation to their Church alone; but though I am no divine I cannot help thinking it absurd to imagine that God Almighty made mankind to damn nine out of ten, which must be the case, if their maxim holds true. Our blessed Saviour died for both Jew and Gentile. But I will not insist upon the subject, as you may guess my meaning, and I hope will not fail to consider seriously of it. I could, and indeed I incline to say a good
*fol.* 418. deal more, but that I don't care to crowd too many thoughts upon you all at once, so shall only further assure you that I am sincerely, A PRODIGY OF WICKEDNESS.

[1] Sir David Murray was bred Popish.

## Copy of the Prince's Summons to the City of Edinburgh to surrender. Directed to the Lord Provost, Magistrates, and Town Council of Edinburgh. 16 Sept. 1745

Being now in a condition to make our way into this capital of his Majesty's ancient kingdom of Scotland, we hereby summon you to receive us, as you are in duty bound to do. And in order to it we hereby require you upon receipt of this to summon the Town Council and take proper measures in it for securing the peace and quiet of the city, which we are very desirous to protect. But if you suffer any of the Usurper's troops to enter the town, or any of the canon, arms, or amunition now in it, whether belonging to the publick or to private persons, to be carried off, we shall take it as a breach of your duty and a heinous offence against the king and us, and shall fol. 419 resent it accordingly. We promise to preserve all the rights and liberties of the city, and the particular property of every one of his Majesty's subjects. But if any opposition be made to us we cannot answer for the consequences, being firmly resolved at any rate to enter the city, and in that case, if any of the inhabitants are found in arms against us, they must not expect to be treated as prisoners of war.

(Signed) Charles, Prince Regent.

*From our Camp,* 16*th September* 1745.

Upon the magistrates receiving the above, the inhabitants 16 Sept 1745 were called together and almost unanimously agreed to surrender the town, and sent deputies out to the Prince to treat with him, viz., Baillies Gavin Hamilton, John Yetts, and David Inglis, and James Norrie, Deacon Convener, to whom the Prince caused deliver the following answer.

His royal Highness the Prince Regent thinks his Manifesto and the King, his father's, Declaration, already published, are a sufficient capitulation for all his Majesty's subjects to accept fol. 420

16 Sept. of with joy. His present demands are to be received into the city as the son and representative of the king, his father, and obeyed as such when he is there.

His Royal Highness supposes that since the receipt of his letter to the provost and magistrates no arms or ammunition have been suffered to be carried off or concealed, and will expect a particular account of all things of that nature.

Lastly, he expects a positive answer to this before 2 o'clock in the morning, otherwise he will find himself obliged to take measures conform. By his Highness's command,

(Sign'd) John Murray.

*At Gray's Mill*, 16 *September* 1745.

17 Sept. 1745 After this a second deputation was sent to the Prince, viz., Provost Coutts and Baillie Robert Baillie, who brought the following answer.

His Royal Highness has already given all the assurances he can that he intends to exact nothing of the city in general, nor
*fol.* 421. of any in particular, but what his character of Regent entitles him to. This he repeats, and renews his summons to the magistrates to receive him as such. By His Highness's command, (Sign'd) John Murray.

*Gray's Mill*, 3 *o'clock in the Morning*,
*Tuesday*, 17 *September* 1745.

## A Narrative[1] given me by Mr. Alexander Murray, Printer, in Burnet's Close, Edinburgh.

About the beginning of July 1746 one Garnet, a dragoon in Lord Mark Ker's regiment, and son of one Garnet, a printer at Sheffield, came to the printing house of William Sands and Company at Edinburgh, and having been asked several questions in relation to the battle of Culloden, said: That he

[1] See ff. 375, 707, 1087, 1323, 1376.

himself was engaged there; that the orders they received were July. *To make no prisoners:* That the reason of this severity was that the Duke had got notice before the armies were engaged that the rebels had given orders—To kill men, women, and children of their enemies, without distinction, for eight days after the battle, in case victory should declare for them; that *fol.* 422. he himself went to the field of battle the day after the engagement in the forenoon; that on coming near it, he heard a doleful noise; that on coming to the place he found that the noise he had heard was several of the wounded rebels who had crawled together were bemoaning one another's condition; that in a short while after he saw some small parties of the king's troops with officers on their head go through the field and shoot the wounded rebels; that six or eight of the soldiers fired together at different rebels, but did not receive the word of command from their officers, though they stood by and saw the service performed; that they went thro' the field thus; that some of the rebels seemed pleased to be relieved of their pain by death, while others begged of the soldiers to spare them, which, however, was no ways regarded; that the soldiers employed in this service were foot, so that he himself was only a spectator; that soldiers went, a day or two after to the field and did the like; that such severity would not have been exercised against *fol.* 423. a foreign enemy, and that at this time the French were treated with great humanity, as they are said to be remarkably human when conquerors; and that a written order was said to be found in the pocket of one of the rebels after the battle agreeing with the accounts above mentioned which the Duke had received before the engagement. This dragoon who named and designed himself as above seemed to be a discreet, ingenuous man.

*Edinburgh, October 30th,* 1746.

An officer of the Broadalbine Militia (who was among those 30 Oct. 1746 who made openings in the stone walls, through which the dragoons passed) being told the above, did not believe it, and gave as his reason that a præmium having been given for every gun and sword brought to the king's camp after the battle, the men under his command were so busied in carrying guns and swords from the field of battle to the camp that he could

30 Oct. scarcely keep a sufficient number of them to do duty, and yet
*fol.* 424. he never heard of the rebels being thus killed in cold blood, which, being a thing very uncommon, he thought his men could not miss to observe and to tell him of it. This gentleman added, that he heard at that time of the order of the rebels for giving no quarter; that a particular serjeant in a certain regiment was said to have it; that he asked it of him, but was answered he heard another serjeant had it, and went to two or three thus, and always found less reason to believe there ever was any such order.

8 Oct. 1747 *N.B.—Edinburgh, October 8th, Thursday,* 1747.

I visited Mr. Alexander Murray, printer, out of whose hand I received a copy of the above in his own hand-writ, and from which I have faithfully made the above transcript. The copy in Mr. Murray's hand-writ is to be found among my papers. Mr. Murray is the person who conversed with the dragoon and the Broadalbine officer in presence of Mr. James Cochran, co-
*fol.* 425. partner in business with Mr. Murray. The said Mr. Cochran vouched to me the truth of the above narrative in every ace of it, as given by the dragoon and the officer.

Robert Forbes, A.M.

14 Nov. 1746

## Copy of a Letter from Charles Gordon of Terperse[1] to his own lady.

Dear Heart,—I now tell you that I suffer death to-morrow for my duty to God, my king, and country. I bless God I

[1] He was 'Younger of Terpersie' in Aberdeenshire, and had engaged as a volunteer. His father, James Gordon, was an officer in the Prince's army. In the *List of Persons concerned in the Rebellion, etc.* (Scot. Hist. Soc., vol. viii.), he is said to have been *made prisoner at Carlisle.* But a story is told of his having been captured at his own house, when, after lurking long among the neighbouring hills, he ventured to pass a night there. His captors, not being sure of his identity, carried him before the minister of the parish, but not getting satisfaction from him, they took him to a farmhouse where his wife and children resided. On his approach his children ran out and greeted him with cries of 'Daddy! Daddy!' and so unwittingly sealed their father's fate. He was tried at Carlisle and executed there on 15th November 1746. As the prisoners taken at Carlisle were sent to London, and those taken in Scotland to Carlisle, the story may be authentic.

die in charity with all men. I think my butchered body will be taken care of and buried as a Christian, by order of Francis Farquharson, who has acted a father to me, and laid out a good deal of money to and for me, whereof you may expect a particular account, which I leave you on my blessing to repay him. I die with the greatest regret that I've been a bad husband to you, and I beg you'll pardon me in your heart, and that you'll express your goodness (as you'll answer to God and me in the everlasting world) by your care of and motherly looking to your children's salvation and right putting them to business in this world. I know not how many are alive; only set the boys to some right imployment while young, and strive to admonish the daughters in the fear of God. I herewith send you a note of what I would have done with the trifles I have a concern in, for you know the lump of my business. 14 Nov. *fol.* 426.

My dearest,—If I should write till my life ends I would still have something to say. But to stop that I end with my dying blessing to you, my young ones, and your poor mother, if alive. Your last from, your unfortunate husband,

CHA. GORDON.

*Carlisle, November 14th*, 1746.

## Copy of a Letter which served to cover the above to LADY TERPERSE from MR. PATRICK GORDON, Presbyterian preacher at Rhynie.

26 Jan. 1747

MADAM,—The inclosed came to me two or three days ago, and I intended to have delivered it to you with my own hand. But as I cannot travel so far for some days by reason of necessary business in my parish, I thought proper, rather than delay it any longer, to transmit it in this manner. My correspondent is a gentlewoman that lives in the neighbourhood of Carlisle, who saw Terperse every day for some time before his death, and says he died as became a truly penitent Christian, to the conviction of all the clergy and others that conversed with him. She writes me that one Wright, by orders from Mr. Farquharson, provided a coffin for his body; that she gave *fol.* 427.

26 Jan. such grave-cloaths as are usual, put them on, and saw him buried in St. Culbert's Churchyard. So that you and all your relations are very much obliged to this gentlewoman. She
fol. 428. desires me further to acquaint you that he never received any letter from you nor any remittance; and the letter I wrote, giving him an account of you and your children did not reach Carlisle till after his death; that she has his stock-buckle, buttons, and a book he left to his son, Charles, which she is ready to send to Edinburgh to any person you shall name there, which you may do by me when you please, for I intend to write her soon. Terperse mentions some note or account in his letter; but it did not come to my hand, nor does my correspondent write anything about it. I am, Madam, your most humble servant, (*Sic subscribitur*) PAT. GORDON.

*Rhynie, January 26th*, 1747.

## fol. 429. Copy of a Letter, said to be written by LORD GEORGE MURRAY or one of his friends, 1746.[1]

IN answer to what you write about the Highland army having not behaved with their usual bravery, or that some of their principal officers had not done their duty, which might be the occasion of their late misfortune, I must inform you by all I can learn, the men showed the utmost eagerness to come to action, nor did I hear of any one officer but behaved well, so far as the situation and circumstances would allow. The truth seems to be that they were overpowered by a superiour force, and their field of battle was ill-chosen, which gave the Duke of Cumberland great advantages, especially in his canon and horse. Another misfortune they lay under was a total want of provisions, so that they were reduced to the hard necessity either of fighting an army a third stronger, or to starve or disperse. As to what happened the day of the battle and the preceding day, I shall let you know
fol. 430. what I could learn.

---

[1] This letter is printed in the *Lockhart Papers*, vol. ii. pp. 523-536.

On the fifteenth, all those of the Highland army as were assembled were drawn up in line of battle upon a moor south from Culloden, facing eastwards. This was done early in the morning, as it was known that the Duke of Cumberland was come to Nairn the night before; but as he did not move before mid-day, it was judged he would not march that day, it being his birthday; and as his troops had made no halt from the time he left Aberdeen, it was reasonable to think he would give them a day's rest. It was then proposed to make a night attack upon the Duke of Cumberland's army in their camp, which, if it could be done before one or two o'clock in the morning, might (though a desperate attempt) have had a chance of succeeding. Several of the officers listened to this, as they knew the Duke of Cumberland was much superiour to the Highland army. The objection to it was that a great many of the army had not as yet joined, particularly Keppoch, the Master of Lovat, Cluny, Glengyle, the Mackenzies, and many of the recruits of Glengary and other regiments, which were all expected in two or three days, and some of them sooner; that if they should fail in the attempt and be repulsed, it would not be easy rallying the Highlanders in the dark; that if the Duke of Cumberland was alarm'd by any of his patrollers, he might have time to put his army in order in the camp (I suppose no spy should give timely notice), and place his canon charged with cartouch shot as he had a mind, and his horse might be all in readiness so as to pursue, if the Highlanders had been beat off; and lastly, the difficulty of making their retreat with perhaps a good many wounded men, whom the Highlanders will never leave, be it possible to bring them off. It is to be remarked that there was no intelligence of the enemy's camp. Add to this, how fatiguing it would be to march backwards and forwards twenty miles, and probably be obliged to fight next day; nor could they make their retreat safe and not be attacked before they joined the rest of the army. 15 April. *fol.* 431.

On the other hand the Prince was vastly bent for the night-attack, and said he had men enow to beat the enemy, whom he believed utterly dispirited, and would never stand a bold and brisk attack. The Duke of Perth, Lord John Drummond, *fol.* 432.

15 April. with others, seemed to wish it; and Lord George Murray, Lochgary, with many others, were induced to make a fair trial what could be done, though they were very sensible of the danger should it miscary. They observed with much concern the want of provisions. The men had only got that day a biscuit each, and some not even that.[1] It was feared it would prove worse next day, except they could take provisions from the enemy; and they had reason to believe if the men were allowed to disperse to shift for some meat (which many of them would do if the army continued there all night), that it would be very difficult to assemble them in the event of a sudden alarm, which, considering the nearness of the enemy, might very reasonably be supposed; and as they must have layen that night in the muirs near Culloden, as they had done the night before, they knew many of them would disperse
*fol.* 433. without liberty to several miles distance for provisions and quarters, and that it would be far in the day before they could be assembled again; and as Keppoch came up and joined the army that afternoon, they flattered themselves that the men they had might do if they could have made the attack by one or two in the morning, especially if they were undiscovered, as they had great hopes they might. For having examined the different roads, of which they had perfect intelligence from the MacIntoshes, who lived in those very parts, they found they could keep upon a muir the whole way so as to shun the houses, and be a considerable way from the highroad that leads from Inverness to Nairn. They also considered that in the event of making the attack, should they even be beat off without the desired success, they might before daybreak get back the length of Culcarick,[2] which was very strong ground, and from thence by a hill they could retire the whole way on the south side of the water of Nairn, till they were joined by their friends whom
*fol.* 434. they expected and by the stragglers. Nor did they believe the enemy would follow them (suppose the Highlanders were beat back) till it were good daylight, so as they could see about them and send out reconnoitering parties to prevent

---

[1] See ff. 157, 659.

[2] So the copy had it, but I think it should be Culraick.—Robert Forbes, A.M.

their falling into ambuscades and snares. And before all this could be done, the Highland army might have reached Culcarick,[1] and the hilly ground on the south side of the water above-mentioned, where regular troops could not easily overtake them, and where their canon and horse (in which their greatest superiority consisted) would have been of little use. That they found the Prince was resolved to fight the enemy without waiting for the succours that were soon expected, and without retiring to any strong ground, or endeavouring to draw the Duke of Cumberland's army farther from the sea, from whence he got all his provisions, that was brought about in ships which sailed along it as his army marched near the shore. 15 April.

For these reasons the gentlemen and most others, if not all, who were spoke to upon the subject, seemed to think the *fol.* 435. night attack might be attempted. But most of them thought they were in very bad circumstances at any rate, and no attempt could be more desperate than their present situation. Lord George Murray, about mid-day, desired Brigadier Stapleton and Colonel Ker to cross the Water of Nairn near where the army was drawn up (not far from the place where the battle was fought next day) to take a view of the hill ground on the south side of the water, which to him appeared to be steep and uneven, consequently much properer for Highlanders, for the ground they were drawn up upon was a large plain muir; and though in some places it was interspersed with bogues and deep ground, yet for the most part it was a fair field, and good for horse. After two or three hours, they returned and reported that the ground was rough and rugged, mossy and soft, so that no horse could be of use there; that the ascent from the water side was steep; and that there was about two or three places in about three or four miles where horse could cross, the banks being inaccessible. *fol.* 436. They could not tell what sort of ground was at a greater distance, but the country people informed them it was much like the other. Upon this information Lord George Murray proposed that the other side of the water should be the place

[1] Scored through and 'Culraick' substituted.—[Ed.]

15 April. for the army to be drawn up in line of battle next day; but this was not agreed to. It was said it was like shunning the enemy, being a mile further from the muir they were then upon and at a greater distance from Inverness, which it was resolved not to abandon, a great deal of baggage and ammunition being left there. This was before the resolution was taken of making the night attack. About seven at night an incident happened which had liked to have stopt their designed attempt, and upon it many were for giving it up as impracticable. The thing was this. Numbers of men went off to all sides, especially towards Inverness, and when the officers who were sent on horseback to bring them back came
*fol.* 437. up with them, they could by no persuasion be induced to return again, giving for answer—they were starving; and said to the officers they might shoot them if they pleased, but they could not go back till they got meat. But the Prince continued keen for the attack, and positive to attempt it, and said there was not a moment to be lost; for as soon as the men should see the march begun, not one of them would flinch. It was near eight at night when they moved, which could not be sooner, otherwise they might have been perceived at a considerable distance, and the enemy have got account of their march. Lord George Murray was in the van, Lord John Drummond in the centre, and the Duke of Perth towards the rear, where also the Prince was, having Fitz-James's horse and others with him. Proper directions were given for small parties possessing all the roads, that intelligence might not be carried to the enemy. There were about two officers and thirty men of the MacIntoshes in the front as guides, and
*fol.* 438. some of the same were in the centre and rear, and in other parts, for hindering any of the men from straggling. Before the van had gone a mile, which was as slow as could be to give time to the line to follow, there was express after express sent to stop them, for that the rear was far behind. Upon this the van marched still slower, but in a short time there came aide-de-camps and other officers to stop them, or at least make them go slower; and of these messages I am assured there came near an hundred before the front got near Culraick, which retarded them to such a degree that the night was far

spent: for from the place the army began to march to 16 April.
Culraick was but six miles, and they had still four long miles to Nairn. It was now about one o'clock in the morning, when Lord John Drummond came up to the van and told there were several far behind; and, if they did not stop or go slower, he was afraid the rear would not get up. In a little time the Duke of Perth came also to the front, and assured *fol.* 439.
that if there was not a halt the rear could not join. There was a stop accordingly. Lochiel had been mostly in the van all night, and his men were next the Athol men, who were in the front. These two bodies made about twelve hundred men. There were also several other officers that came up, there being a defile a little way behind occasioned by a wall of the wood of Culraick, which also retarded the march of those that were behind. The officers, talking of the different places of making the attack, said it was better to make the attempt with four thousand men before daybreak, as with double the number after it was light. Mr. O'Sullivan now having come up to the front, and it being now evident by the time the army had taken to march little more than six miles it would be impossible to make the other part of the road—which was about four miles—before it was clear day-light, besides the time that must be spent in making the disposition for the *fol.* 440.
attack, as it could not be done by the army in the line by their long march. Mr. O'Sullivan said he had just then come from the Prince, who was very desirous the attack should be made; but as Lord George Murray had the van, and could judge the time, he left it to him whether to do it or not.

There were several volunteers present, who had walked all night in the front, such as Mr. Hepburn, Mr. Hunter, Mr. Anderson, and others; and as the Duke of Perth, Lord John Drummond, and other officers seemed to be much difficulted what to resolve upon, Lord George Murray desired the rest of the gentlemen to give their opinions, for they were all deeply concerned in the consequence. It was agreed upon all hands that it must be sun-rise before the army could reach Nairn and form, so as to make an attempt upon the enemy's camp; for one part was to have passed the water a mile above the town, to have fallen upon them towards the sea-side. The *fol.* 441. 16 April. volunteers were all very keen to march. Some of them said that the red-coats would be all drunk, as they surely had solemnised the Duke of Cumberland's birth-day; and that, though it were day-light, they would be in such confusion they would not withstand the Highlanders.

This opinion shewed abundance of courage, for these gentlemen would have been in the first rank had there been any attack. But the officers were of different sentiments, as severals of them expressed.[1] Lochiel and his brother said they had been as much for the night attack as anybody could be, and it was not their fault that it had not been done; but blamed those in the rear that had marched so slow, and retarded the rest of the army. Lord George Murray was of the same way of thinking, and said, if they could have made the attack, it was the best chance they had, especially if they could have surprized the enemy. But to attack a camp that was near double their number in day-light, when they would
*fol.* 442. be prepared to receive them, would be perfect madness.

By this time Mr. John Hay came up and told the line was joined. He was told the resolution was taken to return. He began to argue upon the point, but nobody minded him. This was the gentleman the army blamed for the distress they were in for want of provisions, he having had the superintendency of all these things from the time of Mr. Murray's illness, who had always been extremely active in whatsoever regarded the providing for the army. It was about two o'clock in the morning (the halt being not above a quarter of an hour) when they went back in two columns, the rear facing about, and the van taking another way. At a little distance they had a view of the fires of the Duke of Cumberland's camp; and, as they did not shun passing near houses as they had done in advancing, they marched very quick. Day-light began to
*fol.* 443. appear about an hour after. They got to Culloden pretty early, so that the men had three or four hours' rest. They killed what cattle or sheep they could find; but few of them had time to make anything ready before the alarm came of the enemy's being upon their march and approaching. The

[1] See ff. 158, 661, 1270.

horse of the Prince's army had been all on such hard duty for several days and nights before that none of them were fit for patroling. At that time, Fitz-James's horse and several others had gone to Inverness to refresh, so at first it was not known whether it was an advanced party or the Duke of Cumberland's whole army. However, the Highlanders got ready as quick as possible, and marched through the parks of Culloden in battalions (just as they chanced to be lying) to the muir on the south side, facing eastwards, and about half a mile farther back than where they had been drawn up the night before. Lord George Murray proposed once more to pass the Water of Nairn, as being the strongest ground, and much the fitter for Highlanders. Cluny, who was expected every moment, was to come on that side; but it was not agreed upon for the same reason given the day before. Lord George, speaking to Mr. O'Sullivan, he told him that he was afraid the enemy would have great advantage in that plain muir, both in their horse and canon. But he, O'Sullivan, answered that he was sure horse could be of no use, because there were several bogues and morasses; but the event proved otherwise. Mr. O'Sullivan drew up the army in line of battle (he being both adjutant and quarter-master-general), and having shown every battalion their place, the right closed to some inclosures near the Water of Nairn, and the left towards the parks of Culloden. I cannot justly tell what order they were drawn up in. There had been some disputes a day or two before about their rank, but nobody that had any regard for the common cause would insist upon such things upon that occasion. Those who had gone off the night before and early that morning to Inverness and other parts had now joined, and the Master of Lovat was come up with a considerable recruit of his men. It was observed that upon the right there were park walls, under cover of which so many of the enemy could draw up and flank the Highlanders. Lord George Murray, who commanded that wing, was very desirous to have advanced and thrown them down; but as this would have broke the line, and the enemy forming their line of battle near that place, it was judged by those about him too dangerous to attempt.

16 April

*fol.* 444.

*fol.* 445.

Both armies being fully formed, the canonading began on

16 April. both sides, after which there was some small alteration made
in the disposition of the two armies by bringing troops from
the second line to the first, as both the ends advanced to out-
flank one another. The Highlanders were much galled by
the enemy's canon and were turned so impatient that they
*fol.* 446. were like to break their ranks. Upon which it was judged
proper to attack, and orders were given accordingly. The
right wing advanced first as the whole line did much at the
same time. The left wing did not attack the enemy, at least
did not go in sword in hand, imagining they would be flanked
by a regiment of foot and some horse, which the enemy brought
up at that time from their second line or corps de reserve.
When the right wing were within pistol-shot of the enemy
they received a most terrible fire not only in front but also in
flank by reason of those that were posted near the stone walls,
notwithstanding of which they went on sword in hand, after
giving their fire close to the enemy, and were received by them
with their spontoons and bayonets. The two regiments of
foot that were upon the enemy's left would have been cut to
pieces had they not been immediately supported by other two
regiments from their second line. As it was, these two regi-
*fol.* 447. ments (being Barrel's and that called Monroe's) had by their
own confession above two hundred men killed and wounded.
Two regiments of dragoons coming in upon the same side
entirely broke that wing of the Highlanders, and though three
battalions of the right of the second line were brought up and
gave their fire very well, yet the ground and everything else
was so favourable for the enemy that nothing could be done but
a total route ensued.

I am positively informed that the Highland army did not consist of above seven thousand fighting men,[1] and that the Duke of Cumberland's must have been ten or twelve thousand. In the one army there were not above an hundred and fifty horse, of which one half was of the regiment of Fitz-James. In the other army they had eleven or twelve hundred.

When a misfortune happens people are apt to throw the
blame upon persons or causes, which frequently are either
*fol.* 448. the effect of malice or ignorance, without knowing the real
springs and motives. Severals are of opinion that the night

[1] See ff. 128, 1275.

attack could have been made, but I am convinced of the contrary for the following reasons. The Highland army, when they halted near Culraick, were not above five thousand men. They had four miles to march, and part of them were obliged to have made a considerable circumference so that it would have been sun-rise before they could have made the attack. The ground about Nairn where the enemy lay encamped was a hard, dry soil, and plain muirs three miles round about except where the sea intervened; the nearest strong and uneven ground being the wood of Culraick. Let it be supposed the Highlanders had made an attack in the broad day-light upon an enemy double their number in their camp, who were well refreshed with a day and two nights' rest, with plenty of all kinds of provisions, with their canon pointed as they thought proper, their horse drawn up to their wish in a fine plain, what must the consequence have been? What would have been said of officers that led on men in such circumstances and such a situation? Would it not have been certain death and destruction of all those that made the attack? Would it not have been said and justly said, Why go you on in such a desperate attempt seeing it could not be done by surprize and undiscovered as projected? Why not try the chance of a fair battle by returning and being joined by the rest of the army as well as by those who had withdrawn the night before, and a great many others who were hourly expected; where also they might have canon and choice of the field of battle? By this means there was a fair chance, by others there was none.

16 Apr

*fol.* 449

As to the above-mentioned facts you may rely upon them. I saw the Duke of Perth, the Duke of Athol, Lord John Drummond, Lord George Murray, Lord Ogilvie, Colonel Stewart of Ardshiel, Colonel Roy Stewart, Lord Nairn, and several others, at Ruthven of Badenoch on the Friday two days after the battle, and they all agreed on the same things. *fol.* 450

One thing I must take notice of, that from the beginning of the whole affair there never had been the least dispute[1] or

[1] I am afraid this is not fact, for disputes and canglings arose even in the Abbey at Edinburgh, and I have heard some affirm, who had an opportunity of knowing, that these were owing to the haughty, restless, unaccountable temper of Lord George Murray, some of whose blood-relations fail not to lay blame upon

April. misunderstanding among the officers. Some find fault that the night march was undertaken seeing there was not a certainty of marching to Nairn time enough to make the attack before day-light, as also that they had too few men.

In answer to this. It was not doubted when the march was begun but that there would be abundance of time. Their greatest precaution was not to be discovered. The Highlanders had often made very quick marches in the night-time. The French piquets I believe were in the rear and were not so clever in marching, and the muir they went through was more splashy than they expected, and they were obliged to make some turns to shun houses, and there were two or three dykes that took
*fol.* 451. up a good deal of time to pass. The guides though they knew the ground very well, yet were not judges to tell what time it would take to march the ten miles, as they were called, though by reason of the indirect road, must be more. Notwithstanding of all this I am persuaded most of the army (had not the van been frequently stopt and retarded by repeated orders and messages) would have been at Nairn by two o'clock in the morning. As for the number of men, though not half that of the enemy, they might very probably have succeeded in the attempt had they made the attack undiscovered. Nothing is more uncertain than the events of war. Night attacks are most subject to disappointments. This march and countermarch, to be sure, was, as things turned out, a great disadvantage. It fatigued the men much, and a council of war might have been obtained in which doubtless a resolution would have been taken to chuse a more advantagious field of
*fol.* 452. battle and perhaps postpon'd fighting for a day till the succours that were coming up with the utmost expedition should join. Councils of war were seldom held and were out of request[1]

him. Witness likewise the contest betwixt Keppoch and Lochiel about the right hand before they went out to fight Cope, a particular account of which dispute I had from Major MacDonald in the Castle of Edinburgh.

ROBERT FORBES, A.M.

[1] No wonder that councils of war were out of request, when the Prince was always thwarted in them, and hardly got his will in anything he proposed, though his opinion of things in the event turned out to be the most eligible. Lord George Murray was at the head of the opposition, having got the ascendant of the greater part of the chiftains, and having insinuated himself into the good

from the time the army marched into England. I remember April but of two that were held, the one at Brampton in regard of besieging Carlisle or going to attack General Wade. The other was at Carlisle, where it was resolved to march forwards. What happened at Derby was accidental by most of the officers being at the Prince's quarters, and taking into consideration their situation, they were all unanimous in advising the Prince to retreat. I think there was but one council of war called after they returned to Scotland, and that was near Crieff, the day after the retreat from Stirling, where there was some *fol.* 453 difference of opinion, but it was at last agreed to march for Inverness in two separate bodies, the one the Highland road, and the other by the coast, severals at first being for the army all going one road. The day of the battle of Falkirk the officers were called on the field where the army was drawn up betwixt Bannockburn and the Torwood, and all agreed immediately to march to the enemy; also the retreat from Stirling, it was advised by many of the principal officers, particularly the clans. They drew up the reasons and sign'd them at Falkirk three days before the retreat was made, the chief of which was that a vast number of men had gone off after the battle, and were not returned, and that the siege of Stirling Castle was not advancing; they did not think it advisable to fight in such circumstances.

This letter has been much longer than I intended. But *fol.* 454 before I conclude I must acquaint you that six weeks before the battle of Culloden some officers proposed sending up meal to several parts of the Highlands, and in particular to Badenoch, that in the event of the Duke of Cumberland's army marching towards Inverness before the army was gathered they might retreat for a few days till they could assemble; or if a misfortune should happen by a defeat there might be some provisions in these parts. But this was reckoned a timorous advice and rejected as such, though I have reason to believe that the opinion of mostly all the Highland officers was much

---

graces of all the clans who were ever ready to embrace his schemes. Besides, it was most unlucky that great jealousies and misunderstandings had arisen betwixt Lord George Murray and the French officers. These things are too notour to admit of any denial.—ROBERT FORBES, A.M.

April. the same. There was no doubt the Highlanders could have
avoided fighting till they had found their advantages. In so
doing they could have made a summer campaign without
running the risque of any misfortune. They could have
marched through the hills to places in Aberdeenshire, Banff-
*fol.* 455. shire, the Merns, Angus, Perthshire, or Argyleshire by ways
that no regular troops could have followed them; and if the
regular troops had continued among the mountains they must
have been attended with great difficulties and expence. Their
convoys might have been cut off, and opportunities offered to
have attacked them with almost a certainty of success. And
though the Highlanders had neither money nor magazines
they could not have starved in that season of the year, so long
as there were any sheep or cattle to be had. They could also
have separated into two or three different bodies, got meal for
some days' provision, met again at a place appointed, and have
attacked the enemy where was least expected. They could
have marched in three days what would have taken regular
troops five. Nay, had these taken the high roads (as often
they would have been obliged to do upon account of their
*fol.* 456. carriages) it would have taken them ten or twelve. In short,
they would have been so harrassed and fatigued, that they
must have been in the greatest distress and difficulties; and
at the long run probably been destroyed. At least, much
might have been expected by gaining of time. Perhaps
such succours might have come from France as would have
made the Highlanders to have made an offensive instead of a
defensive war. This I saw was the opinion of many of the
officers who considered the consequences of losing a battle.
They knew well that few of the Highlanders would join heartily
against them, as long as they continued entire, but would upon
a defeat. There was one great objection to this, that the Irish
officers, who were all as brave men and zealous in the cause as
possibly could be, and many of the low-country men, could not
endure the fatigue of a Highland campaign. As to the common
*fol.* 457. soldiers that came from France there were not four hundred of
them remaining. They and their officers, even though a battle
was lost, had but to surrender and be made prisoners of war. It
was very different with the Scots, whose safety depended upon

their not venturing a battle without great probability of success. But any proposition to postpone fighting was ill-received and was called discouraging the army. April.

I have nothing further to add, but am, etc.

*Leith, Saturday, October 17th,* 1747. *fol.* 451

John Hay, captain of the Custom House yacht at Air, came to the house of James Renny, wine-cooper in Leith, about 8 o'clock at night, when the conversation turned pretty much upon Miss Flora MacDonald, whom Captain Hay had seen several times after she was made prisoner, as he had been employed along with the ships and sloops of war, etc., in executing the errands and designs of the government about the west and north coast before the battle of Culloden, and after that in searching for the Prince and his friends. Captain Hay, asking about Miss MacDonald's welfare, said he could not help being surprized how it came about that her stepfather, MacDonald of Armadale, had never been taken up for that he had done very much, and far more, than ever it was in the power of Miss MacDonald to do. When it was asked what Armadale had done, the captain's answer was in these or the like words,[1] 'General Campbell complained to me more than once, that MacDonald of Armadale was the man that had misled him when searching for the Young Pretender; and therefore,' added he, 'I cannot fail being surprized that Armadale was never taken into custody.' 17 Oct 1747 *fol.* 45

Miss Peggie Forbes, who had heard something of Armadale's history, told the captain it was not for want of inclination and searching on the part of the government that Armadale had not been taken up, for that he was under a necessity, after knowing himself to be suspected, to skulk and go out of the way for some time.[2]

*N.B.*—The above narrative I had more than once from Miss Peggie Forbes's own mouth. Robert Forbes, A.M.

---

[1] See f. 770. [2] See ff. 194, 769.

fol. 460. ## Copy of some Omissions in DONALD MACLEOD's Journal.

21 Oct. DONALD MACLEOD, having been long detained in and about Edinburgh by the civilities and kindness of friends, was in my room in the Citadel of Leith, along with James MacDonald, joiner, upon Wednesday, October 21st, 1747, when Donald was pleased to inform me that upon reflection, he found he had forgot some few particulars in giving me his Journal, and therefore he would now take the opportunity of giving me a narrative of them. Accordingly I writ them down from his own mouth.

[See vol. 2d, page 301,[1] near the foot, the paragraph beginning with June 14th.]

From the foot of the mountain of Coradale they set sail in Campbell's boat still, and landed in the Island Ouia, at Benbicula, where they stayed four nights. From thence the Prince and O'Neil, with a guide, went to Rushness, where Lady Clanranald was. Donald and O'Sullivan were left at Ouia, where they abode two nights after the Prince had gone off to Rushness by land. The third night after the Prince had
fol. 461. been at Rushness, he got information that it was advisable he should go back again to the place from whence he had come; but he knew not well what to do, as the boats of the militia had been all the time in the course between Ouia and Rushness. Donald and O'Sullivan, hearing of the Prince's situation, set sail under favour of the night, and brought the Prince off from Rushness, steering their course from thence south again back towards Coradale hill. But meeting with a violent storm, and a very heavy rain, they were forced to put into Uishness Point, two miles and an half north of Coradale. The place they put up at in that night is called Achkirsideallich,[2] a rock upon the shore, in a clift of which they took up their quarters, the storm continuing for a whole day. At night the enemy being within less than two miles of them, they set sail again, and arrived safely at Ciliestiella, from whence they

[1] See f. 301. [2] See f. 336.

steered their course towards Loch Boisdale. But one on board swore that there was a long-boat in their way, no doubt full of marines. Donald MacLeod was positive on the contrary, and assured them that it was nothing else but a little rock in the water, which he was formerly acquainted with, having the appearance of a boat at some distance. But he could not persuade them to take his opinion of the matter, and therefore they steered back to Ciliestiella, and stayed there that night. Next day they set out for Loch Boisdale, where they got the disagreeable accounts of Boisdale's being made a prisoner, etc., and whereabouts they made their abode for about eight days.[1] 21 Oct. *fol.* 462.

At the same time Donald told me that Boisdale was once a whole night with the Prince upon Coradale,[2] and was very merry with him; and desired me still to remark that if Boisdale had not been prisoner, the Prince needed not to have left the Long Isle at all.

Donald likewise told me that when in London he called for his chiftain, who would not vouchsafe him so much as a look; and that one day spying him on the street of Edinburgh, he ventured to make up to him to enquire about his welfare; but his honour never minded honest Donald, and would take no notice of him at all. *fol.* 463.

When I told Donald that I would write down an account of this odd conduct in the Laird, he said, 'O na, lat him be.' But I positively insisted upon it, and would not yield it to Donald, remarking withal that I looked upon him as a great honour to his chiftain, and that therefore he needed not have behaved so to him as if he had been ashamed of him. To which Donald modestly replied, 'Faith, sir, I hope he winna say I am a disgrace to him.'

*N.B.*—The above omissions occasion some variation in the dates at the end of Donald's Journal about the Prince.

ROBERT FORBES, A.M.

---

[1] See f. 303. [2] See f. 589.

## *fol.* 464. Copy of a Letter to me, Robert Forbes, containing a true and genuine account of the case of poor William Baird.[1]

8 Sept. 1747 Revd. Sir,—I am to address you at this time on behalf of William Baird, a very misfortunate man, and now lying prisoner under sentence of death in the jayl at Carlisle, and every moment expecting to be transported with others that are in the same situation with himself there. This poor man went up to Carlisle in September last as an exculpatory evidence for the late Revd. Mr. Lyon, who was execute at Penrith in October last; but he no sooner appeared in Carlisle in this capacity, than he was tried for high treason, and condemned to die with the other prisoners that were tried, though he produced in court a protection from an officer in Montrose, upon the delivering up of his arms in terms of the Duke of Cumber-
*fol.* 465. land's order. But the judges had no regard to this, as they wanted by all means to try and condemn this poor man, in order to debar him from being evidence for Mr. Lyon, whom they were to destroy at any rate. As this poor man is in great misery just now, so I wish you would use your interest in order to procure him some supplies of money from well-disposed persons, which would come in good stead to him, as he is just now in the most miserable condition imaginable, being destitute of cloaths, linen, and everything else that is necessary for him to have, and of bread too, of which he has but a scanty portion every day, and such as keeps in life, and that is all. If you can get any money collected for him, Mr. James Wright will direct you as to the way and manner you are to remit to him. This poor unlucky man has a just title to the regard of every well-disposed person, as he has resigned his own life to preserve Mr. Lyon's; and if he had not done so, he would not have
*fol.* 466. been in so miserable a condition as he is just now. He is a married man, and has a wife and children here, which have no subsistence but from myself. I pity their case very much, as every good person must. May God raise up friends for all

[1] See f. 29.

that are in their situation.—I am, Reverend Sir, your most humble servant, (*Sic subscribitur*) ARBUTHNOTT. 8 Sept.

*Arbuthnott, September 8th*, 1747.

*N.B.*—The original of the above is to be found among my Papers. ROBERT FORBES, A.M.

## Copy of a Return to the above Letter, wherein a character of honest DONALD MACLEOD.

MY LORD,—Your lordship may be justly surprized at me having been honoured with yours of September 8th, without making any return to it before this time. But to tell the truth, as I had a view of this bearer, I delayed writing till I could do it with a good grace. And sure I am I could never do it with a better one than at present, when I gladly embrace the opportunity of affording your lordship the happiness to salute one of the first men in the world. 21 Oct. 1747 *fol.* 467.

I know, my Lord, you feel a sensible pleasure beyond many in the world in conversing with worthies, men of rigid virtue and integrity, and such indeed this man is.

Know then, my Lord, that this will be put into your hands by the renowned SCOTS PALINURUS, Donald MacLeod, tenant at Gualtergill, in the Isle of Sky, that most faithfull and honest steersman of the eight-oar'd boat from the continent to the Isles of Benbicula, South Uist, Lewis, etc., etc., etc., and who had the Prince among his hands for about ten weeks after the battle of Culloden. While a prisoner on board a ship he went through an uninterrupted series of the greatest hardships and severities for several months together. In a word, he was reduced to the lowest ebb of misery, and had the mortification of seeing others dying about him like rotten sheep. But his gray hairs (by a remarkable blessing of Heaven) have survived the trials of adversity, while many younger and in appearance much stronger, submitted to the fate of a lingring death. *fol.* 468.

Although his history be most extraordinary in all the several instances of it, yet, my Lord, when he arrived here from London, he had not wherewith to bear his charges to Sky,

21 Oct. where he has a wife and children (under the Laird of Macleod) whom he has now been absent from for nineteen or twenty months. Something has been done for him in and about Edinburgh, but far from what his merit justly entitles him to, and what his circumstances really call for. So many and frequent are the demands that have been made, that I must frankly own I was turned quite bankrupt in applications before I had the honour of your Lordship's letter; so that it was altogether
*fol.* 469. out of my power, though my inclination was great, to make anything for poor William Baird, whose affecting history and character were no strangers to me.

Take a view, my Lord, of this truly noble (though poor) worthy in this single point—that he had the courage and integrity of heart to despise the tempting bait of *thirty thousand pounds sterling*, and not only so, but that in spite of the infirmities attending the hoary head he struggled through as great
*fol.* 470. dangers[1] and difficulties of life for the preservation of etc., as it is in the power of the most fertil fancy to paint; and then I leave it to your lordship to draw the immortal character of this amiable instance of heroic virtue.

I dare venture to say that no man of bowels can hear honest Donald's interesting story without a mixture of joy and pain, and even without shedding tears. Well do I know all the several parts of it, and the more I think upon it, to the greater height is my admiration raised of the wondrous good man.

He has a large silver snuff-box which serves as an excellent medal of his history, to which I refer your lordship after asking your forgiveness for this too long letter. But while I would fain flatter myself with the hopes I am giving you pleasure, I indulge a self-satisfaction, for I could dwell upon the subject.

I shall be glad to know when this reaches your lordship's

---

[1] Well may honest Donald in a literal sense use the words of the blessed Apostle, 2 Cor. xi. 26, 27: 'In journeyings often, in perils of waters, in perils of robbers, in perils by mine own countrymen, in perils by the heathen, in perils in the city, in perils in the wilderness, in perils in the sea, in perils among false brethren; in weariness and painfulness, in watchings often, in hunger and thirst, in fastings often, in cold and nakedness.' [See Donald's whole Journal, ff. 266-326.]—F.

the few that were then with him? I told him it was Donald MacLeod, an old man of sixty-eight years of age, and who had been along with the Prince for nine or ten weeks after the battle of Culloden. 'That project,' said the Captain, 'happened to miscarry by being discovered, and I have reason to think that the discovery was owing to an information given by a Presbyterian minister.' Upon this I gave the Captain an account of this affair (to the best of my remembrance) as I had got it from the mouth of Donald MacLeod, viz., that a Presbyterian preacher in one of the Uists had writ a letter to a friend in the Harris, who then writ a letter to a Presbyterian preacher in the Lewis, upon which the people of the Lewis conveened at Stornoway to the number of some hundreds, etc.[1] 7 Nov. *fol.* 480.

To this the Captain replied that he had good reason to assure me that that indeed was the matter of fact. 'For,' added he, 'as I was cruizing along with the rest at that time I had an opportunity of knowing how the different informations came about.'

I told him I was exceedingly glad to have his account of the matter to support and confirm Donald Macleod's own representation of it, because that Donald had been reproached by severals for having got drunk;[2] and in his cups for having discovered to some one acquaintance or other the real design for which he had hired the ship, and this acquaintance was said to have blown the whole project. Captain Hay said he did not believe one word of all that, but that the true state of the case was above represented, and that the Prince would have been on board with his few attendants that very night when the discovery was made, had he not met with that unexpected disappointment. *fol.* 481.

Captain Hay asked if I could inform him of the day when the Prince set out from the Isle of Sky to the mainland.[3] I told him it was July 5th, and likewise remarked to him what difficulty I had with Captain Malcolm MacLeod to adjust this matter of a precise date.[4] 'Surely then,' said the Captain, 'we behoved to be very near the Prince in his crossing the ferry to

[1] See f. 288.
[2] See ff. 134, 184.
[3] See f. 267.
[4] See ff. 247, 262.

7 Nov. the mainland.' I told him I did not doubt that at all, and then I gave him an account (as exactly as I could) of that narrative given me by Mrs. MacDonald of Kingsburgh, and afterwards confirmed to me by Malcolm MacLeod himself,[1] anent the Prince's desiring Malcolm MacLeod to have no fear, for that the wind would soon change, and make the ships of war,
*fol.* 482. then in view upon the coast of Sky, steer a direct contrary course, so that it would not be in their power to come near him at that time. At this Captain Hay, with an asseveration, assured the company that that was literally true; for that when they were sailing along the coast of Sky with a pretty brisk gale, all of a sudden the wind changed upon them and forced them to sail a direct contrary course. He said he remembered nothing better.

Here I remarked that some would be ready to attribute this in the Prince to the second sight or some such uncommon supernatural cause; but that for my own part I believed there were some who could tell a little time before that the wind would blow from this or the other point of the compass, being in the use of making observations in that way. Captain Hay replied that sailors and others who dealt in observations of that kind could exactly enough tell from the
*fol.* 483. motion of a cloud, or the like, when the wind would veer about to this or the other quarter; and from what had been said he remarked that the Prince behoved to have skill in that way. I then told the company that Malcolm MacLeod had said that he never knew a man in all his life that had such a firm and steady trust in the providence of God as the Prince was remarkably blessed with.[2]

The conversation happening to turn upon the subject of Rorie MacKenzie's death, it was said that it was certain enough that Rorie MacKenzie had been taken by a party of Cumberland's army for the Prince, and that he had been actually butchered by them; but as to the particular circumstance of the butchery, that was an affair not so easily to be discovered. Here I told the company that particular story given me by Kingsburgh anent the officer's talking to him at Fort Augustus

[1] See ff. 215, 242. [2] See f. 216.

about the young Pretender's head.[1] Upon this Captain Hay said that in visiting his friends lately in the south country he had discovered a story well worth the remarking, and the more so because it had come from the Duke of Cumberland's own mouth. The Captain informed the company that he had met with a gentleman in the south who told him that when the Duke of Cumberland was on his way from the north to Berwick he had gone to that town to wait upon him, that accordingly he paid his court to him, and after he had done so, he asked his highness if he had entirely finished the whole affair, and left the country in peace. The Duke answered he had done so. Then the gentleman asked what was become of the Pretender's oldest son? The Duke replied that he had taken care to leave such orders behind him that the Pretender's eldest son would never be more heard of. Captain Hay said that as he had this particular narrative from the gentleman's own mouth, it deserved the more credit, for he could depend upon the truth of it; but he did not chuse to name the gentleman.

*fol.* 484. 7 Nov.

*fol.* 485.

Captain Hay was pleased to tell the company that when General Campbell came to the Laird of Clanranald's house in search of the Prince (so the Captain named him during the whole conversation) Lady Clanranald happened not to be at home, but that she came home pretty soon after. The General told the lady that he was to dine with her, and then began to interrogate her where she had been? Lady Clanranald answered that she had been visiting a sick child at some distance.[2] The General asking the name of the child, the lady made no stop in giving a name, and said likewise that the child was much better than formerly it had been; and she conversed all along with the General in a very easy, unconcerned way. Here the Captain observed that the visiting of the sick child was only a mere pretence the better to cover the real business the lady had been employed about, for afterwards it was discovered that Lady Clanranald at that time had actually been with the Prince.

*fol.* 486.

I could not fail remarking to Captain Hay that Lady Clan-

---

[1] See f. 146. [2] See f. 527.

7 Nov. ranald's acquitting herself so exactly and wisely in the Prince's preservation was something very singular, and the more extraordinary that (as I had been informed) she happens frequently not to be so well in her health, and therefore (one would be apt to imagine) quite unfit to manage a point of so much delicacy and danger. The Captain answered that Lady Clanranald's conduct in that affair, all things considered, was very extraordinary indeed.

After giving several very remarkable instances of the miseries and dangers the Prince had been exposed to in his wanderings, I begged leave to ask at Captain Hay what notions he

*fol. 487.* would entertain of those folks in and about Edinburgh (people of no mean sense and discretion in the common affairs of life) who when certain accounts had come of the Prince's arrival in France were pleased to say: 'O these Jacobites are strange bodies, who attribute the preservation of their Prince to the providence of God alone, when Providence could have no hand in it at all, seeing the Duke of Cumberland and his army were not willing to take him, but, on the contrary, avoided the laying hands on him when they might have done it.' At this Captain Hay held up his hands and declared his amazement that any such expression could ever proceed out of the mouth of any person whatsomever, and asked seriously if there were any persons that could have the impudence to talk so? I assured him there were such persons as had actually used the above expressions, or words to the same purpose, and that they could

*fol. 488.* be named. He said he was indeed surprised to hear the thing, considering the strict searches that had been made for the person of the Prince, and the many narrow escapes he had made. And, moreover, that it was well known in the army that when any officers happened to bring prisoners into the camp in the north, and after the report being made at the headquarters, the Duke of Cumberland used to be in a very bad humour, and to express himself in these words: 'These officers don't know their duty.'

The whole conversation went easily on, and lasted till between four and five o'clock at night.

There were present who witnessed the above conversation, Richard Seaman, baxter in Leith, John Hay, piriwig maker

in Edinburgh, Mrs. Bettie Seaman and Mrs. Ellie Kendal. 7 Nov.
Mrs. Seaman herself went from the company pretty soon after dinner to look after her business, so that she witnessed but a small part of the conversation. John Hay, piriwig maker, declared his being very much pleased with being present at such *fol.* 489.
a long and so particular a conversation upon the dangers and distresses of the Prince, and at the narrating some of the more moving and interesting parts he was so much affected that he shed tears. He frankly owned that he had never heard so much of the matter in all the several companies he had formerly resorted to where this extraordinary and affecting history happened to be the subject of conversation.

ROBERT FORBES, A.M.

## JOURNAL of the Prince's imbarkation and arrival, etc.,[1] taken from the mouth of ÆNEAS MACDONALD (a banker in Paris, and brother of Kinlochmoidart) when he was in a messenger's custody in London, by Dr. BURTON of York, who was taken up, upon suspicion, the 30th of November 1745, and confined till the 11th of March following in York Castle, and was from thence removed to a messenger's house in London, in whose custody he remained till March 25th, 1747, being in all sixteen months wanting only five days.[2] *fol.* 490.

AFTER the Prince had settled everything for his subsequent 1745. June.
undertaking, the gentlemen who were to accompany him on his voyage took different routs to Nantz, the place appointed to meet at, thereby the better to conceal their design. During

[1] This Journal is printed in the *Jacobite Memoirs* (pp. 1-27) with some omissions, in combination with another by Duncan Cameron, f. 346, *ante*.

[2] Dr. Burton and Bishop Forbes were both enthusiastic Jacobites, and an account of their meeting follows (f. 519). Later, a considerable correspondence passed between them, most of which the latter embodied in this manuscript.

June. their residence there they lodged in different parts of the town, and if they accidentally met in the street or elsewhere they took not the least notice of each other, nor seemed to be any
*fol.* 491. way acquainted, if there was any person near enough to observe them. During this time, and whilst everything was preparing to set sail, the Prince went to a seat of the Duke of Bouillon and took some days' diversion in hunting, fishing, and shooting, amusements he always delighted in, being at first obliged to it on account of his health. By this means he became inured to toil and labour, which enabled him to undergo the great fatigues and hardships he was afterwards exposed unto.

From this place he went to a seat of the Duke of Fitz-James, seemingly upon the same errand, and thence at a proper time went in disguise directly on board the ship lying in the Loire, being the river which goes immediately from Nantz to the sea.
*fol.* 492. Here he found eight gentlemen[1] above hinted at ready to accompany and assist him in his expedition. They were the Marquis of Tullibardine, alias Duke of Athol, Sir John MacDonald (a French officer), Mr. Æneas MacDonald (a banker in Paris), Mr. Strickland, Mr. Buchanan, Sir Thomas Sheridan, Mr. O'Sullivan, and Mr. Kelly. To these I may add a ninth, viz., Mr. Anthony Welch, the owner of the ship which carried the Prince. He (this last) staid on the coast of Scotland about three weeks, and did the Prince considerable service.

Here it will not be amiss to give some short account of the above-mentioned attendants.

The Duke of Athol was made prisoner in Scotland, having surrendred himself (as was given out by our lying newspapers) to Mr. Buchanan of Drumakill, a Justice of Peace. But the real matter of fact is that Drumakill, in his own house, basely betrayed the Duke when he thought himself safe under the protection of Drumakill's roof, having got assurances to that purpose. To confirm the truth of this, Drumakill is so much
*fol.* 493. despised for this breach of all the laws of hospitality and honour that the gentlemen in the neighbourhood and in all

[1] The Prince in his Manifesto from the Abbey of Holyrood-house calls them *seven only*. Perhaps Mr. Buchanan (as I have heard suggested by several persons) was reckoned amongst the Prince's domesticks.

ROBERT FORBES, A.M.

places of Scotland where Drumakill is known will not be seen in his company, nor will they converse with him. From Drumakill's house the Duke of Athol was carried to the Castle of Dumbarton, the latter end of April 1746, whence he was removed to Edinburgh, where he remained till the 13th of May, and then was put on board the *Eltham* man-of-war in Leith Road, and conveyed to the Tower of London, June 21st, where he died on the 9th of July, and was there buried July the 11th, 1746. June.

Sir John MacDonald, a French officer, surrendred himself prisoner of war at Inverness upon the day of Culloden battle. He was suffered to go out upon his parole amongst other French officers at Penrith. He is a man of no extraordinary head as a councillor.

Mr. Æneas MacDonald, a banker in Paris, surrendred himself to General Campbell upon terms which, however, were not performed. He was committed to Dumbarton Castle, whence *fol.* 494. he was conducted to Edinburgh Castle under a strong guard the latter end of August 1746; and the week after, in the same manner, was conveyed to the Duke of Newcastle's office at Whitehall, London, and immediately committed into the custody of a messenger. One day when he was concerting a jaunt to Windsor with Miss Flora MacDonald, he was by order taken out of the messenger's hands and committed to Newgate, and thence to new prison in Southwark. All the time the Prince was in Paris he lodged at Mr. Æneas MacDonald's house.

Mr. Strickland died at Carlisle when it was possessed by the Prince's army.

Mr. Buchanan, Sir Thomas Sheridan, Mr. O'Sullivan, and Mr. Kelly made their escape into France.

The first of these, Mr. Buchanan, upon the intended invasion at Dunkirk in 1743 was sent into England, and upon his return, in attempting to get to Calais or Dunkirk, was taken prisoner. He made a plausible story, and going by a feigned name, pre- *fol.* 495 tending great loyalty, etc., he artfully imposed upon one Captain Aires, who was then going into Flanders with some orders from the government, a person who has signalized himself very much upon a late occasion, though not in his profes-

June. sion as a soldier, yet as an evidence at St. Margaret's Hill in Southwark, etc. etc. etc. This very man, perceiving Mr. Buchanan understood French, and knew several of the French officers, proposed making use of him as a spy in Flanders, which Mr. Buchanan readily embraced, as it gave him a safe conveyance out of British dominions. Accordingly he was conducted to Ostend by Captain Aires, who was greatly surprized and no less chagrin'd to find his fellow-traveller so well known there, and to be the very man he had particular orders to find out, if possible, and to secure him, at the time when Mr. Buchanan had the address to deceive him. After this discovery Aires
*fol. 496.* never offered to make any farther use of Mr. Buchanan, neither could he detain him there. Mr. Buchanan was many years assistant to Mr. Æneas MacDonald at Paris.

The second of these, Sir Thomas Sheridan, was tutor to the young hero, whom he attended through most of his travels. His master had a real and, I may say, filial affection for him, which indeed was mutual, no man having his pupil's interest more at heart than Sir Thomas. He got safe to France. From that he went to Rome, where he waited upon his pupil's father, who reprimanded him for persuading his son to undertake such an expedition without better grounds. This reproof so far affected Sir Thomas that he fell ill and died of grief.

The third of these, Mr. O'Sullivan, an Irishman, is a remarkable man, of whom the world has been greatly deceived, whether we look upon him as a soldier, a councillor, or for honesty and integrity.

The fourth and last of these is the same Mr. Kelly who was so many years confined in the Tower upon a suspicion of having
*fol. 497.* had a hand in the famous plot of Dr. Atterbury, bishop of Rochester. Mr. Kelly's chief employment was to go betwixt his young master in Scotland and the French ministry, with some of whom he was very intimate.

22 June. On Saturday the 22d of June 1745, the gentlemen (of whom the above short account is given) being all incog. to the crew, set sail out of the river Loire for Bellisle on board a vessel of 110 tons, called *La Doutelle*, carrying 16 guns, and commanded by Captain Durbe; having first sent expresses from Nantz to the young gentleman's father at Rome, to the king of France,

and the king of Spain, acquainting them with the expedition, and desiring the two last to send armes, ammunition, and money to Scotland, which request was in part complied with.

On the 23d, being next day, they anchored at Bellisle, 23 June.
where they continued till the 4th of July waiting for the *Elizabeth*, their convoy, a French ship of war of 64 guns and about 500 men, commanded by Captain D'oe or D'eau. During the stay at this island, the Prince took great delight *fol.* 498.
in fishing. The better to conceal himself, he never would be shaved from his leaving Nantz to his arrival in Scotland.

Next morning, being the 5th of July, both ships set sail with 5 July.
a fair wind, which continued so till the 7th, when it blew a brisk gale; but the next day was a dead calm. On the 9th, being in the latitude of 47 degrees 57 minutes north, and west from the meridian of the Lizard 39 leagues, they descryed a sail to windward, which proved to be a British man of war of 58 guns called the *Lyon*, Captain Brett, commander, which immediately bore down upon them. About three o'clock in the afternoon they found what she was, and prepared to engage her, having both of them hoisted French colours and shortened sail. By 4 o'clock they were within two miles of each other, and at 5 the engagement began.

Upon the Frenchmen's first discovering a sail, a council of 9 July.
war was held by the commander, etc., of the *Elizabeth* on board the *Doutelle*, along with the passengers and her officers, wherein it was agreed, if no more sail appeared, that the *Elizabeth* should engage her, but should reserve her fire till she *fol.* 499.
was so near the *Lion* as to stand the chance of all her guns having effect, and then to give her a whole broadside; and if the *Lion* did not sink, to close in with her and board her directly, while the *Doutelle* should attack and assist her in that, not being able to engage so heavy mettle as the *Lion* would carry, but with her small arms would be of great use at close fighting. Accordingly, both ships were prepared to engage as agreed upon.

The *Lion*, being to windward, bore down upon the *Elizabeth*, and began the engagement at some distance. The *Elizabeth* followed the directions of the council of war, and received the *Lion's* shot several times in hopes of putting the plan laid

9 July. down into execution. But finding the *Lion* not only had the advantage of the wind, but that the British sailors worked her better than the Frenchmen did the *Elizabeth*, Captain D'oe
*fol.* 500. then found he could not accomplish his designs, and therefore engaged at a distance; but still tried to get as close to the *Lion* as possible.

The *Elizabeth*, being thus disappointed of attempting to board the *Lion*, rendred all the assistance intended her by the *Doutelle* of no effect, she being too small a vessel to contend with the *Lion's* greatest guns; and therefore, when her commander, Captain Durbe, found he could not assist the *Elizabeth*, he drew off to a greater distance to avoid being sunk till a more convenient opportunity might offer. This gave those on board the *Doutelle* both time and leisure to observe the management and behaviour of both ships.

They fought with equal bravery for several hours, but the British sailors showed their superior skill and dexterity, which were highly praised by all on board the *Doutelle*, as well French as Scotch men; for, though the *Elizabeth* had more men, yet they could not work her so well, nor fire so often as the *Lion* did.

The engagement continued thus till after 9 o'clock, when
*fol.* 501. the *Lion* began to abate of her fire, and, as far as she could, to make a running fight, discharging only now and then a gun. Then the advantage turned to the *Elizabeth's* side, her rigging not being so much damaged as the *Lion's*, though she had more men killed; and she now approached nearer and nearer the *Lion*, who, finding she could not escape, fired a gun and immediately struck. The *Elizabeth*, not going instantly up to board her, but rather slacking her pace, encouraged the *Lion* to set up her colours again. The reason of this behaviour of the *Elizabeth* was owing to the death of both Captain D'oe and his brother, who were killed by the last shot from the *Lion*. This accident, when least expected, and there being but one lieutenant left to command the *Elizabeth*, obliged him to drop sail and to wait for the *Doutelle*, who, finding what had happened to the *Lion*, was making all the sail she could to
*fol.* 502. come up to the *Elizabeth*, which was soon accomplished, and a council of war was held immediately upon what should be

done. It was herein agreed that, as it was ten o'clock, and 9 July.
would be some time before they could get up to the *Lion*, who was making all the haste she could to reach England, they might be in danger of falling in with some other English man of war, and be obliged to engage in the bad condition the ship was in, and then must inevitably be either taken or sunk; and, moreover, would be so much farther from the French coast that, were they to spy a sail, they would not have time to get into any harbour to avoid being taken. Therefore, it was thought proper to desist from pursuing the *Lion*, she being by this time out of sight. It was then asked if the *Elizabeth* was in a condition to proceed in her intended voyage, when her new commander answered in the negative; for, as he could not refit her at sea for another engagement, it would not therefore be safe to hazard their being sunk or taken, more especially as so many British men of war and
privateers were cruizing at sea, and as he had near 200 men *fol.* 503.
killed and wounded. They then determined to return to Brest. Some of the passengers of the *Doutelle* endeavoured to prevail upon the Prince to return also till another convoy could be prepared, or the same could be refitted. To this he would not consent, but resolved to proceed on his voyage.

The *Elizabeth*, though a French man of war, was sent out as convoy to the *Doutelle* by one Mr. Walter Rutlets, an Irishman, and a merchant at Dunkirk.

As it may seem odd that a subject could send out a man of war as a convoy without the king's knowledge where she was going, it is incumbent upon me to explain the nature of such an undertaking. I must therefore remark that when any of the French king's men of war are in harbour and fit for use, but not going upon any immediate business of the king's own, any of his subjects may upon proper application have her, and send her out on a cruize for the time granted, he (the
subject) paying the men's wages during that time. By this *fol.* 504.
means the King of France annoys his enemies without being at the expence of the men, and his ships thereby are kept pretty constantly employed, instead of lying in harbours, and their officers having no other employment than entertaining the ladies on shore.

9 July. But to return. After the engagement above mentioned,
the *Doutelle* proceeded on her voyage soon after the council
of war was ended. But before she set sail for Scotland, all
her lights were put out, except that for the compass, which
still was so close confined that not the least ray could emit.
This caution was observed every night through the whole
voyage till their landing in Erisca. On July 11th she was
chased, and made a clear ship to engage; but trusting more
to their speed than to their military power, they made all the
sail they could and escaped all pursuers. The 15th and 16th
they had a rough sea and tempestuous weather. Then they
*fol.* 505. had fine weather till about midnight on the 20th, which was
very stormy. The 21st being very mild, they sounded and
found ground at 108 fathom. On the 22d they made a
small island called Bernera, being the southernmost of the
western isles of Scotland, near the latitude of 57. On the
23 July. 23d they arrived at the island of Erisca, belonging to Clanranald, which lies betwixt the isles of Barra and South Uist
or Ouist, having been eighteen days at sea from July 5th.

They were scarce arrived when they spied two sail which they apprehended to be ships of war, and therefore got all their money, arms, and ammunition on shore as fast as they could. All went ashore except the Marquis of Tullibardine, who was laid up in the gout and could not stir. Their fears, however, were soon dissipated by finding the ships proved only merchantmen.

The very first night they landed happened to prove
*fol.* 506. violently stormy and wet, and they were obliged to lodge in
one of the little country houses wherein there were already
many others that were weatherbound.

Here they were all refreshed as well as the place could afford, and they had some beds, but not sufficient for the whole company, on which account the Prince, being less fatigued than the others, insisted upon such to go to bed as most wanted it. Particularly he took care of Sir Thomas Sheridan, and went to examine his bed and to see that the sheets were well aired. The landlord, observing him to search the bed so narrowly, and at the same time hearing him declare he would sit up all night, called out to him and said that it was so good a bed, and the sheets were so good, that a prince need not be ashamed to lie in them. 23 July

The Prince, not being accustomed to such fires in the middle of the room, and there being no other chimney than a hole in the roof, was almost choaked, and was obliged to go often to the door for fresh air. This at last made the landlord, Angus MacDonald, call out, 'What a plague is the matter with that fellow, that he can neither sit nor stand still, and neither keep within nor without doors?' *fol.* 507.

From Eriska some of the company sent to Roger MacNeil, Esquire of Barra, as relations, being come thither, and who would be glad to see him: but he happened to be from home. At the same time they sent out several other messengers upon the same errand to several gentlemen in different parts, particularly to Alexander MacDonald of Boisdale, esquire, who went to them the next day.[1] But when he found upon what errand they were come to Scotland, he did all he could to prevail upon them to return to France without making any attempt to proceed. His advice being in vain, he then went to several persons to caution them from being drawn into either any rising or promises so to do. By this means he prevented some hundreds of people from joining them, for which he had a letter of thanks from Lord Loudon and others for the great services he had done the present government. *fol.* 508.

From this place Mr Æneas MacDonald, the banker, took boat and went to his brother of Kinlochmoidart, being at the distance of about forty miles. Kinlochmoidart accompanied the banker back to Eriska. Amongst those who went on board the *Doutelle* at Eriska, and there laid the plan of the operations and contrived the scheme, were the foresaid Donald MacDonald of Kinlochmoidart, esquire, and Ronald MacDonald of Clanronald, junior, esquire, who commanded that clan.[2]

Kinlochmoidart was made a colonel and aid-de-camp to the Prince, and was to have been made a baronet and peer of Scotland. He was an exceeding cool-headed man, fit for either cabinet or field. He was frequently employed in going *fol.* 509.

[1] See ff. 256, 302, 353.

[2] The contents of the above paragraph happened in Lochnannuagh.—(F.)

T

24 July from one friend of the cause to another. Upon one of these expeditions he was either going or had been when both he and his servant were taken by some country people, and sent to the Castle of Edinburgh, whence he was removed to Carlisle, and was there put to death upon Saturday, October 18th, the festival of St. Luke the Evangelist, 1746. The place where he was made prisoner is called Lesmahagoe, and he was committed to Edinburgh Castle on the 12th of November 1745.

Having dismissed several messengers to their respective friends on the continent of Scotland, they set sail about the 26th of
26 July July 1745, and coasting about the isles between Sky and Mull, and landing some of their passengers, proceeded to Lochshiel in
*fol.* 510. Lochabar.[1] Of this the government was informed, as we find by a paragraph in the Gazette of Saturday, August 17th, 1745, from Edinburgh, dated on the 11th of the same month.

Here it will not be amiss to give a short account of the vile and dishonourable method used for seizing the Duke of Perth, who was actually in the hands of the Highland officers, Sir Patrick Murray of Ochtertyre and Mr. Campbell of Inveraa, at his own house of Drummond Castle, but he had the good fortune to make his escape from them. The manner of both was as follows :—

A warrant being out to take the Duke of Perth, it was given to the above officers to put it in execution. They, not daring to attempt it openly without a large force, the sight of which would give a sufficient alarm for him to escape, they therefore thought of the following scandalous method. As they were often hospitably entertained at his table, they sent him word
*fol.* 511. that they were to dine with him at such a time. He sent them word back that he should be proud to see them. The time appointed being come (July 26th, 1745), they went as usual, and according to the Duke's generous temper were entertained at dinner. One of his footmen having spied some men in arms coming towards the house, called the Duke to the door of the room and told him what he had seen, begging his Grace in the meantime to take care of himself. This the servant did more than once; but the Duke always smiled and would not

[1] See ff. 355, 640, for precise day, etc.

suspect any gentlemen to be guilty of any such dirty action. 26 July After dinner, the officers having drunk a little while, and the time being come when they had appointed the soldiers to surround the house at a little distance, were pleased to inform his Grace of their errand, pulling out their orders for that purpose. The Duke commanded his temper very well, and *fol.* 512. seeming not to be much displeased, told them he would step into the closet, which was in the room where they were sitting, and get himself ready. To this they agreed, as they thought he could not go out of the room. He went into the closet and (gently locking the door) slipt down a pair of backstairs, which came to the closet, and got into the wood joining his gardens with much difficulty. In making his way through the wood (which was surrounded), he got all his legs much scratched and wounded with the briars and thorns; and he behoved sometimes to crawl on his hands and feet to keep himself from being seen by the sentinels at their different posts. The officers waited some time, and the Duke not returning, they went to the closet door, which, being locked, they called some of the servants, who told them their master was gone away on horseback in a great hurry. After the Duke got out of the wood he lay squat for some time in a dry ditch till the party should *fol.* 513. be gone. The officers and their command, on their return to Crieff, the place where they quartered, passed so near the ditch that the Duke heard all that they spoke. When the party were all out of sight the Duke rose up to look about him, and spying a countryman with a little horse, he desired to have the use of the horse, which the countryman readily complied with. The horse had neither saddle nor bridle, but only a branks (or halter) about its head. However, in this pickle did the Duke ride to the house of Mr. Murray of Abercairny. From that he went to the house of Mr. Drummond of Logie. At night, when all were in bed, Logie Drummond, entertaining fears he could not really account for, got out of bed, and going to the Duke's bed chamber, awaked him and begged him to be gone speedily to some other place; for that he was afraid of his not being safe to stay all night. Logie would not leave him till he *fol.* 514. saw him out of the house, and the Duke was not well gone when a party came (in dead of night), and searched the house

26 July. very narrowly for the Duke. It is worth remarking here that when Sir Patrick Murray of Ochtertyre was made a prisoner on Gladesmuirfield, the Duke of Perth came up to him, and asking how he did, spoke these words to him very pleasantly, 'Sir Petie, I am to dine with you to-day.'

But to return. At Lochshiel in Lochabar they unloaded their ship, the chief of whose cargo consisted of brandy (a liquor absolutely necessary in the Highlands), a thousand stand of arms, a proportionable quantity of ammunition, and some provisions.[1]

3 Aug. About the 3d or 4th of August they had cleared the ship. The next day it was known that the Prince was arrived, and young Clanranald sent a guard to attend him.

*fol.* 515. During this time all the messengers were very successful, and several of the Prince's friends began to be in motion, and gathered their respective vassals in order to be ready to attend at the setting up of the standard.

While these were busy raising men, etc., others were as much employed in procuring a sufficient quantity of oatmeal, which, being scarce, cost seventeen shillings sterling per boll. In about the space of three weeks, having laid up a large quantity of oatmeal, and having a sufficient quantity of brandy (two of the most grateful things that could be given to a Highlander), the Prince thought it high time to begin to try his fortune.

11 Aug. About the 11th of August the Prince sailed to Kinlochmoidart, about 25 miles farther, where he stayed till the 17th.
As he went from hence he was joined by about 150 men. On
the 18th he crossed Lochshiel and lay at Glensiarich,[2] and from
19 Aug. thence on the 19th they proceeded to Glenfinnan at the head
of the loch in Clanranald's country, and there set up his
*fol.* 516. standard, on which there was no motto at all, and was
immediately joined by Lochiel, Keppoch, and others, with 1400
men in all. Young Clanranald had joined him before.

Here a considerable number of both gentlemen and ladies met to see the ceremony; among the rest was the famous Miss

[1] See f. 640.

[2] See f. 640.

Jeanie Cameron[1] (as she is commonly though very improperly called, for she is a widow nearer 50 than 40 years of age). She is a genteel, well-look'd, handsome woman, with a pair of pretty eyes, and hair as black as jet. She is of a very sprightly genius, and is very agreeable in conversation. She was so far from accompanying the Prince's army that she went off with the rest of the spectators as soon as the army marched. Neither did she ever follow the camp, nor was ever with the Prince, but in public when he had his Court at Edinburgh. 19 Aug

Here it must be remarked that Mr. Anthony Welch, the owner of the *Doutelle*, an eminent merchant of Nantz, after having landed his passengers and cargo as above mentioned, *fol.* 517. (towards which expence the Prince gave him £2000 sterling, and knighted him, making him a present of a gold-hilted sword, which cost eighty louis d'ores, and was bought for the Prince against the intended Dunkirk expedition in 1743), this merchant, I say, after landing his passengers, went a privateering, having a letter of mark, and was of signal service to the Highland army by taking six or seven prizes, the chief of which were loaded with meal. The biggest of these he ransomed for £60 sterling, and also the others in proportion, on condition the owners would carry their lading and sell it to the Prince, etc., but if they did not bring certificates of that then the ransom was to be three times as much. This Mr. Welch chiefly trades to Martinico. He has 24 merchantmen and privateers, one of which took man-of-war in and sold it to the King of France for 15,000 livres. *fol.* 518.

Upon the 20th of August the Prince proceeded on his march towards Castle Blair in Athol. On the 23d he was joined by about 500, on the 26th by 50, on the 28th by 100, on the 29th by 150 at Garviemore. 20 Aug.

---

[1] At the end of a pamphlet, called 'The Life of Dr. Archibald Cameron, brother to Donald Cameron of Lochiel,' etc. [London, 1753, p. 32], there is given as an Appendix a notice and portrait of 'Miss Jenny Cameron, in a military habit.' She is there said to be the daughter of Hugh Cameron of Glandessary, and to have joined the Prince when he set up his standard with 200 well-armed followers, whom she personally led in action at Prestonpans, Falkirk, and Culloden. Mr. Robert Chambers, in his *History of the Rebellion*, 7th edition, pp. 251, 252, footnotes, gives all the additional information about this lady which seems to be known.

When they were at Corierag, hoping to fight Cope, they had been also joined by Ardshiel, commanding the Stewarts of Appin, Glenco, Glengary, and some others. The author of ASCANIUS[1] makes the Prince avoid fighting Cope, but it was quite otherwise.

30 Aug. August 30th they arrived at Dalnacardoch in the mountain of Dirmochter, and on the 31st at Blair Castle, which Duke James quitted a few days before upon receiving a letter from his brother, Duke William, alias Marquis of Tullibardine. On the last of August Old MacGregor, alias Graham of Glengyle, had seized, by surprize, forty men of General Campbell's regiment who were mending the Duke of Argyle's roads.

*fol.* 519. In this route Lochgary, Dr. Cameron, and O'Sullivan were sent to Ruthven in Badenoch to take the Barracks. Neither side had any canon. The Highland party endeavoured to set fire to the door, but the soldiers fired through holes in the door, killed one man and mortally wounded two more; and then the party retired. All this time O'Sullivan hid himself in a barn. This garrison consisted of 12 men, commanded by Serjeant Molloy. About this time a new raised company belonging to Lord Loudon deserted and joined the Prince's army.[2]

1747. 19 Novr. *N.B.*—Upon Thursday, November 19th, 1747, I visited Dr. John Burton [physician] of York, at his lodgings in Edinburgh, where I had the favour of the original draught in the doctor's own hand-writ, from which I made out the above transcript. The Doctor had come into Scotland purposely to make enquiry about matters relating to the Prince's affairs. The above is
*fol.* 520. much more to be depended upon than that taken from Duncan Cameron, because Mr. Æneas MacDonald[3] is a gentleman who got a liberal education, and was one of the Prince's council, and therefore had an opportunity of knowing things distinctly; whereas Duncan Cameron, being only a servant, could know things but imperfectly and at second-hand. Meantime it is worth observing that the journal taken from Duncan Cameron and others is the fullest and exactest of the two as to the

---

[1] A pamphlet history of the Prince's escape, printed in 1746, and not all facts.
[2] See f. 642. [3] See f. 346.

marching of the Prince's army down the country to Edinburgh, which Dr. Burton acknowledged.

Upon the foresaid day I also received from Dr. Burton in his own hand-writ the two following short narratives.

I. The Laird of MacKinnon, after ferrying the Prince over from the Isle of Sky to the continent, took leave of him, and then set out upon his return home. The Prince left Knoidart and went to Glenbiasdale, being about ten miles, where he stayed two or three nights, till he heard of the arrival of Captain Scott with 500 men, and General Campbell with 400 *fol.* 521.
more, who having received notice whereabouts the Prince was, were endeavouring to surround him; they and their men being then within three miles of him on all sides. But notwithstanding all the efforts of his enemies, who had all the reason imaginable to expect to get their prey, yet he, by God's providence, slipt them all once more in the night, and travelled 25 Scotch miles in a few hours over rough mountains into Lochaber. The better to deceive his pursuers, he got two or three different men to personate him and to take different routes, by which stratagem, in all probability, he extricated himself out of the then dangers, and once more preserved his life and liberty.

The above taken by Dr. Burton from the mouth of Donald MacDonald of Garryfleugh, prisoner in London in the same messenger's house with Clanronald, Boisdale, etc.

II. The vessel which carried the Prince over from Scotland was the *Bellona* of St. Malo's, a Nantz privateer of 32 carriage *fol.* 522.
and 12 swivel guns and 340 men. She was afterwards taken on the 2d of February 1746-7 by three men-of-war only, the *Eagle*, the *Edinburgh*, and the *Nottingham*. The Prince, after seeing such of his friends as were present first on board, embarked and set sail immediately for France (September 20th, 1746),[1] 20 Sept.
where he landed safely at Roscort, near three leagues west of Morlaise, on the 29th of the same month, having had a very good voyage. The ship was commanded by one Colonel Warren, and had another privateer along with her.[2]

---

[1] See ff. 640, 1476.

[2] See the *Scots Magazine* for September 1746, the first column of p. 445, and second column of p. 492.—(F.)

23 Nov. Upon Monday, November 23d, 1747, Dr. Burton favoured me with a visit, when he was pleased to tell me that some time in the month of September 1746, he took the freedom to ask at
*fol.* 523. Mr. Æneas MacDonald his opinion of Mr. John Murray of Broughton, particularly whether or not he entertained any fears about his turning evidence, as the common talk in London gave it out? Mr. MacDonald's answer was that he believed Mr. Murray of Broughton to be so honest between man and man, that in private life he would not be guilty of a dirty or dishonest action; but then, he said, he knew him to be such a coward, and to be possessed with such a fear for death, that (for his own part) he was much afraid Mr. Murray might be brought the length of doing any thing to save a wretched life!

ROBERT FORBES, A.M.

## *fol.* 524. Journal taken from the mouth of MISS FLORA MACDONALD by DR. BURTON of York, when in Edinburgh.[1]

1746. June. Miss MacDonald had gone from Sky to Milton in South Uist[2] in order to visit her brother-german, who had about that time taken up house. She had not been long there till Captain O'Neil (by some lucky accident or other) had become acquainted with her.[3] When the Prince was surrounded with difficulties on all hands, and knew not well what to do for his future safety, Captain O'Neil brought Miss MacDonald to the place where the Prince was, and there they concerted the plan. At that time Miss returned to Milton. After Miss MacDonald had (with some difficulty)[4] agreed to undertake the dangerous enterprize, she set out for Clanranald's house, Saturday, June 21st, and at one of the fords was taken prisoner by a party of militia, she not having a passport. She demanded to whom they belonged? And finding by the answer that her step-father was then commander, she refused to give any answers till she should see their captain. So she and her servant, Neil MacKechan, were prisoners all that night.

[1] Printed in *Jacobite Memoirs*, pp. 412-423.
[2] See f. 200.
[3] See ff. 186-7.
[4] See f. 192.

Her stepfather, coming next day, being Sunday, she told *fol. 525.*
him what she was about, upon which he granted a passport for *22 June.*
herself, a man-servant (Neil MacKechan), and another woman Bettie Burk, a good spinster, and whom he recommended as such in a letter to his wife at Armadale in Sky, as she had much lint to spin.[1] If her stepfather (Hugh MacDonald of Armadale) had not granted Miss a passport, she could not have undertook her journey and voyage. Armadale set his step-daughter at liberty, who immediately made the best of her way to Clanranald's house and acquainted the Lady Clanranald with the scheme, who supplied the Prince with apparel sufficient for his disguise, viz. a flower'd linen gown, a white apron, etc., and sent some provisions along with him.[2]

During Miss MacDonald's stay at Clanranald's house, which was till the Friday, June 27th, O'Neil went several times betwixt
the Prince and Miss, in which interval another scheme was *fol. 526.*
proposed, that the Prince should go under the care of a gentleman to the northward,[3] but that failing them, they behoved to have recourse to that agreed upon before; and accordingly Lady Clanranald, one Mrs. MacDonald, O'Neil, Miss Flora MacDonald, and her servant, Neil MacKechan, went to the place where the Prince was, being about eight Scotch miles.[4] He was then in a very little house or hut, assisting in the roasting of his dinner, which consisted of the heart, liver, kidneys, etc., of a bullock or sheep, upon a wooden spit. O'Neil introduced his young preserver and the company, and she sat on the Prince's right hand and Lady Clanranald on his left. Here they all dined very heartily.

Next morning, June 28th, they heard of General Campbell's *28 June.*
arrival at Benbecula, and soon after a man came in a great hurry to Lady Clanranald and acquainted her that Captain Ferguson with an advanced party of Campbell's men was at her
house, and that Ferguson had lain in her bed the night before. *fol. 527.*
This obliged her to go home immediately, which accordingly she did, after taking leave of the Prince. She was strictly examined by Ferguson where she had been? She replied she

[1] See ff. 187, 193, 304.

[2] See pp. 152, 210-218, 594.

[3] See ff. 188, 589.

[4] See f. 149.

28 June had been visiting a child which had been sick, but was now better again.[1] Both the General and Ferguson asked many other questions, such as where the child lived, how far it was from thence? etc., but they could make nothing out of the lady fit for their purpose.

O'Neil would gladly have staid with the Prince and shared in his distresses and dangers, but Miss could by no means be prevailed upon to agree to that proposal.[2]

When all were gone who were not to accompany the Prince in his voyage to the Isle of Sky, Miss MacDonald desired him to dress himself in his new attire, which was soon done, and at a proper time they removed their quarters and went near the water with their boat afloat, nigh at hand for readiness to em-
*fol. 528.* bark in case of an alarm from the shore. Here they arrived, very wet and wearied, and made a fire upon a rock to keep them somewhat warm till night.[3] They were soon greatly alarmed by seeing four wherries full of armed men making towards shore, which made them extinguish their fire quickly, and to conceal themselves amongst the heath.

About two or three days after O'Neil parted from the Prince, a French cutter, having 120 men on board, appeared and sailed towards the Isle of South Uist, intending to carry off the Prince.[4] O'Sullivan went immediately on board, while O'Neil made haste to find out the Prince before he might have left the island. But finding that the Prince had left the island about two days before, immediately he returned to the place where he had left the cutter. But unhappy for him, he found that the timorous Sullivan, having a fair wind, and not having
*fol. 529.* courage to stay till O'Neil's return, being resolved to take care of Number One, obliged the captain to set sail directly, lest he should be taken and should lose his precious life. O'Neil returned in the compass of three hours after Sullivan had set sail, and was taken prisoner soon after and brought into England, after having been prisoner for some time in the Castle of Edinburgh[5], to which place he had been brought from a ship of war; for he had been in a state of confinement at sea for some

[1] See f. 485. [2] See ff. 193, 687. [3] See f. 137.
[4] See f. 191. [5] See f. 189.

time. An English officer, having intelligence of the above cutter, immediately dispatched two wherries after her with thirty men in each, but neither of them could come up with her.

At eight o'clock, June 28th, Saturday, 1746, the Prince, Miss Flora MacDonald, Neil MacKechan, etc., set sail in a very clear evening from Benbecula to the Isle of Sky.[1] It is worth observing here that Benbecula is commonly reckoned a part of South Uist, they being divided from one another by the sea only at high water, which then makes a short ferry betwixt the two; but at low water people walk over upon the sand from the one to the other. 28 June *fol.* 530.

They had not rowed from the shore above a league till the sea became rough, and at last tempestuous, and to entertain the company the Prince sung several songs and seemed to be in good spirits.

In the passage Miss MacDonald fell asleep, and then the Prince carefully guarded her, lest in the darkness any of the men should chance to step upon her. She awaked in a surprize with some little bustle in the boat, and wondered what was the matter, etc.[2]

Next morning, Sunday, June 29th, the boatmen knew not where they were, having no compass and the wind varying several times, it being then again calm.[3] However, at last they made to the point of Waternish, in the west corner of Sky, where they thought to have landed, but found the place possessed by a body of forces who had three boats or yawls near the shore. One on board one of the boats fired at them to make them bring-to; but they rowed away as fast as they could, being all the chance they had to escape, because there were several ships of war within sight. They got into a creek, or rather clift of a rock, and there remained some short time to rest the men, who had been all night at work, and to get their dinners of what provisions they had along with them. As soon as they could they set forwards again, because as the militia could not bring them to, they had sent up to alarm a little town not far off. It was very lucky for them that it was a calm then, 29 June *fol.* 531.

---

[1] See f. 1518. [2] See f. 195. [3] See ff. 138, 205, 598.

29 June. for otherwise they must inevitably have perished or have been taken.[1]

From hence they rowed on and landed at Kilbride, in Troternish, in the Isle of Sky, about twelve miles north from the above-mentioned point. There were also several parties of
*fol.* 532. militia in the neighbourhood of Kilbride. Miss left the Prince in the boat and went with her servant, Neil MacKechan, to Mougstot, Sir Alexander MacDonald's house, and desired one of the servants to let Lady Margaret MacDonald know she was come to see her ladyship in her way to her mother's house. Lady Margaret knew her errand well enough by one Mrs MacDonald, who had gone a little before to apprize her of it.[2]

As Mr. Alexander MacDonald of Kingsburgh was accidentally there, Lady Margaret desired him to conduct the Prince to his house; for it is to be remarked that Lady Margaret did not see the Prince in any shape. Kingsburgh sent a boy down to the boat with instructions whither to conduct the Prince
*fol.* 533. about a mile, and he (Kingsburgh) would be there ready to conduct him.[3] Then Kingsburgh took some wine, etc., to refresh the Prince with, and set forwards for the place of rendezvous, leaving Miss MacDonald with Lady Margaret at Mougstot, where the commanding officer of the parties in search of the Prince was, and who asked Miss whence she came, whither she was going, what news? etc., all which Miss answered as she thought most proper, and so as to prevent any discovery of what she had been engaged in.[4]

Lady Margaret pressed Miss very much in presence of the officer to stay, telling her that she had promised to make some stay the first time she should happen to come there. But Miss desired to be excused at that time, because she wanted to see her mother, and to be at home in these troublesome times. Lady Margaret at last let her go, and she and Mrs MacDonald

---

[1] See f. 138. [2] See ff. 727, 738.

[3] Here is a mistake; for Mr MacDonald of Kingsburgh declared to me more han once [see f. 145], that he sought for the Prince some time to no purpose, and had almost despaired to find him, when at last the accidental running of a flock of sheep proved the occasion of finding him out. [See f. 736.]

ROBERT FORBES, A.M.

[4] See f. 138.

above mentioned set forwards with Neil MacKechan and said *fol.* 534.
Mrs MacDonald's maid and her man-servant. They overtook 29 June.
the Prince and Kingsburgh. Mrs. MacDonald was very desirous to see the Prince's countenance; but as he went along he always turned away his face from Mrs MacDonald to the opposite side whenever he perceived her endeavouring to stare him in the countenance. But yet she got several opportunities of seeing his face, though in disguise, which the maid could not help taking notice of, and said she had never seen such an impudent-looked woman, and durst say she was either an Irish woman or else a man in a woman's dress. Miss MacDonald replied she was an Irish woman, for she had seen her before. The maid also took notice of the Prince's awkward way of managing the petticoats, and what long strides he took in walking along, etc.,[1] which obliged Miss MacDonald to desire Mrs. MacDonald (they being both on horseback), to step a
little faster and leave those on foot, because, as there were *fol.* 535.
many parties of militia in the great roads, it was necessary for the Prince to cross the country, and it was not proper to let Mrs. MacDonald's man or maid servant see it. So on they went, and the Prince and Kingsburgh went over the hills and travelled south-south-east till they arrived at Kingsburgh's house, which was about twelve o'clock at night, and they were very wet. But Miss MacDonald, who had parted with her companions and her man-servant on the road, arrived some short time before the Prince.[2]

Here the Prince got his most material refreshment, and was very much fatigued.[3] Yet he was very merry till the company
parted to go to rest. Morning being come and pretty far ad- 30 June.
vanced, Miss MacDonald was in pain about the Prince's lying so long in bed lest he should be overtaken by his enemies, and therefore she entreated Kingsburgh to go and call him up,
which with much ado he was prevailed upon to comply with, *fol.* 536.
he being desirous that the Prince should take as long rest as he could, not knowing when he could meet with the like again. Accordingly Kingsburgh went into the Prince's bed-chamber and found him in so profound a sleep that he could not think

[1] See ff. 143, 206. [2] See f. 146. [3] See f. 209.

30 June of awakening him, and so retired softly out of the room.[1] But at last the day began to be far advanced, and Miss MacDonald was very uneasy, everything being prepared for the journey agreed upon. Though the Prince was determined (from the observations and persuasion of Kingsburgh)[2] to cast off his disguise, yet it was necessary he should leave the house in the female dress he came in, which would, if enquiry happened to be made, prevent the servants telling the particular dress he had put on when he stript himself of the gown, petticoats, etc., and therefore in Kingsburgh's house Miss put on his cap for him.

The day was far advanced before he set out, and when he
*fol.* 537. arrived at a wood side (as the affair had been concerted), not far from Kingsburgh, he changed his apparel once more and put on the Highland dress Kingsburgh had furnished him with.[3] Then Kingsburgh sent a guide with him to Portree, thro' all byways, while Miss MacDonald went thither on horseback by another road, thereby the better to gain intelligence and at the same time to prevent a discovery. They were very wet, it having rained very much. Here he only dried his clothes, took some little refreshment, and staid about two hours.

Hither Kingsburgh had sent to prepare a boat, and to have it ready to convey the Prince to the place where he wanted to be at, not allowing the people about Portree in the meantime to know anything about the person's being the Prince whom they were to receive and to take care of. Young MacLeod of
*fol.* 538. Raaza came with Malcolm MacLeod to conduct the Prince over to the Island of Raaza. The Prince was very uneasy he had not a MacDonald to conduct him still. He left Portree on
1 July Tuesday, the 1st of July, and landed that very same day at a place called Glam in Raaza.[4]

Miss MacDonald took leave of the Prince at Portree, and from thence went to her mother, after a fatiguing journey cross the country. She never told her mother, or indeed anybody else, what she had done.[5] About eight or ten days after, she received a message from one of her own name, Donald MacDonald of Castleton in Sky, who lived about four miles

[1] See f. 213. [2] See f. 143. [3] See ff. 143, 228
[4] See f. 214, 228. [5] See f. 200.

from Slate or Armadale, to come to his house, an officer July
of an Independent Company (one MacLeod of Taliskar) having desired him so to do. She, a little suspicious of what might happen, thought proper to consult some of her friends[1] what she should do in the matter. They unanimously agreed she ought not to go, at least till next day; but go she
would. Then she was instructed what to say upon an examina- *fol.* 539.
tion; and accordingly, when that happened, she said she had seen a great lusty woman, who came to the boatside as she was going on board and begged to have a passage, saying she was a soldier's wife. Her request was granted, and when she landed in Sky, she went away, thanking Miss for her favour. Miss added withal that she knew nothing of what became of her afterwards.

Miss set forwards, as she proposed, to her friend's house, whither she had been desired to come, and on the road she met her father (Armadale) returning home; and soon after she was taken by an officer and a party of soldiers, who were going to her mother's house in pursuit of her.[2] They carried her on board a ship, and would not suffer her to return home to take leave of her friends. She was carried on board
the *Furnace*, commanded by Captain John Ferguson, a sloop *fol.* 540.
of war, where General Campbell happened then to be, who ordered Miss MacDonald to be used with the utmost respect.

About three weeks afterwards, Miss, in cruizing about, being near her stepfather's house, the General permitted her to go ashore and take leave of her friends, but under a guard of two officers and a party of soldiers, with strict orders that she was not to speak anything in Erse, or anything at all but in the presence and in the hearing of the officers. And therefore she stayed only about two hours, and then returned again to the ship.[3]

*N.B.*—The above I transcribed from Dr Burton's own 1747.
hand-writ. Happening to mention several questions that were 23 Nov.
fit to be proposed to Miss MacDonald, the Doctor desired me to give him them in writing, for that he would endeavour to procure direct answers to them. Accordingly, I gave them

[1] Particularly Donald Roy MacDonald. See f. 768. [2] See f. 201.
[3] See ff. 201, 202.

23 Nov. to him in writing, and he performed what he had promised.
fol. 541. Here follows an exact copy of the questions and their answers.

QUESTION 1ST.—Ask particularly at Miss MacDonald by what lucky accident it came about that she and Captain O'Neil had a meeting at first to concert measures? Whether or not it was by direction of her stepfather, Armadale, or of any other person? For as O'Neil was an entire stranger in the country this is a material question, and must remain a mystery till Miss clears it up.

ANSWER.—When the Prince and his few men were skulking in the Long Isle, O'Neil used to scour about frequently by himself to try what he could learn, and this led him to be several times at Milton before he made the proposal to Miss MacDonald, as they were then skulking thereabouts. O'Neil, by being free and easy with Miss and her brother, came soon to learn their history, and that their mother lived in Sky, etc.

2.—Ask particularly if Armadale had any private meeting (in person) with the Prince while skulking. For it is certain that General Campbell complained that Armadale was the person who had misled him when searching for the Young Pretender in the Long Isle.[1]

ANSWER.—When the Prince first landed upon the continent of Scotland, Armadale, happening to be on the continent, was walking upon the shore just as the Prince and his friends were
fol. 542. sailing towards it. Armadale, spying a sail making towards the very spot upon which he was walking, stopt till he should learn what the ship was, and from whence she had come. When the Prince stept ashore, Armadale was the first man that took him by the hand and kissed it, for he was introduced to the Prince by those that were along with him. The Prince and Armadale conversed some time together. Soon after this Armadale returned to the Isle of Sky, and never saw the Prince again, either before or in the time of his skulking.[2]

3.—It is said that Armadale writ a letter, which he sent by Miss MacDonald to her mother, recommending the Irish girl, Bettie Burk, as a good servant, aud giving an account of her good qualifications as such. It were to be wished that

---

[1] See f. 458. [2] See f. 304.

Miss could recollect the contents of said letter as exactly as possible, in order to give a narrative of the same. 23 Nov.

Answer.—The substance of the writing which Armadale sent to his wife, was as is already mentioned in Miss MacDonald's own journal.[1]

4.—Ask what particular songs he chaunted in crossing from the Long Isle to Sky? if she can give the names of them?

Answer.—He sung 'The King shall enjoy his own again,' and 'The twenty-ninth of May,' etc. *fol.* 543.

5.—Ask whether or not Lady Clanronald furnished the Prince and Miss MacDonald with some bottles full of milk as part of their provisions on board the boat in the passage to Sky? And whether or not the Prince did put the bottle to his head, and drink in common with those on board?

Answer.—Lady Clanronald did furnish them with some bottles of milk, and the Prince (in the passage) putting the bottle to his head, drank in common with those on board *Jock-fellow-like.* Lady Clanronald had but one half-bottle of wine (there being so many demands upon her, particularly from parties of the military) which she likewise caused to be put on board the boat. The Prince in the passage would not allow any person to share in this small allowance of wine, but kept it altogether for Miss MacDonald's use, lest she should faint with the cold and other inconveniences of a night passage.

6.—To the preceeding questions Dr. Burton was pleased to add one of his own, which is what length of time there *fol.* 544. happened to be betwixt the Prince's leaving Kingsburgh's house and Captain Ferguson's coming thither to search for him?

Answer.—About six or seven days; so that the Prince behoved by that time to be actually upon the continent.

*N.B.*—Miss Flora MacDonald was upon the 28th of November 1746 put on board the *Royal Sovereign* lying at the Nore, and upon the 6th of December following, was removed to London and put into the custody of Mr. Dick, a messenger, in whose hands were likewise Dr. Burton, Æneas MacDonald, Malcolm MacLeod, Clanronald, senior, Boisdale, etc. But Lady

[1] See f. 525.

Clanronald was not allowed to be in the same messenger's house with her husband.

ROBERT FORBES, A.M.

fol. 545.

## *TOWNLY'S*[1] *GHOST, Etc.*[2]

When Sol in shades of night was lost,
And all was fast asleep,
In glided murder'd Townly's ghost
And stood at William's feet.

Awake, infernal wretch, he cried,
And view this mangled shade,
That in thy perjur'd faith relied
And basely was betray'd.[3]

Embrew'd in bliss, embath'd in ease,
Tho' now thou seem'st to lie,
My injur'd form shall gall thy peace,
And make thee wish to die.

Fancy no more in pleasing dreams
Shall frisk before thy sight,
But horrid thoughts and dismal screams
Attend thee all the night.

fol. 546.

Think on the hellish acts thou 'st done,
The thousands thou 'st betray'd ;
Nero himself would blush to own
The slaughter thou hast made.

---

[1] Francis Townly, Esquire, of an honourable family in Lancashire, was Colonel of the Manchester regiment, and one of the nine English gentlemen that suffered first upon Kennington Common, July 30th, 1746. [See *Scots Magazine* for July, pp. 326-330.]

[2] The verses are printed with some variations in 'Manchester Collectanea, Chetham Society,' vol. lxviii. p. 235.

[3] Alluding to the capitulation at Carlisle.

Nor infants' cries, nor parents' tears
  Could stay thy bloody hand,
Nor could the ravisht virgins' fears
  Appease thy dire command.

But, ah! what pangs are set apart
  In hell, thou 'lt quickly see,
Where ev'n the damn'd themselves will start
  To view a friend like thee.

In haste, affrighted, Willie rose
  And trembling stood and pale;
Then to his cruel sire he goes
  And tells the dreadful tale.

Chear up, my dear, my darling son
  (The bold Usurper said),
And ne'er repent what thou hast done,
  Nor be at all afraid.

If we in Scotland's throne can dwell *fol.* 547.
  And reign securely here,[1]
Your uncle, Satan 's king in hell
  And he 'll secure us there.

## Copy of several remarkable Narratives taken from the mouth of Dr. Archibald Cameron's lady,[2] by Dr. John Burton, when in Edinburgh.

The Prince in going into the hut where the thieves[3] were 1746. July.
(being forced to do it), having been eight and forty hours

[1] England. [2] See f. 374.

[3] Meaning here I suppose the Glenmoriston men [see f. 172], for these men (as I have often heard) were such infamous thieves and noted lifters of cattle, in a word, such remarkable banditti by profession, that the country people who knew them would not drink with them. And yet they proved most faithful and trusty friends to the Prince in his greatest dangers and distresses. These very men (consider and wonder!) that could at any time risque both body and soul for less than the value of a single shilling, were found proof of *thirty thousand*

July. without any sustenance, was discovered by one of them who knew him well.[1] This trusty fellow, knowing the Prince's condition, *fol.* 548. and at the same time, not daring to tell his companions who their new guest was, had the presence of mind to call out, 'Ha, Dougal MacCullony, I am glad to see thee.' By this the Prince found that he was known to this man, and that the man behoved to be a friend by the expression he had now used. The Prince took the hint and humoured the joke so well that he owned the name given him, and accordingly sat down and ate very heartily of some boyled beef and pottage. The man who knew the Prince found (after talking privately with the Prince) that it was necessary to inform his companions who their new guest was. Upon knowing of this they rejoiced greatly and made it their study how to serve him in the best manner they could, two of them being always employed by turns to keep sentry or a good look-out, and to bring in provisions, which they did in plenty. In short they behaved with the utmost fidelity and respect to him while amongst them.

When the Prince and, I think, Cameron of Glenbean or Glen- *fol.* 549. pain were travelling together, one day the latter after going about three miles,[2] missed his purse,[3] wherein he had forty guineas and would needs go back for it. But the Prince was not at all for his returning upon any account. However, Glenbean was positive not to want the purse, and therefore he desired the Prince to wait behind a hill near the place where they then were till he should come to him again. The Prince was obliged to comply, and Glenpean had not gone far before a party of soldiers appeared and marched the very road they should have gone had not Glenbean left his purse; by which means the Prince must inevitably have been taken. The Prince lay snug and watched the road the soldiers went, waiting Glenpane's return. Glenbean found his purse and returned with joy, the Prince at that time having no money, which was

---

*pounds sterling*, and generously despised the tempting bait, whilst others (gentlemen by birth, improved by a proper education) greedily sought after it. This is a most surprising instance of fidelity and heroic virtue!—ROBERT FORBES, A.M.

[1] See f. 1451. [2] See ff. 172, 620.

[3] See this point corrected afterwards, f. 820.

the chief reason that made Glenpean so positive on returning to seek for the purse. July. The Prince told him what he had *fol.* 55 seen, on which they took a different route, heartily thanking Providence for so lucky and so seasonable an accident.

The Prince, not many days after his return from Sky to the continent, sent one to Glenbean[1] (I think) desiring Glenbean to meet him at such a place. But before the messenger and Glenbean came to him he was obliged to remove from the place appointed upon seeing some soldiers approaching towards it. Glenpane and the guide coming to the place and not finding the Prince, parted and went different roads in order (if possible) to find him out. After the Prince had left the place appointed for the meeting, it became so very misty or foggy that a person could not see a yard before him. During the continuance of this fog Glenbean walking up a vale accidentally met with the Prince, being so near as to rub upon one another before the one could discern the other. The Prince in a bold manner asked the other who he was, the Prince being ready for a defence provided it had been an enemy. The answer being given, the Prince said, You are the man I sent *fol.* 55 for, and I am such an one. Soon after this, another guide being got (for they never heard any more of the former guide, who parted from Glenbean when both of them were endeavouring to find out the Prince), they set out for the place whither the Prince was a-going; and the fog still remaining as thick as before, the Prince happened to fall, and was going headlong down a precipice of above twenty fathoms deep, when the guide most happily catched hold of his foot. But the Prince's weight brought him down also, and both of them must inevitably have had their brains knock'd out had it not been for Glenbean's seizing fast hold of the guide who still kept fast hold of the Prince though in so much danger himself. By the help of Glenbean and some shrubs growing on the side of the precipice they recovered themselves and were both preserved.

As soon as the besiegers of Fortwilliam left the place, a *fol.* 55 party of Caroline Scott's men from within the fort went to the house of Cameron of Gleneavis and plundered it, and stript

---

[1] See ff. 569, 608.

his lady of all her cloaths, one petticoat only excepted, taking the very shirt off her and looking upon it as a favour to allow her to untie her own petticoats. They stript one of Dr. Cameron's daughters, a girl that was staying with her aunt at Gleneavis. They stript Gleneavis's only son, a boy about seven years of age, who having gold loops and gold buttons on his cloaths, the soldiers were so greedy of them though half worn that one of them took out his knife and cut them all off. In his hurry cutting off the button upon the child's shoulder, he cut with so great force that he wounded the side of the boy's neck. The mother seeing the blood immediately swooned away, imagining the villain had cut the boy's throat. But
*fol.* 553. when she came to herself she examined the wound and found it of no great consequence.

This lady with her own and two of her brother's children was forced to go and live in a cave of a rock, where she stayed six months, making the best shift she could for provisions to herself and the poor helpless children. Captain Scott sent her a message, pretending that what was done was without his knowledge or consent, and that if she would go to Fort William she should have such things as belonged to her. She consulted her brother Lochiel, who advised her to go. She went accordingly. The captain gave her her shoe-buckles, her buttons for her shirt-sleeves, which in the hurry of taking the soldiers had broke, and a cloak that had been taken from Dr. Cameron's little danghter.

[*N.B.*—Gleneavis was never out, and only during the siege of Fort William, some of the besiegers took up their quarters at his house].

*fol.* 554. Notwithstanding, Scott pretended he knew nothing of the soldiers' actions, yet he never punished any one of them for what had been done. He wrote to the Duke of Cumberland an account of what he or his men had done, who sent for answer that he greatly approved of what had been done. This letter from the Duke of Cumberland (amongst many others) was taken when the post-boy was seized by some of the Highlanders, and I believe it may be got.

The soldiers, or rather some of the independent companies, being out upon the plundering affair, met with a poor old woman, who instead of a cap had a piece of linen cloath about her head. One of the soldiers rather than have no prey at all, took off the piece of cloath; and one of the officers (a Campbell) seeing a head of gray hairs likely to make a good wig, had it instantly cut off. Upon this the poor woman begged to have her piece of linen cloth again to prevent her catching cold, but in lieu of that the officer gave her a kick in the *fol.* 555. breech and bad her begone for an old bitch. She went to General Campbell to make her complaint; but he said as the officer was not under his command he could not relieve her, but that had it been any of his officers or men he would have made them restore what was taken. In the present situation he said he could not assist her. This the old woman told to Dr. Cameron's lady verbatim.

After plundering every place and destroying all the meal, etc., and driving away all the cattle, etc., they destroyed all ferry boats or removed them, and would neither suffer the people to go out for provisions nor suffer any provisions to be brought to them.

The Prince kept a regular journal.

The Duke of Cumberland gave orders in writing sealed up and not to be opened till they should happen to catch the *fol.* 556. Pretender, and if they should miss him, to return the orders unopened.

A captain asked Kingsburgh at Fort Augustus about knowing the young Pretender's head.[1] The person so killed cried out as he fell, 'You have murdered your Prince,' which so far deceived them that the Duke of Cumberland went up directly for London in full persuasion the thing was done.

The two gentlemen who came over with letters in cyphers to the French ambassador sent to find out Lochiel.[2] A third was taken and hanged immediately by the military, they pretending that he had once been a spy in Flanders, but he was really an officer in the French army. There were about forty volunteers on board the same ship with the said gentlemen. They knew nothing of the battle of Culloden till their arrival in Scotland. The Prince in disguise took a letter to them (as

---

[1] See f. 146.

[2] See ff. 173, 175, 628, 635.

*fol.* 557. from the Prince) desiring they would deliver up their letters to the bearer, whom they might trust, for the Prince was afraid they might be spies, and as he could talk French well he chose rather to go himself under a borrowed name than to send any person to them. When he came to them they delivered to him all the letters, which, being in cyphers, he could not make anything of. They were left by their own vessel, and so Lochiel took care of them till the vessel came for the Prince. When again they saw the Prince and knew him to be such they were greatly ashamed that they had used him like a common man, in which shape he had formerly appeared to them.[1]

Colonel Warren went over to France on purpose to fetch a vessel for carrying off the Prince and such as should be with him.

*fol.* 558. The Prince and Lochiel were obliged to remove their quarters when Monroe of Culcairn[2] was killed, because they apprehended there would be a much narrower scrutiny upon that account.

As the military had destroyed all the provisions in the country, the poor old women used to follow where they had seen the soldiers marched in order to get the bowels and the green hides of the cattle which had been killed. These they used to cut and to boil them upon a fire. The soldiers finding this out used frequently to leave a party concealed, who, when the poor women were regaling themselves about the fire, as above, used to shoot them for diversion and for wagers, etc.

*fol.* 559. Captain Ferguson, having one of Lochiel's brothers as a prisoner, would not allow him a bed to lie on, nor anything else but ropes and cables. He fell ill and was so bad that in his then situation it was thought he could not recover. Complaint was made to Lord Albemarle, who sent a physician to

---

[1] See ff. 173-176.

[2] One day when I was conversing with John Cameron (in Edinburgh), uncle of Mr. John Cameron, Presbyterian preacher and late chaplain at Fort William, I asked him if he could inform me who the person was that had shot Culcairn out of the wood. He answered he had good reason to assure me that the father (an old man) of that Cameron whom Captain Grant had basely murder'd near the same spot was the person, and that his aim was against the said Captain Grant. But as he and Culcairn were walking together the latter had the chance to receive the bullet and to fall for his companion.——ROBERT FORBES, A.M.

see him and make his report of him. He returned and said if Mr. Cameron was not brought ashore or was better assisted he must die soon by neglect and ill-usage. Accordingly, Lord Albemarle sent a party for him with an order to Ferguson to deliver up Mr. Cameron. But Ferguson said he was his prisoner and he would not deliver him up to any person without an express order from the Duke of Newcastle, or the Lords of the Admiralty. On this refusal Mr. Cameron's friends sent a bed *fol.* 560.
and bed cloaths with some other necessaries, with intent to put them on board. But Ferguson swore if they offered to put them on board he would sink them and their boat directly. The captain soon afterwards sailed, and, when in the Thames, poor Mr. Cameron died.

*N.B.*—The preceding Remarkable Narratives, etc., I transscribed from Dr. Burton's own hand writ.

Robert Forbes, A.M.

## Copy of a Letter (of a very singular nature) to Arthur Lord Balmerino.[1] *fol.* 561.

*August* 15, 1746.

My Lord,—The name subscrib'd to this letter may prob- 15 Aug. 1746
ably surprize your lordship as one altogether unknown. However, be it sufficient that it comes from one who (though he had not the honour of knowing you before you were in the unhappy circumstances in which you now are) has nevertheless esteem enough for your lordship, founded on the greatness of your behaviour in these circumstances, as to bear no inconsiderable a part in every misfortune that may happen to you. But as in a very short time I can be no longer serviceable to yourself, I must be obliged to transfer my regard to that only person whom you will regret to leave, I mean your wife; and that Lady Balmerino may be at any time ascertained as to the person who would, in regard to your lordship, do all he could to abate *fol.* 562.
her concern by all the marks of friendship which he can possibly shew, I have inclos'd this little paper as a tally which will never

[1] See f. 58.

15 Aug. be in any other hand than in that of the author of this letter. If your lordship has any particular instructions you may leave them seal'd up for me and to be left directed for me at the bar of the British Coffee House over against the Musegate near Charing Cross, and they shall be punctually observ'd.

I have nothing further to add but to desire that your lordship would signify by some means or other that you receiv'd this letter, and then to wish you, as I do from the bottom of my soul, an easy passage out of this world and eternal happiness in that which is to come. And I remain your Lordship's most affectionate friend.

(*Sic subscribitur*) MATTHEW JOHNSON.

Addressed thus upon one of the corners below the wafers without any impression,

*To the Rt. Honble. the Lord Balmerino.*

*fol.* 563. 1747 10 Dec. *N.B.*—Upon Thursday, December 10th, 1747, from the hand of my Lady Balmerino I receeived the original letter from which I made the preceeding transcript wherein I have carefully observed the spelling and pointing of the original, which was an old coarse hand. The bit of paper inclosed in the letter was the half of a square piece of paper which had been torn from one of the corners to the opposite one. Upon asking some questions about the letter, my Lady Balmerino was pleased to give me the following history of it. Her ladyship said that the letter was delivered to my Lord upon the Friday (the date of the letter) before my lord's execution, and that his lordship made a return to it wherein he acknowledged the receipt of such a missive. A gentleman called for and received the return at the bar of the British Coffee House, etc. Soon after my Lord's death a gentleman called at my Lady *fol.* 564. Balmerino's lodgings desiring to know if her ladyship lodged in that house, and having received information that she lodged there, he said that was all he wanted to know and went off directly. After my lady went to live in Mr. John Walkingshaw's house the same gentleman (as is supposed) came and enquired if Lady Balmerino lodged there. Mrs. Walkingshaw happened to be the person that answered the call, took the

gentleman into a separate room and told him that my Lady Balmerino lodged there, and that her ladyship being then in the house he might see her if he pleased. To which the gentleman answered that all he wanted to know was if my Lady Balmerino lodged in that house; and was then making to go off when Mrs. Walkingshaw informed him that Mr. Walkingshaw was at home and begged him to stay a little and talk with him. But the gentleman refused to see Mr. Walkingshaw. However, Mrs. Walkingshaw pressed the gentleman so much that at last he agreed to see Mr. Walkingshaw. In the course of the short conversation (for the gentleman went soon off) the letter happened to be talk'd of, and the gentleman said he was not *fol.* 565.
the author of the letter, but that he was only employed about that matter. Mr. Walkingshaw then told the gentleman how much my Lady Balmerino would be indebted to such private persons as would be pleased to take notice of her in her present distressed condition; for that her ladyship was positively resolved not to accept of the smallest assistance or favour from the Court, if she should starve for want of bread. To this the gentleman made no reply at all, but immediately took leave of Mr. Walkingshaw. When Mr. Walkingshaw returned to the room where he had left some company who had been dining with him he told my Lady Balmerino and others present what had passed betwixt the gentleman and himself, and withal remarked that the gentleman looked very like one that used to be much about Prince Frederick's Court. But he could not affirm any thing positively about the gentleman at all. *fol.* 566.

Neither my Lady Balmerino nor any person concerned in her has ever heard any more of this matter. Although Mr. Walkingshaw has been at pains to make all the enquiry he could, it has never yet been in his power to make any further discovery about this affair. My Lady Balmerino is determined to preserve the letter and the piece of paper that was inclosed, and if anything cast up relative to the contents of the letter, her ladyship has been pleased to promise to inform me about it.

Robert Forbes, A.M.

My father was at the taking of one of three the 3 parties of the Campbells in Athole, namely the party at the Kirkton of Strowan. Mr. James Stewart, late of Urrard, was one of Lord Loudoun's officers who refused to deliver his sword after the rest had surrendered; and the late Mr. Alexander Stewart, minister of Blair-Athole, was along with the Campbells.

Mr. James Stewart of Cluns was the Captain of the Prince's party who apprehended those at the Kirkton of Strowan in Athole. D. MACKINTOSH.[1]

fol. 567. Upon Tuesday, December 22d, 1747, I waited upon Dr. Archibald Cameron's Lady at her lodgings in Edinburgh when she was pleased to favour me with two papers, exact copies of which are as follows:—

## COPY of the ORDERS given by COLONEL JOHN CAMPBELL to CAPTAIN CAMPBELL of Knockbowie of the Argyleshire Militia, and which was taken from the original order found amongst Knockbowie's papers and baggage, which were seized when the greatest part of his men were made prisoners at Rannoch by Lord George Murray.

*Nairn House, the 20th February* 1746.

Orders for Captain Campbell of Knockbowie. You are to march directly hence with your own company, Carsaig's, Raschelly's, and Ardmenish's to the following parts, where you are to dispose of the men as follows:—

| | Men |
|---|---|
| At Blairfetty, | 60 |
| At Kenichan, where you are to be yourself, | 100 |
| fol. 568. At Glendulichan and Cochivile, | 60 |
| In all | 220 |

[1] This paper is not in Mr. Forbes's own hand, and it appears as if the subscriber had been obtained to write it in and sign it.

It is the Duke of Cumberland's orders you take post according to the above list. 20 Feb.

You are to have the command of the several companies above mentioned.

Such of the rebels as may be found in arms you are to take prisoners, and if any of them make resistance you are to attack them, provided their numbers do not exceed yours. And it is his royal highness's orders that you give them no quarters.

You are to seize upon all kind of provisions that belongs to the rebels or may be designed for their use.

You are to make your report three times a week to the commanding officer at Castle Menzies or Blair of Athol.

(*Signed*) John Campbell.

There is one material circumstance omitted in the Journal given by Mr. John Cameron, and which ought to come in after these words,[1] '*so close to their tents as to hear every word they spoke.*' The material circumstance omitted is as follows:— *fol.* 569.

When the Prince sent for Donald Cameron of Glenpean, the said Donald went along with the messenger to the place the Prince had appointed, and according to the Prince's orders took along with him all the provisions he had, which was no more than two or three handfulls of oatmeal and about a pound of butter. And when the messenger had conducted the said Donald Cameron to the place appointed for meeting the Prince, by some accident or other the Prince had left that place and they missed him. Upon which they were very uneasy and resolved to go different ways to see to find him out. And there happening a great fog or mist to come on at that time they wandered a considerable while in the hill. At last the said Donald Cameron by mere accident met the Prince, who being in great want of provisions, the said Donald gave him the oatmeal and butter he had, of which he ate very heartily, and which subsisted the Prince and other three persons who were with him for four days. As the lines of the regular troops were July. *fol.* 570.

[1] See f. 172.

July. then all formed with a design to surround the Prince, he advised with the said Donald Cameron if there was any possibility of getting through the lines and in what manner. Upon this the said Donald replied that it was a most hazardous attempt and next to an impossibility, as the sentries were all placed so close that they were each of them within speech of the other. But the Prince being determined to penetrate through the
*fol.* 571. lines at all hazards, having nothing else left for his escape, the said Donald told him that there was one pass with a hollow to go down over a very high rock, which was exceedingly hazardous, but was the only place he could advise the Prince to attempt. Upon this they went to the said precipice, being then dark night, and Donald Cameron went first over the pass and the Prince followed. But as he was coming down the hill to the top of the rock where the pass was, his foot slipped, and the hill being so steep he tumbled to the very top of the rock and would certainly have fallen one hundred fathoms perpendicular over the rock had not he catched hold of a tree on the very top of the rock with one of his legs, after his body passed the same and which he kept hold of betwixt his leg and his thigh till the next person that was following catched hold of
*fol.* 572. him by the breast and held him till the said Donald Cameron returned back and came to them and recovered both. At last they got over this so dangerous pass, by which they pass'd the first line of the troops, and different nights after this they passed the other four lines of the troops creeping on their hands and feet betwixt the sentries.

The above account was taken from the said Donald Cameron his own mouth, so it can be depended upon.

After this follows the rest of Mr. John Cameron's journal, the next words being these, 'When they came to Glenmoriston they got six stout,' etc.[1]

*N.B.*—The preceeding narrative appears to be the same with that account which Dr. Cameron's lady gave to Dr. Burton from the best of her remembrance.[2]

[1] See f. 172.

[2] See f. 550.

At the same time (December 22nd) I received from Dr. Cameron's lady a copy of Mr. John Cameron's journal,[1] and as the copy I had made my transcript from happened to be very unexact and confused, so I was not a little desirous to compare my transcript with that copy which I received from Mrs. Cameron; and upon comparing them together I found them to be one and the same, there being no other difference betwixt them than what ordinarily proceeds from the carelessness and inaccuracy of transcribers. Even the copy I had from Mrs. Cameron was none of the correctest as to orthography. 22 Dec. *fol.* 573.

In the course of our conversation Mrs. Cameron said it was a very remarkable thing that the Prince landed (in his course from the island Eriska) in Lochnannua, at Boradale in the country of Arisaig[2] and in the parish of Ardnamurchin, and that at the very same spot he went on board the eight-oar'd boat after the battle of Culloden, to sail for the isles, that he was thereafter coming from the Isle of Sky, and likewise that at the very same spot he imbarked for France upon September 20th, 1746, when he was forced to leave Scotland and to seek for safety in foreign parts.[3] ROBERT FORBES, A.M. *fol.* 574.

## Copy of the Petition of George, Lord Rutherford, etc.[4]

To the King's Most Excellent Majesty the Humble Petition of George, Lord Rutherford.

SHEWETH,—That your petitioner has always been firmly attached to your Majesty's royal person and government, and in testimony thereof was the first man in Britain (for what he knows) that discovered to the ministry in the end of April last that the horrid and wicked rebellion was intended. And

[1] See f. 155.

[2] Or rather Moidart, Lochnannua being the boundary betwixt Arisaig and Moidart. See f. 640.

[3] See ff. 180, 281, 352, 355, 522.

[4] This was George Durie of Grange, who claimed the title of Lord Rutherford as grand-nephew of the first Lord. His claim was disputed by a gentleman of the Rutherford family, and to determine the dispute the Lords' Committee of Privileges ordered both to lodge their proofs, and in end disallowed both claims.

as a further proof of his fidelity and loyalty did upon the fifth of June last cause apprehend Sir Hector MacLean and George Blair of Castlehill, by three o'clock in the morning, being informed they were to set out by five o'clock for the
*fol. 575.* Highlands of Scotland in order to raise all the clans they could influence to rise in an open rebellion against your Majesty in favour of a popish pretender.

That your Majesty's petitioner hath been the butt of the malice of the Jacobites ever since, and was obliged to fly his own house for fear of his life, they having sent a hundred and fifty men three different times to his house, who carried off a great part of his fine armory, cows, and cattle, because they could not apprehend himself and horses, with which he made his escape.

Therefore your petitioner himself hopes your Majestie will not only be graciously pleased to order the arrears of his pension to be paid him, but as a further testimony of your royal favour, to create him a peer of Great Britain, and the more especially as he has the honour to be a remote relation to your Majesty, his grand-
*fol. 576.* mother, the Earl of Teviot's mother, having been niece to King James the Second of Scotland.

And your Majesty's petitioner (as in duty bound) shall ever pray for, etc.

28 Dec. Upon Monday afternoon, December 28th, 1747, Captain Alexander MacDonald, brother german of Æneas or Angus MacDonald of Dalely in Moidart, of the family of Clanranald, and full cousin-german to Miss Flora Macdonald, visited me in my own room and favoured me with a Journal of several sheets in his own handwriting, and in the handwriting of young Clanranald, and in the handwriting of MacDonald of Glenaladale, the Journal having been drawn up in the presence, and by the mutual assistance of all the three. By appointment the said Captain Alexander MacDonald returned
*fol. 577.* to me next day about nine o'clock in the morning and stayed with me till near six o'clock at night, in which time I went through the whole Journal with him at great leisure, not only the better to prevent my making any mistakes in transcribing

of it, but likewise to have his observations upon some parts to render them more plain and intelligible to those who are strangers, either to the subject matter or to the Highlands of Scotland, and to have his additions to other parts, for he had told me there were some few omissions of lesser matters. The whole Journal (from beginning to end) is written in a very legible and distinct letter and the words are well spelled. At the same time the said Captain MacDonald gave me his animadversions upon some parts of other Journals which I read to him, as will appear hereafter. 29 Dec.

[Now begins the Journal in Captain Alexander MacDonald's handwriting.[1]] *fol.* 578.

After the battle of Culloden (which was fought upon the 16th April 1746) his royal highness, attended only by one Colonel O'Sullivan, Captain Allan MacDonald (a clergyman of the Church of Rome)[2], Mr. Alexander MacLeod (one of the Prince's own *aid de camps*), and one Ned Burk, came that night late to Frazer of Gortleg's house in Stratherick,[3] where my Lord Lovat himself stayed at that time. He took some refreshment there and a couple of hours rest, but went off before daylight and tooke his route by Fort Augustus and through Glengary. And though his royal highness was vastly needful of some recreation there after such fatigue, the disconveniences of both time and place did not allow any better accommodations than a piece of a broiled trout he received there from some well-wisher for his supper at MacDonalds of Droynachan. 1746 16 April *fol.* 579.

Upon Friday's morning, being the 18th, he set off, and held through Lochharkaig, where he stayed that night with Donald Cameron of Glenpean, married to MacDonald of Auchtrichatan's daughter. 18 April

---

[1] It seems to have been from this Journal that the 'Account of the Young Pretender's Escape,' in the *Lockhart Papers*, vol. ii. pp. 537-562 is taken. But here it is much fuller.

[2] See ff. 281, 328.

[3] Some difference in this page, etc., from the account of Ned Burk, an eye-witness of the route.—ROBERT FORBES, A.M.

19 April Upon Saturday's morning, being the 19th, he came to Oban in Kinlochmors, a corner of Clanranald's estate, and for their further security contented themselves that night for their lodgment with a small sheal house near a wood.

20 April Early upon the 20th his royal highness got up and went straight to Arisaig to a town called Glenbiastill, where the Prince got a sute of new Highland cloaths from Angus MacDonald of Boradale's spouse, the better to disguise him and to make him pass for one of the country. At Glenbiastill the few gentlemen (that happened to come home from that unlucky battle of Culloden) of Clanranald's men assembled about the Prince, in order to consult and lay their schemes for
*fol.* 580. his present and future safety, being convinced that the enemy would probably soon be about them if not resisted. His royal highness stayed at Glenbiastill for four nights,[1] and upon the 24th then instant his royal highness concurred in their opinions that he should leave the mainland and go to the Isles.

24 April Upon the said 24th day, as young Clanranald was absent at the beginning of their consultation, he finds great fault with his royal highness's resolution of leaving the continent so abruptly, but that he should tarry for some time to see what might cast up; and that he would immediately cause four small bothies to be built at competent distances in different woods where he might with all imaginable security skulk for some time, and that he himself (young Clanranald) and some other chosen men would take a trip to the Isles to look out for a ship for his transportation, if seen requisite. But then his royal highness was so far overswayed by Colonel O'Sullivan, etc., that he would by no means stay. Upon this young Clanranald
*fol.* 581. immediately prepares a boat and shippage (Donald MacLeod of Gualtergill in Sky being appointed pilot and steersman)[2] and got all things in the best order the place and time could admit of. And consequently about the 24th then current,[3] being

[1] See f. 329. [2] See f. 281.

[3] Donald MacLeod in his own account fixes precisely upon April 26th with which Ned Burk's account agrees pretty exactly. See ff. 273, 281, 316, 329. Captain O'Neille in his account, attested by his own subscription, makes the Prince arrive in Knoidart only upon the 28th. See f. 675. But in the copy I formerly took of O'Neille's Journal the Prince came to Knoidart the 26th. See f. 183.

Thursday, they set sail for Uist. The wind blew pretty reev (*i.e.* smart or strong) from south-east, that in weathering the point of Arisaig the bowsprit broke in pieces.[1] It was a most terrible dark night, attended with a violent tempest and some flashes of lightning, and wanting a compass they could not be sure how they steered their course. But at daybreak they providentially found themselves within few leagues of their wished for harbour, and landed at Rossinish in Benbecula[2], where the eight-oar'd boat did not stave to pieces for (to put this matter beyond all doubt) the eight-oar'd boat was lately brought back again from the Island Skalpay or Glass to the owner upon the continent, Angus MacDonald of Boradale.[3] 24 April *fol.* 582

About 8 o'clock in the morning they arrived upon the 25th of April. They refreshed themselves there for three days and were visited by the old Laird of Clanranald. Upon Monday, April 28th, early, they set sail for the Lews, ilk one of them getting borrowed names, his royal highness being called young Mr. Sinclair, the son, and O'Sullivan, old Mr. Sinclair, the father,[4] and Captain Allan MacDonald (the clergyman as forementioned) being named Mr. Graham, but the crew retaining their old designations. But it is to be observed that previous to the parting with old Clanranald it was thought advisable to advertise the whole company they should give out among the Lews people that his royal highness, Colonel O'Sullivan, Captain Allan MacDonald, and O'Neille were the captain, mate, boatswain, etc., of a merchant ship shipwreckt at the Isle of Tiry, and being straitned how to get home to their native country, the Orkneys, came to Uist, where Clanranald's brother, MacDonald of Boystil, advised them distrest gentlemen to embrace the company of his men to the Lews, who were bound for the town of Stornway there, in order to hire a competent vessel to carry some meal from the Orkneys to supply the country. And then, if they should succeed in procuring the 25 April *fol.* 583

[1] Donald MacLeod mentions nothing of this at all. See f. 283.

[2] The forementioned Captain Alexander MacDonald (well skilled in the Earse) assured me these words should be spelled as above.

ROBERT FORBES, A.M.

[3] See ff. 270, 284, 287, 343.

[4] See ff. 133, 286.

said ship, Mr. MacLeod of Gualtergill would land them at their own home in the Orkneys still under the borrowed names above mentioned.

So, after planning their voyage in this order, they set sail for
28 April the Lews as aforesaid upon Monday the 28th, about 6 in the morning, the wind blowing boisterously from the South-west, and they landed, Tuesday's morning the 29th, about seven o'clock, at the Isle of Skalpay, and went to the house of Donald MacEan Oig, *alias* Campbell, tenant, married to a gentlewoman of the name of MacDonald, a rigid loyalist. They took their repose that night at Skalpay whereof they had great need.

30 April Upon Wednesday morning, being the 30th of April, they sent off Donald MacLeod and four Uist people to bespeak a
*fol.* 584. ship at Stornway in order to concert their meal bargain from the Orkneys, etc. Mr. MacLeod went thereabout with the greatest expedition and fidelity, though in the meantime his conduct thereanent did prove unlucky,[1] for after hiring a sufficient brigg of forty tuns carriage for £100 sterling freight, and settled all things for sailing off, the master of the ship would by no means undertake the voyage cheap or dear. Which turn of affairs so far disordered the whole scheme that they were now more straitned than ever in their lifetime; for it seems they scented something about the Prince. However, Mr. MacLeod tried as his last effort to buy the ship, and engaged to give £300 for it. 'Tis probable the captain of the vessel, being tempted by this unexpected offer and his own poverty, was induced to dispose of the vessel, though he could scarcely want it (the ship). But through avarice he exacted £500, which Donald MacLeod's necessity obliged him to promise. But then the exorbitancy of the sum, together with the unlikelihood of Mr. MacLeod's ability to be master thereof, suggested
*fol.* 585. to the seller it was in favour and behoof of the Prince, which he formerly suspected. The bargain was made, but immediately he so far resiled therefrom as to deny he would go himself alongst with them, but would allow the mate and crew to go; but when these were brought present, they likewise refused

[1] See this affair cleared up, ff. 289, 479.

unless the captain would go also. With this the whole project was blasted at once, and not only so, but the carrying the affair on thus far did involve them no greater difficulties and dangers than though they had never broached it; for all kind of people then began to be of such itching ears and sharp-sighted that his royal highness's being at the Lews began to blaze abroad. Donald MacLeod, conceiving the imminency and fatal consequence, without loss of time goes back to his royal highness at Kildun's house at Arynish and apprized him of the whole story.[1] Upon this they took the alarm and go streight to the yawl they left formerly at Loch Seaforth. As they were launching it out Captain MacDonald (the Popish Clergyman)[2] asked some of the country people that followed them to the shore in order to be gazing at them, if there was any amongst them that would accept of a reasonable præmium for piloting them to Loch Fraon, an harbour in the shire of Ross, upon the coast of Seaforth's country, but there was none that would answer. However the meaning of this question was to suggest they were bound for that country whereas they were to take a quite contrary course. May *fol.* 586

They made off late, about six o'clock upon the 5th of May, those upon the shore noticing their course, but the darkness of the night favoured them to disappear, and the wind blowing contrary for their purpose (though favourable for the place given out to the Lews folks) obliged them to skulk that night under the covert of a hollow creek in a small Island,[3] at the very foot of the loch called Loch Shelg, where they were necessitated by a contrary storm to lurk for three nights, having both the comfort and mortification of seeing some Lews vessel passing by pretty near them, bound for Loch Fraon in pursuit of his royal highness. 5 May

Upon Thursday 8th May the wind chopt about to the north and they were that night on sea. They landed Friday's morning at Rairnish, near Rossinish in Benbecula, belonging to Clanranald. They went from Rairnish to Rossinish, where old 8 May *fol.* 587

[1] See ff. 288, 330.

[2] This is a mistake, for he was left at Scalpay and returned to South Uist. ff. 287, 343.—ROBERT FORBES, A.M.

[3] Probably Erwin, f. 291.

9 May Clanranald and his lady came to pay them their respects with all the accommodations the place could afford. It was consulted there whether his royal highness could venture to spend his short time at old Clanranald's house or not.[1] But, being voted by a plurality in the negative, it was determined the Forrest house in Glen Coridale should be repaired for his use, a remote private place, yet centrical, both to maintain a free communication betwixt him and his Uist friends and by its advantageous situation facilitating his ready access either to take sea or hill, in case alarmed upon the coming of an enemy, by the advertisement of their out spies who were planted on all arts of them. For there was still a boat and skippage in
fol. 588. readiness for his reception in case obliged to take sea, as also good guides to conduct him through the mountains.

10 May About the 10th of May 1746, his royal highness with his small retinue and as little grandeur, repaired to his famous palace of Coridale (the house in the forest) in South Uist, attended constantly by Captain Allan MacDonald (Popish clergyman),[2] Colonel O'Sullivan, Mr. O'Neill, the two Rorie's, and Alexander and John MacDonalds, all formerly his royal highness's officers in Clanranald's regiment, with a dozen of other sturdy clever fellows that served as guard, and running several incident errands back and forward. These were all the people that stuck constantly to his royal highness at Coridale.[3]

fol. 589. In the Forrest house the Prince (when resting himself) used to sit on a fail-sunk, *i.e.* an earthen seat, having some fog and

---

[1] Captain Alexander MacDonald, Ned Burke, and Miss Flora MacDonald agree in telling me that the name of Clanronald's house in Benbecula is Ballinnagallioch, *i.e.* the Carl's house, about five miles from Rossinish, which is a kind of a harbour. I told the said Captain Alexander MacDonald that I had asked at several Highlanders about the derivation and meaning of the word Benbecula, but I could never meet with any one that could give me an answer. I then begged him to satisfie me as to that. He answered that he looked upon Benbecula as a corruption of the original, which in Erse was Beinnmhaol (as to the true just spelling) but Beinviol (as to the vulgar way of spelling), *i.e.* a hummle or bare hill, there being such a hill in the island of Benbecula.—ROBERT FORBES, A.M.

[2] This gentleman, no doubt, has joined the Prince upon his returning again to South Uist.—R. F.

[3] At this time 'tis to be presumed from what follows that Donald MacLeod was upon his errand on the continent, f. 301.—F.

plaids under him, and would step into a by-chamber, which served as a pantry, and (when he stood in need of it) put the bottle of brandy or whiskie to his head and take his dram without any ceremony. Upon the 10th day of June MacDonald 10 Jur
of Boystil,[1] Hugh MacDonald of Bailshair in North Uist, of the family of Slate, James and Lauchlan MacDonalds, brothers of the often mentioned Captain Alexander MacDonald, and Ranald MacDonald of Torulum of Clanranald's family, visited the Prince in his Forrest palace,[2] to pay him the compliments of the day. Their drink was only cold brandy out of a clean shell without any mixture at all, and the Prince stood it out better than any one of them in drinking the health of the day. The foresaid Hugh MacDonald of Bailshair is that gentleman whom Miss MacDonald pitched upon as the Prince's guardian[3] for his greater safety, but who refused the important trust from fear of the great dangers attending it. *fol.* 59

The island of South Uist is reckoned the only country best for game in all Scotland, where all species of wild fowls are in great plenty besides deer, etc.[4] His royal highness was pretty oft at his diversion through the mountain, papping down perhaps dozens in a day of muircocks and hens, with which this place abounds; for he is most dextrous at shooting all kinds of fowl upon wing, scarce ever making a miss.

His magnaminous spirit bore all crosses and adversities with the greatest Christian resignation and manly courage.

Now his royal highness's greatest danger was an invasion from Clanronald's continent where then the throng of all his pursuers encamped. And as the enemy were persuaded he once came to thir rough countries of Clanronald's, viz., Moidart, etc., it was natural for them to guess he would pass to the outmost recess of his isles as being environ'd by the sea and consequently a faster refuge. The old laird of Clanronald being pretty oft in his company, the prudent, old, reverend sage did now and then apprehend the dreadful danger that aye *fol.* 59

[1] As to Boystil's seeing the Prince at Coridale and being merry with him, see f. 462.

[2] The Prince had different kinds of palaces, f. 300.—ROBERT FORBES, A.M.

[3] Referred to at ff. 188 and 526, but his name now given.

[4] See ff. 307, 333.

June impended his royal highness's constant abode in an isle, and did (with others) signifie the same to him. But he would not be dissuaded from continuing in South Uist till farther account. Upon this old Clanranald thought it advisable to go to the continent to dive into the doings there, and in case of any apparent danger to advertise his royal highness; all which he did. The people of Uist would have prest him more than they did to leave the island, were it not they feared he might think it was more for their own safety than for the delivery of him they would be so importunate.

June About the latter end of June Captain Ferguson landed at Barra with some hundreds of red-coats. Three hundred of the MacLeods of Sky likewise at the same time arrived at Benbecula, all in quest of his royal highness. General Campbell with a squadron had gone about to St. Gilda, the remotest of all the western Isles, the Laird of MacLeod proprietor, and
*fol. 592.* from thence was to come to Uist. Besides all this the channel between Uist, Skie, and Canna was all full of ships and scooners, so that at once his royal highness and his few adherents were to be attacked from all quarters environed by sea and land.

It was now full time to concert measures for the evading this prominent danger; upon which they sent off Lieutenant John MacDonald (nephew to Captain Alexander MacDonald frequently mentioned) to the south end of the country to reconnoitre Captain Ferguson's motions, and sent Lieutenant Rory MacDonald (brother of the said John MacDonald) to the north end to observe and bring message of the route of the MacLeods; and appointed that both these messengers should tryst them at Lochboystil, a centrical place for making use of any future resolution. The gentlemen came back at the appointed time and place, and told that these two parties were to march forward from both the ends of the Isle in search of the Prince till they would meet in the midst of the country.

The Almighty only knows, and the Divine dispenser of human providence allennarly knows, what inexpressible per-
*fol. 593.* plexity of mind and anguish of soul and body his royal highness and his small retinue laboured under when taking it into their serious consideration that they were now encompassed by no less than three or four thousand bloody hounds, by sea and

land, thirsting for the captivity and noble blood of their Prince, June
the apparent heir of Great Britain, France, and Ireland, and that none of the many thousands that should be in readiness to relieve him at the expence of their lives were then about him either to protect or advise him, but only one O'Sullivan, one O'Neille, and twelve MacDonalds, and that very handfull to be disposed on different posts for fear of being suspected for such a number. However, Providence directed them to the top of a hill called Beinchillkoinnich in South Uist, from whose eminence they might have an ample prospect. They here formed themselves into a committee to consult for the most expeditious methods to leave Uist (though late) and it was here they pitched upon the stratagem of getting Miss *fol.* 594.
MacDonald;[1] and then they severed till they came to the shealling called Alisary within a mile to Milntoun, where Flora MacDonald lived as housekeeper to her brother, young Milntoun. At first the young woman was surprized, but then when spoke to sincerely did condescend to go with his royal highness through the vast world if it should contribute in the least to his safety. She goes off to Benbecula where the lady Clanranald was desired to have suitable cloaths for Bettie Burk who was engaged in the station of a servant with Flora MacDonald to go with her to the Isle of Sky.

The Lady Clanranald upon the advertisement of this noble stratagem provides all necessaries for getting Mrs. Burk cled suitable to her new servile station, and after getting all things in due order that were proper for Mrs. Burk and her mistress, they both go off to Lochuiskava in Benbecula, where his royal highness, Lieutenant John MacDonald, Rory and Alexander MacDonalds, ensigns, Little Rory MacDonald (John's brother) and some other Uist hands met them with a small shallop of a *fol.* 595.
boat of about nine cubits, wright measure, in full readiness to take sea. It was about St. Peter's feast, the 28th of June.[1] The 28 June
Lady Clanranald begged of his royal highness to try on his new female apparel, and after mutually passing some jocose drollery concerning the sute of cloaths, and the lady shedding some tears for the occasion, the said lady dresses up his royal highness in

[1] See f. 524.

[2] See f. 529.

his new habit.[1] It was on purpose provided coarse as it was to be brooked by a gentlewoman's servant. The gown was of caligo, a light coloured quilted petticoat, a mantle of dun camlet made after the Irish fashion with a cap to cover his royal highness whole head and face, with a suitable head-dress, shoes, stockings, etc. So that about 8 o'clock in the evening of
26 June Thursday, June 26th, his royal highness, etc. moved towards the boat, where he took leave of the Lady Clanranald most kindly.

*fol.* 596. It is to be observed that some days before this Donald MacLeod, as also Captain Allan MacDonald and Colonel Sullivan parted from his royal highness at the side of Lochboystil. Sullivan dropt several tears and loudly roar'd when parting with his master. Then all the company was dismist that could not speak Erse but O'Neille, and O'Neille himself two days ere they went off to Skie.

His royal highness at parting with the Lady Clanranald thanks her for her great trouble about him. They[2] go to sea about 8 o'clock at night, and as they had but a small breeze in their sail they made but a very little progress; so that about one o'clock afternoon next day they were inclosed with a prodigious thick fog which made them think it dangerous to continue rowing for fear they might err in their course and perhaps unawares approach the coast of Skie, which they were informed was all hemmed with guards of the enemy to prevent
*fol.* 597. his royal highness's landing, and being safe. So it was thought proper to drop in the oars till the mist dissipated; and soon afterwards the fog disperst by a feeble caver (*i.e.* a breeze) of north-easterly wind against them. They mistook the point of Snod for the point of Watternish; but as they were obliged to row close to the shore for a shelter from the wind that blew sidling, they descry pretty near them, about a musket-shot, a number of men under arms, and to the number of fifty armed men sallying out of a formall guard-house, all rushing to the shore, crying vehemently to land upon their peril. Upon this

---

[1] See ff. 218, 525.

[2] In this account the honest and trusty Neil MacKechan is altogether neglected. See ff. 149, 529, 533.—Robert Forbes, A.M.

they only changed their course a little further from the shore and did not much pull their oars better than before for fear of suspicion.

Lieutenant John MacDonald (nephew of Captain Alexander MacDonald) sat at the helm, and the other four MacDonalds wrought most strenuously at the oars, pulling them most industriously but without the least disorder or hurry. But as the guard saw no appearance of their obeying orders they let fly a thick volley at them, which made more noise than harm. His royal highness rubs up their courage not to fear the *fol.* 598.
villains. The people replied they maintain'd no fear upon their own account if Providence should rescue his royal highness. He repeats no fear of him. Indeed the people were apt to believe all he could say, God aye working on patent passages for their safety from time to time. But having seen three[1] boats on the shore, they were mighty apprehensive they would pursue them. However, they wrought the boat to the utmost of their endeavours, doubled the tedious point of Watternish, and by this they left all MacLeod's country behind them. And though Sir Alexander MacDonald did not join his royal highness they were sure to meet with greater favour among the worst of his men than among the cold MacLeods. Besides that, MacDonald of Kingsburgh was trysted[2] to meet his royal highness upon the shore of Modhstot, Sir Alexander's habita- *fol.* 599.
tion. They landed upon the 29th of June, Sunday, at 29 June
Modhstot Bay, where Kingsburgh met them exactly as soon as they footed Skie. He directs Miss MacDonald and Mrs. Burk[3] to his own house; Clanranald's people that brought his royal highness from Uist were desired by himself to turn home.

His royal highness lodged that night at Kingsburgh. From

---

[1] See f. 530.

[2] This is an error, for there was no tryst in the case at all, nor could there be any such thing. It was all a matter of chance, or rather a wise, unexpected appointment of Heaven, without any foresight or contrivance of man. This is plain and undeniable from Kingsburgh's own words and the words of Miss Flora MacDonald. See ff. 145, 210, 533.—ROBERT FORBES, A.M.

[3] Kingsburgh himself went along with the Prince, leaving Miss MacDonald, etc. who overtook them by the way. See ff. 145, 533.—ROBERT FORBES, A.M.

30 June Kingsburgh he went to Portree,[1] where Captain Malcolm MacLeod received him and conducted him to the Island of Raisa, and from thence back again to Skie, where he delivered him over into the hands of the old Laird of MacKinnon, who without loss of time provided him in a boat. The old Laird and four of his men, viz., John MacRory VicLauchlan, Calum M^cEan Yairs, etc., ferryed his royal highness over from Skie to a place called Buarblach in Glengary's lands. He was but two or three nights upon the MacKinnon's lands. Here it is
*fol.* 600. to be observed, though he happened to be landed upon Glengarie's lands, that he would by no means go to Knoydart, which was very near him, nor to Lochabar, but chused to strike directly to Clanranald's[2] continent to a place called Cross in Morror, from whence he was received and conveyed by Angus MacDonald of Boradale,[3] the first house he entred in the Highlands at his first landing upon the continent.

Veir mi niosh a chorrahimain yuit
fein, gos a faidh mi tuillad Gaosid.

*i.e.* I leave you the Thrawcrook
till I get more hair.[4]

10 July The night before the 10th of July,[5] his royal highness set sail from MacKinnon's country, accompanied by old MacKinnon,[6] and another gentleman of MacKinnon's name (viz., John MacKinnon, a captain in his royal highness's service before), with the crew, and landed by daybreak next morning, being the eleventh, at a bay in Glengary's Morror, where he stayed all that day and the following night. There are two Morors, the
*fol.* 601. one belonging to Glengary and the other to Clanranald.

Early in the morning upon the 12th, MacKinnon parting with

---

[1] See f. 228.

[2] It appears the Prince had a particular affection for the MacDonalds in his wanderings. See ff. 214, 538.

[3] See f. 281.

[4] In the original Journal here ended the handwriting of Captain Alexander MacDonald, and then immediately began the handwriting of young Clanranald.

[5] This is a wrong date. See the true state of the case in ff. 247, 262, 1218, 1224.—ROBERT FORBES, A.M.

[6] See ff. 244-247, 1664, 1831.

him, he (the Prince) sailed into Loch-Naives,[1] when, as he was turning at a point he was met by some of the Slate militia, who put the ordinary questions. From whence they came? Where they were bound? And they undauntedly answering suitable to the time, the militia let them pass without taking further notice. His royal highness pursued farther into the loch, and how soon he got out of sight of them, he landed, and travelling the remainder of the day and the following night through hills and woods, he arrived upon the thirteenth of July in that part of Clanranald's estate called Moror, where being received by the Laird of Moror (MacDonald, of the family of Clanranald, and lieutenant-colonel of the Clanranald regiment) in a small hut, where he lived for the time, his own houses being burned by the enemy sometime before, and having refreshed himself there that night and the next day as well as these troublesome times could afford, he set out the night betwixt the 14th and 15th, accompanied by Captain MacKinnon and a guide, and arrived before day at Boradale,[2] the place of his first landing, and was there received by Angus MacDonald of that place, who, having his houses burnt and effects destroyed by the troops under General Campbell's command, was obliged to remove with his royal highness to a hut in a neighbouring wood, where he refreshed him the best way he could for three days.

12 July

13 July

*fol.* 602.

15 July

Upon the 18th of July his royal highness wrote a private letter (by John MacDonald, junior, son of the foresaid Angus MacDonald of Boradale, and a lieutenant formerly in Clanranald's regiment) to Alexander MacDonald of Glenaladale, major to Clanranald in his royal highness's service, and who was well known to his royal highness before, commanding his attendance at the foresaid place to concert measures for his royal highness's safety. 18 July

Angus MacDonald of Boradale had two sons of the name of John, viz., John, senior, and John, junior, the former of whom was killed at Culloden battle.[3]

Immediately after sending off the above-mentioned express

[1] See ff. 1219-1226, 1831.

[2] Four times at this place, see f. 573.—R.F.

[3] See f. 280.

*fol.* 603. 18 July his royal highness got an account of MacKinnon's being taken, which made it, he judged proper, for his royal highness to remove, upon the 18th, four miles to the eastward to an inaccessible cave (known to very few of the country people), accompanied by the said Angus MacDonald of Boradale and his son (Ranald, formerly lieutenant to Clanranald's own company), where he was to stay till Glenaladale should join him.

20 July On the 20th of July at night, Glenaladale met with the foresaid Angus Macdonald at the place they had formerly agreed upon, from whence he was conducted to his royal highness. On the 21st, Angus MacDonald got a letter from a son-in-law of his own, acquainting that it was whispered about the country that his royal highness was with them, and representing how dangerous it was for them to stay any longer there, and making an offer of a place he had prepared, where they might be more secure for some time. Accordingly Ranald MacDonald
*fol.* 604. was sent to reconnoitre the place.

22 July Upon the 22nd of July, Lieutenant John MacDonald being sent to view the sea-coast and to learn something of the enemy's motions, he returned with the news of their seeing a small boat, something like one of the enemy's tenders, which allarmed that side of the coast. Upon which his royal highness judged it proper to remove from his grotto (without waiting the return of the quartermaster he sent the day before to take up his lodgings) in order to repair to the place prepared for him in the Glen of Moror. His royal highness, being accompanied by Major MacDonald of Glenaladale, Angus MacDonald of Boradale, and his son, John, junior, when they came to a place called Corrybeinicabir, they were met by Angus MacDonald's son-in-law, who, as above mentioned, had a place prepared for them in the Glen of Moror,[1] and who informed that young Clanranald was within a few miles of them, who had come to where he then was, in order to conduct his royal
*fol.* 605. highness to a safe place he had prepared for him: but his royal highness and his small party having gone on too far towards their designed quarters, and it being late to go where Clan-

---

1 In the original Journal here ended the handwriting of young Clanranald, and then began the handwriting of Glenaladale.—ROBERT FORBES, A.M.

ranald was or to send for him that night, they went on, supposing they would have time enough next day to send for Clanranald. Accordingly they pursued their journey to the Glen of Moror, and sent Angus MacDonald to provide some necessaries. Upon his royal highness's arrival at his quarters,[1] an information was brought that General Campbell, with six men-of-war, well furnished with troops, had anchored at Loch Naives (the place where his royal highness landed from Skie in Glengary's country), whereupon two men were sent off by Loch Moror to Loch Naives to observe General Campbell's motions. But before they had time to return, Angus MacDonald came back upon the 23rd early, without waiting for the necessaries he went for, and brought intelligence that Captain Scott had come to the lower part of Arisaig from Glengary's Moror. July *fol.* 606.

His royal highness and the small company that was with him, finding upon this information that Clanranald's country was surrounded on all sides by the troops, and that in all probability there could be no further security for his person in that country, it was resolved that his royal highness should leave it with the utmost dispatch, especially since it was impossible to join young Clanranald,[2] the enemy being already between them and the place where he was. Accordingly he sets out, accompanied only by Major MacDonald of Glenaladale and his brother (Lieutenant John MacDonald), and the other Lieutenant John MacDonald, junior, Boradale's son, being obliged to part with Angus MacDonald of Boradale, and his son-in-law (Angus MacEachine), surgeon formerly to Glengary's regiment, that they might the more easily pass undiscovered by the guards placed on their way,[3] and by twelve o'clock they came to the top of a hill in the outmost bounds of Arisaig called Scoorvuy, where having taken some refreshment it was thought proper to send Lieutenant John MacDonald (Glenaladale's brother) to Glenfinin, the outmost bounds of Clanranald's country, and Major MacDonald of Glenaladale's property, as well for intelli- *fol.* 607.

[1] In the original Journal here ended the handwriting of Glenaladale, and then began again the handwriting of young Clanranald.—ROBERT FORBES, A.M.

[2] See f. 1837.

[3] In the original Journal here ended the handwriting of young Clanranald, and then began the handwriting of Glenaladale.—ROBERT FORBES, A.M.

July gence as to bring two men Glenaladale kept still on guard there, and appointed them to meet him about ten o'clock at night on the top of a hill, above Lochharkaig in Lochiel's country, called Scoorwick Corrichan.

Lieutenant MacDonald being sent off, his royal highness set out, and by two o'clock came to the top of a neighbouring hill called Fruighvein, where, observing some cattle in motion, his royal highness and the other Lieutenant MacDonald stood back, and Major MacDonald of Glenaladale went to examine what that might mean; who upon examination found this to be some of his own tenants removing with their cattle from the troops, who by this time, to the number of five or seven hundred, *fol.* 608. had come to the head of Lochharkaig, in order to inclose his royal highness in Clanranald's country, while the search was going on very narrowly within it. This being the route they were resolved to hold, pretty much disconcerted their measures. Major MacDonald of Glenaladale bringing back word to his royal highness of what he had heard, they resolved to alter their course, and accordingly the Major sent off one of his own tenants express to Glenfinnan about a mile off, to call back Lieutenant MacDonald and the guard if he had found them, and sent another of his tenants to an adjacent hill for one Donald Cameron of Glenpean,[1] where he had removed with his effects upon the approach of the troops, in order to learn from the said Donald Cameron the situation of the forces that were at Fort Augustus, and if he would undertake to guide his royal highness by their guards, if possible.

While his royal highness and Major MacDonald of Glenaladale, with Lieutenant MacDonald (Boradale's son), waited the return of both the expresses, one of the Major's tenant's wives, regreting the condition she saw him in, and willing to refresh him the best she could (she suspecting nothing of his *fol.* 609. royal highness being in company with him), milked some of her cattle, and brought the fresh milk to them. Upon observing the woman coming up to them, the Prince covered his head with a handkerchief and passed for one of the Major's servants that had got an ache in his head. Notwithstanding the

---

[1] See ff. 172, 569.

refreshment was very seasonable, the day being excessively hot, they could very well have dispensed with the good woman's compliment. However, the Major thanked her and used some policy to dismiss her, having first taken care to have some of the milk reserved for his royal highness, which he drank with pleasure. Soon after the express sent to Glenfinnan returned, but could find neither Lieutenant MacDonald (Glenaladale's brother), nor the two men, they having run express with intelligence to where they expected to have found the Major. The said express brought word that a hundred of the Argyleshire militia had come to the very foot of the hill where his royal highness stayed; whereupon it was thought proper to tarry no longer there; and, as there was no time to wait for Donald Cameron, their expected guide, trusting in the great Guide that directs all, his royal highness, full of courage and confidence, set out about sun-setting with his small retinue, and travelled pretty hard till about eleven o'clock at night, when, passing thro' a hollow between two hills, they observed a man coming down one of the hills. Upon which his royal highness and Lieutenant MacDonald (Boradale's son), stept aside, and Major MacDonald of Glenaladale[1] went to the man to examine whether he might be a friend or a foe, and as Providence would have it, found him to be their intended guide, Donald Cameron, whom after some short conversation he conducted to his royal highness. Donald Cameron gave a relation so far as he knew of the situation of the forces, and undertook to guide them by the guards. Upon this they pursued their way through roads almost impassable even in day light, and travelling all night they came at four o'clock in the morning upon the 24th of July to the top of a hill in the Brae of Lochharkaig, called Mamnynleallum, from whence they could (without the help of a prospective glass) discern their enemy's camp, being not above a mile distant. But being informed by the guide that that hill was searched the day before by the troops, they supposed there would not be a second

23 July

*fol.* 610.

*fol.* 611.

24 July

[1] As this narrative proceeds from Glenaladale himself, so it deserves more credit than that in f. 550, for Mrs. Cameron narrated the matter only from the best of her remembrance, and that too from report that had passed from hand to hand.——ROBERT FORBES, A.M.

24 July search that day, and therefore they resolved to pass the day
there; and choosing the fastest place in the hill they took a
little rest. After two hours sleep the Major, Lieutenant Mac-
Donald, and the guide got up to keep sentry, and by ten
o'clock of the day they observed a man at a distance, and as the
guide (Donald Cameron) being in his own country, and very
near his own place of residence, knew the inhabitants best, he
was sent to converse with that man, and upon examination
*fol.* 612. found him to be Lieutenant MacDonald, Glenaladale's brother,
who not meeting his royal highness at the place appointed and
getting no intelligence of the enemy's being so near till he
himself came within sight of their camp, he turned apprehensive
of what might happen to be the case, and regretting his misfortune in parting with his royal highness, went on wherever
Providence directed him, which (most happily) brought him
directly to the place where the Prince was, who was well pleased
to find the lieutenant safe, as the whole company had given
him over for lost.

His royal highness continued in the top of the said hill all
that day, and about nine o'clock at night set out with his
retinue to the northward, and by one o'clock in the morning of
25 July July 25th, came to a place called Corrinangaull on the confines
betwixt that part of Glengary's country called Knoydart, and
that part of Lochiel's country called Lochharkaig, where the
guide expected some Lochharkaig people to have fled with their
*fol.* 613. effects, whom he had confidence in, and which was very much
desired, as they had entirely run out of provisions, excepting a
very small quantity of oatmeal, and as small a remainder of
butter, which they could not dress or prepare in any shape, as
they travelled continually (for the most part) in view of the
enemy if in day light;[1] their camps being (in a direct line pitched
from the head of the Lochiel in Lochiel's country to the head
of Loch Uirn, dividing Knoydart of that part of MacLeod's
country called Glenealg), within half a mile's distance of one
another, their sentries being placed within call of one another,
and patrols going about every quarter of an hour to keep their

---

[1] See f. 1450.

sentries alert, that so his royal highness might be surely catched should he attempt to pass through them. 25 July

Being pinched in provisions as above, his royal highness stood back with the two lieutenants, while Major MacDonald of Glenaladale and the guide (Donald Cameron of Glenpean) went to some shealing huts where they expected to meet some people. *fol.* 614 But finding none, they chused a fast place in the face of a hill at the head of Lochqhuaigh, to which fastness they came about two o'clock in the morning, having only about a mile in walking to it. After taking an hour's rest there, the guide and Lieutenant MacDonald (Glenaladale's brother) were sent off to the hill above them to furnish some provisions if possible, the Major and his cousin, the other lieutenant (Boradale's son), standing sentries, while his royal highness took some rest. When the sun shined they observed distinctly a camp pitched at the head of Lochqhuaig, and though they did not like the prospect they waited the return of their provisors, who came back to them about 3 o'clock, having got only two small cheeses, that would not be a morsel to the piece of them; and brought intelligence that about one hundred of the red-coats were marching up the other side of the hill his royal highness lodged in, in order to destroy and carry off such of the poor *fol.* 615. inhabitants as had fled to the hill for shelter. Notwithstanding this alarm (the search for his royal highness being general and very narrow all around), they stayed in the same place till about eight o'clock at night, when, setting out, his royal highness travelled stoutly till it became dark, and climbing a steep hill called Drimachosi to the top,[1] they observed the fires of a camp directly in their front, which they could scarcely shun, at Glenqhosy. However, being resolved to pass at any rate, they came so near without being observed as to hear them talk distinctly; and ascending the next hill, no sooner was his royal highness at the top than he and his small party spied the fires of another camp at the very foot where they were to descend. But turning a little westward they passed between two of their guards betwixt one and two o'clock in the morning of July 26 July 26th. After travelling two miles, as they judged, beyond *fol.* 616.

[1] See ff. 1448, 1474.

26 July them, they came, betwixt two and three o'clock in the morning, to a place on the Glenealg side of the head of Lochuirn called Corriscorridill,[1] where having chosen a fast place they took such refreshment as the exigency of the time afforded them, his royal highness covering a slice of cheese with oatmeal, which, though but dry fare, he ate very comfortably, and drank of the cold stream along with it.

His royal highness passed the whole day in the above place till about eight o'clock at night, and the guide (Donald Cameron), knowing the road no further in the course the Prince intended to hold, he expected to find some people thereabouts he could trust. Glenaladale and the guide accordingly went about in order to find them; but no sooner did they get out of their fasthold than they found they had lodged all day within a canon-shot of two small camps, and spied a company of red-coats getting in some muttons to a cot and chusing out some
*fol.* 617. for slaughter. Upon which they brought[2] back word to his royal highness of what they had seen. Upon this his royal
27 July highness set out, and by three o'clock in the morning of July 27th they came to Glensheil in Seaforth's country. As they had run out entirely of their last supply of provisions, the Major and Lieutenant John MacDonald (Boradale's son) were sent off as well to furnish some as to provide a guide to conduct them to Pollieu in Seaforth's country, where his royal highness had heard some French vessels to have been; and coming to the place where the inhabitants were, the Major bought some provisions, and made application to one of the inhabitants for a guide, which he undertook to provide. In the meantime that the Major was talking about the guide, a Glengary man appears coming towards them who that morning had been chased by the troops (they having killed his father the day
*fol.* 618. before) from Glengary to Glensheil. Upon seeing this man the Major knew him, who upon conversing with him found him to have formerly served in his royal highness's army, and conceiving

[1] See f. 1450.

[2] In the original Journal here ended the handwriting of Glenaladale, and then began the handwriting of Captain Alexander MacDonald, which continued to the end of the Journal.——ROBERT FORBES, A.M.

him to be a trusty fellow, resolved to make use of him[1] as a reserve in case they should be disappointed of the intended guide, and would be thereby obliged to alter their course, though at the same time Glenaladale did not disclose his mind to the Glengary man. 27 July

The Major after furnishing what provisions he could get, returned to where his royal highness was, and taking some refreshments, they went to the face of an adjacent hill to take some rest and sleeping, till about four or five o'clock in the afternoon, when they got up and dismist their old faithful guide, Donald Cameron.[2] Soon after whose departure, the Major, upon seeing the Glengary man passing by on his way to his country, slipt out of his den and brought him to a byplace, till he would be sure about his intended guide, and returning to his royal highness consulted with him what should be done in regard of the Glengary men, and the Prince approved of *fol.* 619. keeping by him till their fate with regard to their other guide should be known. About seven o'clock at night, the man who undertook to furnish the guide was seen coming to the place which had been appointed for meeting at betwixt him and the Major, who immediately stept out to the place appointed, and after some conversation he found that the only French ship that had been there was gone off, and that no guide could be procured. The Major finding it needless to proceed further towards Poolieu made the man believe that he intended to return again to his own country and so dismist him.

Immediately Glenaladale returned to the Prince and told him what had passed; whereupon it was resolved to change their course, and accordingly the Glengary man was introduced to his royal highness, and most chearfully undertook to guide him. And, preparing to pursue their journey, they set out late *fol.* 620.

---

[1] Who could have thought that the troops would have furnished the Prince with a guide to make him escape their own clutches at the very nick of time when they were hunting after him like a partridge in the mountains? For their chasing the Glengary man proved the means of bringing him to the place where Glenaladale was. An instance of Providence most adorably conspicuous that made these very men who were eagerly panting after his blood, become (quite opposite to their intention) the principal instruments of the Prince's preservation.
ROBERT FORBES, A.M.

[2] See f. 1451.

27 July at night, and going on about a quarter of a mile, they stopt a little, which was occasioned by the Major's clapping his hand to his side and missing his purse,[1] wherein he had another purse of gold he had got the charge of from his royal highness in order to defray his charges, and which he had forgot when they had been preparing for their journey. Upon this Glenaladale and Lieutenant MacDonald (Boradale's son) returned, and coming to the place found his purse, but opening it miss'd the inner purse in which the gold he had got from the Prince was contain'd. In the midst of his surprize he reflected it might have been taken away by a little boy sent by their landlord, Gilchrist MacCrath, with a compliment of milk, as the landlord supposed to the Major, who had not allowed him to know anything about the Prince at all. He was the more confirmed in this opinion, as they had left the boy at the place where the
*fol.* 621. purse was forgot. Accordingly the Major and Lieutenant MacDonald went all the way to MacCrath's house, which was more than a mile off, and calling for him represented to him the inconveniency of the accident that had happened, and intreated him to oblige the boy to restore the purse, which he did to a trifle. They returned by a different road from what they had gone before, and came to the Prince, who was in great pain for them, fearing they might have been intercepted by an officer and two private men that pass'd under arms by the place where his royal highness was in their absence; which made him reflect how much the hand of Providence guided him in all his ways,[2] and particularly in this late lucky accident of losing the purse, which stopt them in their progress: whereas if they had pursued their journey they would inevitably have fallen in with these persons, in which case any thinking person may
*fol.* 622. easily judge how fatal the consequence of such a meeting might have proved. The Prince likewise used to think much upon the happy undesigned event of his enemies, chasing a guide to him for no less than thirty miles whom Providence led in his way to conduct him safe out of their hands.

---

[1] This is the same narrative with what is contain'd f. 549 of this volume, and serves to correct a mistake there as to the person who lost the purse: for 'tis plain that Glenaladale has been the man.——ROBERT FORBES, A.M.

[2] See f. 550.

Having once more got together, his royal highness and his 27 July
small retinue set out, and travelling all the remainder of the night came early in the morning of July 28th to a hill-side 28 July
above Strathchluaine, and, chusing a fast place, took some rest till towards three o'clock afternoon, when they set out, and travelling by a hill-side about a mile from the place they rested in, they heard the firing of small arms in the hill above them, which they judged to be some of the troops chasing people that had fled with their effects. They steered their course northward, and mounting up a high hill betwixt the Braes of Glenmoriston and Strathglass came late at night to the very top of it, and being very dark they were obliged to lodge there all *fol.* 623.
night, the only shelter his royal highness could have being an open cave where he could neither lean nor sleep, being wet to the skin with the heavy rain that had fallen the day before; and having no fuel to make a fire, the only method he had of warming himself was smoking a pipe.

About three o'clock in the morning of July 29th the 29 July
Lieutenant (Glenaladale's brother) and the guide (the providential Glengary man) were sent in quest of some trusty people they intended to find out in order to conduct his royal highness to Pollieu,[1] and were appointed to return to the top of a neighbouring hill where his royal highness and the remainder of his retinue were to meet them. Accordingly about five o'clock in the morning his royal highness set out, and by seven came to the top of that hill, where meeting with *fol.* 624.
the guide on his return he told he had found out his intended trustees,[2] who had given him directions to the Major (they knowing nothing at all of his royal highness, only suspecting that a young man they were told was in company might be young Clanranald) to repair into a cave in the Brae of Glenmoriston in a place called Coiraghoth, where they promised to come at an appointed hour with a refreshment. Accordingly his royal highness set out, and by the time appointed came to the place and meeting with these few friends (who upon

---

[1] See ff. 1451, 1661, 1664.

[2] The faithful Glenmoriston men. See f. 172.

29 July sight[1] knew his royal highness, having formerly served in his army) they conducted him to the grotto where he was refreshed with such chear as the exigency of the time afforded; and making a bed for him, his royal highness was lulled asleep with the sweet murmurs of the finest purling stream that could be, running
fol. 625. by his bedside, within the grotto, in which romantic habitation[2] his royal highness pass'd three days, at the end of which he was so well refreshed[3] that he thought himself able to encounter any hardships.

Having time in that space to provide some necessaries and to gather intelligence about the enemy's motions, they removed,
2 Aug. on the 2d of August, into a place within two miles of them, called Coirmheadhain,[4] where they took up their habitation in a grotto no less romantic than the former. After taking some refreshment, they placed their sentries and made up a bed for his royal highness in a closet shaped out by nature, and seemingly designed by her for the reception of his royal highness. He rested comfortably all night. In this place he resided four days; but, being informed that one Campbell (factor to Seaforth

---

[1] Perhaps the circumstance of 'Ha! Dougal MacCullony' etc., mentioned by Mrs. Cameron is not literally true. But I have often heard that these men used to call the Prince by the name Dougal the better to conceal him. See f. 1451.
ROBERT FORBES, A.M.

[2] Here begins vol. iv. of Bishop Forbes's Manuscript Collection. It is entitled: 'THE LYON IN MOURNING, or a collection (as exactly made as the iniquity of the times would permit) of Speeches, Letters, Journals, etc., relative to the affairs, but more particularly, the dangers and distresses of. . . . Vol. 4th. 1748.

*Extera gens nostro passim dominatur in orbe,*
SCOTORUM PRINCEPS *vix, ubi degat, habet!*

On the inside of the back board there is one piece of wood, an inch long by about $\frac{3}{4}$ broad and $\frac{1}{8}$ thick (and there has been another piece, but now it is not) and underneath is written:—

The above are pieces of that identical eight-oar'd boat, on board of which Donald Macleod, etc., set out from Boradale on the continent with the Prince (after the battle of Culloden) for Benbecula in the Long Isle. The above pieces were sent to me from Major MacDonald of Glenaladale to the care of Captain Alexander MacDonald in Edinburgh, brother-german to Dalely. The said Alexander MacDonald delivered the above pieces to me on Wednesday evening, December 28th, 1748, he having come under a promise upon our first acquaintance to procure me a bit of the eight-oar'd boat. See vol. 2, ff. 270, 284, vol. 3, ff. 581, 582. Vol. 4, ff. 677, 678.——ROBERT FORBES, A.M.

[3] It is very remarkable that the Prince made little rest serve him at any time, and that he was almost indefatigable in walking and in undergoing hardship. [See ff. 238, 244, 291.]——ROBERT FORBES, A.M.

[4] See f. 1664.

in Kintale, and captain at that time of a company of militia) had gathered a throng herdship of cattle and pitched his camp within four miles of them, it was then resolved his royal highness should remove his quarters. Accordingly, upon the 6th of *fol.* 626.
August, he set out to the northward, and, by break of day upon 6 Aug.
the 7th, came in upon the Brae of the Chisholm's country, called Strathglass, having left one of their party behind in the Brae of Glenmoriston to wait Campbell's motions.[1] That friend came up to them that night (August 7th) and brought 7 Aug.
word that they needed not be afraid for that night. Upon this his royal highness repaired to a neighbouring sheally hut, when they prepared a fire, and, taking some refreshment, they made up a bed for his royal highness, which consisted of a long divot or fail (that was found lying in the hut) of six or seven foot long; and, laying it flat upon the floor, the grass side uppermost, with a pillow of the same kind, his royal highness slept on the earthen bed all night. They remained in this place two days, and in that time the prince sent an express to Pollieu[2] to know the certainty about some French vessels being there.

Early in the morning of August 9th, his royal highness set *fol.* 627.
out to the northward so far on his way to Pollieu in case of 9 Aug.
any encouragement[3] from that quarter, and, travelling a muir road unfrequented, came that night into another sheally hut, about the distance of five or six miles from where they had set out. There they remained all night, and set out about two o'clock in the morning of August 10th, and came about twelve 10 Aug.
o'clock into a place called Glencanna, where, passing the remainder of the day in a wood, they repaired late at night to a neighbouring village, where they stayed only the dead of night.

About two o'clock in the morning of August 11th, they set 11 Aug.
out and climbed a hill on the northmost side of Glencanna,[4] where they pass'd the day and sent off two of their party to

---

[1] See f. 1665.

[2] The Prince used to insist upon it that the French would still send him succours. This I heard from severals. See ff. 175, 214.—F.

[3] See the preceding note.——Robert Forbes, A.M.

[4] See f. 1665.

11 Aug. furnish a fresh supply of provisions. At night they repaired into a neighbouring sheally hut, where they remained two days,
*fol.* 628. expecting the return of the express sent off to Pollieu, who accordingly came to them and brought back word that the only French ship that had come there had sailed off again, and that a couple of gentlemen who had come on board of her had actually landed and were making the best of their way for Lochiel's country in search of the Prince.[1] He, becoming anxious to know if they had dispatches for him, resolved to return towards the place from whence he had come in order to meet with them.

13 Aug. August 13th, at night, they set out cross the water of Canna back again, and boldly by young Chisholm's house, came by two o'clock in the morning to a place called Fassanacoill in Strathglass; and, consulting what was best and fittest to be done, it was resolved (before his royal highness should venture any further) to send some spies to the Braes of Glengary and Lochiel's country, in order to get sure information
*fol.* 629. whether or not the search for him in these bounds was all over, and if the troops had gone into their camp at Fort Augustus, which being done, his royal highness remained there for three days in a very fast wood, the inhabitants dreaming nothing of his being so near them.

They waited the return of the spies, who brought notice that the forces had returned to their camp. Whereupon his
17 Aug. royal highness set out by six o'clock in the morning of August 17th, travelled through an unfrequented road, and came by ten o'clock to the Braes of Glenmoriston, and, passing the day on the top of a hill, they set out at night, and had not travelled above a mile when they learned that a strong party had been detached to the Braes of Glengary in quest of the Prince. Upon this it was resolved to proceed no further on their journey untill the motion of the enemy should be farther known; and then they repaired into a neighbouring sheally
*fol.* 630. hut, where they passed the remainder of the night.

18 Aug. Upon August 18th, in the morning, three expresses were sent off—two to Lochiel's country, Lochharkaig, who were to

---

[1] See ff. 173-176, 356.

seek out Cluns Cameron,[1] and to tell him from Major MacDonald of Glenaladale that he wanted to meet with him in a convenient place; and the third express was to return at the Brae of Glengary and to bring back word if the party they were informed of the night before had returned to their camp or not; that so, if the road should happen to be clear, his royal highness might be pursuing his journey, even while the meeting betwixt the Major and Cluns Cameron was a concerting. 18 Aug

Accordingly the expresses were sent off, and, upon the 19th, 19 Aug
the one that was to return brought word that the road was clear. Whereupon the Prince and his small party, being then ten in number, set out under the advantage of a foggy afternoon, and, passing through Glenmoriston and Glenlyne, came *fol.* 631
late at night to the Brae of Glengary. In their way to the water of Gary, the rain came on so heavy that the water swell'd to a great height. Two of the company went first to try if they could wade the water, and they found it passable, even though it came up to their very middle. Whereupon, his royal highness and the rest of his party entering the water, they forded it safely, and, travelling about a mile from the water of Gary, the night being very dark, they were obliged to pass it on the side of a hill, without any cover, though it rained excessively.

In the morning of August 20th the Prince set out, the rain 20 Aug
still continuing very heavy, and, travelling six miles cross hills and muirs, came about ten o'clock to the Brae of a place called Achnasaul,[2] where the other expresses had been appointed to meet them. There they pass'd the day in a most inconvenient habitation, it raining as heavy within as without it. Towards *fol.* 632
the afternoon they began to despair about their expresses, and, being entirely run out of provisions of any kind and being quite strangers to the situation of Lochiel's country for the present, they began to concert what should be done, when, in the midst of their concert, the expresses came to them and brought word to the Major that Cameron of Cluns could not

[1] See f. 173.

[2] It is omitted in this Journal that Auchinsaul himself was with the Prince. See f. 173.——Robert Forbes, A.M

20 Aug. wait upon him that night, but had directed him to lodge all night in a certain wood within two miles of them, where he would come to them next morning. Accordingly, two of their number were detailed to take a view of their intended habitation, who, coming to the place, found it to be very fast.

And here it must be observed that that wonderful providence which always prevented his royal highness's difficulties seemed in a particular instance remarkable here. He and his faithful few, as has been observed above, running entirely out of all manner of subsistence and being at a loss to know which
Fol. 633. way to be provided, they were immediately supplied by the small detachment, they having shot the finest deer (a large hart) that could be, at the very place where the Prince intended to pass the night.

The two returning with their approbation of the place to his royal highness, he (after permitting Major MacDonald of Glenaladale to acquaint D. MacDonald of Lochgary of their arrival at that place, and to send for him) set out for the intended quarters with his party, and coming to the place, they were most deliciously feasted with their late purchase. Lochgary joined them that night, after which they took their rest.

21 Aug. About ten o'clock in the morning of August 21st, Cluns Cameron joined them, and, remaining there till towards the afternoon, Cluns conducted them into a wood at the foot of Lochharkaig, where they lodged all night, etc.

22 Aug. Timeous in the morning of August 22d, an express was sent
Fol. 634. off to Lochiel[1] to command his attendance. His royal high-

[1] The affair of the Prince's sending expresses to Lochiel, and of Lochiel's sending proper persons to seek out the Prince, and at last of their meeting together as they both intended, appears to me not to be so distinctly and accurately narrated in this Journal as in that of Mr. John Cameron [See ff. 173-179]. As I have made some enquiry into this matter, I shall note down all I have discovered about it as exactly as possible. Dr. Archibald Cameron (Lochiel's brother) and Mr. John Cameron (late Presbyterian chaplain at Fort William) were the persons despatched by Lochiel to use all the endeavours they could to find out the Prince, in which they were happily successful. Lochiel was by this time recovered of his wounds [See f. 1479] as is evident from Dr. Stewart Threpland's leaving him and making his way to Edinburgh in the habit and character of a Presbyterian probationer, in the month of July, long before the Prince and Lochiel could meet. The foresaid Mr. John Cameron was the person dispatched

ness stayed in the foresaid place three days, till the return of the express, who brought word that Lochiel, not being recovered of his wounds and being at too great a distance, could not come, but he sent his brother, Dr. Cameron, to make his apology, who came to his royal highness upon August 25th.

August 26th. The Prince set out with his attendants, and travelling about a mile came to a wood opposite to Achnacary called Torramhuilt or Torvauilt. Dr. Cameron and Lochgary having parted with his royal highness about three or four o'clock in the afternoon to avoid suspicion, as did also Cluns Cameron, how soon he had conducted his royal highness into this last habitation. In this place the Prince remained for eight days, during which time the forementioned French gentlemen were sent for and were brought to the place where his royal highness was, and after staying two or three days with him, were sent to a safe place to be taken due care of till such time as they could get a passage to their own country.

26 Aug.

*fol.* 365.

---

by Lochiel (after meeting with the Prince) to Edinburgh in order to hire a vessel to take him and whom he should bring along with him off the east coast. Mr. Cameron (by the assistance of proper friends) succeeded in this negotiation, as is well known to some. But when he returned to inform the Prince of his success, he, with Lochiel, etc., had set out for the place where the French were landed upon the west coast to take off the Prince, etc. So that Mr. Cameron was left to shift for himself. He made his way back to Edinburgh in disguise, and at last got off under a borrowed name in the same coach with Lady Lochiel and her children for London, the lady passing under the name of Mrs. Campbell, for she could have no pass. They all got safely to France. When I happened to be conversing with John Cameron, uncle of the said Mr. Cameron, in Edinburgh [See f. 558], he told me that he himself attended Lochiel in his skulking. I told him it was surprizing to me how any person could find out the Prince when the ship landed in the west, because he was so far down the country in his way southward, and then asked him if he could inform me what miles the Prince might be from the ships when notice came to him. He said that he himself was then on an errand enquiring about some of the distressed gentlemen, but that he was persuaded the Prince was no less than 60 miles from the ships in a direct line over the tops of hills, etc., as by that time he behoved to be in the confines or in the county of Athol. I said no doubt he meant Highland miles. He said he meant so, for that it would be no less than 70 or 80 ordinary miles; and if one was to travell it by the common roads [See f. 1475], it would make no less than 90 or 100. The indemnity did not make John Cameron (the uncle) safe, because he had carried arms abroad in the first Highland regiment, and when the Prince landed had a pension from Chelsea. He got off to Holland, and from thence to France. He said the Prince, when skulking, used to retire some time morning and evening by himself.——ROBERT FORBES, A.M.

Sept. The Prince seeing himself in a manner out of danger, having got intelligence that all the forces which had been encamped at Fort Augustus were dispersed up and down the kingdom, and that no more was left there but Loudon's regiment; and besides that all the militia were returned home, having delivered back their arms; and supposing that a chance party might come near the place where he was still, he had a safe retreat, south and north as would be thought most convenient; upon all these considerations put together he thought proper to
*fol. 636.* dismiss Major Macdonald of Glenaladale home to his own country near the coast, there to look out for the arrival of French vessels which his royal highness expected daily for conveying him safely off, and to bring him intelligence upon their arrival, the Prince himself being resolved to remain in the same place (unless he was surprized) to wait that event.

3 Sept. Accordingly upon September 3d the Major set out, leaving his royal highness attended by Lochgary and Cluns Cameron, and arrived in his own country upon the 5th, where he remained till the 13th, when Captain Sheridan and Lieutenant O'Burn landed from on board two French ships that anchored in Lochnannuagh upon the Arisaig side in order to carry off his royal highness, they coming to the place where Glenaladale then was and expecting to find the Prince with him.

Lochnannuagh is the boundary between Arisaig and Moydart,
*fol. 637.* so that people can arrive upon either of these places out of that loch.

13 Sept. Glenaladale set out that very night (September 13th) to acquaint the Prince of the arrival of these ships and to conduct him safely on board. But coming to the place where he expected to have found him, to his great disappointment he could get no person that could give any certain account whereabouts his royal highness might happen to be. The Prince had been obliged to retreat by a party that had come out of Fort Augustus under the command of Culcairn and Captain Grant; and Cluns Cameron, who had been appointed to acquaint the Major where the Prince was to be found in case he should be obliged to retreat, having gone out of the way without leaving any directions for the Major either about his royal highness or
*fol. 638.* himself, these things put the Major in the utmost pain, con-

sidering the many disappointments and inconveniencies this piece of inadvertency in Cluns might be the occasion of. Whilst he was taken up with these melancholy thoughts, a poor woman came accidentally where he was and told him the place where Cluns was to be found. Immediately he set out with all diligence and arrived at a shealling whither Cluns came soon after, with whom he concerted measures for sending an express to his royal highness, who by this time had gone where Lochiel was for the reasons abovementioned, that so he might be speedily informed about the arrival of the ships. When the concert about sending an express was adjusted, the Major returned with all possible expedition to the ships to inform the gentlemen of the reasons of the delay, and that the Prince would be with them as quickly as possible. 13 Sept. *fol.* 639.

As soon as his royal highness was informed that the vessels were at Lochnannuagh he set out with all possible diligence for that place, where he arrived about the 28th of September,[1] accompanied by Lochgarry, John Roy Stewart, and Lochiel, and went on board the *Happy*, a privateer of St. Malo's, which set sail instantly upon his royal highness's being on board. 28 Sept.

Here ends the Journal.

*N.B.*—When Captain Alexander Macdonald was in my room (Tuesday, December 29th) I read to him those passages in Mr. Æneas Macdonald's Journal which relate to the landing and the marching down the country, and upon which he gave me his observations. I took them down in writing from his own mouth, and they are as follows :— *fol.* 640.

Vol. 3, page 509, 514. It is an oversight either in Mr. Æneas Macdonald or in Dr. Burton not to have mentioned that the Prince actually landed in Lochnannuagh upon the Arisaig side,[2] and went to Boradale, which was the first roof he July 1745

---

[1] This certainly is a wrong date, for by the best intelligence that can be had the Prince arrived in France on the 29th or 30th of September, having set sail from Scotland on the 20th of said month: [See ff. 522, 1476].

ROBERT FORBES, A.M.

[2] I asked particularly at Captain Alexander MacDonald whether the Prince arrived on the Arisaig or Moidart side, and he assured me he landed on Arisaig. This serves to clear up any doubt in Vol. 2, f. 355, and Vol. 3, f. 573.

ROBERT FORBES, A.M.

July was under upon the continent of Scotland, Boradale is in Arisaig. The landing at Lochshiel must be a mistake, as no ship can land there, seeing it is only a fresh water loch. This will be better cleared up in the following paragraph.

Aug. Vol. 3, page 515. Before the Prince marched to Glenfinnan he was at Glenaladale where old Glenbuicket joined him and delivered over to him Captain Switenham (an English gentleman,
*fol.* 641. one of the prisoners taken by Major Macdonell of Tiendrish.[1] The foresaid Captain went to London upon his parole and strictly kept it till the time prefixed was expired. At Glenfinnan the Laird of Moror, of Clanranald's family, came up to the Prince (before the standard was set up) with 150 men who were joined to the fifty men of Clanranald's following, that had been for some time keeping guard upon his royal highness, the Prince himself thinking fifty men sufficient for that purpose, the rest of Clanranald's men having been employed in carrying the baggage and luggage from the head of Lochshiel[2] (up which loch they had been brought in small boats) to the head of the Loch-iel; which service kept the most of Clanranald's men back for four days from joining the main body at Moidh or Moy in Lochabar.

Captain Alexander MacDonald was on board the frigate in
*fol.* 642. Lochnannuagh before the Prince set his foot on the continent, but he acknowledges he did not then know that the Prince was among the passengers, who being in a very plain dress, Captain MacDonald made up to him without any manner of ceremony and conversed with him in a very familiar way, sitting close by the Prince and drinking a glass with him, till one of the name of MacDonald made him such a look that immediately he began to suspect he was using too much freedom with one above his own rank. Upon this he soon withdrew, but still was in the dark as to what particular person the young gentleman he had been conversing with might be.

Aug. Vol. 3, page 519. Captain MacDonald declared that he could not help looking upon the affair of O'Sullivan's hiding himself in a barn, etc., as a romance.

At the same time I read in the hearing of Captain Alexander

---

[1] See f. 68. [2] See f. 356.

MacDonald the passages in the Journal of Duncan Cameron, etc., that relate to the landing and the marching down the country. He owned they were very exact, and he made only two short remarks upon them, which are as follows. *fol.* 643.

Vol. 2, page 356. Captain MacDonald said it was most certain that if Keppoch, Lochiel, and young Clanranald had not joined the Prince, he would have been forced to shift for himself in the best manner he could.

Vol. 2, page 359. A night at Dalquhinnie before marching to Dalnacardoch.

I then read in the hearing of Captain Alexander MacDonald the conclusion of Captain O'Neille's own subscription, which had been lying by me for some time till I should find leisure to take an exact transcript of it.[1] In the forementioned conclusion Captain O'Neille complains of one in Benbecula that had betrayed him even after he had entirely confided in him, but he does not name the person. I asked at Captain MacDonald if he could inform me who that person was. He told me he knew the whole affair well, and that he would give it me faithfully and honestly. He said that Ranald MacDonald of Torulum in Benbecula was the man there meant,[2] and that the whole story had taken its rise altogether from a jealousy in Captain O'Neille. Ranald MacDonald happened unluckily to have an outcast with Captain O'Neille, who, though a very clever fellow, was heartily threshed by a MacDonald, they having had a boxing bout together. This unlucky difference made O'Neille strongly believe, when he happened to be seized, that Ranald MacDonald had actually betrayed him, whereas Ranald refused to betray him when a sum of money was offered him for that purpose. Upon this Ranald MacDonald has given his oath of old Clanranald, who questioned him upon the report of his having betrayed O'Neille, and was very hard upon him for it, swearing that he deserved to be shot through the head if he had done any such dishonourable thing. June *fol.* 644. *fol.* 645.

As to the story of General Campbell and Campbell of Skipness, Captain MacDonald declared to me he did not in the least doubt the truth of that, for this single reason, because all the

[1] See f. 690. [2] See ff. 589, 923.

Campbells, from the head to the foot of them, had discovered a most avaritious, greedy temper in the matter of pillaging and plundering their native country.

29 Dec. Captain Alexander MacDonald spoke excellent things of Donald MacLeod of Gualtergill in Sky, and saying that he did not know an honester man or a stauncher loyalist.[1] He told
*fol.* 646. me that Donald MacLeod's wife is aunt to the present Glenaladale.

Captain MacDonald had all his effects plundered and pillaged. After everything was destroyed or carried off, the party happening to spy a living cat, immediately killed poor harmless puss, and threw it out of the way, lest the poor mother and her children should have eaten the dead cat in their necessity. For Cumberland and his army were exceedingly desirous that the young and old (women and infants not excepted) they did not murder might be starved to death, which was the fate of too many, and their endeavours were fully equal to their desires.

Captain MacDonald and his wife and children wandered through hills and mountains till the act of indemnity appeared, and in the time of their skulking from place to place his poor wife fell with child, which proved to be a daughter, and is still alive. He is a very smart, acute man, remarkably well skilled in
*fol.* 647. the Erse, for he can both read and write the Irish language in its original character, a piece of knowledge almost quite lost in the Highlands of Scotland, there being exceedingly few that have any skill at all in that way. For the Captain told me that he did not know another person (Old Clanranald only excepted) that knew anything of the first tongue in its original character; but that the natives of Ireland (particularly in the higher parts of the country) do still retain the knowledge of it. Several of the Captain's acquaintances have informed me that he is by far the best Erse poet in all Scotland, and that he has written many songs in the pure Irish. Robert Forbes, A.M.

---

[1] See ff. 266, 466, 760-776.

## Copy of COLONEL KER of Gradyne,[1] his Account. *fol.* 648.

IN order to judge of the state of the Prince's affairs at the time of the battle of Culloden, it will not be amiss to look back to the time of his coming to Inverness, where the Earl of Loudon commanded before his highness's coming there.

The Earl of Loudon hearing of the Prince's coming, and 16 Feb. that he was to quarter that night at Moy[2] (the seat of the Laird of Mackintosh, about seven miles from Inverness), formed a design to surprize him and to carry him off, as he was to have but a few men with him for his guard. The Earl marched from Inverness with most of the garrison, and was within about two miles of Moy, where accidentally five of the Prince's people[3] going about their own private affairs met with Loudon's *fol.* 649. advanced guard, and being under night called to them. But the five, finding who they were, called out loudly for Lochiel and the other clans to advance. Lord Loudon's people, not doubting but they were there, took flight and returned to Inverness in great confusion, and left it next day on the Prince's appearing on the rising ground above the town, returning with his men to the shire of Ross, where they continued till the Earl of Cromarty with a party was sent in pursuit of them.[4] Upon his approach they retired towards Tain, where we shall leave them for a while and return to Inverness.

The Prince coming before the place, summoned the castle to 17 Feb. surrender, and on being refused a battery was raised; but the canon being but small, had little effect upon it, which obliged the besiegers to have recourse to a sap, which being brought *fol.* 650. near the angle of one of the bastions, the castle was surrendered and the garrison made prisoners. This being done, Brigadier Stapleton, with Lochiel's and Keppoch's regiments, Lord John Drummond's (which was not compleat, a great many of them

[1] See f. 669. This narrative is printed in *Jacobite Memoirs*, pp. 131-144.

[2] See f. 380.

[3] Ker's account of this affair agrees most exactly with that of Captain Malcolm MacLeod, but the account given by the Captain is much more exact and circumstantial, as may be seen in [see ff. 258-261, 273, 989, 1207, 1256.]

ROBERT FORBES, A.M.

[4] See f. 156.

Feb. being made prisoners in their passage to Scotland), and the French piquets, were sent to besiege Fort Augustus, which surrendered likewise, and the garrison were made prisoners. After which it was thought proper to leave part of Lord John Drummond's regiment there, and to send Lochiel's and Keppoch's regiments, the French piquets and some of Lord John Drummond's regiment (in all not 300 men) with Brigadier Stapleton to invest Fort William, where we shall leave them and return to the Earl of Cromarty in pursuit of the Earl of Loudon towards Tain, where the said Earl crossed the ferry with his
*fol.* 651. men and went over to the shire of Sutherland; where we shall again leave him for a while and return to Inverness, from which the most of the Prince's troops that were not employed as above were sent to Speyside, under the command of Lord John Drummond, to guard that river against any surprize from the Duke of Cumberland, who by that time was come with his troop to Aberdeen, and had sent some of Kingston's horse and some of the Argyleshire men to Keith[1] (a small village about six miles from the river Spey), where they were all surprized and made prisoners.

As it had been assured that the Duke of Cumberland was to stay at Aberdeen (where he had thrown up some works to prevent a surprize) till all the forces he expected should join him, the Prince on his part took his measures, and in order to secure a retreat in case he had no mind to fight till he should get all his men together, or to march into Perthshire if needful
*fol.* 652. for the better support of his army, was advised to endeavour the recovery of Blair Castle (which he would not allow to be burnt when he passed that way), which was then possessed by Sir Andrew Agnew with some regular troops under his command, as were most of the principal posts in Athol by the Campbells; whilst the 6000 Hessians and St. George's dragoons lay at Crief and places adjacent. Lord George Murray was ordered to march with the Athol men to Badenoch to join the MacPhersons that lay about Ruthven of Badenoch (from the time the Prince had passed that way) to guard the passes leading to and from Athol and to get intelligence on that side.

---

[1] See f. 1138.

As soon as Lord George had joined the MacPhersons they marched with such expedition into Athol that they surprized a great many of the Campbells at Blairfetty, Keinochin, and other posts possessed by them, and made most of them prisoners.[1] Sir Andrew Agnew,[2] being alarmed by his out-sentinels, retired into the castle, in which he was shut up for seventeen days, some part of which time it was battered with two pieces of canon,[3] one of three, the other of four pounds, which made but little impression upon the walls, though they ruined the roof. March *fol.* 653.

During this time the Hessians marched to relieve the castle, and some of the Athol men being advanced as far down as Dunkeld to get intelligence and to guard that with other passes on the river, where were frequent skirmishes between them and the Hessian hussars, and some of St. George's dragoons who had come to reconnoitre some days before the foot came up. But when they were come up, the Athol men were obliged to retire (as they could not be supported at such a distance) to Pitlochrie, near the famous pass of Killicrankie, where, with some others that were sent from Blair, they continued about eight days (the MacPhersons with some of the Athol men keeping Sir Andrew and his men still shut up in the Castle), always skirmishing with the hussars and dragoons till their foot came up, which obliged the Athol men to retire into the above pass, where they continued that day. But as they were few in number, Lord George called a council of the officers, who were of opinion that the pass was not tenable, since it might be surrounded on all sides by such a vastly superiour number. It was therefore resolved to abandon both it and the Castle, which was accordingly done that night. And having sent the canon away, they marched to Ruthven of Badenoch without the least interruption from the enemy.[4] Here the MacPhersons were left as formerly, and the Athol men were ordered to the Speyside. Lord George went on to Inverness, and upon his arrival there, intelligence being brought that Lord Loudon had repass'd with his troops *fol.* 654.

---

[1] See ff. 567, 902.

[2] Who pillaged the house of Lude (the widow lady living in it), breaking to pieces all the doors and windows, and the finishing of the rooms and some of the floors.——Robert Forbes, A.M.

[3] See f. 907.

[4] See ff. 907, 1267.

March from Sutherland to Tain, he was ordered to march with some
fol. 655. troops to join the Earl of Cromarty and to give Lord Loudon battle if he would stay for it. But he, hearing of Lord George's march, returned to Sutherland again. Lord George, having given the necessary orders to Lord Cromarty (who continued to command in that country), returned to Inverness, where it was resolved the Duke of Perth should be sent to take upon him the command,[1] and if possible to get as many boats together as would ferry over his men, and to drive Lord Loudon out of Sutherland if he would not stay to fight. The boats were got together, and the Duke of Perth with his men passed over without being perceived and surprized Lord Loudon's people,[2] obliged them to capitulate, and made them prisoners. Lord Loudon and the President of the Session of Scotland made their escape. After which the Duke of Perth seized some ships that lay in the Firth of Tain, on board of which were all the valuable effects that were shipt on board at Inverness before Lord Loudon left it, the military chest excepted, which had
fol. 656. been conveyed on board a frigate which lay in the bay. This done, the Duke of Perth returned to Inverness, leaving the command to the Earl of Cromarty.

About this time, the *Hazard* sloop returning from France with money, arms, and ammunition, and several French and Spanish officers on board, was chased on shore by an English man of war in Lord Rae's country,[3] where they landed their cargo, and, apprehending no danger from the country people, they provided themselves with a guide to conduct them and their cargo to the Earl of Cromarty. But as they were on their march they were set upon by Lord Rae's people, who, after a good resistance, made them prisoners and carried off the cargo, which was thought could not have been done without the treachery of the guide, who disappeared before the action began. The news being brought to Inverness, orders were sent to the Earl of Cromarty to send a party into Lord Rae's country to demand satisfaction. But his Lordship, being some-

[1] These particulars represent the Earl of Cromarty in a very indifferent light. See f. 1259.—F.

[2] It should be *some* of Lord Loudon's.—Robert Forbes, A.M.

[3] See f. 1261.

what dilatory in executing his orders, Lord Rae's people gathered *fol.* 657.
together with some of Lord Loudon's officers at their head. April

About this time advice was brought to Inverness that the Duke of Cumberland (being joined by all the forces he expected) had begun his march from Aberdeen northwards, and had ordered the ships that attended him with provisions for his army to coast along in sight of him to Inverness. Upon which, orders were dispatched to the Earl of Cromarty to call in all his detachments, and to march with all expedition to join the Prince.[1] He gave his orders accordingly, and went himself with some of his officers to Dunrobin Castle to bid adieu to the Countess of Sutherland, and to thank her for the civilities they had received from her. Whilst they were there amusing themselves, the castle was surrounded by Lord Sutherland's and Lord Rae's people, who, having had intelligence of their being there, made them all prisoners. Orders were likewise sent at this *fol.* 658.
time to the MacPhersons, and to those that were at Fort Augustus and Fort William, to join the Prince as soon as possible. Those from Fort Augustus and the French piquets joined on Saturday, and Lochiel from Fort William on Sunday.[2] Advice was brought on Monday that the Duke of Cumberland was coming to the Spey, and that Lord John Drummond, with the troops under his command, was retiring. Upon which the Prince ordered the drums to beat and the pipes to play to arms. The men in the town assembled as fast as they could, the canon was ordered to march, and the Prince mounted on horseback and went out at their head to Culloden House, the place of rendezvous; and Lord George Murray was left in the town to bring up those that were quartered in the neighbourhood of Inverness, which made it pretty late before he joined the Prince at Culloden. Orders were likewise sent to Lord John Drummond to assemble there likewise, which he did the next day, *fol.* 659.
being Tuesday.

Tuesday,[3] being April 15th, the whole army marched up to 15 April

[1] See ff. 156, 1261. [2] On Monday, says Mr. John Cameron [see f. 157].

[3] The copy from which I transcribed had here the words, viz.: 'Wednesday, being the 16th of April,' which certainly behoved to be an error, as it is well known that the battle of Culloden was fought upon Wednesday, April 16th. See ff. 126, 157, 181, 430, 439.——Robert Forbes, A.M.

5 April the muir, about a mile to the eastward of Culloden House, where they were all drawn up in order of battle to wait the Duke of Cumberland's coming. Keppoch's men joined in the field from Fort William, and the whole was reviewed by the Prince, who was very well pleased to see them in such good spirits, tho' they had eaten nothing that day but one single bisket a man, provisions being very scarce, and money too.

The Prince (being informed that the Duke of Cumberland had halted that day at Nairn to refresh his men, and that the ships with his provisions were coming into the bay of Inverness that evening) called a council of war, and, after great debates
l. 660. (although neither the Earl of Cromarty—who by that time was prisoner, tho' not known—nor the MacPhersons, nor a great many of the Frasers, were come up) it was resolved to march and endeavour to surprize the Duke in his camp at Nairn, about twelve miles distant. Accordingly, the march was begun between seven and eight o'clock at night, the first column commanded by Lord George Murray, the second by the Prince. The night being dark occasioned several halts to be made for bringing up the rear. When about half way, Lord George ordered Colonel Ker, one of the Prince's aid-de-camps, to go from front to rear and give orders to the respective officers to order the men to make the attack sword in hand,[1] which was thought better, as it would not alarm the enemy soon, and that their fire-arms would be of use to them afterwards. When he
l. 661. returned to the front to acquaint Lord George Murray of his having executed his orders, he found they were halted a little to the eastward of Kilravock House, deliberating whether or not they should proceed (having then but four miles to march to Nairn, where the enemy was encamped) or return to Culloden, as they had not an hour at most, or thereabout, to daylight; and if they could not be there before that time the surprize would be rendered impracticable, and the more so as it was not to be doubted that the enemy would be under arms before daylight, as they were to march that morning to give

[1] Mr. John Cameron says sword and pistol [f. 157]. But certainly Colonel Ker, who carried the orders from Lord George Murray, must know that point best.——Robert Forbes, A.M.

the Prince battle. The Duke of Perth and his brother, Lord John, who had been sent to advise the Prince, returned to Lord George.[1] Lochiel and others, who were in the front, hearing that there was a great interval between the two lines, which would take up most of the time to daylight to join, it was resolved to return to Culloden, which was accordingly done; which, some say, was contrary to the Prince's inclinations. They marched the shortest way back by the church of Croy, which, though but scarce two miles from the place where the halt was made, yet it was clear daylight before the front arrived there, which makes it clear there was no possibility of surprizing the enemy before daylight, as was designed.

16 April

*fol.* 662.

The march was continued to Culloden, from whence a great many, both officers and soldiers, went to Inverness and other places in quest of provisions, which were very much wanted. The Prince, with great difficulty having got some bread and whiskie at Culloden, where, reposing himself a little after having marched all that night on foot, had intelligence brought that the enemy was in sight, whereupon those about Culloden were ordered to arms, and several officers sent to Inverness and places adjacent to bring up what men they could meet with.

Whilst those about Culloden were marching up to the muir above the house, where they were join'd by about three hundred of the Frasers just then come up, Colonel Ker went out to reconnoitre the enemy. When he returned, he told the Prince and Lord George that their foot were marching up in three columns with their cavalry on their left, so that they could form their line of battle in an instant. The Prince ordered his men to be drawn up in two lines, and the few horse he had in the rear towards the wings, and the canon to be disperst in the front, which were brought up with great difficulty for want of horses.

*fol.* 663.

As there was not time to march to the ground they were on the day before, they were drawn up a mile farther westward, with a stone inclosure on the right of the first line, and the second at a proper distance behind; after having reconnoitred

---

[1] See ff. 158, 441, 1270.

16 April the inclosure, which ran down to the Water of Nairn[1] on the right, so that no body of men could pass without throwing
fol. 664. down the wall. And to guard further against any attempts that might be made on that side, there were two battalions placed facing outwards, which covered the right of the two lines, and to observe the motion of the enemy, if they should make any attempt that way.

The Duke of Cumberland formed his line at a great distance, and marched in battle-order till he came within canon shot, where he halted and placed his canon in different places, at some distance in his front, which outwinged the Prince's both to the right and left without his cavalry, which were mostly on the left, some few excepted that were sent to cover the right. As soon as the Duke's canon were placed, he began canonading, which was answered by the Prince's, who rode along the lines to encourage his men, and posted himself in the most convenient place (here one of his servants was killed by his side) to see
fol. 665. what pass'd, not doubting but the Duke would begin the attack, as he had both the wind and weather on his back, snow and hail falling very thick at the same time.

Here it is to be observed that neither those that had been with the Earl of Cromarty (he, with his son and some of his officers being only made prisoners, his men having marched on before), nor the MacPhersons, nor between two and three thousand men that had been on the field the day before, were come up. Notwithstanding all these disadvantages, and the Duke's canon playing with great execution,[2] Lord George Murray, who commanded the right,[3] sent Colonel Ker to the Prince to know if he should begin the attack, which the Prince accordingly ordered. As the right was farther advanced than

---

[1] In the copy which I made, my transcript from the word here was Ern, which behoved to be a mistake, the water of Ern being in Perthshire. The same mistake was in the said copy a second time—viz., in the fourth line of page 667 in the volume.——ROBERT FORBES, A.M.

[2] See ff. 129, 445.

[3] As this proceeds from Colonel Ker himself, who behoved to know this matter best, so it is more to be depended upon than other accounts, which differ from this, and some of which tell it in such a way as to leave an insinuation of some blame upon Lord George Murray, whose bravery can never be called in question. See ff. 129, 160, 182, 328, 446, 675.

the left, Colonel Ker went to the left and ordered the Duke of Perth, who commanded there, to begin the attack, and rode along the line till he came to the right, where Lord George was, who attacked at the head of the Athol men (who had the right of the army that day) with all the bravery imaginable, as did indeed the whole line, breaking the Duke's line in several places, and making themselves masters of two pieces of the enemy's canon. Though they were both fronted and flanked by them, they, notwithstanding, marched up under a close firing from right to left to the very points of their bayonets, which they could not see for the smoak till they were upon them. 16 April *fol.* 666.

At the beginning of the attack the Campbells[1] threw down a great deal of the wall of the inclosure for the dragoons on the Duke's left to pass to the rear of the Prince's army, which they were suffered to do without receiving one shot from the two battalions that were placed to observe their motions. This being observed, and the constant fire kept up by the Duke's foot in the front, put the Prince's people in disorder and rendered the defeat of his army compleat. *fol.* 667.

The Prince retired in good order with some few of his men, and crossed the Water of Nairn at the ford on the highway between Inverness and Corryburgh, without being pursued by the enemy, where he parted with them, taking only a few of FitzJames's horse and some gentlemen along with him up that river, the rest taking the highway to Ruthven of Badenoch, where they stayed some days expecting an answer to a letter that was sent to the Prince; but it not coming in the time expected, they all separated, every one to do the best he could for himself. Most of the clans had gone from the field of battle towards their respective countries.

The publick has been no ways favourable to Lord George Murray,[2] but if they had been witnesses of his zeal and activity

---

[1] This says very ill for the corps posted to guard the park walls in order to prevent the Prince's army being flanked by the enemy from that quarter.

ROBERT FORBES, A.M.

[2] Here Colonel Ker vindicates Lord George Murray from villainy, an imputation which no man in his right senses could ever entertain against Lord George, because no villain would have exposed his person so remarkably as he did where danger called upon all occasions. Besides, if Lord George had acted the double

April from the time he joined in that affair to the last of it, his
exposing his person wherever an occasion offered, and in par-
*l.* 668. ticular at the battle of Culloden, where he went on with the
first and came not off till the last, they would have done him
more justice. And whatever sentiments they have been pleased
to say the Prince had of him, they are hardly to be credited,
and for this reason; because when, after the battle, Colonel Ker
went to acquaint the Prince how affairs were going, his highness enquired particularly about Lord George Murray, and,
being told that he had been thrown from his horse in the time
of the action, but was no way hurt, the Prince, in presence of
all that were there, desired Colonel Ker to find him out and
*ol.* 669. take particular care of him, which it is to be presumed he would
not have done if he had had the least suspicion of what has
been laid to *his charge by his enemies.*

*N.B.*—The above faithfully taken from a copy transcribed from another copy, which other copy was transcribed from Colonel Ker's own handwriting. As Colonel Ker has an excellent good character, and is acknowledged on all hands to be a gentleman of strict veracity and honour, so his account of things justly merits a place in the esteem of every lover of truth. He was taken prisoner (if I rightly remember) somewhere in the shire of Angus, about the beginning of May 1746 (see *Scots Magazine* for said year, page 238), and was found guilty, November 6th, 1746 (see *Scots Magazine* for said year, page 529), and accordingly was condemned upon November

---

and dishonest part, why should he have skulked, and, at last, have gone to foreign parts? But, then, it is worth noticing that Colonel Ker says not a word with respect to the insolence and haughtiness of Lord George's temper, his great misfortune and fault, in which alone he can be justly blamed, and with which he stands charged by the Prince's own words to more than one [see ff. 150, 236, 450, 453]. However, to do Lord George justice, it is affirmed by some who have an opportunity of knowing, that Lord George, before he left Scotland, did declare his surprize to a friend (Murray of Abercairney) how it could enter into the head of any person to charge him with treachery. But at the same time that he acknowledged with concern and regret that he had been too often guilty of contradicting and thwarting the Prince in the measures he proposed. Certainly, tho' both be bad enough, there is a great difference 'twixt villainy and pride.

ROBERT FORBES, A.M.

15th of said year (see page 530 of the foresaid magazine). He is under a reprieve, and continues still to be a prisoner in a messenger's house by the interest of the Prussian ambassador, who did much good in that way. ROBERT FORBES, A.M.

## Copy of CAPTAIN O'NEILLE's Journal, taken from a copy attested by his name subscribed with his own hand.[1] *fol. 670.*

HAVING heard and seen many scandalous libels given out in my name of the conduct and retreat of the Prince since the battle of Culloden, I have thought myself obliged in duty and honour to give an impartial and true account of the same during [the][2] time that I had the honour to be near his person. This I don't pretend in justification of that great Prince, whose inimitable virtues and qualifications as well render him the darling of his friends as the astonishing surprize of his greatest enemies, and whose valour and calm intrepidity in heretofore unheard of dangers will usher down his fame to the latest posterity; but to convince and assure the world that all accounts as yet given, either under any name or otherwise, have been as spurious[3] as defective and infamously false. I moreover *fol. 671.* assure this to be the first and only account that I have given or will give, and affirm the contents to be true upon my honour.

April 15th, O.S.—Prince Charles marched his army in three 1746 columns from Culloden Muir in hopes to surprize the Duke of 15 April Cumberland in his camp at Nairn, ordering at the same time two thousand men to pass the river Nairn and post themselves between Elgin and the camp of the enemy. To deceive the ships that were in Inverness Road he ordered several fires to be made on the mountain where he drew up in battle. At eight at night he began his march, and about two next morn-

[1] Printed in *Jacobite Memoirs*, pp. 348-362.

[2] Thus the attested copy had it, without the word 'the.'

[3] If this be so, how then came I by the copy in vol. i. p. 181? For I can declare I was master of that copy upon July 14th, 1747, *i.e.* exactly a month and a half before the date of the Captain's letter, along with the attested copy, to the Countess of Dundonald. [See ff. 692-700 *postea.*]

6 April ing, being the 16th of April, within a mile [1] of the enemy, our van halted. The Prince, who marched in the centre, dispatched an aid-de-camp to know the motive of the halt. Colonel [2]
*fol. 672.* O'Sullivan (who marched in the van) immediately hasted to the Prince and told him Lord George Murray and some other of the chieftains, as they wanted some of their men, did not think themselves sufficiently strong to attack the enemy, and upon a strong belief the Duke of Cumberland was apprized of their design, refused to advance, maugre the instances he (Colonel O'Sullivan) made use of to engage them to the contrary. Upon this the Prince advanced to the head of the column, where, assembling the chiefs, in the most pathetic and strong terms demonstrated to them the visible and real advantages they had of an enemy who thought themselves secure of any such attempt, and descending his horse,[3] drew his sword, and told them he would lead them to an enemy they had as often defeated as seen. But, deaf to his example and intreaties, the
*fol. 673.* major part declin'd, which so sensibly shocked the Prince, that, remounting his horse, he told them with the greatest concern [4] he did not so much regret his own loss as their inevitable ruin. He immediately marched back to the former camp at Culloden, where he arrived at five in the morning. At ten he was informed the Duke of Cumberland was in full march towards him. Whereupon the Prince gave the necessary orders for the attack, riding from rank to rank encouraging his troops and exhorting them [with his usual sprightliness] [5] to behave as they had done at Prestonpans and Falkirk. Between twelve and one the Prince engag'd the enemy, commanding himself in the centre. The right wing immediately broke the left of the enemy, but their flank being exposed to seven [6] squadrons of

---

[1] Three or four miles, say other accounts, and justly too, as must be confessed by those who know anything of the country about Nairn, where the attack was to have been made. See ff. 158, 448, 661.—F.

[2] This page contains several particulars not so much as mentioned in any of the accounts given by others, as may be seen by making a comparison.—F.

[3] The Prince marched all that night on foot, says Ker of Gradyne, f. 662.—F.

[4] With tears in his eyes, says the other copy, f. 181.—F.

[5] These words are wanting in the foresaid copy. See f. 182.—F.

[6] Nine squadrons, says the foresaid copy, f. 182.—F.

horse, who attack'd them while they were in pursuit of the enemy's foot, was put into so much confusion that it was dispers'd. The Prince gallop'd to the right, and endeavouring to rally them[1] had his horse shot under him.[2] The left followed the example of the right, which drew on an entire deroute in spite of all the Prince could do to animate or rally them. Notwithstanding which he remained upon the field of battle untill there were no more hopes left, and then could scarce be persuaded to retire, ordering the Irish piquets and FitzJames's horse to make a stand and favour the retreat of the Highlanders, which was as gallantly executed. Previous to the battle the Prince had ordered the chieftains that (in case of a defeat) as the Highlanders could not retreat as regular troops, they should assemble their men near Fort Augustus. In consequence of this, immediately after the battle the Prince dispatched me to Inverness to repeat his orders to such of his troops as were there. That night the Prince retir'd six miles from the field of battle[3] and went next day as far, and in three days more arrived at Fort Augustus, where he remained a whole day in expectation his troops would have join'd him. But seeing no appearance of it, he went to the house of Invergary and ordered me to remain there to direct such as pass'd that way the road he took. I remained there two days and announc'd the Prince's orders to such as I met, but to no effect, every one taking his own road.

16 April

*fol.* 674.

*fol.* 675.

I then followed the Prince, who was so far from making a precipitate retreat [as has been maliciously reported][4] that he retired by six and six miles and arrived the 28th of April[5] O.S. at Knoidart, where I join'd him next day and gave him an account of the little or no appearance there was of assembling

28 April

*fol.* 676.

---

[1] Here in the foresaid copy these following words, 'but to no purpose. See f. 182.—F.

[2] Not true. See f. 1161.—F.

[3] The foresaid copy says here, 'And next day arrived at Fort Augustus.'—ROBERT FORBES, A.M.

[4] These words are not in the other copy, f. 183.—F.

[5] The 26th of April, says the foresaid copy, which day Donald MacLeod fixes upon for their departure from the continent to the Isles. See ff. 273, 281, 316. Ned Burk says much the same. [See p. 329.]—F.

28 April his troops, upon which he wrote circular letters to all the chiftains, enjoining them, by the obedience they owed him, to join him immediately with such of their clans as they could gather; at the same time representing to them the imminent danger they were in if they neglected it. After remaining some days there in hopes his orders would have been obeyed, and seeing not one person repair to him, the extreme danger his person was in, being within seven miles [1] of Lord Loudon, Sir Alexander MacDonald and the MacLeods, it was proposed to evade it by retreating to one of the islands near the continent. After repeated instances of the like nature he reluctantly assented, leaving Mr. John Hay behind to transmit
fol. 677. him the answers of his letters, with an account of what should pass, and parted for the Isles in an open fishing boat at eight at night, attended by Colonel O'Sullivan and me only.[2] About an hour after we parted a violent hurricane arose, which drove us ninety miles [3] from our designed port; and next day running for shelter into the Island of North Uist,[4] we struck upon a rock and staved to pieces,[5] and with great difficulty saved our lives. At our landing we were in the most melancholy situation, knowing nobody and wanting the common necessaries of life. After much search we found a little hut uninhabited, and took shelter there, and with a great deal of pains made a fire to dry our cloaths. Here the Prince remained two days,
fol. 678. having no other provisions but a few biskets we had saved out of the boat, which were entirely spoiled with the salt water.

---

[1] Says Donald MacLeod, 'ten or twelve miles by sea, but a much greater distance by land.' See f. 278.—ROBERT FORBES, A.M.

[2] Honest Donald MacLeod, the pilot, and Allan MacDonald, Clanranald's relation might have had a place here, to say nothing of the poor rowers. See f. 281.—F.

[3] This must be a mistake, tho' it be so in the other copy too, for none of the lochs has so much bounds as to allow of such a drive from an intended harbour. I remember Donald MacLeod called this 'nonsense,' for he makes the whole course but only 96 miles. [See f. 284.]—F.

[4] This should be Benbecula, but I think not so much of his mistaking names, being a stranger. See f. 284.—F.

[5] This is altogether an error, as plainly appears, not only from the words of Donald MacLeod and Ned Burk [see ff. 270, 343], but likewise from a remarkable token given me by Captain Alexander MacDonald, which puts this point beyond all doubt. See f. 581.—F.

As this island belonged to Sir Alexander MacDonald, and not judging ourselves safe, we determined going elsewhere, and by the greatest good fortune, one of our boatmen discovered a boat [1] stranded on the coast, and, having with great difficulty launched it into the water, we imbarked for the Harris. In our passage we unfortunately met with another storm which obliged us to put into an island near Stornoway. Next day the Prince dispatched me [2] for Stornoway to look for a ship, ordering me to imbark on board the first I could get, and to make the most diligent haste after my landing on the Continent to the Court of France, ordering me to give an exact account to his most Christian Majesty of his disasters and of his resolution never to abandon the country untill he knew the final result of France, and if it was not [3] possible once more to assemble his faithful Highlanders. Unluckily the person that the Prince sent with me [4] getting drunk, told the master of the ship somewhat that induced him to refuse taking me on board, and immediately alarmed the country, which obliged me to return and join the Prince, who upon what I told him resolved for the continent by way of Seaforth's country. But the boatmen absolutely refused to comply, which made us take the road we came. And meeting with three ships of war we were constrained to put into a desert island where we remained eight days [5] in the greatest misery, having no sustenance but some

1 May. fol. 679. fol. 680

[1] One error never fails to prove the foundation of another, if not of many.—F.

[2] This whole affair is represented in quite a different manner by Donald MacLeod, who caused me remark more than once that O'Neille did not accompany him to Stornoway (See ff. 270, 287), and I have heard Ned Burk affirm the same thing.—F.

[3] Here either 'not' should be wanting, or the next word immediately following should be 'impossible' to make sense of the words which were precisely as above in the attested copy, but in the other copy they happen to be right. See f. 184.—F.

[4] One error must be the foundation of another at least. See this whole affair cleared up by Donald MacLeod himself (See f. 289), and that, too, according to the expressions of Captain John Hay upon the head who could have no interest or by-view in what he spoke. See f. 479.—F.

[5] Four days and four nights, says Donald MacLeod, and not in so very great misery as Captain O'Neille represents them to have been in, though indeed their case was bad enough (See ff. 291-297). And Ned Burk's account of this matter agrees with that of Donald MacLeod (See f. 331). One day I read this

6 May dried fish that Providence threw in our way in this island. When the ships disappeared we put to sea again, and next morning met with another ship of war just coming out of one of the lochs, who pursued us for near an hour; but the wind rising we made our escape. In the afternoon we arrived at the Island of Benbecula, and one of the boatmen, being acquainted with a herd of the island, led us to his house, where, passing for friends of the boatman, we remained four days, and then the Prince sent the boat to the continent with a Highland gentleman whom he charged with letters to the chiefs, Secretary
*fol. 681.* Murray and John Hay, requiring an exact account how affairs stood.

Not thinking ourselves secure in the cottage, by the advice of a friend we retired to the mountain of Coradale to wait the return of the gentleman, where we remained two-and-twenty days, when the gentleman returned with a letter from Secretary Murray importing that the clans had almost all delivered up their arms, and, consequently, were no more to be depended on. He likewise acquainted the Prince of two French ships who had arrived at the continent with money and arms, and in which the Duke of Perth, his brother, Sir Thomas Sheridan, and John Hay had imbarked for France.

Here we remained some days longer, till the Duke of Cumberland having intelligence that the Prince was concealed in the Long Isle, ordered the militia of the Isle of Sky and the Independent Companies to go in search of him. As soon
*fol. 682.* as we had notice of their landing we retreated to an island about twelve miles distance, called Ouya, where we remained till we found they had followed us, and then we went for Loch Boisdale, and stayed there eight days, when Captain Carolina Scott landed within a mile of us, which obliged us to separate, the Prince taking me to the mountains, and O'Sullivan remaining with the boatmen. At nightfall we marched towards Benbecula, being informed Scott had ordered the militia to

---

particular of the desert island to Ned Burk when he used this remarkable expression, 'What deel needs a man mack mair wonders than we had. Faith we had anew o' them.' Words tho' coarse, yet very significant.—ROBERT FORBES, A.M.

come and join him. At midnight we came to a hut, where by good fortune we met with Miss Flora MacDonald, whom I formerly knew. I quitted the Prince at some distance from the hut, and went with a design to inform myself if the Independent Companies were to pass that way next day, as we had been informed. The young lady answered me—Not—and said that they would not pass till the day after. Then I told her I brought a friend to see her, and she, with some emotion, asked me if it was the Prince. I answered her it was, and instantly brought him in.[1] We then consulted on the imminent danger the Prince was in, and could think of a no more proper and safe expedient than to propose to Miss Flora to convey him to the Isle of Sky, where her mother lived. This seemed the more feasible, as the young lady's father being captain of an Independent Company would accord her a pass for herself and a servant to go visit her mother. The Prince assented, and immediately propos'd it to the young lady, to which she answered with the greatest respect and loyalty; but declined it, saying Sir Alexander MacDonald was too much her friend to be the instrument of his ruin. I endeavoured to obviate this by assuring her Sir Alexander was not in the country, and that she could with the greatest facility convey the Prince to her mother's, as she lived close by the waterside. I then remonstrated to her the honour and immortality that would redound to her by such a glorious action, and she at length acquiesc'd, after the Prince had told her the sense he would always retain of so conspicuous a service. She promised to acquaint us next day when things were ripe for execution, and we parted for the mountains of Coradale. Next day at four in the afternoon we received a message from our protectress, telling us ALL WAS WELL. We determined joining her imme-

June

*fol.* 683.

*fol.* 684.

[1] In all this Captain O'Neille is exactly right, for I have heard Miss MacDonald declare more than once that the Captain came to her (bringing the Prince along with him) when she happened to be in a shealling belonging to her brother; that the Captain was the contriver of the scheme, and that she herself was very backward to engage in it; and indeed no wonder (whatever some may say), when one seriously considers the important trust, and the many dangers attending it. Something of all this may be gathered from her own Journal. See f. 524.

June. diately, but the messenger informed us we could not pass either of the fords that separated the island we were in from Benbecula, as they were both guarded. In this dreadful situation a man of the country tendered us his boat, which we readily accepted, and next day landed at Benbecula, and immediately marched for Rossinish, the place of rendezvous, where we arrived at midnight, and instead of our protectress,
*ol.* 685. found [ourselves within fifty yards of][1] a guard of the enemy. We were constrained to retreat four miles, having eat nothing for thirty hours[2] before. The Prince ordered me to go to the lady and know the reason she did not keep her appointment. She told me she had engaged a cousin of hers in North Uist to receive him in his house, where she was sure he would be more safe than in the Isle of Sky.[3] I immediately dispatched a boy with this news to the Prince, and mentioned him the place of appointment, whither he came. But the gentleman absolutely refused receiving us, alleging for a motive that he was vassal to Sir Alexander MacDonald. In this unexpected exigence, being within a small half mile of a captain and fifty men, we hastened for Rossinish, being apprized the enemy had just
*ol.* 686. abandoned it. The Prince sent me to acquaint Miss Flora of our disappointment and to intreat her to keep to her promise, as there was no time to lose. She faithfully promised for next day, and I remained with her that night, the Prince remaining at Rossinish attended by a little herd. Next day I accompanied Miss Flora to the rendezvous, where we had not long been when we had an account[4] that General Campbell was just landed with 1500 men.[5] We were now apprehensive that we were betrayed, and instantly got to our boat and put to another place, where we arrived at daybreak. We dispatched to Clanranald's house to learn what news, who brought us word that General Campbell was there with Captain Ferguson,

---

[1] In the other copy these words are wanting. See f. 187.—F.

[2] In the other copy thirty-four hours.—ROBERT FORBES, A.M.

[3] See ff. 526, 589.

[4] It is truly a matter of much wonder that the Prince should escape the clutches of so many in such narrow bounds, especially when the coast was swarming with ships, sloops, etc.—F.

[5] See ff. 485, 526.

and that he saw Captain Scott's detachment coming to join June
them, and that they amounted in all to 2300 men. The *fol. 687*
Prince intreated the young lady I should accompany him, but she absolutely refused it, having a pass but for one servant. The Prince was so generous as to decline going unless I attended, untill I told him, if he made the least demur, I would instantly go about my business, as I was extremely indifferent what became of me so that his person was safe. [With much difficulty and after many intreaties][1] he at length imbarked, attended only by Miss Flora MacDonald.[2]

Here my hard fate and the Prince's safety, which was my only object, obliged me to share no longer the misfortunes of that illustrious hero, whose grandeur of soul and intrepidity, with a calmness of spirit particular to himself in such dangers,
increased in these moments when the general part of man- *fol. 688*
kind abandon themselves to their fate. I now could only recommend him to God and his good fortune, and made my way amidst the enemy to South Uist, where we had left Colonel O'Sullivan.[3] Next day I joined O'Sullivan, and found (four days after the Prince parted) a French cutter, commanded by one Dumont, and who had on board two captains of the Irish brigade with a number of volunteers. Here Colonel O'Sullivan and I concerted what were the properest measures to be taken. We agreed that he should go on board the cutter, as he was so reduced by the long fatigues that he had undergone in the mountains, as not to be able to walk, and that he should bring the cutter to Loch Seaforth, nigh the Isle of Rasay, where the Prince ordered me to join him by a billet he had sent me the day before by one of the boatmen who had rowed
him to the Isle of Sky. After having seen my friend on board, *fol. 689*
and after innumerable difficulties, I got a boat and went round the Isle of Sky to the Isle of Rasay, place of rendezvous; but at my landing had intelligence that the Prince was returned to the Isle of Sky, whereupon I hasted to said Isle of Sky again,

---

[1] These words are not in the other copy. See f. 189.—F.

[2] The faithful MacKechan might have been named here.—F.

[3] Captain O'Neille speaks more respectfully, and is more favourable in his accounts of Colonel O'Sullivan than some other hints that are given in this Collection. (See ff. 496, 519, 528.)—ROBERT FORBES, A.M.

July and there too had the grief to learn that he had departed
that island, but for what place nobody could inform me in
the least. I then repaired to Loch Nammaddy in North Uist,
where by our agreement Colonel O'Sullivan was to come to
me in case that in eight days I did not join him at Loch Seaforth; but not meeting my friend there, after a delay of four
days I returned to the Island of Benbecula, where I promised
l. 690. myself greater safety than any where else; but I met with a quite
different usage. For the very person [1] in whom I had entirely
confided, and under whose care I was, betrayed me to Captain
MacNeal (induced thereto by a great sum of money offered for
me), who was in that country under the command of Captain
Ferguson of the *Furnace-Bomb.* I was taken by this Captain
MacNeal in a rock over a loch, where I had skulked for four days,
and brought to Captain Ferguson,[2] who used me with all the barbarity of a pirate, stripped me, and had ordered me to be put
into a rack and whipped by his hangman, because I would not
confess where I thought the Prince was. As I was just going
to be whipped, being already stripped, Lieutenant MacCaghan
of the Scotch Fusileers, who commanded a party under Cap-
l. 691. tain Ferguson, very generously opposed this barbarous usage,
and coming out with his drawn sword threatened Captain
Ferguson that he'd sacrifice himself and his detachment rather
than to see an officer used after such an infamous manner.

I can't avoid acquainting the public that four days after I was taken [3] General Campbell sent me word upon his parole of honour that if I had money, or other effects in the country, in sending them to him they should be safe. Upon which (always imagining that the word of honour was as sacredly kept in the English army as 'tis in others) I went with a detachment for my money and gold watch which I had hid in the rock when I perceived the party searching for me, and sent to General

[1] See the person named and the whole affair cleared up in this vol. f. 644.—F.

[2] A man remarkable for his cruelties. See ff. 192, 216, 257, 309, etc. Even in his younger years he was remarkable for a cruel turn of mind among his school-fellows and companions, and therefore he is the fitter tool for William the Cruel. He was born at Old Meldrum in the shire of Aberdeen.—ROBERT FORBES, A.M.

[3] See ff. 191, 645.

Campbell by Captain Skipness Campbell 450 guineas, with my July
gold watch, broadsword, and pistols, all which he has thought
proper (to be sure consistent with his honour) to keep from me *fol.* 69
upon diverse applications made to him to that purpose.

I hope the public will excuse this long digression, that I have made since my separation from the Prince, the moré so that I have only made it to show that I did everything in my power as well to fulfil my duty as to endeavour to deserve the confidence with which the Prince was graciously pleased to honour me.

(*Sic subscribitur*) F. O'NEILLE.

A coppy.

*N.B.*—After getting notice that Captain Felix O'Neille, after 1747 8 Dec.
his being removed from the Castle of Edinburgh to some part in England, had transmitted an attested copy of his Journal to one of his friends in Edinburgh, I was at no small pains to find it out. At last I discovered that it was in the hands of the Countess of Dundonald. Upon Tuesday, December 8th, 1747, I did myself the honour of paying my respects to lady Mary Cochran in Edinburgh. I begged to know of her ladyship if
it was true that the Countess had any such Journal and if I *fol.* 69
could have the favour of seeing it. Lady Mary said it was very true that her mamma had the Journal with O'Neille's own subscription at it, and that it was transmitted to her from O'Neille himself, and that she would endeavour to procure it for me from her mamma and send it down to me as soon as possible. But, then, her ladyship was pleased to observe that the Countess would not allow any copy to be taken of it, as Captain O'Neille had desired that no copy should be given of it, till he should send a letter to the Countess from France, wherein he would give allowance for copies to be taken of it at a proper time. And therefore Lady Mary added that all the favour I could obtain was only the reading of it. To this I answered that I had heard the Journal was made a great secret, and seeing it was so, I did not chuse to have the trust of it; for that if copies should happen to appear from other quarters it might be said that I had taken a copy without any allowance,
and thereby had become the occasion of spreading it. And *fol.* 69

8 Dec. therefore I would much rather chuse to read it in her ladyship's presence and return it directly into her hands, if her ladyship would take the trouble of procuring me a sight of it while I had the honour of being with her. Lady Mary was so good as to say that though my Lady Dundonald was confined to her apartment with a severe cold, she would step to her and ask a reading of the Journal. Accordingly, in a very short time, Lady Mary returned and gave me the Journal. After reading of it I could not help declaring my surprize that the Journal should be made a matter of so much nicety when I could assure her ladyship that I had been master of a copy of it (the preface and conclusion only excepted) for about six months past, and that several such copies as mine were in Edinburgh and other places of Scotland. Lady Mary said that certainly Captain O'Neille's touching so severely upon General Campbell behoved to be the reason why he made his Journal an affair of such secrecy. To this I answered that the reason
*ol.* 695. was good so long as Captain O'Neille remained in any part of Scotland or England, because the making such a particular the subject of common conversation might have brought rough enough treatment upon Captain O'Neille. But now that he was safe in France, I could not help looking upon it as a point of justice to make that particular part of the Journal known to the world, that so General Campbell might have an opportunity of vindicating himself, if there was any mistake in the case, and that if the charge was a fact, the truth might be fixed. Then I added that if my Lady Dundonald could be prevailed upon to allow me the use of the attested copy to compare it with my own, and to take transcripts of the preface and conclusion, I would promise to give her ladyship in return for that favour a copy of Ker of Gradyne's account; and withal I said I should not give copies of the preface and conclusion or have any hand in making them common. Lady Mary was so good as to assure me that she would faithfully report *that* to
*fol.* 696. my Lady Dundonald, and would employ her interest to procure that favour for me upon the conditions I had mentioned. I then took leave, and said I would do myself the honour of waiting upon her ladyship some day next week.

Upon Thursday, December 17th, I again made my court to

Lady Mary, who had most faithfully performed her promise, 17 Dec.
and had procured what I so much desired. Upon receiving the attested Journal at Lady Mary's hands, I repeated the conditions and assured her ladyship I would observe them.

I had been promised the use of Ker of Gradyne's account from the right reverend Bishop Keith in the Canongate, who at that time had the only copy of it in Scotland. Lady Mary informed me that the Countess was very much surprized to hear that I should have a copy of O'Neille's Journal, the preface and conclusion excepted, for that her ladyship had firmly believed that there was no such thing in all Scotland as the copy of a single sentence of it. Upon this I informed Lady Mary that Mr. William MacDougal, Wine merchant,
was master of a transcript of O'Neille's attested Journal, which *fol.* 697
he had got when taking a jaunt with his lady in England for her health sometime in the month of September, from one of the French officers then prisoners upon parole at Berwick, but that Mr. MacDougal had given his promise not to communicate it by giving a copy to any one whatsoever, even though O'Neille had before that time set out for France, the officers that were left behind being much afraid that they themselves might feel the effects of resentment, should the animadversion upon General Campbell be publickly known before they should be exchanged and set free. Upon comparing the attested copy with the one I had formerly transcribed [vol. i. f. 181] I found no other difference betwixt them than what might proceed from a multiplicity of copies and from the unskilfulness and inattention of transcribers. And therefore at first I intended only to remark the differences of the two copies and to take transcripts of the preface and conclusion. But, upon second thoughts, I
judged it more eligible to take an exact and faithful transcript *fol.* 698
of the whole of the attested copy, that so I might have it all as it had come from the hands of Captain O'Neille, who had sent it to my Lady Dundonald wrapped up in a cover with two seals upon it, and with an address in the following words precisely:—

'To the right honble. the Countess of Dondanold, Edinburgh.'

17 Dec. The remarks I have made[1] still hold good even as to the attested copy: for (to omit other particulars) considering the long time that Captain O'Neille was with the Prince after the battle of Culloden (about ten or eleven weeks), and the great variety of difficulties and dangers they had to struggle with during all that time, certainly the Captain behoved to have much more to say than what he has given an account of in his Journal, had he only been at the trouble of taking time and leisure to recollect himself with that accuracy and exactness

*fol.* 699. which the importance of the subject justly calls for. In such an uncommon and interesting scene of life the minutest occurrence that has the smallest tendency to illustrate the character of the *suffering hero* should not be omitted. Let this piece of history be cooly and impartially considered only from April 16th to September 20th, and I dare venture to say one will not find a parallel to it in any history whatsoever. For a prince to be a-skulking five long months exposed to the hardships of hunger and cold, thirst and nakedness, and surrounded on all hands by a numerous army of blood-thirsty men, both by sea and land, eagerly hunting after the price of blood, and yet that they should miss the much coveted aim, is an event of life far surpassing the power of words to paint. In a word, I presume it may be asserted with great truth that the Prince (all circumstances considered) could not have been safe in any other place of the three kingdoms but in the Highlands of Scotland. Let any one compare O'Neille's Journal

*fol.* 700. with Donald MacLeod's,[2] and I am persuaded he will find the Captain's account of things dull and wanting when put into the balance with that of the old honest Palinurus, whose simple unadorn'd sayings have a peculiar energy and beauty in them.

ROBERT FORBES, A.M.

*Tuesday's forenoon, February 2d,* 1748.

1748 2 Feb. I paid my respects to the Countess of Dundonald and Lady Mary Cochran, when I delivered back to the Countess the attested copy of O'Neille's Journal, and likewise gave to her

[1] See f. 189.

[2] See ff. 277-307.

ladyship the copy I had promised of Gradyne's account. I then asked the Countess if her ladyship remembered at what time she had received the attested copy from O'Neille. Her ladyship was pleased to answer that as she had received a letter along with the Journal from Captain O'Neille, so she could fully satisfy me about that; and going to a cabinet her ladyship fetched O'Neille's letter out of one of the drawers and showed me the date of it, which was as follows: 'Berwick, August 30th, 1747.'

Robert Forbes, A.M.

# APPENDIX

## A.—A Coppy of a Letter from a Soldier in Cobham's Dragoons sent to his Brother at Cirencester.[1]

*May* 11*th*, 1746: *Stonehive,*
80 *miles this side Inverness.*

To which we marched since that glorious 16th of April which gave liberty to three kingdom. These rapacious villains thought to have destroyed their prisoners, and by their orderly books, had they got the better, we were to have been every soul of us cut off, and not have had one prisoner, and for the Duke he was to have been cut as small as herbs for the pot, thus they and their books declare. But, God be praised, he wou'd not suffer such inhumanity and such barbarous villains to thrive, and I pray God our young hero is preserved to be a second deliverer to church and state; he beeing the darling of mankind, for we had certainly been starved had it not been his care to bring ovens and bakers with him. I say, Down on your knees all England and, after praise to God who gives victory, pray for the young British hero, for had he been at Falkirk these brave Englishmen that are now in their graves had not been lost, his presence doing more than five thousand men; and every man stands an equal chance for his life without partiality; which has not been the case for these six months last past. Your news papers give you a tolerable account, so I shall not, nor can I, give you a better within the compass of a letter. Since the last I sent you we find kill'd amongst the rebels no less than ten colonels, seven majors, fifteen captains, and as to lieutenants and ensigns, a volume of them. I leave you to guess at the number of rank and file that must fall. In short, 'tis mine and every bodie's opinion no history can brag

[1] See footnote, p. 50, *ante*.

of so singular a victory and so few of our men lost, that we lost but one man; 'tho I fear I shall lose my horse, he having at this moment of writing a ball in his left buttock. 'Twas pritty near Enoch that time, but, thank God, a miss is as good as a mile, as we say in Gloustershire. And now we have the pleasure of a bed and not hard duty; but for six weeks before the battle few of Cobham's heroes (thank God, that is our caracter from the Duke and the general officers, except General Hawley, who does not love us because our regiment spoke truth about Falkirk job), I say for six weeks before I had not my cloaths off once, and had it not been for our dear Bill, we had all been starved, only for the good loaves he order'd for the army, and some provisions that came by shipping. But thank God, I am well and in good quarters for this country, and I hope I shall live to see you once more. I have the vanity to believe Cobham's will be welcome to England now; for the regiment has always been in front upon all occasions where hard and dangerous duty was to be done: from our first setting off to Stonefild where the sneaking dogs stole away in the night, at Clifton-Moor where we dismounted and fought on foot and the Duke thanked us at the head of the regiment and so he has done several times. I shou'd be glad to hear what the caracter of Cobham's is in England. Direct for me at Stonehive or elce-where. 'Tis impossible for me to tell you what hard duty we have done since we have been in the north, but had we done ten times more, 'tis what I shou'd think of with pleasure so as we serve our King and country. We are all hearty that is left of us, and we thank and praise God for our deliverance. We have not lost above one troop and one hundred horses, which I think a miracle. As to what you say about agents, you must think I tried long ago. But, in short, the officers dont care how little cash they have about them in these parts, especialy in war; for every time we thought of a battle the officers' servants had all the regiment's cash, rings, and watches. I sold my watch a little before Falkirk's battle, and the dear lad that bought it was kill'd the first fire, so that he and all he had fell to these inhumane dogs. He was my particular friend. I hope all is now over. We are guarding the coast that Charles may not get off. I pray God I had him in this room, and he the last of the Stuart race; it wou'd be my glory to stab the villain to the heart. Beside it wou'd look well in history for him to fall by the hand of a Bradshaw. I dare say did the rankest Jacobite in

England know the misery he has brought on the north of England, he wou'd be sick of the name of Stuart; for I have a shocking story of their villainy, which wou'd make even a papist tremble at the reading of it. My humble service to all friends in general. I pray God I had a flicth of your bacon, but am well, and we have bread and brandy in plenty.—Yours,

ENOCH BRADSHAW.

Lightning Source UK Ltd.
Milton Keynes UK
21 March 2011

169613UK00001B/153/P